Journalistic Standards in
Nineteenth-Century America

Journalistic Standards in Nineteenth-Century America

Hazel Dicken-Garcia

The University of Wisconsin Press

The University of Wisconsin Press
114 North Murray Street
Madison, Wisconsin 53715

3 Henrietta Street
London WC2E 8LU, England

5   4   3   2   1

Printed in the United States of America

Library of Congress Cataloging-in-Publication Data
Dicken Garcia, Hazel.
   Journalistic standards in nineteenth-century America/Hazel
Dicken-Garcia.
   352 pp.   cm.
   Bibliography: pp.
   Includes index.
   1. Journalistic ethics—United States—History—19th century.
2. Journalism—United States—Objectivity—History—19th century.
3. Journalism—United States—History—19th century.   I. Title.
PN4888.E8D5   1989
174'.9097—dc20   89-40252
ISBN 0-299-12170-4   CIP
ISBN 0-299-12174-7 (pbk.)

For the students
who asked the questions

The News

The News, *Indeed!* —*pray do you call it news*
When shallow noodles publish shallow views?
Pray, is it news that turnips should be bred
As large and hollow as the owner's head?
News, *that a clerk should rob his master's hoard,*
Whose meagre salary scarcely pays his board?
News, *that two knaves, their spurious friendship o'er,*
Should tell the truths which they concealed before?
News, *that a maniac, weary of his life,*
Should end his sorrows with a rope or knife?
News, *that a wife should violate the vows*
That bind her, loveless, to a tyrant spouse?
News, *that a daughter cheats paternal rule,*
And weds a scoundrel to escape a fool?—
The news, indeed! —such matters are as old
As sin and folly, rust and must and mould!
                    —*John Godfrey Saxe (1816–1887)*

Contents

Charts and Graphs

Acknowledgments

All research efforts are collaborative, and I am deeply indebted to many for assistance with this project: the University of Minnesota for a quarter's leave from teaching that finally permitted meaningful progress in the reading of newspapers; the University of Minnesota Wilson Library staff, especially in the Office of Inter-Library Loans, who handled so many requests so efficiently and courteously over such a long period of time; the staff of the Wisconsin State Historical Society Library, especially in the microfilm room, who have always given invaluable assistance; and the University of Minnesota School of Journalism and Mass Communication for research assistant support during the summer and fall of 1987.

Space does not permit me to name every individual who contributed in some way to completion of the manuscript, but I am especially grateful to Nathaniel Hong, Jean Olson, and Tom Volek, graduate students in the University of Minnesota School of Journalism and Mass Communication, who assisted with research and the inevitable computer problems that beset me at intervals; Professors Gerald Baldasty, University of Washington, and John Finnegan, Jr., and MaryAnn Yodelis Smith, both of the University of Minnesota, who read and commented on early drafts and discussed relevant issues with me; Professors James Boylan, University of Massachusetts–Amherst, and James Baughman, University of Wisconsin–Madison, who offered especially cogent suggestions for revisions; University of Minnesota Professors Donald Gillmor and Ted Glasser, who offered encouragement during the project's developmental stages; Dawn Bremseth, whose ever-cheerful, ever-superior assistance with other of my tasks during the past year made sustained effort on this project possible; and Jane Rasmussen, Victoria Smith, and Julie Tillotson, who on occasion helped locate elusive bits of information. Words cannot adequately express my special appreciation to Ann Brill, Don Gillmor, Junko Fang, John Finnegan, Jr., Jeanine and Glen Halva-Neubauer, Jean Olson, and MaryAnn Yodelis Smith, whose generosity and capabilities provided matchless aid during the difficult months of my father's illness and death during the

research. Finally, deepest gratitude goes to my students; without the persistent questions they raised in various courses the project would never
have been begun. It is for this reason that the book is dedicated to them.

H.D.-G.
Minneapolis, 1988

Journalistic Standards in
Nineteenth-Century America

Chapter One

Journalistic Standards in History

PENNYBOY. . . . *Come in* Thom: *set thy things vpon the Boord,*
  And spread thy clothes, lay all forth in procinctu,
  And tell's what newes?
THOMAS.   *O Sir, a staple of newes! . . .*
PENNYBOY. *What's that?*
FASHIONER. *An* Officer, *Sir, a braue young* Office *set vp. . . .*
PENNYBOY.   *For what?*
THOMAS. *To enter all the* Newes, *Sir, o' of the time.*
        ·   ·   ·   ·   ·   ·   ·   ·   ·   ·   ·   ·
PENNYBOY. . . . *What is't, an* Office, *Thom?*
THOMAS.   *Newly erected*
  Here in the house, almost on the same floore,
  Where all the newes of all sorts shall be brought,
  And there be examin'd, and then registred,
  And so be issu'd vnder the Seale of the Office,
  As Staple Newes; *no other newes be currant,*
PENNYBOY. *'Fore me, thou speak'st of a braue busines,* Thom.
                    Ben Jonson; The Staple of Newes *(1631)*

Following a lecture on the dual role of editors as journalists and politicians
and the often tasteless newspaper content in nineteenth-century America,
a student asked, with some indignation and incredulity, "But weren't those
people concerned with telling the truth? Didn't they ever talk about that?"
The question highlights important issues about journalists' concern with
truth and other moral principles over time, what that has meant in how
they carried on their work, how it affected the development of journalism,
and how the accumulated experience relates to the contemporary debate
on journalistic ethics. But the question has not really been answered, despite the fact that perhaps no topic has ever been so prevalent in journalism
as has ethics during the past decade. After years devoid of literature on
the subject, numerous books have appeared in recent years; centers for
the study of media ethics have been established, courses developed, con-

ferences organized, and each year seems to bring increased intensity and momentum to the debate.[1]

Intense interest in how information is handled seems a natural outgrowth of the vast expansion of communications industries over recent decades. More of the nation's labor force now work with information than any other occupational concern, and more do so now than at any time in history.[2] Technological changes have rapidly altered methods of gathering, presenting, and distributing information. It is incumbent, therefore, perhaps as never before, to examine and understand conduct connected with something so integral to society's functioning as information dispersal.

But the absence from the debate about media ethics of a historical perspective—that is, reference to the past to inform, direct, and give continuity to the discussions and the purposes they serve—is conspicuous and limiting. No literature deals to a significant degree with the history of journalistic ethics. None examines what journalists have viewed over time as "right" and "wrong" practices, appropriate and inappropriate conduct, or the role of ethics in their work. No literature examines criticism of the press and how it may have changed over time, or discussions among journalists that might show what they have collectively emphasized in how they have gone about their work over the centuries. This void seems striking, considering the relationship of other contemporary discussions to journalism's past. For example, our understanding of freedom of the press in America would be deficient indeed without knowledge of the centuries of struggle for that freedom and the thought it generated over time. Contemporaries resort to that history to clarify issues and inform the present on countless occasions. U.S. Supreme Court justices cite John Milton; attorneys search the historical record to strengthen arguments in First Amendment cases; and journalists frequently refer to practices of the Star Chamber in the sixteenth century as a way of emphasizing the specter of threats to the press's position and role.

Were there discussions in the past among journalists about their practices, and what effect, if any, did these exchanges have on the kind and quality of media functioning in America at any given time? Might knowledge of such previous concerns reveal patterns useful to contemporary discussions and media direction? What might be the implications of such knowledge for journalistic performance and the media? If significant debates preoccupied journalists and press critics at other times as they do today, what were their premises, issues, and conclusions, and what effect did they have on journalism and on society? If such debates affected journalistic performance and media, how was the change defined? In short, has there been an evolution of journalistic standards and the rationales underlying them over time—that is, a building of a store of thought and experience that may be instructive in the present?

Such questions prompted study of the development of concepts of journalistic standards—broadly defined as the rules governing journalistic practices—in nineteenth-century America. The task proved gargantuan, for references to standards and press criticism appear only fleetingly in the literature, usually as interesting sidelights in work addressing other subjects. An array of scholarship addressing related issues has, however, proved valuable.[3]

The research reported here is immeasurably indebted to these and other sources, particularly works by the historians Donald Stewart and James Pollard on, respectively, the American press in the 1790s and presidential-press relationships.[4] Although neither directly addresses the question of journalistic standards, both Stewart and Pollard are intrigued by practices and their rationalization, and they each provide a wealth of material, insight, and source references.

As research progressed, it became clear that studying criticism of journalism in nineteenth-century America meant entering a story that was well under way. The earliest published nineteenth-century press criticism was British, and a cursory search of secondary sources revealed much even earlier.[5] Although beyond the scope of this work, study of earlier British and European journalism would be important to what has been attempted here. The bulk of the present research has focused on past discussions of press behavior, including particularly press criticisms and the newspapers they referred to. Although a modest beginning, the work should nevertheless contribute to filling a long-standing gap in the record, and will perhaps stimulate further efforts to make that record more complete. Moreover, understanding of the development of journalistic standards may provide useful insights and reveal distinctions that become apparent only through historical analysis.

Study of press criticism raised questions about patterns and models: do nineteenth-century data reveal patterns in concepts of journalistic standards that may be described with models? If so, did those models change in the course of the century? And if they did, what was associated with or might account for changes? Pursuing such questions called for exploring why concepts of journalistic standards changed and how the models relate to present-day concepts at the broadest theoretical level: for example, from what assumptions about the press, journalists, and society are standards derived? And to what aspects of society's structure are standards related?

Exploring these questions required a broad perspective, one extending beyond but not detached from the structure established in journalism history of the party press era, the penny press era, and similar divisions. Borrowing from the title of a recent book by the historian Charles Tilly, the view here is of journalism in its broadest contours—as a "big structure" and a "large process."[6] Histories of journalism have generally emphasized the press traits of differing eras. The present work, however, aims to pose a framework for analyzing press changes over time within that larger perspective, for as research quickly made clear, examining journalistic standards requires first considering society's purposes for that part of its communications system called journalism. And this, in turn, requires considering how journalism functions in the larger society. What a society intends its communications system to do relates to notions of standards, for standards imply expectations. On the highest level, whether an entity accomplishes what is expected is a measure of its conduct and performance.

Press criticism becomes the intersection between society and journalism, for it represents how people think about and discuss journalism. And such discussion reveals reference points—values—by which people judge journalistic conduct. This makes study of press criticism important to any examination of standards over time, for every criticism of the media implies assumptions about what the press can and should do; that is, a notion of press function inheres in criticism, for the critic implies both dysfunctions and corrections, at least according to her view. Such criticism evolves, however, with changes affecting the press and its role, and identifying that evolution requires examining journalism's broad historical contours.

Focusing on these contours emphasizes the social and institutional aspects of journalism. That is, it requires considering journalism as carrying out essential functions both to perpetuate its own existence and, through interaction with other social institutions, to aid in preserving and maintaining society. And this draws attention not only to its own development but also to its connection, broadly, with America's national development. Journalism's capacities, which determine its social and institutional reach, are ultimately determined by the cultural context.

American journalism has been shaped by the nation's changing economic and political structures, the emergence of new ideologies and cultural trends, evolving schools of ethical thought and values, and historical shifts in the composition and distribution of population. As such changes occurred, notions of the press's function and role themselves evolved, in turn shaping concepts of journalistic standards. Thus, notions of right and wrong journalistic conduct at any given time are products of dominant cultural strains.

Changes in culture (ideas, politics, religion, technology, values) lead to changes in social institutions (in structure, purpose, function, role), and these then lead to changes in the procedures and rules governing the work carried out by those institutions. Furthermore, changes in culture are reflected in discussions of social institutions—in expressions revealing changed perceptions of their roles, purposes, and functions. Ideas of standards governing the conduct of the tasks of social institutions are related to these perceptions and will likewise change over time.

It is important to stress at the outset that the scope of this book is limited to the journalistic standards of the newspaper press. The purpose is not to attempt a history of journalistic *ethics;* the focus has been on the ideas, notions, and concepts expressed in nineteenth-century publications of what constituted right or wrong journalistic conduct. Since ethics lies in the realm of philosophy, a study of the history of journalistic ethics would necessarily deal with philosophy and with how journalistic activity was related to the evolution of ethical thought. Although occasional references to ethics appear throughout, this book is not *about* ethics.

People have expressed concern about journalistic conduct since the first newspapers were published, and from the beginning some recurring themes can be readily identified with ethical principles. But generally, although most of the discussion emphasized the press's potential harm to the larger society, and although journalists had themselves begun to use such phrases as "code of ethics" by the 1840s, the debate was not in the realm of ethics.[7] Some writers did lament that philosophers had neglected such a pervasive institution as the press. In 1834, for example, one writer began an article:

THAT the great changes of recent times have been mainly owing to the influence of the press, is a matter of universal observation; but it is extraordinary, that while so great and important an element has now for the first time been brought fully to bear on public affairs, the attention of philosophers and statesmen should have so little turned to the principles by which it is governed. . . .[8]

An article published more than sixty years later echoed the same theme, as the author Aline Gorren commended the French critic M. Ferdinand Brunetière's remarks on journalism upon his admission to the French Academy. Gorren wrote:

he made in his address certain remarks upon modern journalism that were note-worthy because uttered on a subject from the treatment of which anything like a philosophy is, as if by common consent, excluded. To take any but the shortest and most immediate views of this topic, that is of such incalculable importance to every side and aspect of modern life, appears to be one of the things that is tacitly understood must not be done. The Fourth Estate has . . . become . . . practically removed from any searching criticism and from the peril of being tested by the standard of the general idea.[9]

The first article of press criticism located that used the word *ethics* in its title appeared in 1889.[10] The first located "code of conduct" for journalists appeared in 1890, and although crude, broad "maxims" were recorded in the late nineteenth century, no one seems to have offered a more formal code until 1911.[11] Since this initial effort to develop a history of concepts of journalistic standards examines what people wrote about most, the scope has been confined to the nineteenth-century press and contemporary critical discussions to determine patterns and their evolution. Furthermore, although some nineteenth-century press criticism encompassed magazines and books as well as newspapers, the present work focuses only on what was written about the latter. The term *press* is used to avoid monotonous repetition of *newspapers*, and *journalist* to refer to all those involved in gathering, preparing, and presenting newspaper content.

Because no systematic rules governing journalists' work appeared until very late in the period under study, several assumptions guided the research. One such assumption was that, whether written or systematically spelled out (and regardless of how crudely), certain procedures or rules existed—either as understood among those in the occupation or as instructions transmitted by supervisors. In the 1840s, for example, Horace Greeley, editor of the New York *Tribune*, established rules governing read-

ers' contributions, and George W. Childs listed twenty-four rules of journalistic conduct at the Philadelphia *Public Ledger* after he bought it in
1864.[12] Another research assumption was that, regardless of the crudity
of the rules, both journalists and their readers had notions of appropriate
journalistic conduct and that discussions of the press reveal at least some
of these. An important underlying assumption, therefore, has been that
any press criticism suggests notions of what is right and wrong in journalistic conduct. Related assumptions are that discussions of the nature of
journalism, the press, and the news also reveal—explicitly or implicitly—
perceived functions and purposes of the press and that those are related to
concepts of journalistic standards. That is to say, certain words describing
the press recur in the discussions, and over a long period the descriptions
form patterns in that particular ones prevail for a time, then give way
to others. Such descriptions thus represent perceived press functions and
roles at any given time, and the recurring patterns may be described as
models. After the Civil War, for instance, descriptions of the press as a
"business" and vocabulary associated with industry emerged in discussions
and prevailed throughout the late nineteenth century. Hence the press
model for this period, as identified in people's perceptions of newspaper
journalism, may be called a business model. These models of how the press
is perceived form the basis or reference point for either criticism or defense of journalistic procedures. To illustrate, an Ohio publisher in 1893
blamed the press's business development for the "poor" journalistic practices of the period. He told the eighth annual meeting of the Associated
Ohio Dailies:

But the marvelous development of the newspaper, in the machinery which turns
it out, in the gathering of news, the equally marvelous increase in circulation and
number of newspapers, and the elevation of the business of newspaper publishing to business standards, have attracted the sensitive attention of capital and
made many of our leading metropolitan papers the object of speculative interest.
	Herein lies a danger. It will be a sorry day for journalism if our leading papers
pass out of the control of trained, professional newspaper men, and their policy
be dictated and guided by men who look upon the business of journalism as the
pork packer does upon his. . . . Is it not already foreshadowed—a press pandering to the low and vicious, to the love of scandal for the sake of larger money
returns. . . ?[13]

	Obviously, the ideas of functions and standards revealed in the discus-
sions studied may not have been in fact the only—or even the prevailing—

ones. Rather, the discussions disclosed only what those involved asserted, which may have been minority, majority, or only singular views. Nevertheless, patterns in these ideas do emerge, providing more than has thus far been known about past journalistic criticism and standards.

Since this book emphasizes standards and specifically excludes historical treatment of ethics, the distinction between standards and moral principles requires some explication. As used here, *standards* has a broad, twofold meaning—one relating to function, the other to the ideal. The term is used to mean the criteria, or rules of procedure, governing the accomplishment of an occupational end—those "rules," for example, that define how information is to be collected, incorporated into a report, and presented in published form. The rules also include a range of related activities that affect the quality and substance of what appears in a newspaper, such as Greeley's "ground rules" for publishing readers' contributions, or Chicago *Daily News* editor Melville Stone's "principles" for what would *not* appear in his newspaper. And they define the norm of press content—that is, values and journalistic ends as manifested in content, reflecting what is acceptable at any given time. For journalists, standards although unwritten, are linked with journalistic ends or goals in three ways: (1) they inhere in procedures for accomplishing the goal; (2) they are reflected in what constitutes the "norm" of press content at any given time; and (3) they form measures against which to judge whether or not work is done well. (Note that the first two points relate to function whereas the third is connected to the ideal, although some overlap does occur between points 1 and 3.) Standards are thus central to, and an overriding part of, a journalist's activity; she must be constantly thinking about them. A philosophical dimension is not explicitly incorporated—nor is the connection between standards and ethics a central concern here, for two reasons: first, press critics throughout the nineteenth century did not apply the philosophical concepts of ethics to journalism, and second, a study of standards seems essential before the history of journalistic ethics can be fully examined. The fact that no philosophical dimension is included does not deny its existence nor the relation to ethics.

Standards are part of the journalist's routine, part of the daily work; they are more readily subject to proof than are moral principles, and they are more apt to change over time. Ethics, or moral principles, transcend the practical; they are abstract constructs that are not easily proved, and they are more stable, more enduring than standards. The moral principle of telling the truth, for example, is ancient; although every society allows certain "permissible" lies, the basic principle has remained virtually the same.[14] By contrast, the "rules" (stated or implied) for gathering information, assimilating it into a report, and presenting it, along with the norm reflected in content, have changed. Values also have changed, as have, in turn, judgments about whether the conduct and report "measure up" to expectations (ideals or values). In sum, then, although standards are tied to practical everyday procedures, moral principles are constructs representing ideals equally incumbent on all professions; they are relatively few and can be stated with little dispute about their desirability in any human activity.

It must also be stressed that the purpose here has not been to uncover practices likely to be considered wrong under any circumstances. For example, an article by the journalism historian Ted Smythe presents valuable evidence that reporters surreptitiously inflated stories in the 1880s and 1890s because they were paid by the amount published.[15] The intent of this work, however, is not to document such practices or deliberate falsifications of news, but rather to examine broad concepts of standards and how these were related to changes in the role of the press in the nineteenth century.

The issues confronted by the earliest journalism were simple compared with those with which the present-day ethics debate is concerned. Nevertheless, an example from the beginning of the eighteenth century may illustrate the distinction being made here between standards and moral principles. An item that appeared in 1702 in the world's first successful daily newspaper suggests a notion of standards governing the printer's conduct. Publisher Elizabeth Mallett explained that the editor would not

under Pretence of having Private Intelligence, impose any Additions of feign'd Circumstances to an Action, but give . . . Extracts fairly and Impartially; at the beginning of each Article he will quote the Foreign Paper from whence 'tis taken, that the Publick, seeing from what Country a piece of News comes with the Allowance of that Government, may be better able to Judge of the Credibility and Fairness of the Relation: Nor will he take upon him to give any Comments or Conjectures of his own, but will relate only Matter of Fact, supposing other People to have Sense enough to make Reflections for themselves.[16]

Mallett emphasized "fairness" and "truth" especially, suggesting that readers must use their own knowledge about the information's source when judging its worth. (It should be noted that the word *fair* did not carry today's connotation of balance but rather seemed to mean "good" or "accurate.") Clearly, the editor had thought about whether the journalist should intervene in conveying a source's version of the truth, and decided that, even though the information might not be truthful (that is, it might be "partial," or what is today called "biased"), any intervention would be inappropriate. Clearly, too, the moral principle of truth-telling concerned the editor—hence the warning that people be wary that the information might not be true. But, beyond that warning, the conduct and method of proceeding were simple and defined routine practice. The journalist's procedure was defined very narrowly as simply conveying information as "matter of fact"—that is, whatever news came into the editor's hands.

The direction for proceeding is clear: publishing without changing or adding to the news. Before judging such procedures, however, we must remember that the first daily newspaper appeared long before the editorial emerged, before news-gathering methods (beyond clipping items from other newspapers) developed, and when fears for press freedom impinged on what journalists published.[17] All of this had implications for how journalists' roles, tasks, conduct, and criteria for achieving journalistic ends got defined and carried out.

Since standards are related to practices at one level and to broader concepts and functions of the press at another, the research followed two lines of investigation. At the broader level, questions were, What were broad trends in America over the course of the nineteenth century? How was the press's role as a social institution related to these? How were notions of journalistic standards related in turn to the press's role and to cultural trends? (see fig. 1.1) The second line of investigation focused directly on journalistic standards through three source categories: press criticism published in secondary sources throughout the nineteenth century; content in samples of newspapers from the beginning, middle, and final decades of the century to deduce, from news presentation, the standards in use and to try to ascertain changes; content in newspapers or in any relevant secondary sources discussing journalism, the press, and news to identify concepts of press functions, purposes, and roles and of journalistic conduct.

Press development is surveyed in the context of American national development, with special attention paid to the press's role in relation to trends. The press in the nineteenth century is then examined in each of three eras: the early era of the new nation, from 1789 to 1850; the second era, overlapping the first, which extended from the early 1830s into the

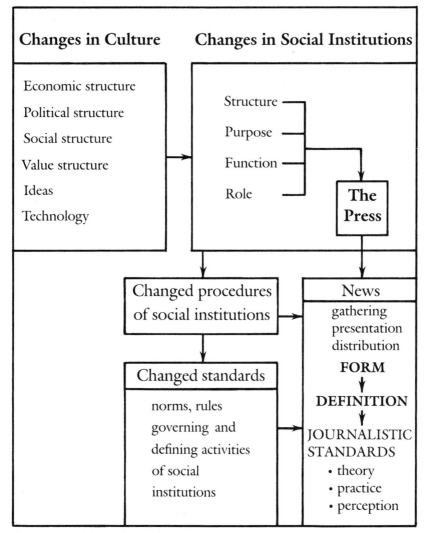

Changes in Culture   **Changes in Social Institutions**

Economic structure

Political structure

Social structure

Value structure

Ideas

Technology

Structure

Purpose

Function

Role

The Press

Changed procedures of social institutions

News

gathering
presentation
distribution

FORM

Changed standards

norms, rules
governing and
defining activities
of social
institutions

DEFINITION

JOURNALISTIC
STANDARDS

• theory
• practice
• perception

Fig. 1.1. Relationship of Journalistic Standards to Culture

1870s; and a third era, overlapping the second and extending from 1860 to the turn of the century.

The eras thus demarcated are defined by broad cultural shifts under way, and time boundaries serve only as convenient marking devices. Time is not causal, nor is the sum of each era assumed to fit neatly within a specific period. In any given historial period, a core of ideas and trends emerges out of a mix of forces, takes on a definite pattern, and dominates for a time, influencing both institutions and events.[18] The set of trends and ideas does not necessarily originate in the designated era; rather, some portions may have originated long before and, through interaction with other ideas and events, were altered, reshaped, and crystallized; these in turn gave rise to others, which were also affected—intensified, deemphasized, or otherwise altered—over time.

For example, the influence of Enlightenment ideas on the institutions formed during the eighteenth century is readily discernible. As another example, ideas about the nation's direction and government intensified and coalesced in the 1820s around a few central issues; proponents fixed on Andrew Jackson as symbolizing or representing these concepts, and the dominant trends of the time have been characterized as the Jacksonian era in American history.[19]

One final example illustrates the role of events in giving rise to points of view on emerging issues that, in turn, initiate other events. U.S. military activity in Vietnam from the 1950s into the 1970s included events against which opposing views emerged, and these propelled other events that in turn spawned issues. Opposing views—that the U.S. government should or should not be involved in Vietnam—created issues that incited public demonstrations, bombings of buildings as symbolic protests, and the deaths at Kent State University in 1970. The very debate of U.S. activity in Vietnam spilled over into areas of long-held values, leading to other events and issues affecting the course of American development. The interconnection of events, issues, and ideas related to U.S. military activity in Vietnam has thus become identified with an era in American history.[20]

The delineation of three journalistic eras in the nineteenth century is based on the dominant ideas, trends, and cultural strains of each. The first era was an age of political experimentation, a working out of the functioning of a new form of government in general and of the party system in particular. The second period, generated by movements that accelerated beyond the first era, was characterized by reform movements, technological advances in transportation and manufacturing, and growing urban-based commercial and political activity. Finally, the third era was marked by a changed national economic base from agriculture to industry; it was a period of what some have called nationalization, one in which third parties (other than the two that emerged out of the Civil War crisis ending America's party-building stage) made the last serious showing in the political system, and a time of preoccupation with scientific discovery and business. Concomitant with broad societal changes in each era, values shifted—and, as sets of receding and emerging values competed, the resulting tensions were reflected in press content and criticism.

The term *values,* the broad dominant social attributes, behaviors, and larger goals that are advocated, promoted, and defended by a society, generally follows the definition by John Finnegan, Jr., in his study of defamation law as a product of "larger cultural values about the control of communication behavior." Such values, he notes, "are influenced by political, social and economic conditions affecting the organization of society and communication activity. . . ."[21] Drawing on several sources, Finnegan defines *culture* as "shared ideation behind social behavior among groups"; *society* as a "group of people in social and behavioral interdependence"; *social structure* as the manifestation of "the nature of social and behavioral independence"; and *values* as "ideals"—"desirable, preferable ends that . . . correspond to a pattern of choices or actions."[22] The term *values* would, then, designate the attributes of social deference characteristic of eighteenth-century society, the social goal of establishing a purely "American" form of government, a republic, in the late eighteenth and early nineteenth centuries, and the aspiration to make political participation more democratic during the 1820s, 1830s, 1840s.[23] Such values would also encompass subsidiary values growing out of such movements as abolition during these same decades. The slavery issue represented two sets of competing values in antebellum America: some valued slavery and sought to maintain and expand it, while others valued a society proscribing human bondage. The tension between these competing values is clear: the former prevailed as the new government was formed, but the latter—already being articulated at the founding of the nation—emerged, gained strength, and ultimately overtook and dominated the value condoning slavery. Hence, the American value system during the early nineteenth century advocated the support, promotion, and defense of slavery; by the end of the Civil War, however, the value that slavery was untenable had triumphed.[24]

In an open society, media content is the most immediate and visible indication of changing values. While informing citizens of daily affairs, it also conveys broad contours of social change that become visible only over the long term, as cumulations form patterns. Part of what provokes media

criticism are elements embedded in daily reflections of the world that unsettle and obtrude because they deviate, even if only barely perceptibly,
from established values. When the state of tension between competing
sets of values is fairly even, some press content will be in harmony with
each. In other words, some journalism—more likely of comparatively recently established newspapers—will be ahead of the times, so to speak,
foreshadowing future values, whereas some will be at one with established
values, or even somewhat behind, holding to receding values. Press criticism is thus greatest when the tension between sets of competing values
is at its height; the anxieties generated by change draw attention and even
blame to the press as at least diffusing if not actually originating the unsettling current. The broad changes themselves are obscured from view,
but the press is not, and therefore the press or its conduct, not the actual
change in values, may be seen as the cause of the problem.

In advocating journalistic standards, press criticism contains, whether
explicitly or implicitly, elements in harmony with both declining and
emerging values. In other words, those critics who resist change see content and behavior as injurious and advocate established norms; those who
are in step with change suggest or imply standards opposed to, or out of
tune with, traditional patterns and promote "new" press definitions and
functions. Such elements are revealed in critics' discussions (see Chapters
5, 6, and 7). Although this tension in values does not account for all instances of media criticism, it implies a kind of analysis that might prove
productive. (This and other implications are considered in Chapter 8.)

Values not only significantly affect the press's role, they largely determine it. And both values and the role of the press affect concepts of standards. Each nineteenth-century era reshaped the press, producing significant changes and implications for its role. The press's role is defined by the
conjunction of the overall nature of its content, articulated perceptions of
what the press does or should do, and its relationship to the larger polity.
For example, the dominant content of the press in the early years of the
nation was political; discussions of the press reflected perceptions that it
existed to inform about and debate political issues; and its relationship to
the larger polity was characterized by ties to parties and government. Di-
vergences may, of course, occur between these. What people say the press
does or should do may diverge from what it seems to do and from how
it relates structurally to the larger polity, as appears to be the case in the
late nineteenth century (see Chapters 2 and 3). But in periods of dramatic

change, because of conflicts in the perceptions resulting from competing values, dominant content will likely correlate more closely with the press's place in the larger social structure than with articulated perceptions of what it does or should do.

Since conceptions of the press's role are products of ideas and trends in a given society at a given time, notions of this role, shaped by dominant trends, differ in each era. These conceptions in turn shaped standards—the criteria governing the way journalists conducted and viewed their work, and the norms as manifested in content. Related to this, the press's own development as a social institution also influenced conceptions of its role. In other words, its level of development and activity as a social institution determined, in large part, how its role was conceived, for—in concert with the influence of society's value structure—people's view of its capabilities depended on its level of development. Furthermore, views of its capabilities influenced notions of the way it should function and what "rules" or norms should govern its conduct.

At this point, it may be helpful to separate the two emphases—the press's own development and its role as a social institution—as conceptualized here in relation to standards. The press's development will be considered first, followed by discussion of the press as a social institution and how changes in the press expanded that role.

The argument here follows the principles of press change that have been articulated by Robert Park and Bernard Roshco, extending them to assert that journalistic standards evolve through the same process.[25] Park enunciates a "natural" sequence of newspaper evolution, whereas Roshco maintains that changing social conditions create news-gathering procedures. In Roshco's words, Park refers to the manner in which "institutions evolve in response to changing circumstances . . . within a particular society"; the newspaper is thus "the outcome of an historic process. . . . In spite of all the efforts of individual men and generations of men to control and to make it something after their own heart, it has continued to grow and change in its own incalculable ways. . . ."[26] Again citing Park, Roshco argues that "the introduction of new procedures of news gathering and the emphasis on new categories of news content are at least as much the result of changing social conditions as of innovating individuals."[27] Journalistic standards, products of society and institutions, follow the contours of this process of change.

The earliest press criticism implied a small set of journalistic standards substantially the same as those at the core of many present-day issues. C. Edward Wilson, for example, in a study of seventeenth-century criticism, concludes that most critics focused on accuracy, fairness, and profit seeking, all of which are recurrent themes today.[28] As the press expanded and developed in complexity—in structure, journalistic tasks, perceived role, and as a social institution—journalistic standards also grew in number and sophistication. Although early statements reflect themes readily recognizable today, consideration of these themes must recognize the vast differences between the press then and today. Identifiable standards in the earliest press criticism are simply stated, narrow, and limited in depth and scope, and they focus on few issues and reflect little or no analysis. Over time, however, issues multiplied and their complexity was increasingly recognized, so that present-day analyses probe and explore their many facets, often focusing on one at a time but from many perspectives—philosophical, sociological, psychological, economic, and political.[29]

Although early journalism was simple compared to present procedures of gathering, presenting, and distributing news, its evolution over nearly six hundred years along multiple lines increasingly raised questions about standards unimagined when the first newspapers appeared. Historical developments altered journalism as an occupation and a social institution, and they altered the nature of news as its sources, styles, forms, and substance changed with cultural trends.

The evolution created and expanded jobs, tasks, and roles, which, in turn, also contributed to changing the nature of news. Colonial American newspapers, for example, were one- or two-person operations headed by a printer. The concept of news gathering as it is understood today, or even that held in 1870, was virtually nonexistent; procedures were those identified by Elizabeth Mallett for her early eighteenth-century newspaper in the example cited above. News and newspapers were circulated through the mail. Rarely leaving the shop to gather news, printers culled items from other newspapers and letters.[30] Since operating a printing press was laborious and time-consuming, the one or two people publishing a newspaper hardly had time to go in search of news, even if such a concept had existed.[31]

Dramatic changes in these procedures began in the early nineteenth century, and over the ensuing decades news gathering evolved to include (in approximate chronological order of development)

— clipping items from other papers and gleaning excerpts from letters;
— attending congressional sessions to take notes on political developments;
— hiring men to row small boats to meet incoming ships, in order to collect news from captains and passengers and newspapers from abroad;[32]
— using pony express, carrier pigeons, and trains—separately or in combination —to reduce the lag between events and published reports of them;[33]
— traveling to local events to collect eyewitness accounts;[34]
— traveling out of state or across states to collect nonpolitical news;[35]
— seeking out and interviewing individuals whose positions made them central to news;[36]
— investigating for news below the surface—for example, to gather information about treatment of patients in institutions;[37]
— researching background, context, and implications of events to provide interpretation and analysis;
— studying specific subjects to gain expertise for reporting on "specialized" fields.[38]

Developments in news gathering created the role of the reporter, whose tasks and procedures also evolved over time. Distinguishing between news gathering and reporting, for example, one could focus on changes in reporting tasks that were propelled by the changes in news gathering procedures. Reporting evolved from conveying other newspapers' items, letters, and government documents to traveling—short distances at first and then across states and nations—to collect and prepare information for publication. It also evolved from culling published materials to directly observing events and composing eyewitness accounts, seeking out and interviewing persons and incorporating the information into news reports, and pursuing developments in complex national events, as when the country was at war. And it went from relying on the relatively simple thought processes involved in selecting newsworthy content from published documents or letters to explicating complex issues, investigating (with the reporter as detective) to discover and relate elusive information, interpreting events in relation to other occurrences and issues and their implications, and mastering and reporting specialized subject areas.

Each development represents changing journalistic *procedures*, regardless how slight. Though changes accrued gradually, aggregations in the periods 1830–1850 and 1860–1890, superimposed on the accumulation over decades, shaped and reshaped journalists' procedures. Changes in the kinds of sources used, for example, which evolved from other newspaper accounts as well as letters and documents to interviews and eyewitness observation and from the willing to the uncooperative, led reporters to find ways to gather elusive, hidden, or withheld information. Whether in the nature of news and its collection, in the industry, or in the social institution of journalism, each development impinged on methods of collecting, presenting, and distributing news while at the same time it raised new issues about journalistic conduct and standards. By the late nineteenth century, for instance, the journalistic goal of exposing corruption and inhumane or unjust conditions led reporters to "undercover" procedures—methods that themselves raised previously unheard-of questions, such as what criteria should govern journalists' activities when they do not wish to be recognized as journalists.[39]

As these broad changes occurred during the course of the nineteenth century, journalism developed from a small-scale, one-person operation, often pursued as a sideline, to an industry composed of various departments, to the corporation and ultimately the multimedia corporations of today. As a social institution, American journalism developed from a political forum for an educated elite to an educational and socializing force for individuals throughout society to a component of the nation's economic structure that markets "news" in a variety of forms to attract consumers. Since changes in journalistic procedures and press structure are linked to this expanding role as a social institution, the following discussion will focus on that relationship.

Several years ago a communications historian, in an institutional approach to advertising, defined a social institution in a self-governing society as an entity created to implement a society's decisions about how it intends to govern itself. Social institutions, he wrote, help meet "problems of human existence"; they "act as agencies of social control providing information and norms of conduct which protect society against chaos, and which lend stability to social life and viability to society." Institutions represent the "embodiment of ideas" and of society's values—views of the nature of humanity, of morality, and of life's meaning.[40] Social institutions, then, help preserve and maintain society, moving it from stage to stage as they serve to socialize new generations; at the same time, they temper the rate at which change occurs. Transmitting norms of accepted behavior, they provide mechanisms for society's persistence.

Although all social institutions, in this wide-ranging definition, work toward the same goals, specific institutions, of course, serve different roles. Because they are first and foremost creations of society, institutional roles are determined by society; their histories are interwoven with the society's history, and they reflect its cultural shifts. As a society's collective views and values change, institutions—both subject to and interacting with changing trends—may change along any number of dimensions, in structure, substance, purpose, function, and role.

Tracing a social institution's evolution, then, requires evaluating its capacity to fulfill its functions of embodying collective values and helping meet needs of society's existence. Studying the press means assessing social norms and expectations about content, production, distribution, reception, and use. It also means examining cultural norms and expectations; proscriptions about who has access; who may or may not, who should or should not, be involved in the production, distribution, and reception of communications; what ought or ought not be communicated; patterns of information flow, authority, responsibility, and accountability; links between press operations and other institutions; and who has ownership or control. Finally, the implications of all these aspects must be weighed against how the press functions in society. These factors depend in part on economic and other considerations and the stage of press development under study; but at bottom they are based on society's values. The historical questions then become, Over time, how has the American press embodied society's ideas, values, and beliefs? What were those ideas, values, beliefs, and norms at given times? How has the press operated to transmit norms of accepted behavior? How has it served as an agent of social control? In any given era, how did the press perform these functions?[41]

How does one judge a social institution's capacity to fulfill such a role at given times? Several dimensions immediately suggest themselves as useful guides to broad changes and their implications. It is important to note that these dimensions overlap, and only bare outlines are offered in the framework that follows, which forms the backdrop against which the evolving journalistic standards of the nineteenth century will be analyzed.

1. *Function: Whether, and at what point, society has defined (explicitly or implicitly) what the institution's function is to be.*

The U.S. Constitution implicitly defined the purpose of the press as providing a forum for ideas and debate—especially of political issues— and set a course for its development during the nation's first thirty years (see Chapter 2).

2. *Agreement on Function: The degree to which the institution (or the larger part of it) takes on an appearance of an agreed-upon function.*

3. *Place in Social Structure: The degree to which the institution's functioning is a part of the way the society is ordered.*

Until at least the end of the seventeenth century in England and through-out the colonial period in America, press function was limited to what those in authority permitted. Viewed as a potential threat to government, newspapers embodied the beliefs, values, and ideas of those in power. Although it reflected the way society was ordered, the press cannot be characterized as embodying the entire society's beliefs, ideas, or values. The many printers punished for stepping outside boundaries of permitted expression belie any widespread agreement on at least some values. A major issue was seditious libel—criticism of government—so the press hardly had freedom to comment on society, let alone represent divergent interests.[42] The press therefore could not develop independent power of social control, although it surely served as a tool of social control for those in authority.

4. *Interaction and Integration: The degree to which the institution interacts with society and is an integral part of the way it is ordered; that is, the degree to which it is manifestly part of the function of keeping society going while at the same time reflecting and shaping the society.*

This and the previous dimension overlap considerably, but it will be seen that the earlier point refers to an institution's *reflection* of the social order, whereas the latter measures the institution's self-conscious *interjection* in society's maintenance and preservation. Here the press's involvement in social controversies gives us insight about its interdependence with and its role in maintaining society. Before the American Revolution, there is little evidence of ongoing press involvement in larger issues; occasional examples appear to be one-time events.[43] With national independence, however, the press became deeply involved in political issues, establishing a pattern that continued.[44] The era of reform, 1830–1860, saw the press taking positions on an array of social issues that, although permeated with political implications, were not tied to government and party structure as had been true previously.[45] For example, newspapers led the campaign for reforms in education, they were deeply involved in the abolitionist (and proslavery), the anti-Catholic, and the American nativist movements of the day, and they worked to promote the notion of American Manifest Destiny and continental expansion.[46] The degree to which the press represented all groups in society also changed. Although the early American press was inaccessible to some groups, during the late 1820s and 1830s newspapers serving blacks, American Indians, labor, and various reform and religious groups were founded and came to symbolize the interjection of the press in shaping society.[47] Despite the fact that the penny and party press were closed to some groups, the redefined press began, however imperfectly, to reflect a diversity both of social composition and of ideas, while at the same time it helped mold a society more responsive to that diversity.

5. *Reinforcement and Promotion of Society's Goals: The degree to which the institution, is (or is capable of being) an integral part of reinforcing and promoting the widely held goals of the society.*

6. *Preservation and Maintenance of Society: The degree to which the institution's work and emphasis reflect a conscious sense of its role in keeping society going.*

Until the eve of the American Revolution, the colonial press was unable to fulfill these functions of promotion and maintenance because both it and colonial society were as yet limited in their development. There were few colonial newspapers; those that existed were small and scattered, and few people could read them.[48] Furthermore, the colonies did not constitute a cohesive society. They were disparate and sometimes in conflict with one another, and their populations represented differing backgrounds.[49] The colonies seemed to unite around only one common goal: defense against external threats.[50] The press did not begin to address issues concerning all colonists until just before the American Revolution, beginning with the Stamp Act of 1765.[51]

7. *Reflection of the Larger Society: The degree to which the institution's work reflects society's composition and diversity.*

During the nation's first decades, the press was tightly tied to government. Blacks and American Indians had little or no access, for example, and had to establish their own newspapers to get their views circulated.[52] Women were scarcely considered an audience, and little content dealt with them.[53] Furthermore, newspapers were not aimed at the wider society in cost, distribution methods, or content. Circulated predominantly through the mail at high cost, they were hardly accessible to any except the well-to-do. Also, in a population with a low literacy rate, content emphasized politics in esoteric essays that could hardly have been intended for the less educated.[54]

8. *Stability: The degree of permanence of the institution.*

Until the 1830s, newspaper failures outnumbered successes. Although political patronage offered financial success, it put journalists in a precariously dependent position. The direction, tone, and content of a newspaper usually came from sources other than policy designed by journalists alone, and any misstep regarding party positions could bring abrupt ruin to the printer and newspaper.[55]

Technological changes during the 1830s fostered greater stability. Printing technology had remained unchanged from Gutenberg's time until the early nineteenth century, and publishing a newspaper was too slow and laborious to permit high circulation. Minor changes, which began to emerge in 1814, culminated by 1832 in a steam-driven press that, by 1846, could produce 12,000 sheets per hour.[56]

Until the 1830s, methods of gathering and circulating news also worked against stability. Distribution relied on mail, carried by ships from port to port and by horseback overland. In the 1820s, journalists began to use the pony express for special, limited kinds of news; then, after the first thirty miles of track were laid in 1830, the expanding railroad network gradually superseded the pony express.[57] Until 1838, ships bringing news from Europe required five to six weeks to cross the Atlantic Ocean; with the beginning of transatlantic steamship service, the time was reduced to less than three weeks, and later to less than two.[58] In 1844, an even more significant support for permanence appeared: the telegraph. Initially ignored by newspapers because of the high cost of transmission, the telegraph was so crucial to meeting the demand for news during the Civil War that, by 1865, it had become an appendage of news gathering and distribution.[59] Successful completion of the transcontinental railroad and transatlantic cable soon after the war secured a network for news gathering from across the nation and Europe, laying to rest problems of press stability linked with difficulties of distribution.[60]

9. *Internal Mechanisms of Permanence: The extent to which the institution's own means of permanence and persistence have developed.*

Such internal mechanisms require, at least to some extent,

— a developed and relatively stable structure, organization, and policy;
— a sense of community among those engaged in the institution's work;
— shared notions of purpose and standards among those engaged in the institution; and

— the institution's self-concept that it serves the whole society, addressing a diversity of groups and expressing a wide range of ideas, and that it is involved with social issues and movements in the larger society.

Journalists had little sense of community or brotherhood before the 1820s, when an "association" of New York journalists and merchants pooled resources to support a boat to gather news from incoming ships.[61] Such cooperative efforts continued, despite fierce competition, and in 1848 the formation of what became the Associated Press began a new stage of journalistic partnership in working toward common goals.[62]

Shared journalistic notions of news values did not clearly emerge until the second decade of the nineteenth century, when innovative methods of news gathering were tried and new stress was placed on the timeliness of news items. Up to that time, except for attending legislative sessions to transcribe proceedings, only rarely would printers leave their shops to gather news firsthand.[63] But in 1811, during the conflict leading to the War of 1812, a Boston coffeehouse owner who assembled "newsbooks" for patrons to read began hiring men with rowboats to meet incoming ships to collect news and return ahead of the ship—and the practice spread.[64]

The War of 1812 also highlighted the importance of timeliness. When three weekly mails failed to arrive, New York merchants with investments in Louisiana cotton spent an anxious January in 1815 while waiting for news of the fate of New Orleans. Reports in early February that Andrew Jackson's army had saved New Orleans, and a week later, that a treaty had been signed two weeks before the battle, poignantly emphasized the significance of timeliness.[65]

The values of news gathering and timeliness became entrenched over the ensuing decades through energetic and sometimes unscrupulous competition, including "scoops," news stealing, exchanges of insults, and interference with rivals' news distribution.[66] Although this competition reflects other developments, it also indicates shared notions of news. Other news values that were subsequently to emerge included prominence, proximity, and local and human interest.[67]

10. *Interdependence of the Institution and Society: The degree to which a balanced relationship between the institution and society has developed, such that continuance or advance of either depends on the other.*

11. *Differentiation: The degree to which an institution is distinguished from other institutions, with a clear and separate purpose, function, body of knowl-*

edge, set of skills, boundaries of expertise, and experience, and the extent to which the institution meets needs of society not met by any other entity.

Interdependency must exist, and differentiation does not mean absolute autonomy. Differentiation can be observed in an institution's interactions with others, especially in defending itself against encroachments from others. In the 1830s, for example, an appeal arose for all journalists to band together to fight a state legislative bill calling for published bylines, and again to oppose court strictures on trial news.[68]

Another way to examine differentiation, however, is to look at structure, the set of skills, body of knowledge, boundaries of expertise, and experience peculiar to the institution. During the mid-nineteenth century, structure and skills took on exclusionary status. For the first time news became a full-time job, and news policy, decisions, and organization, separated from the "mechanical" and business tasks of the press, became the province of one person—the editor. Although printing skills remained the foundation of those associated with journalism, the printer lost status.[69] As needs expanded, other roles emerged: that of the reporter, the correspondent (world, national, or war), and a variety of editors—from associate to managing editor, plus editors for different departments, including a city department.[70]

The financial and editorial sides of running a newspaper diverged, and people with business acumen were sought for the former positions.[71] Still other tasks were added as advertising sales—converted from the "square" to a line rate—became a significant source of financial support, and as a street sales circulation system superseded reliance on the mail.[72]

A final test of differentiation is whether an institution meets social needs that are not met by other institutions or in any other way. It might be argued that the press always serves this function, regardless how limited its development. But in the American experience, it was not until the Civil War that the essential function served only by the press was clearly demonstrated. If antebellum Americans regarded the press as an interesting and amusing but nevertheless dispensable institution, that view changed with the war. Some have in fact asserted that the American press only *became* a social institution with the Civil War.[73] The public depended on the press as never before for news of events that affected families, neighbors, homes, and livelihoods, and national leaders depended on it to gain information for formulating and carrying out policies for saving the union.

The present work examines press development, content, and structure during three distinct eras in the nineteenth century to reveal its function, whether it reflected the larger society, and what role it assumed in maintaining society. The dominant content, tone, and direction of the press convey its function (whether tacitly or overtly established). Groups and ideas acknowledged or encompassed by its operation indicate its place in the polity and the degree to which it reflected the larger society. Last, relation to social movements reveals any acknowledged roles it took in maintaining and perpetuating society. Whether one assumes that the press has always constituted a social institution or took on that status over time, the dimensions outlined have relevance for its role in society. Stages of development of these dimensions have significance for press function, purpose, and direction—defining, limiting, expanding, or altering them; and perceptions of the press's role change with changes along any of these dimensions. Changed conceptions of journalistic standards, in turn, follow those changes in perceptions.

Examining the press along these dimensions across nineteenth-century America calls attention to previously obscured paths of growth and change. Although developments along any dimension had implications for changing the role of the press as well as journalists' tasks and the standards governing their work, neither changes nor perceptions of change emerged full-blown to be readily identified. But when aggregate changes occurred, as happened in certain periods, shifts in values, news definitions, and the press's role—and ultimately changes in concepts of journalistic standards—were inevitable and may be discerned over the long term.

To summarize, then, research surveyed journalistic standards across nineteenth-century America, examining the role of the press and its relationship to standards. Changes in standards were expected to be virtually imperceptible except when viewed over the long term, in part because change in practices is always gradual—it takes at least a generation to *begin* to change an older generation's way of doing things—but also because lag times occur between changes in society at large and accompanying adjustments in its institutions. To observe these changes, nineteenth-century newspapers were examined in each of three distinct eras for evidence of shifts in content, tone, and practices, and press criticism throughout the century was scrutinized to ascertain perceived press functions and journalistic standards.

The book's chapters follow two formats. Chapters 2 and 3 survey nineteenth-century American journalism from different vantage points; the subsequent four chapters focus on time periods within the century; and the final chapter returns to the survey format. Chapter 2 recounts press developments, emphasizing role, and sets the historical context for the press criticism discussed in later chapters. Chapter 3, relating press content to roles and standards during three decades across the nineteenth century, elaborates this context, especially for understanding what prompted the criticism discussed in later chapters. Chapter 4 examines discussions of journalistic conduct, particularly what journalists said, in relation to changing press roles up to 1850. Chapter 5 discusses press criticism during the same years, and Chapters 6 and 7 summarize criticism and journalistic standards from 1850 to 1889. Finally, Chapter 8 summarizes the findings and considers the implications of the research.

Chapter Two

The Role of the Newspaper Press in Nineteenth-Century America

—The Federalists *are down at last,*
The Monarchists *completely cast,*
The Aristocrats *are stripp'd of power,*
Storms on the British *faction pour.*
Soon we Republicans *shall see*
Columbia's slaves from bondage free.
Lord! How the Feds will stare
At JEFF *in* ADAMS' *chair!*
What glorious times! When great men wait;
And little men *direct the state;*
When Tom *and* Dick *and* Harry, *rise*
Two feet above their common size;
. . . .

When Rulers must in turn obey,
That "every dog must have his day;"
And we, whom now the laws expose
To pillories, or the halter's noose,
May then the seats of Honour grace,
And hang our Rulers in our place.
. . . .

The people hold the sovereign sway,
Rulers are chosen to obey;
Their President and Congress-folks,
Are only Tom *and* John-a-nokes,
Their servants, by themselves appointed,
To shew they're not the Lord's annointed . . .
        "Triumph of Democracy," Walpole, N.H.,
        Farmer's Museum, or Literary Gazette, *January 19, 1801*

Early American conceptions of the press's role are clearer than those of any other period. A political role dominated until the 1830s, when changes in press structure and journalism affected ideas about the press's function. Then, slowly, other notions of the press's role competed over the decades through the Civil War, with the information model gaining strength. By the 1860s, although the information model steadily took root as changes expanded and remolded the press, Civil War demands entrenched and extended it while fostering a third conception—the business or market model—that dominated by the end of the century. By century's end, discussions hinted of still another conception of the press—the responsibility model—that was not clearly formulated until decades later.[1] This chapter discusses the changing press roles in relation to American developments from 1800 to 1890. To bring evolution and trends into focus, each era is considered in turn, beginning with the press in the years of the new nation.

The Role of the Press, 1800–1850

The dominant concept of the press's role in early America was political and is clearest during the first three decades of the nineteenth century.[2] The press served other purposes, but its content, function, and role reflected Americans' primary interest in fashioning a new form of government and debating ideas for the country's development. Whether politics really was the all-consuming interest may be debated, but the press emphasized it above all else. In his book published in 1969 dealing with the press in the nation's first decade, the historian Donald Stewart writes:

Despite the unevenness of its influence, the press almost from its inception in America came consistently to reflect the life and interests of the nation's citizenry. At times it both molded public opinion and mirrored it. Seldom has it accomplished both functions so completely as in the years immediately following the ratification of the Federal Constitution.[3]

The political role established a pattern of press evolution and influence, fostering practices and molding expectations that fed on each other well into the twentieth century as journalists pursued active involvement in politics. Whether or not they received financial support from parties, many journalists aided party organization and campaigns—from establishing and leading political societies, to holding public office, to serving as confidants and advisers to political leaders and generally exercising powerful influence. Such individuals were informally supported by parties or political leaders. Stewart lists thirty printers who were connected with political societies in nine states in the 1790s. Among additional printers he mentions, Philip Freneau's brother Peter published the Charleston *City Gazette* and served as secretary of state for South Carolina; Thomas Greenleaf, the *New York Journal* editor, was a "sachem of the Tammany Society" and closely associated with Aaron Burr in party affairs; several printers, including Philadelphia *Aurora* editor Benjamin Franklin Bache, were active in the American Philosophical Society, viewed by some as the organizing center for the Jeffersonian party's emergence; Bache and Eleazer Oswald were members of the Corresponding Committee of the Democratic Society of Pennsylvania; and John Bradford founded the Democratic Society of Kentucky.[4]

The pattern held at mid-century and after. *National Intelligencer* editor William Winston Seaton served as the mayor of Washington, D.C., during the 1840s.[5] Horace Greeley, editor of the *New York Tribune*, served in Congress in the 1840s, wanted to run for New York governor and lieutenant governor during the 1850s, and ran for president in 1872.[6] Henry J. Raymond, founder and editor of the *New York Times*, was elected to the New York House of Representatives (where he served as Speaker), and was subsequently elected lieutenant governor and U.S. congressman; he also chaired the National Union Executive Committee during the Civil War, and served in various nonelective capacities throughout his career.[7] Thurlow Weed, the *Albany Journal* editor and a founder of the Anti-Masonic party, later earned recognition as a powerful "boss" in the Whig party. Several journalists were deeply involved in political campaigns and in the Republican party's emergence in 1854.[8] In addition, journalists were often called on to carry out specific political tasks. President James K. Polk appointed *New York Sun* editor Moses Y. Beach as a special agent empowered to negotiate for peace during the Mexican War.[9] Charles Dana, a veteran journalist and a successor to Moses S. Beach as editor of the *New York Sun*, was appointed assistant secretary of war during the Civil War. That appointment was withdrawn when news of it leaked prematurely, but Dana was then appointed a special commissioner in the War Department.[10] When Abraham Lincoln gave his famous Cooper Union speech in 1860, five of the seven persons on the dais with him were newspapermen, and *New York Evening Post* editor William Cullen Bryant introduced him.[11] The examples could be multiplied, for every nineteenth-century journalist of note had powerful political influence.

Political journalism habits became so entrenched that, although many advocated an "independent" press during most of the century, the issue of the press's proper role in politics was never resolved, and articles late in the century reveal an inability to comprehend a nonpolitical press. Present-day standards discourage journalists' direct involvement in politics, but ambiguity about indirect involvement and an inability to define the press's role and effects are part of the legacy of patterns established in early America.[12]

Because of newspapers' political nature and party affiliations, historians have called the early period of American journalism the era of the party press.[13] The purpose here is not to retell that history, but to focus on the conditions fostering and entrenching such a political role. Conditions in four broad areas created an especially conducive climate: the origins of the nation's press, the course of national development, social conditions, and the financial status of and prospects for the press.

The Origins of the Nation's Press

This book emphasizes the American press after the government was formed, but any discussion of its political origins must acknowledge the English influence. A pattern of partisanism had long existed in England's press, and a ready model—along with many transplanted English printers —favored a similar pattern in America.[14] The John Peter Zenger case in the 1730s, which emerged out of use of the press in behalf of a political faction, demonstrates that the pattern was not new to American printers.[15] And the long-established role of the public printer was also transplanted from England. Patronage evolved from this English practice of designating someone to "publish" laws and official proclamations to the realm—tasks performed by the royal secretary before printing. Soon after printing appeared in England, the first "public" printer was named in 1504 to publish such information.[16]

Such precedents augmented late eighteenth-century conditions conducive to the development of a political role for the press. These conditions included the American revolutionary experience, the special status accorded the press in the Constitution, the public printer tradition, and the respect for the press as a symbol of advancing civilization.

Until events in the 1760s precipitated the American Revolution, the press was shaped by a view that it potentially threatened social order and government stability. Under threat of seditious libel charges for content interpreted as critical of government, printers limited political coverage largely to foreign news, to what colonial officials permitted, or to what they believed would not offend sufficiently to threaten their livelihoods. During the colonial era, for example, at least five kinds of controls operated at various times. From 1636 to 1730, royal governors were instructed to prevent printing in "our said territory under your government."[17] After the law had expired in England, colonial printers were nevertheless required to be licensed, and although "printed by authority" disappeared from mastheads after James Franklin's defiance in the 1720s, occasional persecutions for publishing "unauthorized matter" continued.[18] The power of the royal courts was deflated after the John Peter Zenger case in 1735, but it remained a threat.[19] Although apparently rarely used, the ability of anyone to lodge complaints against printers through filing an "information" still existed.[20] Finally, legislative breach-of-privilege citations could be used to restrict journalistic coverage.[21] Consequently, foreign news dominated what has been referred to as the "bulletin board" journalism of the colonial press, which presented isolated items without commenting, filling in background, explaining, establishing connections among items, or providing anything like what is today called "follow-up."[22]

But after passage of the Stamp Act in 1765 threatened an already financially weak press with a heavy tax, colonial American printers went on the political offensive. Filling columns with criticism of the act while flouting it, printers aroused sentiment that led to successful organized opposition. The Stamp Act was repealed, and no newspaper ever paid a cent of the tax.[23] The triumph and experience gained in resisting the law were inevitably incentives for increased political activity, and the press turned advocate as printers passionately took sides during the American Revolution by printing the political tracts of nonjournalists. The press came to be a vehicle for influencing and manipulating public opinion to support and agitate for desired ends;[24] in fact, it was viewed as virtually the only vehicle for doing so.

Thus the new nation's leaders, journalists, and citizens had used the press for political purposes in a history-changing event and won, learning unforgettable lessons. The recognized value of the press as a political weapon, combined with experience in using it as such—to advocate, promote, persuade, and manipulate opinion—make the early party press seem a natural result as America's political system developed following the Revolution.

Although the prerevolutionary American press functioned according to the cultural value that rulers were "masters" to a "servant" constituency, the new government's reversal of this tenet—the new emphasis that those in government were servants of the people[25]—gave the press special status under the Constitution that aided development of a political role in two ways. First, the stipulation in the First Amendment that Congress could make no law abridging freedom of the press gave journalists, in the opinion of contemporaries, greater freedom than ever before. Especially after the first test of this principle in the Alien and Sedition Acts ordeal of 1798–1800, journalists could, for the first time anywhere, publish about political matters with relatively little fear of intimidation, imprisonment, or loss of livelihood.[26] Such freedom was no doubt heady. As happens whenever strictures are loosened, journalists could be expected to plunge headlong into publishing on political subjects; thus, merely exercising this newfound right portended a political press.

Second, the constitutional guarantee implied protection precisely for political discussion. Perhaps because of Enlightenment values emphasizing reason, the Founding Fathers intended to quash traditions restricting political content and, in guaranteeing press protection, assured freedom to discuss primarily political matters. The amendment has been extended over the years through judicial interpretation,[27] but because of the framers' preoccupations with freedom to discuss political affairs, the Constitution's conferring on the press the role of forum for such discussion set the stage for linking the press with the party system.

The long tradition of the public printer provided, by the late eighteenth century, a ready means for attaching the press to the political system. By the end of the century the position had become one of formal patronage, meaning appointment or election to publish (for payment) the laws of the United States, states, and government departments at all levels. As parties developed, printers who showed aggressiveness in promoting and advancing the ascendant party in any area were most likely to win these public appointments or elections. Incentives were thus created for politicizing the press, and a network of informal patronage also emerged as partisans rewarded, with financial support, politically useful printers who may or may not have won positions through formal patronage.[28]

Last, awe of the press as a symbol of advancing civilization and progress dominated discussions, which were infused with notions of its immense political power, through mid-century. In his autobiography, the journalist Joseph T. Buckingham wrote that Connecticut had no more than five or six newspapers when he was a boy, and the first in his hometown (Windham) in 1793 created "a memorable epoch in our village history." He continued:

> In the general opinion it seemed to add much dignity and importance to the town. For several weeks I was greatly exercised with a desire to see the operation of printing . . . when an opportunity to gratify my curiosity was presented, I stood in one position . . . for an hour, to see a compositor work at his case, and another hour . . . with intense interest watching the operation of the press.[29]

By 1800, great numbers of people had not experienced the press as part of their lives; certainly, newspapers were not commonplace, as they are today. But anyone curious to observe present-day "new technologies" can readily identify with the feeling the passage conveys.[30] For the people of early America, some of their awe of the press flowed, no doubt, from satisfying long-held curiosity about something that must have seemed incomprehensible at second hand. Although it had functioned in some parts of the world for centuries, the press remained unfathomable until it was actually seen. Other sources of such awe, as the record attests repeatedly over the next decades, were the respect the press earned in America's struggle for independence, along with the recognition that it linked one to the rest of the world. Over the decades, this awe reflected increasing public preoccupation with the press's power to reach and therefore influence thought and opinion in the nation's every nook and cranny. Finally, a newspaper in one's own community meant direct access to political news—the pre-eminent news in this era when a new government and a nation's destiny were being shaped. Seeking sound financial bases and knowing political matter interested readers, printers obliged by filling columns with it. It must be noted in this context, too, that the conception of the audience reinforced and perpetuated the political role. Newspapers were expensive, sold by subscription primarily via the mail, and aimed at the educated elite.[31] In making political content dominant, printers evidently viewed the political leadership as their primary audience.

The Course of National Development

The nation's beginning endowed the press with an unending stream of political content as leaders debated critical issues. After the American Revolution, the new republic's leaders confronted issues of national development and whether government's chief purpose was to promote equality and justice or to preserve order and security. The two major groups that formed on either side of the debate in the 1790s—Federalists and Anti-Federalists—shaped the early press agenda as they advocated different sets of values. The Federalists feared anarchy and democracy. They argued that inequality was natural, that government and property were interdependent, that strong central government was essential, and that the United States should pursue internal improvements and manufacturing. The Anti-Federalists feared tyranny and concentration of power in too few hands. They sought equality, simplicity, and frugality while opposing special privileges. Fearful of government managed from the nation's capital, the group stressed states' rights and advocated public opinion as a restraint on power. Unconvinced of the need for industrialization, the Anti-Federalists envisioned an America based on an agricultural economy and opposed government action to promote industrial forms of economic development.[32]

These opposing values are at the foundation of the emerging and increasingly inseparable roles of the press and the political system in the early years of the nation. Alexander Hamilton and Thomas Jefferson, both members of the first cabinet, represented these divergent views; when Jefferson could find no way of expressing his disagreement with Federalist policies, he resigned in 1793, marking the formation of an opposition "party" in America.[33] In the meantime, the Federalists used the patronage system to establish John Fenno as editor of the *Gazette of the United States* in the first capital in New York on April 15, 1789. At the time, the new Constitution had been sent to the states for ratification, and the Federalists believed a newspaper essential to gaining public support for it. On October 31, 1791, the Anti-Federalists established the *National Gazette*, edited by Philip Freneau, and newspapers supporting either party proliferated throughout the 1790s.[34]

But the Federalists, with control over a host of government positions opening across the nation, went even further in linking the press with the party. In power during the early period of the Post Office's expansion, they appointed approximately a thousand editors as postmasters by 1800 and established criteria governing appointments, selecting these postmaster/printers on the basis of political views. The advantages of the Federalist postmaster/printer over the Anti-Federalist printer served the party well. A printer who was also a postmaster had free and certain delivery of his newspaper, was assured of receiving news first since it came via the mails, and was in a position to exercise some control over Anti-Federalist newspapers. Anti-Federalists charged Federalist postmaster/printers with opening, confiscating, diverting, and suppressing their newspapers.[35]

The climate was right, then, for the emergence and development of a political press in America. Beginning with the debate over ratification of the new Constitution, each side used the press, and any new or controversial idea could become the basis for establishing a newspaper to promote it. Some newspapers came into being only for a political campaign and ended with the election—a pattern that continued at least into the 1840s. Often newspapers were established to expound views that might draw a following sufficient to coalesce into a party.[36]

This symbiotic beginning of the nation's first political parties and newspapers to promote them forged a solid foundation for the press's political role. But other trends in national development, especially in politics, entrenched and fostered such a role. These included changed attitudes about campaigning, office holding, and requirements for political leadership, along with the emergence of professional politicians, party organizations, and political strategies.

In the late eighteenth and early nineteenth centuries, it was viewed as improper for political aspirants to campaign for office,[37] so newspapers served as campaigners, disseminating parties' ideologies and candidates' views. At times when passions ran high about the correct course of national development, those espousing one view zealously promoted it and debunked others. Printers serving parties thus filled newspapers with polemics, making the press primarily a vehicle of political views.

The emergence of what have been called the first "professional" politicians also abetted the press's political role. Initially, Americans did not seek office, regarding such public service as simply a duty. As this notion of public service changed in the early nineteenth century, however, political strategies and party organization developed, and the new kind of politician saw the press as central to these activities.[38]

Changed conceptions of how best to achieve political ends, of what was good strategy and what political leadership required, accompanied the professionalization of politics. By the 1820s, the traditional belief that political leaders must be eloquent orators able to persuade the educated elite had given way to the view that they must appeal directly to the public and be capable of persuading the masses and shaping public opinion.[39] Supporting a candidate with popular appeal, a newspaper was viewed as essential for making and maintaining the connection with the public.

Such a belief entrenched a view of newspapers as central to party organization. The newspaper was a vehicle for conveying party views to the public, convincing the public of the rightness of those views and the errors of opposing views, achieving party cohesion and solidarity, maintaining party organization, "winning" public debates of issues, and winning elections.[40] As professional politicians built party organization around the newspaper, they sought editors more for their political astuteness than for their journalistic training, patronizing those they saw as the most capable, persuasive writers and the most politically adept.[41]

Social Conditions

The historian Edward Pessen, citing Walter Bagehot's introduction to *The English Constitution* (1872), has discussed the significance of a malleable citizenry in the emergence of early American leaders. Learning how to function in a new form of government, the citizens of the new nation were very dependent on leaders. People needed direction, and any direction offered would likely have far-reaching influence.[42] Since leaders used the press to disseminate views and ideas, people relied on it to learn the course and trends of national government, and this increasing reliance in the nation's early years continually reinforced the political role of the press.

Because the great focal point of interest was the government and the newspaper was the only "national" medium through which government policy and directions could be learned, the press's place in the larger polity defined it as part of the political structure. The chief party newspaper in the nation's capital became especially powerful. Because other newspapers were scattered and unable to keep their own reporters in the capital, they relied on the national party paper for news of government. Also, because newspapers were small, such news could dominate their space, making their content primarily political even if they did not publish debates of local issues. The administration newspaper's standard of partisanism was imitated, and the national paper became a main link in what inevitably emerged as a "network" of party papers across the nation. Unlinked to the capital's administration newspaper and composed of groups surrounding specific newspapers, sometimes called "juntos," the network first made the press instrumental in national elections in Andrew Jackson's 1828 campaign[43] and made journalists powerful in determining political appointments and policies thereafter. In ensuing years, Jackson's chief editor, Francis Preston Blair, used it to disseminate Jacksonian policies and cement support for them.[44]

Financial Status of the Newspaper

Financial difficulties of early American newspapers also favored their political role because patronage, one of five chief sources of income, offered the best possibility for survival. Subscription income, averaging about one-third of publishing expenses, would not support a newspaper—in part, because fees were not paid. After the canvassing of a community, a newspaper was normally established on the basis of the number of people saying they would subscribe; but many receiving newspapers never paid. Printers complained about thousands of dollars owed them for subscriptions, and early newspapers' columns reveal the problem as constant.[45]

Advertising would not support a newspaper because rates were too low and advertising had not been "discovered" as a way to ensure a solid financial base. Amounts varied, of course, but printers generally charged 50 cents per square (twelve lines) for the first insertion and 25 cents for each succeeding insertion; yearly rates were $32 to $40—with a newspaper subscription included for the advertiser. Advertising typically filled half, and often three-fourths, of newspaper space; with rates so low, heavy advertising was necessary and often made the difference in a newspaper's survival. Job printing, another income source, was also very important, but such contracts frequently became the privilege of those few printers favored by the stronger party in a community.[46] Printers who held appointments as postmasters had an economic advantage because, in representing the national government at the local level, they often got contracts to print congressional laws, whereas the postmaster's income, averaging approximately $800 a year in the early nineteenth century, helped keep a newspaper in business. In addition, other income often came from operating a book and stationery store in conjunction with the Post Office and press.[47]

But the most certain way to keep a newspaper going—and the most lucrative source of income—was patronage. Printers sought government contracts, and most who got them had few financial worries. The journalism historian William Ames has found that editors of the *National Intelligencer*, the administration newspaper during the first three decades of the nineteenth century, received $299,622.78 for Senate and House printing contracts during the 1820s.[48] Printers who received no such contracts could depend on party support to see that they stayed afloat financially so long as they remained loyal and useful. Parties often set editors up in business and assured patronage in return for party service.

The political role of the press during the nation's early decades had significant implications for American journalism throughout the century. Such an entrenched role could not diminish quickly, and as late as the Civil War, more than 80 percent of the nation's four thousand–plus periodicals were partisan.[49] Throughout the century, patterns of journalists' political involvement, set in motion in the earliest decades, persisted in the holding of public office and influence on national policy.

The Role of the Press, 1830–1870

Emerging conceptions of the press competed with its established political role in the 1830s, and aggregate changes, especially during that decade and again in the Civil War era, led increasingly away from a strictly partisan function. The appearance of the penny press, which posed the first serious challenge to the political newspaper, in the 1830s has been examined from many perspectives.[50] Emphasis here is on the changing role and perceptions of the press during the century's middle decades.

Especially important in altering both the actual and the conceived role of the press during the middle decades were a spirit of reform and an emphasis on the individual. As America's great reform era (1830–1860) began, an aggregate of changes reshaped virtually every aspect of journalism. It could be argued, in fact, that the penny press was itself a reform movement, while at the same time it was a product of broader drives sweeping the country, for every aspect of journalism was affected. Political reformers emphasized individual rights, advocating broader class representation among government officials, the rights of women and free blacks, abolition of slavery, and elimination of property qualifications for voting. Economic reformers sought to end the inheritance system, monopoly in landownership, child labor, and the institution of the debtors' prison; they pushed for equalization of property ownership, a homestead law, the ten-hour workday, better working conditions, and labor rights. Educational reformers sought universal education, improved teaching and classroom facilities, and compulsory school attendance laws; humanitarian reformers sought improved conditions in prisons and institutions for the mentally incompetent.[51]

Such activities grew out of serious questioning of the new government and its effects on society; some argued that the government was not working because, despite rhetoric about democracy, portions of society were left out or adversely affected. As every institution's function and effectiveness came under scrutiny, Americans' collective set of assumptions about government, individual roles, society, and the world changed. The advent of the industrial revolution changed ideas about the economy; urban growth changed relationships and affected people's thinking about politics and society; Jacksonian Democracy changed people's view about their role in government.[52] And underlying all, a celebration of the individual marked the age.

Contemporaries have been credited with outlining the phenomenon of "individualism"—Alexis de Tocqueville as conceptualizing it, and Ralph Waldo Emerson as defining its parameters. Often treated in contemporary literature as up against society and its institutions, often as superior to those, and often as at one with the world, the individual was paramount. In Emerson's words, "The private life of one man shall be a more illustrious monarchy, more formidable to its enemy, more sweet and serene in its influence to its friend, than any kingdom in history."[53]

In concert with such views, the press's role changed from an orientation to groups—parties, elites, the commercial class—to the individual and the information citizens needed to understand and participate in the community, nation, and world. By mid-century, journalism reflected reform preoccupations and the increased concern with the individual, resulting in changes in the nature of news, news style, newspaper work, conception of audience, means of financial support, and press structure and role. In effect, journalism was redefined.

News

News became event oriented, which is not to say that previous journalism did not report events; rather, dominant newspaper content began to focus on events, as opposed to political views. Furthermore, news categories increased, from foreign, political, party, and national government reporting, to include crime, sports, and local "beats" such as the courts and police. And news of violence and a flurry of sensational journalism also appeared. Substance changed from esoteric polemical essays typical of the party press era.[54]

News Style

More concise items, often reported in a comparatively light, entertaining style, came to dominate. A type of story intended purely to entertain also became part of newspaper content; and some events were reported with wit and humor, making news enjoyable to read, even though it often trivialized events and people.[55]

Newspaper Work

The printer's role diverged from that of editor, and other roles became defined—reporters, paid correspondents, associates, assistants, and managing and city editors became common by 1860. For the first time, news was a full-time job as the tasks of news decisions and policy became the province of one individual—the editor.[56] Reporters began serving a role closely akin to that of today, and their tasks, no longer limited to reporting legislative proceedings, included presenting eyewitness accounts and interviews about a diversity of news items.[57]

Conception of Audience

The conception of the audience changed. Whereas newspapers had previously aimed at the educated elite throughout the country, they now began to target an audience in an expanse of city blocks in some specific proximity to the newspaper office. In addition to providing a link outward to the rest of the world, the newspaper became community-centered, thus connecting individuals to both their immediate surroundings and the larger polity.

Financial Basis

A sounder financial base was built by changing advertising sales to a line rate and organizing an efficient distribution system based on carriers and street sales. Carriers were charged a lower rate per hundred if they paid for their newspapers in advance, which solved the problem of unpaid subscriptions.[58] Sales no longer depended primarily on the mails, and the timeliness of news in papers bought daily on the streets added a quality that an inefficient mail system could never guarantee. And, of course, the price of one penny per paper increased accessibility to a wider audience.

Press Structure

Industry structure took shape out of a division of labor among departments and the emergence of numerous journalistic positions. The business and editorial departments became more clearly demarcated. Other areas also became defined, such as, for example, the literary and "home" departments.[59]

An observer writing in 1842 provides insight into the press's new direction. Comparing the British and American milieus of journalism, he outlined the importance of a geographically well-defined audience, an efficient means of gathering and distributing news, competitiveness within the urban setting, payment of contributors for news items, and the division of tasks. Noting Great Britain's newspaper circulation advantages over America's breadth of space and sparse settlement, he wrote:

The compactness of the British population enables editors to concentrate their patronage within a narrower compass, which brings them nearer to their readers, aids them in acquiring a more intimate knowledge of their interests, opinions, wishes and feelings, and places more readily within their reach, those pecuniary returns, upon which the existence of the Press, as well as of every art, trade and profession essentially depends; while . . . their modes of inter-communication ensure despatch and safety to the circulation of important intelligence. The lively, and even fierce competition that exists between the leading newspapers in London, enhances greatly their value, as mere vehicles of news;—in proof of which emulation, we would mention their establishment of expresses at a large expense . . . to place at the disposal of editors, within the least possible time consistent with the nature of the case, reports of the latest, rarest, and most important information that occurs in the country, near and remote—a practice . . . first commenced by the "London Times," but which has been followed advantageously, and with great perseverance and public spirit, by other newspapers. The same journal was the first to set the example of paying a high rate . . . to those who contributed acceptable articles. . . . The division of labor system, . . . emphatically the British system . . . has been extended to the operations of the Newspaper Press, and has contributed more to its improvement than any other cause. The same has been adopted to some extent, in the principal cities of our own country, by the employment of sub-editors and of correspondents who are paid for their services.[60]

The passage suggests that the changes under way were channeled; that audience conception, news value, competition, emerging structure, news-gathering developments, and writing quality were studied; and that American journalists benefited from knowledge of press developments in other nations (especially England). The nineteenth-century journalism historian Frederic Hudson noted the outlines of the "London plan" in the structure of the penny press. Hudson quoted an article from the New York *Journal of Commerce* for June 29, 1835, that the penny papers were "less partisan in politics than the large papers, and more decidedly American, with one or two exceptions." They were "circulated on the London plan, the editors and publishers doing no more than to complete the manufacture of the papers, when they are sold to the newsmen or carriers at 67 cents per 100." The *Journal of Commerce* writer finally remarked that the "manner in which their pecuniary affairs are conducted shows how much may come of some details."[61]

With these changes, the press's role in the larger polity also shifted. Although many have emphasized the growing attention to news in this era, the journalism historians Dan Schiller, Frank Luther Mott, and Michael Schudson have called attention to a shifting model.[62] Of particular relevance here are Schiller's and Mott's views. Schiller argues that the era's press was committed to a broader concept of the public good, attempting to define and protect the larger society and emphasizing individual rights and American ideals as values. The press, providing "cheap, value-free information," emphasized a common belief of the time—that "knowledge, like property, should not be monopolized for exclusive use by private interests. . . ."[63]

Mott suggests the new orientation to the individual by arguing that the penny press represented a great democratic movement. The papers were easy to read and accessible in cost to everyone, and hence more people could be informed and better prepared as citizens; the papers were easy to handle, to carry around and read at leisure; in short, they recognized a mass in society not previously recognized by the press in cost, content, and style. The emphasis on human interest stories, Mott notes, dealt with "persons who were interesting merely as human beings, and not for their connection with either significant or sensational news," and crime news in the era often represented the first press attention to persons lacking social standing.[64]

The new orientation, especially the emphasis on the public good, along with other qualities Schiller and Mott cited permeate discussions of the press in the 1830s. Individuals offered various ideas of journalistic functions and sought to distinguish and justify something beyond a political role for the press. Generally, they defined it as important to everyone, outlining its functions in serving the broader society. The first successful penny newspaper announced in its first issue that it intended to serve all, aiming "to lay before the public, at a price within the means of everyone, all the news of the day."[65] Don Seitz describes the second successful penny newspaper, the *New York Herald*, as a "little paper" that was "so individualistic that it at once made headway."[66] James Gordon Bennett, editor of the *New York Herald*, also emphasized that his newspaper was intended for everyone: "There was plenty of room . . . for a cheap paper . . . calculated to circulate among all ranks and conditions; to interest the merchant and the man of learning, as well as the mechanic and the man of labor."[67]

Writers stressed the centrality of overcoming the prohibitive cost of published materials in expanding their accessibility. Because the earliest books were expensive and difficult to publish, the writer of an article appearing in the *Southern Quarterly Review* in 1842 said, most people were "deprived of the benefits . . . from this most useful discovery, and it became necessary to devise some method" to provide access for "all classes" to a "cheaper kind of literature . . . better suited to the popular needs." And this "gave rise to periodical issues, first of newspapers," then essays and magazines.[68] Bennett, after founding the *New York Herald* in 1835, referred to this new accessibility: "there is not a person in this city, male or female, that may not be able to say—'well I have got a paper of my own which will tell me all about what's doing in the world—I'm busy now—but I'll put it in my pocket and read it at my leisure.'"[69] Seven years later the *Southern Quarterly Review* writer quoted above, lauding the press's information function, declared:

Men knew little, formerly, of what was passing beyond . . . their own immediate neighborhood, but now, through the . . . newspaper . . . , town and country, state and nation, and the most distant parts of the world are brought together, and whatever is new, rare and important, is conveyed with rapidity to every reader . . . set forth in the most succinct manner, and in a style adapted to the comprehension of all.[70]

Although some decried attention to so many individuals as trivialization, many—especially journalists—hailed it. Samuel Bowles III, editor of the *Springfield* (Massachusetts) *Republican*, argued in 1858 that such attention motivated people and stimulated progress and good works:

The mention of a notable deed in the public press is the highest public honor that can now be awarded. . . . The ribbons and orders bestowed by royalty are of small account compared with the fame created by the newspaper press for him who conceives a great thought, or does a brave or noble deed. The press carries his name on the wings of the wind to every land, and makes it a household word. . . .[71]

The orientation to the individual had implications for criticism and standards, but as a broad direction it meant that the press not only provided reports on government but became the individual's "eyes and ears," informing him about all levels of society, the gradations of human behavior, and matters that might be of interest in hundreds of places he could not be. The results were reports of crime, violence, sexual liaisons, and other content that shocked some. But aiming to be eyes and ears for the individual affected news-gathering and reporting techniques: eyewitness and interview accounts became important for the first time, and speed of transmission became ever more crucial. A style of vivid, graphic description laden with detail also emerged that was intended to provide the "true" sense of a place or event, the style often referred to as realism.[72]

But the new role remained shrouded by the overshadowing implications of the entrenched political role, by people's confusion about the press's unprecedented growth and what it could or should do, and by their conceptual inability to separate a political from an information role.

Implications of the Political Role

The deeply rooted political role had far-reaching implications that sustained it, despite the claims of the new journalism. Those aspiring to a journalistic career in the era of the political press found that the surest route was through political sagacity. If they wanted to advance in journalism, political activity was the way to gain attention; if they sought financial success in their careers, political affiliation—although not perfectly reliable—offered the most certain means; if they aspired to a comfortable life-style (and who didn't?), political support promised it; if they sought visibility and influence, the paths to follow were political. To prepare for achieving any of these aims, however, meant learning politics and participating in party activities from an early age. Henry J. Raymond had read Horace Greeley's newspapers, and when he left college around 1840 he pursued two avenues to support his journalistic aspirations: working for Greeley (whom he had never met) as a "go-fer" and aiding in political campaigns.[73] Thus, a crop of aspiring journalists schooled in politics had prepared themselves by the 1840s according to what they understood as the required qualifications. Becoming journalists just when the press's role was changing meant they brought all their political preparedness to a journalism that was on a shifting course. It was logical that they would use the only training they knew, and therefore the newspaper press—although veering in a new direction—was infused with the political preoccupations resulting from their training. Hence, even as they debunked partisanship in the 1830s and 1840s, journalists sought political roles and used newspapers to advance political views and parties.

Another implication of the political role, born of the American revolutionary experience, concerned the press's power over public opinion. After the Revolution, Americans believed that the press directly influenced and molded public opinion, a view that dominated into the 1880s, even though some began to question such power as early as the 1830s. The English philosopher Thomas Carlyle's familiar statement, published in 1840 and attributed to Edmund Burke, epitomized views in both America and England at the time. Claiming that the press constituted a "fourth estate" among government branches and was "more important far than all," Carlyle wrote:

Writing brings printing . . . every-day extempore Printing, as we see at the present. Whoever can speak, speaking now to the whole nation, becomes a power, a branch of government. . . . Those poor bits of ragpaper with black ink on them;—from the Daily Newspaper to the sacred Hebrew Book, what have they not done, what are they not doing! . . .

All this, of the importance and supreme importance of . . . how the Press is to such a degree superseding the Pulpit, the Senate, the *Senatus Academicus* and much else, has been admitted for a good while; and recognised often enough, in late times, with a sort of sentimental triumph and wonderment.[74]

Discussions through the 1880s charged the press with usurping the roles of other institutions (such as the church and the state and national legislatures), as Carlyle had implied. But through the Civil War, by far the more prevalent theme concerned the press's power over public opinion. By the 1860s, a belief prevailed that the press created and shaped public opinion. The journalist Lambert Wilmer, in a book published in 1860, typified this view, citing several sources to stress the press's power. American political philosopher and statesman Edward Everett, for example, said on the eve of the Civil War, "The newspaper press of the U.S. is, for good or evil, the most powerful influence that acts on the public mind,— the most powerful in itself and as the channel through which most other influence acts." A judge addressing a jury in the Philadelphia Court of Quarter Sessions called the newspaper press "all powerful." A *Washington Union* item called the press the "Greatest power in the state"; holding that the press controlled "the state and the church" and directed "the family, the legislator, the magistrate and the minister," the writer said, "none rise above its influence" or "sink below its authority" . . . from its very nature, it places every other power, to a greater or lesser extent, in subjection to its laws." Congressman Charles J. Ingersol, in a letter dated July 5, 1858, called newspaper editors "*the real sovereigns of our country*" (emphasis in original).[75] The 1860 census took notice of the press's power and importance. Among several comments on the press in an introductory section of the census report, the response to the question "What is it that controls the different departments of the government and all the varied industrial and social interests within the . . . republic?" was "The answer is, emphatically, public opinion enunciated through the Press. . . . The press is the real representative of the people, the great conservative power held by them to guard public and individual liberty."[76] As Wilmer wrote,

Are not public opinion and newspaper opinion identical? And is not public opinion evidently manufactured by the public journals? If the newspapers form public opinion, they govern the country; they control the elections and direct the choice of our executive, legislative and judicial officers; for public opinion is the instrument by means of which these operations of our government are effected.[77]

Inability to Conceptualize a Nonpolitical Role

Through the 1830s and following decades, Americans decried the partisan press, enumerated its weaknesses, and increasingly lauded the inde-

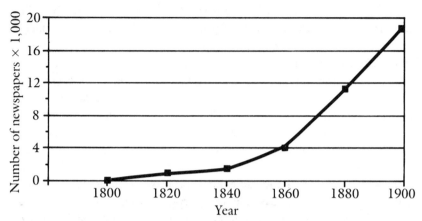

Fig. 2.1. Growth of Newspapers in the United States, 1800–1899.
Source: Based on U.S. census data and information in William A. Dill, *Growth of Newspapers in the United States* (Lawrence: University of Kansas Press, 1928)

pendent newspaper. But what they called "independent" papers generally supported particular parties and manifested other political propensities. At most, *independent* seemed to mean that a paper had no formal party alliance; in practice, it did not mean that it would not in other ways play the same role or one similar to that of the party papers. And indeed, some newspapers that claimed to be independent still looked to a party for financial aid.[78] As late as the 1880s, writers attempted to explain how a newspaper could maintain party loyalty and be "ethical" at the same time —suggesting difficulty in comprehending a press function divorced from partisanism.[79]

Confusion About Growth and Power

Discussions near mid-century suggest that people were overwhelmed by a phenomenon they could not understand. Preoccupied with unprecedented press growth (see fig. 2.1), their statements reflect an almost pious awe that glorified the press's capabilities and infused it with near omnipotence in its multiple functions and capabilities.

Apparently, aiming to impart understanding through long-term perspective, many traced press history in detail, but such exercises typically seemed to confound and defy any clear articulation about the press. In 1833 one writer said it "would be trite to enlarge . . . on the immense influence of the press, or the great change . . . it has wrought in the destinies of mankind";[80] another, a year later, remarked that everyone knew the press had "effected a greater change in human affairs, than either gunpowder or the compass."[81] Recounting the tale of Faust's persecution for magic when he appeared in fifteenth-century Paris with copies of the Bible, because the bare notion of printing was so incredible, an American minister wrote in 1844 that Faust escaped death by his accusers, but "the secret art was made known. An agency had been discovered which could multiply copies of books with astonishing facility and cheapness, and to a boundless extent. This agency was the Art of printing. This secret was the POWER OF THE PRESS."[82]

Often acclaimed as the greatest invention of civilization, the press was credited with multiple, quasi-magical functions: it was touted as capable of speedily educating people, advancing scientific knowledge, determining political outcomes, powerfully shaping opinion, and effecting world peace—in general, as being essential to the conduct of human affairs. The writer of the article cited earlier from the *Southern Quarterly Review* called the newspaper a "vehicle of news,—of intelligence,—of knowledge" and a shrinker of boundaries; he asserted that its value to commerce was incalculable, for newspapers provided "indispensable" information on the "state of the markets and of the wants of mankind"; without them, "neither foreign nor domestic trade could be carried on advantageously, if at all. . . ."[83] A few of the more articulate attempted to define the press's role as other than partisan although still distinguishing a political function. The *Southern Quarterly Review* writer called the newspaper's political power "immense" because it provided for dissemination of opinions, explained and upheld government principles, promulgated and discussed reform measures, debated rival candidates' claims to office, was the first to disseminate to the world "discoveries of men of science," and investigated and set forth "in a lucid, faithful and able manner" all other "matters bearing upon the welfare of the community in its most important relations."[84]

Many in this era cast the press in the role of protector and defender of people's rights. Again, the writer in the *Southern Quarterly Review*, distinguishing the American press's function from that in other countries, especially England, emphasized this role:

it is the peculiar province of the Newspaper Press, in this country, to maintain the principles of a free government; to advocate popular rights; to be, in a word, in all respects, the champion of the people; its chosen protector from internal and external foes; its pioneer in removing difficulties and leading the way to peace, happiness and national fame.[85]

Virtually all observers remarked on the pervasiveness of the American press, which was wedded, in their minds, to a direct, potent influence on thought processes and opinions. Perceptions that the press powerfully affected public opinion, whether it in fact did or not, meant that the press's expanded role during the Civil War only increased its influence. To the degree that perceptions influence behavior, actions based on such beliefs gave the press enhanced power.

The Role of the Press, 1860–1900

As the Civil War approached, the American press had been significantly remolded by various changes during the 1830s, 1840s, and 1850s. The new emphasis on information and the traditional political functions were just two enduring trends. The "alternative" media—the black and American Indian press and the abolitionist, women's, and labor publications that emerged beginning in the 1820s—added dimensions, infusing the press with content and views that had previously remained submerged. The abolition crisis in the 1830s over freedom of expression and other First Amendment rights created a new sensitivity to the press's role and its protection. During the Civil War, the press became a body of organized activity, distinct, more independent, and with interests and functions identifiably different from those of other institutions such as political groups and structures. Because the press met one of the nation's greatest needs, a need no other institution could satisfy, its institutional role, or place in the larger polity's structure, was crucial and its information role became crystallized. Only the press could provide information about the course of the war, policy, and potential outcomes of the conflict—and hence, some sense of whether the nation might endure. It was indispensable in providing information needed by a whole nation, from the frontier to the farm to the village to the highest levels of authority. Such dependence on the press solidified its expanded role.

As a result of the war, a number of changes coalesced with trends already under way to elevate the press's importance and commercial value. By the war's end, the contours of a new business model were clear. Among such changes were the press's establishment as part of people's lives, subordination of opinion and partisanship to facts, modification of reporting form, developments in news gathering, and adoption of organized business techniques to handle demand, supply and costs.

Establishment of the Press as Part of Daily Life

The press became a "habit" as Americans, perhaps for the first time, recognized a vital need for it and established it as part of lives in a way that was unprecedented. Families sought news of relatives fighting in the war, and national leaders needed information about events as a basis for making decisions and forming policies for conducting the war. The insatiable demand for news created thousands of new newspaper readers and established reading habits and reliance on newspapers that would not readily lapse after the war. Since everyone had a stake in the war and thus a driving need to know about events, the newspaper became primary reading material as never before.[86]

Subordination of Opinion and Partisanism to Facts

Whereas partisanism received its greatest blow up to that time, people ironically seemed to believe even more strongly in the press's power over public opinion. It is also ironic that the expanded place of the press in people's lives intensified belief in this power at a time when newspapers' party alliances were dissolving, for the Civil War era marks the beginning of the end of party dependence. Partisanism weakened before the war as newspapers confined criticism less and less to the opposing party. As the press criticized all parties after the collapse of the second party system in the early 1850s, deviation from party lines increased. During the 1850s, articles discussed the superiority of the so-called independent over the partisan press, and as the 1860 campaign split the Southern wing of the Democratic party into three fragments, the Southern press, in criticizing both the political system and Southern candidates, inevitably deviated from party lines.[87] Press supporters and opponents of Lincoln criticized him tirelessly. Lincoln rejected using a party newspaper to serve his administration, becoming the first president to do so; his action has often been pointed out as sounding the death knell of the party press, and surely it had some influence.[88] Finally, the 1872 presidential campaign symbolized the press's changed role. When Horace Greeley ran for president, journalists from all parties supported him, signifying that party lines no longer accurately described or divided the press.[89]

The public appetite for war news also played a part in subordinating another characteristic of the press. The public, uninterested in opinions of what happened, demanded facts about the war, deemphasizing the traditional opinion function of the party press and increasing its emphasis on events.[90]

The Civil War signaled the end of the kind of journalism associated with the penny press era, in which an editor's personality dominated and people read the newspaper for his views. Correspondents' central role during the war overshadowed that of the editor. Reporters' bylines presented many more names associated with a paper, and readers began to identify them with their overriding interests. Reporters met people's immediate needs for war news, and readers looked less for editors' views and more for what correspondents reported.

News came to be treated as a product; volumes of newsprint, often a third of a paper's columns, were devoted to the war. In fact, more news space was given to covering the war than to any other single subject or event up to that time.[91]

Changes in News Form

As news came to be treated as a product, a nascent form of "packaging" it emerged. News items became increasingly standardized as they took on the form that is today called the inverted pyramid, emphasizing the lead, featuring bylines, and depending on Associated Press reporting—a structure that guides readers in finding the most important elements. Before 1860, newspapers had little display material, publishing negligible numbers of cartoons or illustrations (except for the small woodcuts occasionally used in advertisements). During the war, however, magazines hired artists on a massive scale to draw pictures of battles, making illustration part of the news. Before the war, headlines were one column wide and often the same from day to day—for example, "By Telegraph"—rather than tailored to the story.[92] But multi-deck headlines became common during the war.

Some have credited the telegraph with being responsible for new reporting techniques that changed news story form.[93] Because telegraph lines were often cut during the war, reporters began to transmit the most important information first: who won what battle, how many soldiers were killed, the maneuvers used, and so on. Then if they lost telegraph access while transmitting further details, their newspapers would at least have the gist of the story. Multi-deck headlines in turn became a part of the packaging, paralleling major points of the story as they arrived over the wire.[94]

Writing style also changed. Some have in fact argued that the Civil War drastically affected reporting forms. Certainly, the demand for speedy news prompted a terse writing style, but historians disagree about the effect of the war on news writing. John Finnegan, Jr., has noted two broad arguments—one, that the war's chief effect on journalism was to create news stories more like modern than earlier forms, and another, that the war only accelerated developments that were already begun. According to the first view, use of the summary lead, direct quotations, interviews with major political and military figures, and descriptive techniques as in fiction or poetry emerged during the war, especially in battle reports and in stories about war policy and potential outcomes. The other view holds that all these changes were well under way in American journalism by the time of the Civil War.[95]

Schudson, advocating the latter view, maintains that two basic types of news form, the "story" and "information," emerged before the Civil War. The story form appears to have had primarily an entertainment function and to have been aimed at a working-class audience. The information form emphasized facts, minimized opinion, and developed mainly out of patterns set by newspapers that aimed at a more educated audience.[96] Evidence seems to support Schudson's position, for it is clear that journalistic procedures during the war built on developments already in progress. But some effects can be attributed to the war.

Developments in News Gathering

The Civil War helped the press build the basic organization of modern news gathering techniques that defined the later industrialized press. During the war, the product quality sold was newness; hence being first to report an event became paramount. Demand thus speeded up the tempo of news dissemination. As the historian J. Cutler Andrews has noted, antebellum journalism was geared to the slower stagecoach, horse, and ship, and people were more accustomed to hearing another's opinion of what happened weeks earlier than facts about events of the previous twenty-four hours.[97] Study of news gathering between 1820 and 1860, however, shows a steady reduction in time lags between event and published report. The average lag for papers in the Deep South dropped from twenty-nine days in the 1820s to ten in 1850, and items actively gathered by newspapers increased from 30 to 70 percent over clipped contributions.[98]

The distinction made by visual communications scholars between the record and the report of an event is useful here in its implications for news form and value.[99] If information is thought of as a record, its value is principally the same whether it is a week or a year old, and this value may, in fact, increase with time. But if it is regarded as a report, recency is its most valuable quality. During the Civil War, demand for the most recent accounts put behind forever the reliance on "records"—especially of foreign news, regardless of how old—as primary press content. The rapid succession of history-changing events fueled a daily demand for news, putting unprecedented pressure on the press to organize news-gathering methods and expand sources.

The press had never before systematically organized coverage of a war —or much of any kind of event—away from its home offices, but the Civil War allowed no other choice as it stretched across time and vast distances. The speed of events made reporters ingenious in finding ways, at virtually any personal cost, to get their stories—and procedures expanded, with consequences for journalistic standards. Reporters made news more accessible than ever. Riding with the troops gave access to news of battles, generals' performances, military strategies, camp life, and troop behavior. Use of eyewitness accounts and interviews as sources, which had developed before the war, became usual, and reliance on multiple sources became an established practice. Reporters also cultivated high-ranking officials to maintain good relations and keep access to sources open.[100]

The press incorporated previously ignored techniques and technologies, such as illustration and the telegraph, into news gathering. Used little by the press before the war, the telegraph was largely responsible for improved access to news. Newspapers that before had only two or three columns of telegraph news contained two and three pages during the war and often kept offices open to receive late-night telegraph news. (Before the war, morning papers regularly closed their offices at 10:00 P.M.)[101]

Some scholars have also attributed changes in news story form to the nature of news gathering necessitated by the war. The war's complexity forced reporters to use many sources, including individuals whose views differed. Not only did news items increasingly include multiple sources; presenting a diversity of views in the same article—a new journalistic procedure—gained strength. In addition, Northern correspondents' practice of traveling in disguise to avoid detection in the South provided a model for the undercover investigative reporting that developed in the 1880s.[102] Participating in the action as "specials" armed as soldiers reinforced the undercover model.

Organization of Business Techniques to Manage
Demand, Supply, and Costs

The total effect of these and other forces fostered a new business model of the press. During the war, the press began to form clearly industrial organizational patterns. Paralleling the North's industrialization, which was abetted by the need for war materiel, press expansion was stimulated by the need for up-to-date war news, which forced its business organization to manage demand, supply, and costs more efficiently.

The war brought higher press costs than ever. Estimates of the *New York Herald*'s war news expenditures between 1861 and 1865 range from $500,000 to $750,000.[103] In November 1862, the *New York Times* reported a 5 percent rise in newsprint prices in three months, at a time when newspapers needed more newsprint than ever.[104] Before 1860, most dailies were four pages, but during the war newspapers had to expand in size, increase the number of editions, and add Sunday issues, which were rare before the war. In effect, the war made the Sunday paper a fixture of American journalism.[105]

Costs of gathering news skyrocketed. Although some journalists had begun vigorous news gathering in the 1830s, most metropolitan newspapers in the 1850s still relied primarily on Washington correspondents, brief telegrams from the Associated Press in New York, items from local papers, and occasional letters from volunteer correspondents. But such news-gathering methods would not suffice for covering a Civil War. Major papers placed correspondents at important points in the South, with the army, and in Washington, D.C.—and correspondents were especially expensive in salaries, outfits, horses, and telegraph dispatches. Large papers spent an average of $60,000 to $100,000 a year on correspondence alone. Horses and uniforms were expensive and both soon wore out; some correspondents exhausted half a dozen horses a year, and still more horses were often shot or stolen; transfer between campaigns meant buying new uniforms and, generally, property left behind was a lost investment.[106] Telegraph rates were based on mileage—five cents a word from Washington, D.C., to New York City, three cents a word from Washington to Philadelphia.[107] The *New York Herald* paid $250 a column for the account of the Battle of Chickamauga and $1,000 for news of the capture of New Orleans.[108]

On the other hand, profits rose as circulations soared. Circulation of the *New York Times* went from 45,000 to 75,000 after the firing on Fort Sumter.[109] As Northern businesses boomed, constructing new factories, houses, schools, and hospitals, advertising mushroomed, and the *New York Times* soon had more than it could handle.[110] According to Andrews, "Few newspapers on the eve of the Civil War netted . . . more than $25,000 per year."[111] The *New York Tribune*'s profits for 1850 had been considered enormous at $60,000 (New York's population was more than half a million by then). But for the year ending May 1, 1865, the *Tribune*'s gross income was $252,000—third after that of the *New York Times*, which had a gross income of $383,150, and the *New York Herald*, with more than $1 million.[112]

Discussions of the press from the Civil War through the remainder of the century characterized it as a business. Lincoln Steffens, writing in 1897, compared it to a factory or department store.[113] News was the commodity being sold and, indeed, competition for circulation by the 1880s led to manufactured as well as marketed news as editors staged promotional events to report.[114]

As the press grew in sheer numbers, it also expanded in social and political functions, becoming both more national and more international in scope. Historians have dealt with post–Civil War America's shift from concern with state-national government relationships to a focus on the effects of industrialization.[115] The press reflected this shift. Whereas the antebellum press, following contours broadly conforming to states' rights philosophy, emphasized state and regional interests, the war's central issue —survival of the union—fostered a consciousness of the United States as a broader society with interests transcending local and state politics. During the war, some had appealed to journalists to use the press's influence on behalf of preserving the union.[116] This wider range of interest was also stimulated in part by the Associated Press's cooperative news-gathering service that brought news of battles and events to central locations for distribution, and by the dispersal of journalists throughout the nation.[117] A large body of traveling reporters thus emerged who saw and understood more of the nation than had any journalists before them. Their perspectives would influence their work, and thus American journalism, through the ensuing decades. This new focus was reinforced during the immediate postwar period, when attention to restoring the South perpetuated national concern as a daily expression and preoccupation. Moreover, having recognized during the war that other nations had interests in what happened in the United States, the press expanded its attention to foreign events, with a view to their effects on America.[118]

Additionally, the war indirectly promoted a greater diversity of newspapers. For decades women had subordinated their claim to an enlarged role in society and politics to other causes. Now, having been defined as nonvoting citizens by the Fourteenth Amendment, they were stirred to call for an independent movement. Women's rights leaders founded America's first feminist newspaper, the *Revolution*, in 1868.[119] Black publications mushroomed after the war, with a dozen begun in the nine months after April 1865—half of them in the South, representing the first real breakthrough for the black press in Southern states. In 1887 alone, 68 black publications began, and by 1890, 575 black periodicals had been established.[120]

Agricultural journalism also flourished following the war as farmers struggled to keep pace in an industrial society. Farmers no longer aimed to be self-sufficient, and they began to grow cash crops; in order to do so they needed factory-made equipment, more capital, and scientific knowledge about farming and markets. The Grange, a farmers' organization established in 1867 to disseminate scientific information about farming and to assist farmers, fostered the agricultural press.[121]

With the marketing model that emerged after the Civil War, news was at least tacitly defined as a commodity. News "manufacturing" in the form of stunts and other techniques to promote sales were common by the 1890s. News gathering by contract, which had begun in the 1860s, expanded. Increasingly, too, circulation itself became a commodity—a medium for "buying" advertising.[122] The press's place in the larger polity moved toward corporate organization. In these trends as previously, the press reflected the cultural changes affecting it after the Civil War.

One of these changes was rapid industrialization. As the nation moved from an agrarian to an industrial economy, manufacturing increased sevenfold from 1865 to 1900, the number of industries nearly quadrupled (from 140,000 in 1860 to 500,000 in 1900), the proportion of the labor force in industry rose from 41 percent in 1860 to 62 percent in 1900, and national wealth more than quadrupled—from $20 billion in 1865 to $88 billion in 1900.[123]

Industrialization brought increasing mechanization of production, which in turn brought overproduction, heightened competition among industries, displaced workers, ruined many small businesses, and saw many others amalgamated into corporations. Mechanization also brought the need for production controls and led to the setting of production quotas and selling prices, the formation of trusts, and the elimination of competition in the age of industrial barons. With greater industrialization came growing urbanization; cities became power centers where political machines reigned and corruption spread.[124]

Another change was in values. Entrenched in American culture by 1870, values favoring business had evolved from Hamilton's vision for the United States as a nation of manufacturers through the "American system" that had been promoted by Henry Clay. Historians have emphasized the elevated role of business during the late nineteenth century and the growing disparity of wealth among classes. The 1890 census revealed that 9 percent of the nation's families controlled 71 percent of its wealth, and less than half of all American families owned their own homes.[125] In post–Civil War America, the business ethic emphasized industrialization along with protection from foreign interference and for self-development. Leaders saw prosperity as lying in railways, mines, and manufacturing because it was believed that these would attract the nation's most capable individuals and that they promised national strength.[126]

The constitutional historian Paul Murphy has shown that business interests dominated interpretation of the Fourteenth Amendment, adopted in 1868, through the final years of the nineteenth century. Efforts to use that amendment's due process and equal protection clauses to ensure personal rights failed, Murphy writes, because "they flew in the face of the climate of the period and its general value structure." He continues:

In many ways, the search for the traditional meaning of liberty and first amendment guarantees was lost in the dynamism of social and institutional change occurring during the last quarter of the nineteenth century. This change affected both American values and public law. . . . At the time when a small group of liberal attorneys and public statesmen sought some answer to the relationship of first amendment rights to the new fourteenth amendment, the vast majority of American statesmen and the conservative members of the bar sought to convert that amendment into a new bastion of protection for an emerging entrepreneurial class. This class was already . . . converting the nation from an agrarian, decentralized, and informal society, into an industrial, urban, and centralized modern state. The conservatives won.[127]

An accompanying set of values opposed government intervention in individuals' affairs or in the economy as a whole. By 1880, the long-held value of laissez-faire assumed that individual enterprise led to national progress, wealth, and power, and that government should not interfere. Rather, the purpose of government was to protect the kind of society in which the individual could best achieve. This view was buttressed by the "social Darwinism" that emerged following the publication of Charles Darwin's *Origin of Species* in 1858, which emphasized the survival of the fittest.[128]

By 1880, however, competing values began to challenge the laissez-faire doctrine, holding that individual enterprise could bring poverty to some and result in national weakness, that cooperation—not raw competition—was necessary for the public good, and that government should serve the common good and actively try to improve society.[129]

Business ethic values dominated, however, during the last years of the nineteenth century, and the emerging values would not supersede them until well into the twentieth century. Nevertheless, virulent conflicts between these values in the late nineteenth century resulted in social movements such as populism, progressivism, socialism, and unionism that challenged traditional ideas about society and government and sometimes erupted in violent confrontations.[130]

The press reflected the competing values in content and in the changes shaping it during the last decades of the nineteenth century. Emphasis shifted from news *persons* to news *selling,* and an editor-centered, personal structure gave way to corporatism, focused on advances in technology, increased competition, large circulations, diversification, and advertising as a means to profit. The changes resulted from the press's incorporation of the business-centered goals of American culture. As the nation moved from agrarianism to industrialism, the press left behind the old "personal school" that revolved on the editor. As the great editors of the penny press era died, a larger generation of well-educated journalists arose, tested by their covering of the Civil War and trained in reporting facts and drama that sold papers. The idea of news as central that emerged from the Civil War experience devalued the expression of editorial opinion that had been the foundation of the previous generation's supremacy in American journalism.[131]

Structural developments moving toward corporate journalism also devalued the approach of the great editors of the past. The press of the 1830s through the 1850s defined journalistic jobs and increased staff size; Civil War coverage required greater expansion, and by 1880 staffs had grown so large, with forty or fifty reporters plus a half-dozen desk editors on major newspapers, that an editor's name was hardly known beyond the immediate circle.[132] During the 1870s writers emphasized the reporter's role, and a writer in the 1880s, calling reporting the most important job on a newspaper, mentioned numerous well-known correspondents and remarked that no one would know their editors' names.[133]

The prewar press showed the way to profits through building circulations and advertising, but this required increased investment, making an expanded business organization and structure inevitable. Used presses could be bought cheap in the 1830s and 1840s, although a new one might cost $4,000 to $5,000; by the 1880s, the cost had risen to $80,000.[134] Technological developments increased printing speed while paper costs declined, making greater circulations possible and ultimately inevitable. Paper costs decreased from 15 cents a pound in 1810 to 8½ cents in 1860 and, with the adoption of a more efficient paper-making machine, from $416 a ton in 1863 to $60 a ton by 1892.[135] Such circulation increases, requiring more and more sophisticated business techniques and management expertise, enhanced the business department's position. Average circulation, for example, grew from around 1,000 in 1830 to nearly 5,200 by 1890, with the largest papers showing circulations significantly above 100,000. In 1892, for example, one paper had a circulation of 374,741, and seven others were well over 100,000.[136]

Diversification not only expanded journalistic roles; it also subordinated the role of the great editor. Beginning with the Civil War and Reconstruction, as already suggested, the age of the reporter replaced the age of the editor. Moreover, managing editors first appeared in the 1840s, city editors in the 1850s. The latter, at first usually identical with the chief reporters, dominated the news editorial organization by the 1870s. Other departments, such as sports and arts, emerged in the 1880s.[137]

Competition for the market fostered diversification beyond the newspaper into a larger journalistic structure. Agencies and bureaus developed to sell news; city news bureaus also emerged in the 1890s; and press associations began to incorporate.[138] The trend toward concentration of ownership, begun before the Civil War, was defined by the 1880s.[139] Other media—magazines, agricultural journalism, black publications, the women's press—also grew. As competition for the market increased, the nation's newspapers nearly quadrupled in number between 1870 and 1900, with dailies increasing sixfold and daily copies sold increasing fivefold.[140] The advertising revenues of periodicals grew from approximately $1.1 million in 1850 to $95.8 million by 1900. In 1847, approximately 11 million advertisements appeared in two to three thousand American newspapers; in 1897, 350 million appeared in some sixteen thousand publications.[141]

Circulation competition increased sales, and profits created barons of the press parallel to those in other industries. Joseph Pulitzer and William Randolph Hearst, the most visible newspaper editors of the 1880s and 1890s, exemplified the success to be gained from a career in journalism.[142]

The greater investments and huge circulations shifted the press's emphasis from newspersons to news publishing (or selling). Components of the press's function, spurred by the business ethos of the era, were increasingly defined as selling the news, the facts; serving the economy through healthy, robust circulations and advertising sales; and serving the political system by supporting entrepreneurialism. And, spurred by the competing "progressive" values, components of press function were increasingly defined as providing editorial opinion independent of parties; investigating and exposing corruption and injustice; and crusading to improve society. Concern about the press's role and its responsibility to society—especially responsibility in the manner of presenting information—reached a new level.

In short, discussions of the press show that it was perceived as a business while its function was seen as providing the news. But the apparent divergence between the press's place in the larger polity as a business and the claim that its purpose was to disseminate news is not great. Content reflected the same business role, as we shall see in the next chapter.

Having surveyed successive press roles through three eras of the nineteenth century, from a political to an information to a business role, we now turn our attention again to the relationship of press roles to standards as these were perceived and as they operated within newspaper policy.

Chapter Three

Changes in News during the Nineteenth Century

The transfer of our newspapers from personal to corporate ownership and control was not a matter of preference, but a practical necessity. . . .

These newcomers . . . naturally looked at everything through the medium of the balance-sheet. Here was a paper with a fine reputation, but uncertain or disappearing profits; it must be strengthened, enlarged, and made to pay. Principles? Yes, principles were good things, but we must not ride even good things to death. The circulation must be pushed, and the advertising patronage increased. More circulation can be secured only by keeping the public stirred up. Employ private detectives to pursue the runaway husband, and bring him back to his wife; organize a marine expedition to find the missing ship; send a reporter into the Soudan to interview the beleaguered general whose own government is powerless to reach him with an army. . . . If nothing new is to be had, refurbish something so old that people have forgotten it. . . .

. . . A craving for excitement was first aroused in the public and then satisfied by the same hand that had aroused it. . . . In such a race for business success . . . can we marvel at the subsidence of ideals? . . . is not the wonder rather that the moral quality of our press has not fallen below its present standard?

Francis E. Leupp, "The Waning Power of the Press,"
The Atlantic Monthly *(1910)*

Newspaper content during the three eras we have identified in nineteenth-century journalism reveals dramatic shifts in "news" across the century, confirming major changes in the role of the press in American society. Content in the earliest decades was idea-centered; by mid-century, it was event-centered; and by the 1890s, it represented an amalgam of event, idea, and "story" or drama. Although these marked changes occurred, content across the century also shows continuities. Furthermore, it shows what press critics were discussing, as we might expect when we view criticism as an intersection of press and society. Finally, content shows the relation of journalistic standards to the press's role in each era. This chapter considers press content in the three eras of the nineteenth century.

Regarding press role changes and criticisms throughout the century, the earliest critics emphasized partisanship and the press's great power over ideas in the polity, as Chapter 5 will show. Newspaper content reveals that partisanship and ideas did indeed dominate the press in the first decade of the century. As we shall see in Chapter 6, critics at mid-century emphasized a trivialization of news and had begun to consider journalistic taste and the press's intrusions into individuals' lives. Content during this era emphasized individuals and detailed descriptions of events. Post–Civil War critics focused on several excesses: profit seeking, invasion of privacy, sensationalism, and reporting that jeopardized the accused's right to a fair trial. Content of the 1890s shows journalists driven to get every detail that might satisfy curiosity, heighten thrill, and sell newspapers. Newspapers in the last decade of the century reveal several changes, all of which seemed dictated by the era's emphasis on business and the press itself as a business. Among these changes was the development of a clear story model that significantly affected news reporting.

Several elements of continuity emerge from a long-term view of newspaper content. From 1800 through the 1850s, for example, partisanship continued to characterize the press, while at the same time content emphasis shifted from ideas to events. From 1850 to 1890, partisanship diminished, especially after the Civil War, and reporting of events was increasingly stressed—at the expense of airing ideas—until it dominated newspapers in the 1890s. Interest in individuals represents a kind of continuity, although subtle shifts occurred in the nature of that interest. In the earliest decade, the interest was in important personages; by mid-century, the "ordinary" individual figured prominently. In the 1890s, the important personage (what today would be called the celebrity more than the statesman emphasized in newspapers of the first decade) again received much news space, but the ordinary person continued to draw a great deal of attention—although by that time it seemed that, to merit news space, such individuals must be part of an event that yielded significant drama. Also, the importance of ideas in news represents continuity. In the earliest decade, discussion of ideas dominated virtually all content, but by 1850, its place had diminished and it was beginning to be relegated to editorial commentary. By the 1890s, the idea—as *the* reason for a newspaper item

—almost never appeared outside the editorial page except as the basis of fictional pieces.

Content also correlated with issues of journalistic conduct raised by critics in each era. Content in turn flowed from the press's role as perceived by contemporaries and as defined by the press's place in society's overall structure. This means, in effect, that drama (or the "story") as a journalistic goal was to late-nineteenth-century American journalism what partisanism was to the press of the first decades, and what trivialization was to mid-century journalism. When considered as part of journalistic goals dictated by the press's role, excesses such as the sensationalism of the 1880s are more understandable. That is to say, although this perspective makes excesses no more acceptable, it does make sense of them. Viewed as part of a larger framework of forces rather than as simple, individual instances of base conduct (although, as is always true, some journalists upheld, higher—or lower—standards than others), excesses are revealed as by-products of the press's role as it was interpreted and understood at different times. Such a perspective may help in interpreting excesses, and therefore in arriving at decisions about changing them.

Samples of newspapers across the century were studied with attention to what journalists intended newspapers to do. In other words, what role did newspaper content itself suggest the press served? Did that role change with time? And if so, how did it change? In this work, evidence about the press's role was gathered through examining whatever purposes journalists seemed to intend newspapers to serve, and through analyzing newspapers' content and form. Changes in these purposes and in content and form over time would indicate a changing press role. But equally important, newspapers were studied to determine what kind of journalistic standards might have governed their production; to collect and analyze any discussions of the press, news, or journalism that appeared; and to determine the dominant message, in the largest sense, the press conveyed in each era. Finally, content was examined to see what critics were discussing and to gain perspective on press criticism across the century.

Newspapers from the first, middle, and last decades (1800–1810, 1850–1860, and 1890–1900) of the century were read because they marked significant points in the eras studied. The first decade coincided with early efforts to determine the course of a new government and nation; the middle decade was a period when significant changes affecting the press and the nation were under way—and it was chosen also to avoid the unique decade of civil war; the final decade represented a time after the nation's economic base had shifted, technological developments had spiraled, and the press had moved toward a corporate structure. Although press criticism was studied only up to 1890, newspapers of the 1890s were examined because the decade marked the near-culmination of post–Civil War changes in society and the press. Furthermore, it was assumed that content in the 1890s was of the same genre as that addressed by critics through the 1880s. The study thus presupposes that newspaper content for the three eras would reflect trends and values across the century, and that shifts in the press's role and standards resulting from changed trends would be visible. The study also assumes that examining the press in decades at wide intervals would make changes more readily discernible.

Sample titles were drawn from lists of newspapers published throughout each of the three decades.[1] Newspapers that had published for at least ten years were judged as more indicative of prevailing conduct than short-lived papers or those that began or ended during the decade. For the first decade, all newspapers were included. For the other two decades, only those with the highest circulations were selected; here it was assumed that because these papers reached more people they had more influence and are thus a better index to what others either did or strived to do. Although not tested in this research, evidence suggests that today's "umbrella" hypothesis, that other newspapers tend to imitate those in high-circulation markets, holds true for the nineteenth century. The sample weighs heavily toward the eastern United States because fewer newspapers were published in other parts of the country, because high-circulation newspapers were concentrated there, and because of availability. To diversify geographical representation, noneastern newspapers were substituted for those unavailable in the sample, but this did not significantly alter the predominance of eastern papers among those read.

Samples were selected from two years in each decade—one near the beginning and one near the end to avoid distortion by any phenomena that might be passing fads. After sample newspaper titles were randomly selected, sample issues of each were drawn, and all were then read thoroughly.

The first-decade sample constituted approximately one-fifth of the newspapers published throughout the ten years, and every issue of each was read for three months—January, June, and December—in each of two years (1801 and 1809). Some were dailies and others biweeklies, but most were weeklies. For the other two decades, six titles were selected and three issues a year of each was drawn randomly and read for the years 1852 and 1858; for 1891, the sample was three issues of four titles; for 1899, three issues of two titles.[2] The results are preliminary, since the number is insufficient to support statistically valid conclusions. Nevertheless, the findings, although tentative, are important. First, nothing so far suggests that additional research will significantly alter them. Second, the patterns discovered correlate to what critics discussed in each era. Third, they support the thesis of this work, that press role is dictated by culture and that standards are by-products of that role and, in turn, of culture.

Before proceeding, some comment regarding standards is necessary. Reading the papers in the sample to deduce standards governing news presentation and to collect discussions of journalism presented immediate problems. First, the sample issues contained little discussion of the press, news, or journalism—even though journalists frequently berated each other through newspaper columns in the early years. Journalists did often discuss the press, news, and journalism in newspapers throughout the century; the sample selected for this research, however, simply turned up little of that discussion. Additional newspapers selected at random—as well as secondary sources—yielded many such discussions. A second problem is that standards cannot be realistically assessed on the basis of what appeared in newspapers so long ago. Accuracy, for example, is elusive. We simply do not know today what was precisely true about an event reported in 1850.

News items did not identify sources, or did so so rarely—even as late as the 1890s—that it is impossible to search out whatever sources might still exist. News items did not specify how information was gathered; this in itself says something about standards and values at the time, but it leaves little basis for studying what standards might have governed news collection, preparation, and presentation. The absence of indications of how information was gathered suggests a definition of news that would also have affected views about its presentation. As this definition evolved away from partisanism, the validation of information through explication of sources, for example, became more important. Although by the 1890s some indications point toward such explication, the shift from partisanism was not yet so complete as to change underlying assumptions about presentation dramatically. Lack of explanations of sources may also have related to journalists' "protected" status. An embedded American tradition, for example, had operated against the use of journalists' bylines until the Civil War. Although this practice may have protected them, it also absolved them of accountability. It is easy to see how such a long-engrained habit of nonaccountability might lead to proceeding as if accountability on other counts—such as source identification—was superfluous. In short, it seems most likely that sources were not identified simply because the significance of doing so had not yet become clear.

The lack of information about sources and how material was gathered nevertheless leaves the historian without a basis for assessing standards governing procedures. A further difficulty is that distortions can hardly be judged without perspective—which is perhaps even more elusive than accuracy. To determine what might have been a balanced perspective (an undistorted account) virtually requires being there.

Sources used by journalists, then, are, except for government proceedings, generally unknown and unavailable. In rare instances in which multiple accounts of an event exist, newspaper stories of the event might be compared with the various accounts, but even multiple accounts may have come from the same general sources.[3] In any event, the researcher is left with rare, isolated news content that may not have appeared in all—or even a few—of the newspapers at the time. Hence, one cannot generalize regarding accuracy, either about one newspaper's entire contents from one story, or about several newspapers from multiple reports of the same event.[4]

Focusing on the press as a product of cultural context therefore quickly made specific late-twentieth-century standards inappropriate measures for newspapers in the 1800s, 1830s, or even 1890s. There is no way of knowing what was unreported; and accuracy, for example, is in any case irrelevant as a measure of content that was intended to argue political points of view—as was true of most content up to the Civil War. These circumstances confirm the importance of examining social developments, journalistic purpose, and press role to understand nineteenth-century standards. Some judgments can be made, of course; to illustrate, whether the reporter was at the scene or not can often be ascertained by looking at details in a story. And general judgments can be made about bias and taste based on what appeared. One can examine content for tone, substance, and excesses in emphasis and speculate about the extent to which these may have offended taste or opposed values of the time. And, of course, one can look for manifestations of what critics emphasized, such as partisanism, crime reporting, or sensationalism.

Another important area of interest in reading the sample newspapers was to examine how content changed over time, and how any changes related broadly to the press's role and journalistic standards. In other words, what was the medium's dominant message form in any era? As a medium, or vehicle, did it predominantly emphasize ideas? events? life's substance? individuals? And what interests does newspaper content emphasize that might reveal the press's institutional role in society?

Newspaper content for the three decades was studied for topic, tone, form, and some indication of the intended audience. *Content topic* involves categories—political, business, social—and whether reports were local, national, or international. *Tone* is defined as the overall impression conveyed: that is, whether content is personal or impersonal, and what the emotional impact is, whether factually straightforward or dramatic (accusatory, derogatory, titillating, suspenseful). *Personal* items address specific individuals directly or focus primarily on one or more individuals, with attention to character. Personal items include, for example, the invective hurled by one editor against a rival (quoted below), in which he addressed the other with "Halloo, Billy Brown" and accused him of lying as well as having other character flaws, and the story of Brackenridge's drunken spree in which he repeatedly removed all his clothes. Impersonal items report simply that something occurred or discuss ideas as to their soundness, basis, or implications. Such discussions of ideas, if they called into question another's views (or the views of a group) without aspersing character (such as calling people deluded), were straightforward. If they did asperse character in any way, they were classified as personal. The excerpts below, claiming that property is essential to government, and that Americans had erred in assuming they could successfully establish a republic, are straightforward items.

Definition of *form* involved two dimensions: whether the item was idea- or event-centered, and whether it presented a "story" or simple information. Idea-centered means the reason for the item's being in the newspaper was an idea or ideas, whereas event-centered means that the reason for the item being in the newspaper was a specific occurrence at an identifiable time and place. "Story" was defined as any news item emphasizing what might generally be called fictional techniques—suspense, conflict, plot, central character, dialogue. These elements were defined as "drama." In some cases, these were event-centered—that is, an event (or events) was the reason for the news item—but dramatic elements dominated the reporting; in other cases, items would not have been reported if the occasion for them had lacked dramatic elements. In other words, in the latter, an item's dramatic quality was the reason for its inclusion in the news. Finally, items with simple, factual information were defined as straightforward accounts of events, ideas, or processes—without any effort to provoke or involve the reader's emotions. The example below about the woman committed to an insane asylum by her sister is a "story"; an example of simple information reported in a straightforward manner is the account under the headline ARCHBISHOP IRELAND TO BE HONORED that tells that Ireland would be asked to preside over French festivities honoring Joan of Arc.

Intended audience was deduced from the categories and kinds of items published. What sector or sectors of society did the newspaper address —government, institutions, individuals? And what composition of society did the content reflect—were ethnic groups, minorities, and women recognized as newspaper consumers? Obviously, this dimension calls for speculation that is risky, although it was clear by the 1890s that journalists recognized women as newspaper readers. Minorities and ethnic groups, however, were rarely reported on, which might suggest that these groups were not viewed as intended audiences; nevertheless, there is evidence that some editors did aim content to minority groups, especially to immigrants.

In broad outline, the characteristics of press content paralleled those of American culture in the nineteenth century. For two reasons, it was assumed that the early American newspaper press would be idea-centered. First, journalists had been active in the Revolution and increasingly involved with issues afterward, and such activities heightened their emphasis on ideas involved with issues. Second, the fact that the new government was itself a new idea, and that debates about its—and the nation's —future shape were dominated by competing ideas, made press content idea-centered. If this was true for the first era under study, how did press content change in the other eras?

After 1830, the press increasingly emphasized events and individuals over ideas. By the middle decades of the nineteenth century, the succession of events in the nation's own history shaped its course of development. Very conscious of many of these events and their implications, Americans were increasingly drawn to consider them.

Because the press by the last decade of the century was driven by a compulsion to "market" news, diversity came to characterize content. By the 1890s, press content reflected an amalgamation of ideas, events, individuals, and groups.

Newspapers, 1800–1810

The sample newspapers confirm that the early press was, indeed, idea-centered. Excluding foreign items, virtually every page—except of course those given over to advertising—of every newspaper read contained political content in which ideas were presented or exchanged and debated: Concepts of democracy, federalism, republicanism, office seeking, parties, factions, policies, "monarchical" and "aristocratic" tendencies, qualities needed for leadership, law and order, equality. The debate almost always spilled over into aspersions on persons advancing opposing ideas, but the content remained idea-centered.

Although the discussions were often tasteless, the participants could not have been more serious about the underlying purpose. They were, however, inexperienced in this kind of debate. They were having to learn several momentous lessons in the process of doing: how to debate political issues, how to function in a new kind of government, how to use the press in a new kind of political milieu, and how to ensure that public opinion would serve as a check on government, as the new order decreed. Therefore, what they said and how they said it might be better judged on the basis of their inexperience rather than how distasteful the exchanges were. In fact, some evidence suggests that what would now be considered distasteful was not then viewed by the majority as beyond acceptable limits in such debates.

To journalists of the early nineteenth century, the best journalistic conduct was whatever succeeded in making points for their party and advancing its views. As one historian has noted, to have failed their party would have been, in their minds, tantamount to treason.[5] Passion for their convictions often outdistanced reason, but every generation since has been a beneficiary of their tenacity and assiduity in earnestly debating issues of paramount importance to the nation's future.

It is difficult to arrive at a description of the "typical" newspaper of this period because papers varied so much in news placement and format. Some included editors' comments, for example, but in different locations, and they differed also in treatment of news from other states; some contained clearly identifiable entertainment sections; most faithfully reported congressional and state legislative news, but treated these items differently; most included ship news, and all emphasized foreign news. Furthermore, numerous items duplicated material from other papers.

Newspaper issues selected randomly from those read show five to twenty items in a four-page newspaper (excluding advertising items and foreign news). (Foreign news items are not enumerated for the early papers because the focus of interest is on how the papers reported on or reflected *American* society.) The low number of items in a paper is indicative of length of items published. Political essays especially often ran more than a page and frequently continued from issue to issue. One issue, for example, contained ten items, of which four and a half columns (excluding two columns devoted to Congress) contained idea-centered items. (According to the categories set forth above, reports of Congress are technically idea-centered, but they are here identified as event-centered since the session —occurring at a specifiable time and place—led to the report.) The idea items included an essay on the change in government, comment about opposition to the newspaper's views, an article by Thomas Cooper examining the logic behind the Alien and Sedition Acts, and a letter from Aaron Burr explaining why his views were not Federalist. Five columns were filled with advertisements, two were devoted to Congress, and one contained entertaining items—a poem and anecdotes. One other item was event-centered—reporting an unfavorable response to Samuel H. Smith's request for permission to report on proceedings of the House of Representatives from inside the bar. Another issue contained twelve items, five of which were idea-centered and occupied more than three columns. Two columns were devoted to foreign news, one reported on Congress, two reported news from "the Mails," and one entertainment column contained anecdotes and short essays. The remainder of the newspaper was advertising. Another newspaper issue selected at random from 1809 yielded five items, with three devoted to ideas and two to events (one was the printer's announcement that Bonaparte was at Madrid; the other gave ship news). Twelve and three-fourths columns were devoted to advertising; three-fourths of one column reported news of Congress; five and a half columns gave foreign news.

The examples included below convey the passion and sense of responsibility for the new nation (if not for the press) of early American journalists, competing values, exultation in freedom to debate (as rawly as they might), and the often very personal desire to triumph in debate.

A printer in 1801 succinctly stated what seemed to typify views of the press's function during this era. In a long article, he wrote that presses had "been multiplied on the American continent from the Delaware to the Ohio . . . not to print books and diffuse a love of literature, but to publish newspapers and disseminate intelligence." His definition of intelligence (used synonymously with "news") revolved on party principles, for he continued, "It is from newspapers that the mass of the people derive their knowledge; and the principles of many thousands have been determined in support or opposition of federal measures, by the accidental perusal in youth, of a federal or antifederal paper." In concluding, he took a swipe at those who sneered at newspaper content, saying, "Indeed many persons of wealth and reputation . . . have gotten their knowledge from no other source than . . . a newspaper, tho' by some silly shame none will confess it."[6]

Newspaper content also, of course, reveals competing values. And a personal tone permeated content as individuals tried to outwit opposition spokesmen and undermine those advocating rival views and values. Federalists and Anti-Federalists denounced each other, and the intense competition continued throughout the decade. The examples are mostly taken from newspapers published in 1801, in part because competing values were clearer then than later, but as the few excerpts from later in the decade show, tone and substance did not change much by 1809.

Discussion of the changed administration dominated newspapers in 1801. Federalist printers bewailed Thomas Jefferson's election as president and then seized every opportunity to berate his administration. Using his inaugural speech as a basis for ridiculing him and all he stood for, they lifted phrases from it to illustrate just how "dangerous" the new administration would be. A Boston newspaper item that also appeared in several other Federalist papers shows the consternation over the incoming administration and suggests the era's underlying competing values and notions of government. In part, the item said:

To the Public

The time has at length arrived, when the administration of our government is about to pass out of the hands of those, who have been in the councils, and confidence of our departed *Washington*! Men who are principally known, only as the leaders and favourites of a *faction*, composed in a great measure of *discontented, fortune-hunting,* foreigners, are now to succeed. This is a serious and portentious moment. . . .

We have all observed . . . that this country has been tranquil, prosperous and happy, in proportion as the faction now about to predominate, has been restrained. . . .

Men of uneasy and turbulent tempers have existed in the country from the first . . . ; but they have been . . . men of little personal character, and deserving of little consideration. At length, however, from the alliances of numerous men of *desperate fortunes,* of *corrupted morals, aliens, desperados, expatriated [patricians?], refugees* from European justice, together with many well meaning but mistaken and deluded persons, they have increased to a formidable, and regularly organized phalanx. . . .

Such is the faction, against which the good and the wise have now to contend:—a noxious, poisonous weed, which . . . has sprung up and gained its maturity during the night of neglect . . . till its spreading branches have become co-extensive with the nation, threatening to smother the growth of our morals, religion, liberty and national dignity. . . .

In a land of universal suffrage, like ours, it is not the conduct of one or two individuals that we have most to dread. It is the general ascendency of the worthless, the dishonest, the rapacious, the vile, the merciless and the ungodly, which forms the principal ground of alarm. These are the men who have incessantly maligned the officers of our government, collectively and individually, our courts of justice, our laws, our clergy, and our seminaries of learning. These are the men who called Washington a *murderer,* and these are the men to whom Mr. *Jefferson* and Mr. *Burr* are indebted for the two highest offices in the nation. . . .

It is a consideration sufficiently deplorable in a Christian country, that a reputed infidel, an open scoffer at the person and character of the Saviour, and a reputed sharper, speculator and libertine, should be elevated to the highest stations in the government. . . . their administration will certainly be dangerous to the peace and constitution of this country. . . .[7]

Several Federalist printers published an article calling Jefferson's inaugural speech a "net to snare popularity" that adumbrates sentiments in 1830s criticism. One printer lamented, "It is with reluctance, with painful reluctance, that we are compelled to declare the sincerity of our belief that 'a political intolerance as despotic as wicked,' is about to become the disgraceful and contradictory comment of an amiable text of the President's fallacious speech. . . ."[8]

Ideas about government and who should control it were frequent themes of articles, and the views expressed do not differ substantially from those in British and American press criticism into the 1830s. An article in a

Maine newspaper, calling on society's propertied sector to bring the disintegrating polity under control, asserted that the "daring [persons] must be over-awed by an union of the wise; and, above all, the ignorant and misguided must be instructed and set right, by industry unremitted and extensive as that which has been used for their delusion." The author warned, "If men of property and integrity will not stoop to these means, they will be bowed under [by] the consequences."[9] An article in another issue declared, "The ruling part of any state must always have considerable property" because "property has such an invariable influence, that whoever possesses property must have power." Furthermore, "Property in a state, is also some security for fidelity, because interest then is concerned in the public welfare."[10] In a later issue of the same newspaper, another writer called it "the strangest doctrine ever promulgated by a statesman and philosopher [i.e., Jefferson], that *the offices of government are created for the benefit of individuals.*" He also rejected the idea that "minorities have equal rights," arguing that "by the very construction and nature of our government, a *majority* constitutes, or is, in legal understanding, the *whole* [word illegible] *or body politic.*" This body's "will" and "rights" were "indivisible" and "cannot be separated even in idea," the writer contended, arguing: "A will of the majority is a will of the whole. There is no such thing as will, or rights attached to a minority as such. The individuals who compose a minority have the same personal and political rights of a majority."[11] And a New York newspaper article said in part:

One fundamental error, in the opinions of Americans . . . on which has been reposed an undue . . . confidence in the practicability of a free elective government, is the belief that the citizens . . . enjoy . . . the *fairest* opportunity, of founding and rendering durable a republican form of government. This error is of the more consequence, as it has led the legislators . . . to neglect to raise those barriers against popular violence and corruption. . . .[12]

Renewal of the Alien and Sedition Acts of 1798, or institution of similar laws, received much debate during the decade and was always an occasion for arguing the merits and demerits of self-government. A Maine newspaper reported John Randolph as stating during the "late debates of Congress upon the Sedition Law" that "how strongly soever the gentleman supposed that question to have been decided by the Congress who passed the law; the judges who gave their opinion upon it, or the juries who had settled cases exhibited to them, he would tell that gentleman and all his adherents, that he had a still higher tribunal to appeal to, and higher

than than [*sic*] they could produce." The printer, to emphasize the important implications to his readers, told them that "he meant the *American
People*," saying Randolph was arguing that "their voice was more powerful than those courts, these two branches of the legislature, these judges,
and this president, to whom the gentleman referred." The printer scoffed,
"This sounds like revolutionary language, and comes with a bad grace
from a legislator," continuing:

When a law has passed both houses of Congress, been approved by the President and declared to be constitutional by the judges, is there still an appeal to
the people? Does our constitution recognize the people, as a forum competent
to decide upon the constitutionality of a law? —Should this new doctrine of
Mr. Randolph's come into operation, the constitution would be annihilated, the
people erected into a *revolutionary tribunal,* and a new order of things begin.[13]

Anti-Federalists were equally adamant in condemning Federalists. A
New Jersey printer exclaimed, "The many pretensions of the *federalists*
to the title of *exclusive friends to order,* is as hypocritical as it is false and
deceptious."[14] And a Maryland printer complained in 1809, "The Federalists will exert every nerve to divide," saying, "They pursue this course
in their endeavors to shew a change of conduct in the present administration. . . ."[15] A long article addressed to "Americans" said, in part, "I
appeal to my fellow citizens, if men who possess such opinions as these
[Federalists], are fit to represent you in any office of trust? No, they now
begin to receive the just detestation of all true Americans."[16]

The Anti-Federalists especially denounced the Alien and Sedition Acts
and efforts to revive them or establish similar laws. A New York paper
reported resolutions in the Virginia House of Delegates against any such
laws—resolutions that emphatically declared English common law had no
force in the United States:

And whereas the said . . . General Assembly by their resolution passed on the
12th day of Januaray last, instructed the Senators from the state in the Congress
of the United States to oppose the passing of any law founded on or recognizing
the doctrine lately advanced that the common law of England is in force under
the government of the United States, a doctrine which they truly declare to be
novel in its principle and tremendous in its consequences. . . .[17]

The remainder of the item can't be completely deciphered, but a final
resolution urged senators and representatives in Congress to take "every
opportunity" to oppose the law and any resolution containing a recognition of "the said doctrine."[18]

Personal invective and aspersions on individual character permeated most of the writing in both Federalist and Anti-Federalist papers, and it seems that nothing was too gross for publication. A Federalist paper in Connecticut, for example, reported an event-centered item on the return of an American diplomat from France that was the context for ridiculing the incumbent administration's efforts, policies, and personnel. The item noted that "Col. Swift, the late Secretary of the Legation to France has (we are sorry to say it) returned," and continued:

We have it from Federal authority that the Col. peremptorily asserts [that] every woman in France is without exception, a prostitute. Does the Col. *Know* this to be true? If he does not, it will be agreed that he ought not to say it. —And if he does, Lord bless us, what a hero he must be! . . . What, every woman in France! Why there must be seven or eight million of them! No, no, the Col. does not know quite so much. But if we will give the Col.'s assertion that construction which reason and charity demand—that is to say—that his acquaintance was confined to Ladies of that description, it will appear by no means improbable. . . .[19]

An example from the *Maryland Herald and Hagers-town Weekly Advertiser* for 1809 is quoted at length below because it exemplifies the personal tone in addition to the very common taunting among printers through the first half of the century. However, this exchange is more good-natured and less malicious than most. William Brown, the printer of a new Hagerstown paper, the *Gazette*, used its prospectus and first issue to lambast the Anti-Federalists, or Republicans. Thomas Grieves, an established Hagerstown printer, responded by trying to goad the rival printer into a debate of Anti-Federalist versus Federalist views, and kept it up in every issue in the sample for June of 1809.

The editor of the Hagers-Town Gazette takes a long time to "arrange the business of his office." When we noticed the shameful and barefaced falsehoods and assertions . . . in his paper three weeks ago, we thought he would have made some justification. But lo! he is contented to stand forth convicted before the citizens of this country, of having asserted the most palpable falsehoods.[20]

Continuing, apparently playing on a statement Brown had made, Grieves asked Brown if he believed his actions would please "*us poor ignorant people*," and asked what confidence people could have "in a paper, which in its very first publication makes the most false charges against a virtuous administration, without the least shadow of a justification." Writing that he had "promised to jog" Brown's memory about promising to prove his assertions "*as soon as he had arranged the business of his office,*" Grieves noted that two weeks had passed without a word from Brown; so, he wrote, he was keeping his own promise and reminding him. He added:

> Halloo, Mr. Brown, have you forgotten your promise? —Do keep up appearance, by a sort of defence if no more. We are anxious to hear from you. —For these two last weeks we have been much disappointed. We promised ourselves much amusement from your great talent at *punning*. Your witticisms must always divert and amuse the public. As we are an *ignorant set of people* in this county, suppose you give us further specimens of your *punnings* and *witticisms*[;] perhaps we may profit by them and in time become as *witty* as yourself.[21]

The following week, Grieves, still awaiting a response, goaded Brown further:

> Halloo, Billy Brown, halloo! Awake from your sleep. —Do not forget your promise. —Remember that truth is a virtuous guide. —Although we do not agree with you in your political creed, still as a brother editor, we will remind you of your promise and endeavor to save you from ruin.[22]

Grieves asked what people would think if Brown did not honor his promise, and answered his own question: "Why . . . as they ought," that Brown was "a base asserter of falsehoods" and his "paper is the vehicle of pestilential doctrines." Grieves reminded Brown of his charges against the administration, of his own denial of them, and of Brown's promise to respond. But, Grieves surmised, Brown's silence must mean he could not substantiate the charges and feared Grieves would show the public the *Gazette*'s "true colors—the channel of falsehood and party-lies." And he would, Grieves asserted, adding that he would "never fail to expose" Brown's party and the "sentiments" he advocated. However, Grieves concluded, perhaps Brown's silence meant that he had "repented of . . . error," so "why not confess . . . ?"[23]

And still the following week, Grieves again taunted:

> Halloo Billy Brown!! They have started you again Billy, have they? Well done Billy, your correspondent has a turn for blackguarding—for you did not write the paragraph in your paper of yesterday afternoon Billy—although it seems on perusal, to be one which might come from a man of about your size and understanding.[24]

Saying he was pressed for time to "set up" for his morning paper, Grieves wrote that, "still, however, we must find time and room to insert a few lines, by way of congratulating the Hagers-town Gazette's correspondent, on his *sobriety*—his *great wealth* and talent for writing." He continued that he saw "by the paper" that "Mr. Bourne of Baltimore" was writing a history of the United States, and if he might "be permitted to give advice," he recommended Brown's correspondent as co-author. Saying that "a small difference" might occur in that neither Brown nor his correspondent knew anything of the civil, political, or religious state of the country then or before, he added that they did have "great talents of a certain kind"—as "yesterday's *Gazette*" showed. But he asserted that when he had asked for proof of Brown's charges, he wanted an answer based on reason instead of invective. He asked Brown not to allow himself to be misled, saying he knew Brown's party formerly "pretended to all of the piety, wealth and wisdom in the country," but "those days are gone"; so, Grieves warned, "be careful . . . how you indulge warm-headed, misguided and uninformed young men with a place for invective in your columns." He added that "none but frothy minds actuated by malice, could either have originated or given currency to the remarks, stamped with the sanction of editorial insertion [in] yesterday's Gazette." Grieves continued:

> Take warning, Sir, and do not begin too soon to throw your fire-brands among neighbors. —If it be *reasoning* you want, republicans, having truth with them, are *at all times prepared;* if it be scurrility, they will yield the palm of victory, and hail you with the "ID TRIUMPHO!" but if true *wit* and *genuine humor,* be your object, we'll meet you on your own or middle ground. However, for your own sake Mr. B. beware both of ill nature and *sarcasm,* for, in either case, both you and your correspondent might enter into a very unequal contest.[25]

Grieves concluded he was disinclined to "take further notice" of Brown's paper, but the following week, he again addressed Brown, who had apparently threatened "vengeance" if he did not print a certain *Gazette* item. The *Gazette* editor, Grieves wrote, was further revealing himself, acting "the part of a little dictator" who "prescribes . . . our conduct . . . tells us what to print and . . . when," continuing:

> This order of Billy the 1st by the Grace of God not *yet* Emperor of the West, puts us in mind of an anecdote, told by . . . *Peter Porcupine* of himself. When the federalists were in the saddle, Peter always riding before, and long John Fenno, of the United States Gazette behind, (for in those days they rode double) one of the leaders . . . thinking Peter galloped too fast, and dreading lest the whole batch might get a tumble—wrote him a severe letter of reprimand—this raised

the mettle of Peter, and only served to make him whip and spur the harder, till at last, sure enough, the whole cavalcade were "unhorsed"—and have not remounted even until this day.[26]

After much more of the same, Grieves wrote that he was wary of copying public documents from "Billy's" paper, "not having implicit faith in the truth of all he says," and concluded with what he called a "jog": "William why doest thou not endeavor to substantiate the calumnies . . . in thy prospectus, against republicans?"[27]

Such goading may well have continued uninterrupted through succeeding weeks. The sample omitted subsequent issues, but sure enough, Grieves was still taunting in the December 13 issue: "Billy Brown has again let fly at us in his last week's Gazette, but in a manner so vile, low and ungentlemanly, as renders it scarcely worthy of notice." Brown had apparently written that Grieves had no genius, for the latter continued that he was "led to reply to the very wise question—'Does he pretend to deny our assertion that he has no genius?'" In response, Grieves said he had received what talents he had from God, and he trusted that they, "such as they are," had "never been devoted to or sullied by the invention and propagation of calumny." Brown had gone beyond "vague and indefinite abuse," Grieves wrote, and had directly charged "fraudulent stuffing the Herald upon our subscribers." Brown had apparently asked if Grieves wished "to assert" that he had "either honor or honesty," for Grieves retorted, "Dare you, Billy, assert the contrary?" and added, "There is a measure of subtlety and cowardice in the dark insinuation, which must have proceeded from the basest malice, and to give it vent, we challenge Billy and the world to point out the smallest deviation from the paths of honor or honesty."[28]

Although ideas dominated these early papers, printers did report events. Generally, however, they simply told that an event had occurred, without elaboration or description. Vivid descriptions were the exception. If the information's source was a letter, the letter writer's description appeared; but such descriptions were terse because of the editor's haste and lack of space. Aside from reports on congressional proceedings, eyewitness news accounts were extremely rare. Furthermore, reports were fairly anonymous and impersonal—that is, neither the person publishing the account nor those reading it had actually seen the event. Event reports were generally created out of secondhand knowledge, assembled from accounts of one person—who may have been reporting hearsay from several sources—or from several persons, who also may have been reporting from second or third hand. Generally, the rare accounts that did feature individuals and events did so in the context of a political argument or idea (exceptions were tributes to "great" figures, such as George Washington). The tone was very personal, often ridiculing the individuals involved, and one suspects that details (or even whole stories) were frequently fabricated. The following, from a newspaper in 1801, illustrates:

> In July last Mr. Brackenridge, desirous of displaying his new dignity of Judge among his old acquaintances, came over to Washington dressed with unusual neatness. Finding . . . no decent person of the place called to see him, he walked through the town, accosted the people with studied courtesy as he passed the streets in some instances advanced to the door of his former friends but was received with marked coolness, and although not directly insulted, yet he found himself so much detested, that with all his insinuating civilities no person invited him into his house. Mortified beyond measure at this treatment, he returned to his tavern, called for brandy to cure his vexation, and after drinking hastily and usual portions of that [word illegible] liquor he rode away to Canonsburg.
>
> Although evidently intoxicated when he alighted there, yet he went on drinking whiskey to great excess and abusing the gentlemen of Washington. Sometimes he pretended to be asleep in his chair, suddenly would start up with some incoherent exclamation, and take another drink. After a while he said he had a fever, proceeding to strip himself naked, took a sheet and hung it over his shoulders, and walked before the door thus exposed. This soon collected a multitude of boys, to whom he addressed many pleasant things affecting to talk and act like one of themselves. —Presently he ordered water to be carried to the stable, and compelled a black smith's boy to throw several buckets of cold water on him. The other boys, and even men, gathered round the stable and diverted themselves with this whimsical figure of a naked judge upon all fours among the horses . . . washing and rubbing. One lad said he should be drenched also.— Others said he was already drenched with whiskey.[29]

The report continued that the judge, offended by "these fellows'" laughter, ordered them away, threatening to "commit them." Telling them he was a judge, he promised the blacksmith's boy something for staying with him and sent the others home. Leaving the stable, wrapped in a sheet, he drank more whiskey at the tavern, then dressed and started for Pittsburgh, although he was "altogether unfit for travelling" and almost unable to mount his horse. By then having heard he was either drunk or mad, the townspeople laughed as he passed. The report continued, "Near the end of the Village he saw several men . . . with sickles. . . . Fancying them to be enemies, he damned them to clear the road for a Judge of the Supreme Court; then clapping spurs to his horse he raised a frightful warshoop, and dashing through the midst of them, went off at full speed yelling wildly. . . ." According to the report, Brackinridge repeated the drinking, disrobing, and drenching when he arrived at a Mr. Agga's and again at a Mr. Hamilton's taverns. The printer concluded that, with such actions by officials, "we can't expect reformation of the dissolute among us," and wrote that "office is degraded, religion dishonored" and "good men everywhere will lament the misfortune to society when such men are appointed." [30]

In summary, newspaper content in the first decade of the nineteenth century was primarily idea-centered and permeated with personal invective; when printers emphasized individuals, they reported on "important" people—most often officeholders. Event-centered items did appear, but they were often prompted by or used as a basis for discussing ideas. These news traits shifted significantly by 1850.

Newspapers, 1850–1860

By the middle decade of the century, content of papers reflected the changed role of the press—the information model oriented to the individual and the community—and the movement toward democratization that emphasized the individual's role in society and government. No longer idea-centered, most items were local and event-oriented. The newspaper press informed individuals about the society they were part of to increase their knowledge of their surroundings, institutions, and government, providing what they needed to participate as citizens. At the same time, the newspaper press emphasized the individual and individual perspectives in content.

Criticisms during this era that the press was destroying values, creating an injurious current in society, and encroaching on firesides indicate the attention attracted by changed reporting procedures resulting from the press's changed role. Charges of distortion, damage to individuals' reputations especially, and invasion of privacy emerged as a natural consequence of the changed press role. To inform individuals about their environment required a journalistic procedure of description. Any description of an event would naturally lead to charges of distorted reporting, for no two persons ever see an event exactly alike, and those who saw and also read a report of an event were likely to believe that the journalist had distorted the news. But reading descriptions of unfolding events that one had witnessed in person was a new experience. Furthermore, describing events to inform individuals of the kind of society they lived in naturally raised charges of immoral reporting, for the press had begun to describe matters traditionally reserved only for conversation—and even then not for "polite" conversation—views that were not intended to circulate. Describing events meant portraying both the good and the bad of society, and the latter was presumed by those attached to traditional values as unfit to be published. Many believed that such material was injurious even if published as part of novels. Humankind's baser instincts were not to be dignified by being committed to print and commonly circulated. This kind of reading matter did not elevate or ennoble, nor did it provide the most meritorious record to pass on to future generations or the rest of the world. Some saw such news not only as poor reading material that lowered general erudition but also as tending to corrupt those who read it. Second, the focus on individuals, their milieu and who they were, naturally led to charges of invasion of privacy, for to describe individuals' behavior more closely than would be offered in the barest sketch meant intruding into their lives further than the values of many at the time condoned.

The typical high-circulation newspaper of the 1850s was four to eight pages long, with half or more devoted to advertising.[31] By the 1850s, the press had become centered on the event—that is, an occurrence at some specific time and place occasioned most reports. A typical four-page paper contained thirty-five to forty items about events, whereas items dealing purely with ideas per se were few. In one issue, only two items—one having to do with women's role in society, and the other with the institution of slavery—were identified as idea-centered. Through a generous interpretation, one could classify some of the political pieces as idea-centered when, for example, they focused on political platforms; however, these articles primarily aimed to report an event, such as a convention or meeting.[32]

The newspapers of the 1850s were published to serve the individual, and they emphasized local news—events in the city where the paper was published. Thirty-five to forty items reported local news as opposed to twenty to twenty-five nonlocal items. Foreign or international news was rare; in one issue only four international items appeared. Twenty-five to thirty items were political.[33] The emphasis on individuals and local news no doubt also flowed from newspapers' need to interest people and to achieve greater circulation. Changes in the press made higher circulation possible; the use of new equipment, however, made publishing more expensive, so the need to increase circulation led to studied attempts to reach the greatest number. Whatever content sold papers was emphasized. The event orientation probably had to do with such changes; as journalists tried to achieve greater circulation, they published dailies and even separate weekly editions. This and the editor's expanded role as policymaker did not leave time for the contemplation necessary to write idea-centered articles. A daily demanded quick production. Finally, the development of news gathering took journalists outside the office and kept them on the go more than ever before, and the new reporting practices left little time for preparing idea pieces. It must be noted here, however, that many of the first decade's idea articles may have been contributed to the newspaper and not actually prepared by the editor. Contributed articles were scarce in papers in the 1850s, probably because of the drive for circulation and its consequent emphasis on events, which crowded out "think" pieces except for the editor's own commentaries.

Trying to convey what was happening in the world for the individual's edification meant creating as complete a picture of any event as possible. Hence, new writing techniques emerged in news reports, influenced to a great extent by the employment of literary figures as journalists. Linda Patterson Miller notes that Edgar Allen Poe, for example, working in New York as one of the first urban journalists, brought literary elegance to descriptions of the city, including street noise and social inequalities, in a series called "Doings of Gotham," which appeared in the *Columbia Spy* between May 28 and July 6, 1844; soon after, a series called "Slices of New York," by a reporter for the *New York Tribune*, followed "almost exactly, the plan . . . Poe had established." A series published in the 1850s, "Hot Corn Sketches," imitated the pattern in trying to describe "city life and its effect on people."[34]

Politics remained important, as indicated by the large number of items devoted to it—even if the pieces were more event- than idea-centered— but journalists in the 1850s in effect attempted to describe what occurred on a daily basis, and aimed as often as possible to describe the process. Reports of social context—that is, descriptions of city life and physical surroundings—were common, and more substance of events in process began to appear. A New York newspaper's report of a riot illustrates the emphasis on event, the eyewitness account, and the description of process. Inclusion of the color of people's shirts and other minutiae suggests that the writer saw the event in person. Under headlines, in the following order, the editor reported "CITY INTELLIGENCE / Riot Among the Firemen —Paving Stones and / Politics—Engines Taken From the Bellige / rants by order of the Chief Engineer":

> Yesterday morning, at about half-past eleven o'clock, the fire bells rang out an alarm for the Fifth district, and the Bowery was soon filled with engines and hose carts, making their way up town. Engine 41, which lies at the corner of Delancey and Attorney streets, was going up under full headway, when, at the junction of the Bowery, Third avenue and Sixth street, engine No. 6 came up with a very strong force, and ran into No. 41, taking off one of the forward wheels of the vehicle, thus crippling the apparatus so as to bring it to a stand still. . . . it was at once understood that a fight was to ensue, and so the members of No. 6 followed up the attack upon the engine by an attack upon the men, who had it in charge. At this time the company of No. 6 far outnumbered their adversaries, and the members of 41 were obliged to give way. Presently, however, other engines and hose companies came up, and were soon engaged, taking different sides, according to their predilections. As the alarm spread, the friends of both sides came up, and the war became general. Conspicuous among those who were actively engaged were, besides the members of 6 and 41, many . . . whose caps bore the numbers 4, 16, 26, 15 and 44. The battle ground was in the open space at the head of Sixth street, known as the Hay Market. A few rods down Sixth street was a large pile of bricks, placed there for building purposes. The party of No. 6 took possession of this lot of ammunition, and commenced to pour in a lively shower of brickbats upon their opponents. No regard was had for passing vehicles. The stages, railroad cars, and wagons, were obliged to take the chances of getting hit, and considerable damage was thus done by the flying missiles. Many persons were injured who had nothing to do with the fight. A man standing quietly in the corner of the Bowery and Sixth street, received a blow from a brick which knocked him down. . . . Some . . . bystanders took him up, and conveyed him out of the reach of danger. . . . Very conspicuous among the rioters were a set of rowdies dressed in red shirts, and armed with axes, cleavers, iron bars, and clubs. . . .
>
> While the fight was going on, and when it was at its height, a detachment of police officers . . . made their appearance, and went boldly into the midst of the rioters, and behaved with such coolness, and courage that a check was soon put to firing of missiles.[35]

The journalist of the mid-nineteenth century emphasized individuals in reporting, often describing their appearance, activities, feelings, thoughts, and conversation. An element of continuity, however, was the interest in "important" persons, which coincided with the increasing emphasis on "ordinary" people. Another new element was that of quoting individuals directly.

Reports of Daniel Webster's death illustrate these points, especially in their emphasis on individuals—in this case, an important personage. The article that follows, excerpted from the *New York Herald*, also illustrates careful explication of the details of Webster's last days, along with exposure of what some surely at the time considered trivial—as well as overly intimate, private, and personal. The story is quoted at length because it is in many ways characteristic of 1850s reporting. Pages and pages of an issue of the *New York Herald* were devoted to Webster's last days and hours.

ANOTHER NATIONAL CALAMITY

DEATH OF

DANIEL WEBSTER,

the

GREAT NEW ENGLAND STATESMAN.

THE expounder of the constitution NO MORE

HIS SICKNESS, AND LAST MOMENTS.

SAD AND TOUCHING DEATH SCENE

Biographical Sketch of the Great Man

The Effect of his Death Here and Elsewhere

&c., &c., &c.

When news reached here on Friday morning that Mr. Webster's indisposition, by which he had been affected for some ten days previously, had suddenly assumed a dangerous and alarming phase the deepest solicitude and anxiety was manifested by all classes of citizens, and the most intense excitement existed to learn, from time to time the contents of each succeeding despatch.

The melancholy tidings were first communicated by . . . a special messenger . . . from Mr. Webster's residence at Marshfield, carrying the sad intelligence that the distinguished statesman could not survive the day. On the previous Tuesday not the slightest danger had been apprehended from Mr. Webster's illness which was disease of the bowels, accompanied by dropsical affection of the stomach, and his physicians anticipated that he would be able to resume the duties of his office in a few days; but on that afternoon the disorder unexpectedly assumed a more menacing aspect, and he gradually grew worse and worse, until Thursday, when Dr. Jeffries, the physician in attendance, began to feel alarmed. . . .

On Thursday night Mr. Webster had a very severe attack of vomiting, but at five o'clock on Friday morning, when the special messenger left Marshfield, he had sunk into a sleep.

The Hon. George T. Curtis, who had been in attendance on the dying states-man, returned to Boston on Friday morning, and confirmed the sad intelligence of the hopelessness of Mr. Webster's recovery; and on the same morning a letter was received from his private secretary, by the Hon. Edward Everett stating that he was not expected to survive many hours. . . .

Mr. Webster, fully sensible of his approaching end, but looked forward to it with magnanimous resignation. . . . His intellectual faculties were as bright and powerful as in their most halcyon days, and among all the sorrow-stricken friends, relatives and admirers, who surrounded his couch, and with whom he conversed freely, he was of all the most placid, serene, and unaffected.

Nor in this last scene and preparation for eternity was the great man unmind-ful of his duties to his family, his household, and his country. On Thursday forenoon he received his mail as usual and gave the directions for answers to his letters. . . . To the workmen on his farm he also gave directions . . . and . . . proceeded to complete various matters of business.

On Thursday evening he executed his last will and testament. . . .

During Friday, the dying statesman had three attacks of vomiting—one at two o'clock in the morning, one at eight . . . and one at four o'clock in the afternoon. From that time up till seven o'clock he lay in a placid state apparently free from pain, and conversing a little. . . . His physician . . . forbade general conversation, as talking produced nausea. . . .

. . . At eleven o'clock on Friday night he was again seized with vomitings, though they were not very severe; but between one and two o'clock on Saturday morning, vomiting recurred and continued for three quarters of an hour, during which time he suffered terribly. . . .

About half past five o'clock [on Saturday afternoon], Mr. Webster was again seized with violent nausea and raised considerable dark matter tinged with blood. Exhaustion now increased rapidly, and his physicians held another con-sultation which resulted in a conclusion that his last hour was fast approaching.

He received the announcement, and requested that the female members of his family might be called in. . . .

Next he had called in the male members . . . and the personal friends. . . .

He now had Mr. Peter Harvey called in again, and said to him:—

"Harvey, I am not so sick but that I know you. . . . I am well enough to love you . . . don't leave me till I am dead. . . ."

Then as if speaking to himself, he said—

"On the 24th of October, all that is mortal of Daniel Webster will be no more." . . .

At half-past seven o'clock, Dr. J. M. Warren arrived from Boston. . . .

Shortly after he conversed with Dr. Jeffries, who said he could do nothing more for him than to administer occasionally a sedative potion. "Then," said Mr. Webster, "I am to be here patiently till the end; if it be so, may it come soon."

At ten o'clock he was still lower, but perfectly conscious . . . and at twenty-two minutes before three o'clock yesterday morning, "the 24th of October, all that was mortal of Daniel Webster was no more."[36]

Historians would expect James Gordon Bennett to report such details, but might be surprised that other editors of the mid-nineteenth century would. Comparison with another newspaper on the same day, however, showed that such reporting was not unique. The Boston *Daily Evening Transcript*, the most staid paper in the sample, published a report so similar to the *Herald*'s as to suggest that the news came via the telegraph in both cases. But neither account appeared under the telegraph headline. Webster had called for "poetry—Gray—Gray," and both stories reported this and that the "Elegy in a Country Churchyard" was read to him; both also reported, "The last words of Webster are said to have been the remarkable ones, 'I STILL LIVE' "[37]

Although newspaper content was no longer dominated by politics and no longer idea-centered, the degree of partisan bias hardly differed from that of the early newspapers. An item selected at random from the *New York Times* illustrates:

Our fastidious neighbors of the *Evening Post* are not pleased with the Whig City nominations. We are very sorry, but the thing cannot be helped now. Two of the leading nominations are from the working classes. This loses the party the countenance of the philosophers and poets of the *Post*. Their ideas run upon the ideal—not the practical. Alderman (Sheriff, that is to be) Kelly is "a *baker* in Beekman-street!" "generally liked by those who know him," but only a bread-baker, and no one knows him in the *Post*'s "set." He drives an honest trade in Beekman-street, not a turn-out above Bleecker!

And the *Post* is not pleased with Morgan Morgans either. This surprises us. Mr. M. is an older worker in *brass*. Respect for a metal constituting no mean ingredient in their own composition, should otherwise incline our neighbors—it should.[38]

But even though editors' public animosities toward each other had lessened, many items showed that exchanges of insults remained common. Under the headline FUNNY NEWSPAPER WAR, for example, an editor noted in 1852:

The Pick and the Picayune, two flashy weekly journals, are at war, both in their columns and in the police office. The Pick is the new one started by Joe Scoville

—the Picayune is the old one, owned by two or three nobodies. The Pick began with a circulation of 25,000 at the first step. This frightened the old boys, and they retaliated by two or three arrests of the Pick man for libel. This is a mean mode of putting down a new rival, and will hardly succeed. Let master Pick keep cool, stick to his text, say nothing of his rivals, make a good paper, amuse all the pretty girls with funny stories, and he is in no danger of damnation.[39]

Common in the first decade, such editorial insults had decreased by the century's middle decade and virtually disappeared by the last decade.

Newspapers, 1890–1899

By the 1890s, the definition of news had changed even more, emphasizing events, dwelling on individual personalities, and using drama to lure readers. In other words, the stress on events, the individual perspective, and the use of drama as a lure had merged into the "story," a product that was marketed and sold. However, the merging blurred the significance of each element, obscuring distinctions and the purity of focus of any one strand. The event was, at one level, the hard news story—the accurate, factual information; at another level, it was the "plot" or part of a plot around which drama was woven to create the thrill that would make people want to read and therefore buy the newspaper. The role of ideas in newspapers was relegated principally to the editorial page, which developed after the 1850s; but even so, ideas were less identifiable in papers at the end of the century. Editorials most often departed from actions—which ideas underlay, to be sure, but the ideas were, if only ever so slightly, out of focus.

Press content of the 1890s reflected a further changed role. The news "packaging," the tightly crowded pages of variety and diversity, and the story model are only three broad traits that signify a press engaged in selling and marketing news. The evidence of drama—what most at the time called sensationalism—to lure readers and sell papers is overwhelming; this, however, did not suddenly burst upon the scene.

In a sense, although the story model preceded the Civil War, the postwar infusion of drama in news may be attributed to the war. The events journalists conveyed to the public during those four years of crisis and during the preceding decade had been constantly thrilling—not pleasant, but thrilling nevertheless. Regardless of how bad or good it was, the news was always exciting; and readers became habituated to looking to newspapers for excitement as well as information. The effect was no doubt similar to the much shorter American media experience during the Watergate hearings in 1974. In that case, a story built over months about whether the president had possibly violated the public's good faith, at the very least, and at the worst, his oath of office, the nation's Constitution, and federal laws. The revelations increasingly cast suspicion, culminating in the hearings that kept the nation riveted to the news media to learn the truth and whether the president might be impeached. The president's resignation and the swearing in of a new president, who then pardoned his predecessor, ended a series of electrifying events. The news had thrilled and excited Americans, keeping the public rapt through a national crisis. But when the crisis was over. . . . A certain sense of letdown followed because the news no longer excited on a daily basis; journalists recognized this anticlimax and the pressure it signified to find a way to keep the public's attention when such absorbing events no longer occurred daily.

Surely, such was the situation of journalism after the Civil War, although no one may have recognized it then as representing a media problem. But surely, too, journalists who had "grown up" during the war and whose experience had necessarily taught them how to thrill readers continued to try to do so as they aimed to fulfill the public's desire for excitement that the war had so elevated. "Sensational" postwar stories about corruption and reforms provided a way to continue to thrill. Journalists simply adapted wartime lessons to a time of peace. And as they adapted newsgathering and other techniques learned during the war—such as using multiple sources, interviewing, ferreting out stories against all objections and odds, disguising themselves for safety in order to pursue the Southern story, and describing events so that readers might almost feel that they were there—they increasingly went beyond what some at the time believed were the appropriate bounds of journalistic conduct; hence the shrill denunciations of the press during the 1880s.

Criticisms focused on these several excesses: invasions of privacy as journalists tried to get every detail that might satisfy what many saw as the most tasteless curiosity; sensationalism that heightened thrill at the expense of perspective and facts; and jeopardizing the accused's right to a fair trial by publishing details that seemed virtually to convict outside the justice system. But considering news drama of the late nineteenth century as part of journalists' efforts to package news for marketing, we can understand it better than by simply excoriating it as sensationalism. It was journalistic conduct dictated by press role.

Newspapers in the 1890s were eight to sixteen pages long, page size was larger than earlier, and up to three pages of an eight-page paper were devoted to advertising. Several new elements were apparent in the papers, each confirming the late-nineteenth-century business model of journalism, which was dedicated to selling news as a commodity:

1. Drama in the reporting was intended to excite and entice readers to buy papers.

2. Personals columns and vital statistics were intended to meet specific interests and attempt to offer something for virtually everyone. This effort to please all readers was a holdover from the mid-century emphasis on the individual. It may be that journalists had tried to meet the charges of trivialization by reducing the space allotted to each story of this type; still, they saw such news as important because it appealed to many readers. It seems worth noting, however, that these short items seemed a far greater trivialization of news than had earlier articles that unabashedly celebrated individuals—ordinary or not-so-ordinary. In the 1890s, however, "personals" attracted those interested in tidbits about the "rich and famous," flattered readers who found themselves mentioned, and injected a personal element in what had become an increasingly impersonal journalism.

3. Reporting on business indicated the press's role in supporting and promoting that trend in American society. Significant designated space devoted to financial news was a new element; in fact, a well-defined financial page appeared in most newspapers of the 1890s. The amount of attention given to business should not have been surprising since national interests were preoccupied with the subject at the time, but it was. A close study of business stories would likely reveal a great deal about competing values during the latter part of the century. It is interesting, for example, that the tone of some articles on American business was mocking whereas that of others was laudatory.

4. Significant space devoted to international news, especially compared to papers of the 1850s, confirmed the "internationalization" of the press following the Civil War.

5. Fashion pages, well defined in some newspapers, showed that journalists were consciously trying to appeal to women.

6. Well-defined sports pages also appeared—another signal of the intent to meet diverse interests.

7. Advertising was interspersed with news columns throughout the

newspaper, indicating clear intentions to ensure that readers would not overlook ads or read only the news and throw away pages given over entirely to advertising. Single ads were also larger—often multiple-column—and contained display type, illustrations, and copy that appealed to the emotions more than any previous ads had. Fewer ads ran on front pages, although some newspapers devoted as many as two of seven front-page columns to advertising.

8. Well-defined editorial pages kept alive a function of dealing with ideas. However, the original idea-centered emphasis of the early national press was gone. Although editorial pages of course involved ideas, editorials themselves most often focused on particular actions of groups, organizations, or companies rather than underlying ideas. Thus the activity or the group—not the idea—was the reason for an editorial's having been written.

9. Inclusion of fiction—that is, short stories—reflected the effort to entertain and provide yet another reason for readers to buy papers. This element capitalized on what journalists had learned about readers' interest in "stories"—demonstrated by journalists in the 1830s who reported the "moan hoax" and coopted literary figures such as Edgar Allan Poe. Fiction also complemented and paralleled the use of drama in news. Both were part of 1890s trends.

The three most striking new elements, in larger terms, were the abundant number of items crowded onto a page, the degree of often contrived drama interwoven in reports of every kind, and the packaging of the news.

The abundance of items is overwhelming. Newspapers commonly fit twenty-five to sixty-five items on the front page, which seemed intended to offer something for everyone—although society's ethnic diversity was hardly recognized. An average number of front-page items calculated from eleven issues of different newspapers was 40.5—and some of those papers gave two front-page columns to advertising. One particular issue had thirty-seven items on the front page, of which nine were local, eleven national (most dealt with events in other states, with two about general national affairs) and seventeen international. Three were political, and four were about business. Thirty were event-centered; none was idea-centered. Twelve of the total front-page items were infused with drama and told as suspenseful stories. The lead story, under the headline AWAITING THE SHOCK, told of crowds waiting for the electrocution of prisoners at Sing

Sing.[40] Another entire issue contained thirty dramatized items. Twenty-six items were business news and twenty were political. The breakdown according to locality was twenty-six local, fifty-eight national, and twenty-five international items.[41]

Obviously, most items were short; however, the most dramatic stories got most space. Front pages commonly had one or two long stories (filling a column or more and continuing on the inside), so additional items crowded into remaining space were short and numerous, indeed.

Regarding form, one may cautiously say that the story dominated—more because of its stronger impact, perhaps, than because it outnumbered straightforward items. Certainly, journalists seized every opportunity to inject drama into their reports; although they did not dramatize every account, they dramatized every kind at one time or another —from political to business to international. News items in the 1890s were, indeed, *stories*. Their headlines were crafted to draw attention to their inherent drama, and those without strong emotional overtones were nevertheless often infused with drama. The headlines for a Philadelphia newspaper's leading front-page story illustrate:

ANNA DICKINSON
She Has Been Declared Sane and a Victim of a Plot.
Taken Away by Force.
She Tells a Startling Story of Alleged Cruel Persecution.
Cut Off from the World—The Horrors of a Mad House—Charges
Against Her Sister.[42]

The story, which filled two columns and continued on page 2, told about an apparently wealthy woman committed to an asylum by a sister who she said was insane.

Other headlines on the same page included

THEY ARE PIRATES
So Ex-leader Barry Called the Knights of Labor Whitty's Unpaid Bill
Evidence Produced to Show that He Has a Just Claim—
How the Organization Expends Its Money.

The story was about the trial in William Whitty's suit against the executive board of the Knights of Labor.

FIRED THE BUILDING
Terrible Charge Against the Proprietor of a Burned Hotel

THE DEED OF A BRUTAL PARENT

TURNED THE HOSE ON HIM
Then There Was a Riot, in Which Men, Irrespective of Station, Participated

LYNCHED BY A MASKED MOB
A Hundred Men Take Murderer Bales from Jail and Hang Him to a Tree.[43]

The lead story in an Ohio newspaper, about a meeting of Methodist ministers, ran under the headlines

GRAVE SUBJECT
How Shall the Dead Be Buried?
M. E. Ministers Discuss It
Undertakers Again Hauled Over the Coals
The Brethren Start the Jury Wheel A-rolling[44]

Some other headlines were

DISAGREEING DOCTORS
An Asylum Superintendent Defiantly Trails the Tail of His Coat.[45]

BOY BRAINS A MAN[46]

AN INHUMAN MOTHER?
She Sells Her Daughter's Virtue and
Then Pleads for Mercy[47]

MURDERED BEFORE THE ALTAR[48]

HACKED TO PIECES[49]

Headlines in 1899 reached for even more drama, as these examples illustrate:

GROUND TO PIECES IN REVOLVING SHAFT[50]

—a particularly gruesome story about a twelve-year-old boy's death in an elevator;

Complaints of Gardiner
Newburger Adjourns Court, De-
Clining to Try Dead Men
Judges Besought by the Dry Goods District

To see that Bachrach and Wereter Are
Tried. Merchants Declare There is Some
Hidden Influence Behind the Thieves[51]

Pronounced a Leper By the Man She Loved[52]

Was "Excited" When He Stole Trousers, Three Months a Pair[53]

A Woman Burned by a Bonfire[54]

Cabin Boy M'Kinley Was a Girl[55]

Not all headlines or stories in this era were "sensational" or contained the drama reflected in these. Many newspapers, in fact, had little excessive drama, but most—if not all—included drama. Even headlines that were mere labels—as many were—included some element of drama (suspense, humor, or punning) intended to hook readers. These headlines illustrate: A CHEEKY REQUEST; A FIRM OLD FIRM; BOTH EYES OPEN; FATAL KICK; AWFUL FATE; THIS IS AWFUL; STOLE A SECRET; NO LONGER A SECRET; CAME TO BLOWS? BOUNCED BY DOCTORS? SMASHED WITH A SANDBAG.[56] Drama was, of course, a part of packaging the news. But packaging included several other elements, the most important of which was confining particular kinds of content to special pages. Journalists in the Civil War era began the packaging of selected *items* with multi-deck headlines and leads; by the 1890s they had expanded this practice to the entire newspaper. Dividing news according to broad categories and interests, they designated places for each—sports, financial reports, editorials, fashion—packaging and labeling it to create systematized order and facilitate readers' ease in finding what interested them most. Lincoln Steffens' description of newspapers in the 1890s was apt: the pattern did indeed imitate a department store, where commodities were separated into different areas. Other packaging elements included illustration to "dress up" a story, multiple headlines to provide the gist of a story quickly, and the many short items that enabled one to read "complete items" in quick takes. All these techniques helped to sell the news.

Newspaper content over the course of the nineteenth century confirms changes in the press's role in each era. Constants throughout were the relationship of press role to journalism's expansion as a social institution and to values. As values changed, role changed, and journalistic standards changed in turn. When journalistic standards are viewed as part of a larger framework of forces—against a background of social developments, changing values, press criticism, and newspaper content, they come into focus. From partisanism to trivialization to sensationalism, journalistic excesses were by-products of how the press fulfilled particular roles as these were interpreted at different times. Since the press's role has implications for standards, discussion now turns to that issue, beginning with a consideration of journalists' views.

Chapter Four

Journalistic Standards and the Press's Role to 1850: What Journalists Said

READER, *it has given me much pain to write such lies as I have presented you in this number. If it has been such a task for me to fill one little paper with them, how the devil does Holt get along with such a piece of work from year to year? Perhaps by being accustomed to it. However, I despair of acquiring the habit; and therefore must give up the idea of becoming a democrat.*
H. Croswell, The Wasp, January 1803

Early American conditions entrenched a political role for the press and established a pattern that, although weakened by the decline of formal patronage in the 1840s and decreasing respect for partisanism, continued throughout the century.[1] In these early decades, the press predominantly supported, promoted, and aided political parties. In supporting a party, an editor generally berated the opposing party and leadership, so using any current measures of standards—such as accuracy or balance—is therefore irrelevant. No "balance," as meant by present-day ideas of objectivity, existed, and accuracy was sacrificed with the use of any successful means to detract from the opposition.[2] The content of party newspapers was deliberately one-sided, filled with political essays that were almost always on the attack. In the historian Donald Stewart's words, "To American political parties, the gazettes were as tools to the machine."[3] The content was often tasteless, including name-calling, ridicule, accusation, deliberate falsity, and rumor intended to damage the opposing party.[4] But as long as journalists held political positions, the practice overshadowed the scant discussion of possible conflicts of interest or related issues.

At the outset of this work, it was assumed that journalists' views would differ significantly from those of critics who were not journalists. But the evidence did not support that assumption. The "inner circle" of journalists, closer to the press and its operations than were nonjournalists, simply represented more contracted views that nevertheless flowed from society's larger values. Looking at journalists' positions separately is important, but it quickly becomes clear that, although they generally dealt carefully with specific issues, their work merely "operationalized" implicit social standards. Perhaps no particular situation makes this clearer than journalists' participation in efforts to suppress the abolitionist discussion of slavery during the 1830s. Most journalists espoused the same values as a large portion of the population at the time.[5] This chapter emphasizes what journalists and a few others especially close to the press said about issues related to standards during the first half of the century.

Tracing the evolution of journalistic standards presents obvious problems because word connotations in the earliest years are lost, and one is left to decipher meanings from context and approximation to current usage. For example, those concerned about press content apparently believed it should be truthful, but evidence of analysis of truth and its meaning for journalists is scant before the twentieth century.[6] The word *objectivity* did not appear until the late nineteenth or early twentieth century.[7] Earlier journalists used the term *impartiality* in a way that seems to embody the core idea that evolved into what we mean by *objectivity,* but it did not include all the dimensions now conceptually attributed to the latter word.[8] *Impartiality* embodied meanings attached to the era in which it was used, just as *objectivity* has been imbued with meanings of its own era, particularly preoccupations with science and scientific method.[9] Consequently, although their core ideas may be similar, they are not equivalent, for their meanings are tied to the concepts of the press's role and the cultural values that prevailed when they emerged, and to the shadings imparted by subsequent usage.

During the early years of the nineteenth century, impartiality, often cited as a standard, was the primary journalistic issue discussed, but it seems to have referred to equal treatment of opposing parties and whether this was desirable. The following discussion, which is indebted to Stewart's work on the early American press, emphasizes journalists' views, but the views of nonjournalists, considered later, show no appreciable differences.

The Early Years, 1790–1840

In 1799, a New York printer, praising several editors who "published for the country" for trying to be impartial, defined impartiality in light of the tension between England and France and of American patriotism. He wrote:

By impartiality we mean the method which they adhere to in editting [*sic*] their papers; instead of Printing only in favor of one nation, they publish as they receive the information, both against France and Great Britain: this conduct discovers the real American.[10]

Some printers of both parties, however, ridiculed impartiality as an unattainable ideal—if indeed it was even desirable. In 1798, a New Jersey Federalist printer called impartiality in politics "curious," referring to printers who advocated publishing both sides. Calling this an evasion and a "folly that should not be tolerated," he likened those printers to witnesses who would lie in testimony to avoid taking a stand for either the accused or the plaintiff:

The times demand decision; there is a right and a wrong, and the printer, who under the specious name of impartiality jumbles both truth and falsehood into the same paper is either doubtful of his own judgment in determining truth from falsehood or is governed by ulterior motives.[11]

The Kentucky printer James Lyon, in launching a national magazine, said treating parties equally was impossible, and that printers' "pretended" neutrality misled people.[12] A Maryland printer called any claims of detachment "all delusion," saying "every party will have its printer, as will every sect its preacher."[13] Another New York printer rejected impartiality as "injurious to the best interests of mankind" if it meant equal attachment to the principles of aristocracy and republicanism.[14] William Cobbett, although not the most respected printer of the era, emphatically denied the merit of impartiality in an early issue of *Porcupine's Gazette*:

PROFESSIONS OF IMPARTIALITY I shall make none. They are always useless, and are besides perfect nonsense, when used by a newsmonger, for, he that does not relate news as he finds it, is something worse than partial; . . . he that does not exercise his own judgment, either in admitting or rejecting what is sent him, is a poor passive tool, and not an editor. For my part, I feel the strongest partiality for the cause of order and good government . . . and against everything that is opposed to it. To profess impartiality here, would be as absurd as to profess it in a war between Virtue and Vice, Good and Evil, Happiness and Misery. There may be editors who look on such a conflict with perfect indifference, and whose only anxiety is to discover which is the strongest side. I am not of these, nor shall a paper, under my direction, ever be an instrument of destruction to the cause I espouse.[15]

Although many printers criticized journalism frequently during the period, those who disagreed with these views about impartiality either did not state them or were rare. The general criticism is typified by examples from the first Federalist paper and from the editor-cum-scholar Isaiah Thomas a decade later. John Ward Fenno, the editor of the *United States Gazette*, said in 1799:

The American newspapers are the most base, false, servile and venal publications, that ever polluted the fountains of society—their editors the most ignorant, mercenary, and vulgar automatons that ever were moved by the continually rusting wires of sordid mercantile avarize [sic]."[16]

Stewart quotes Isaiah Thomas, editor of the *Massachusetts Spy* through the American Revolution and early nation years and author of the first history of American journalism, who called partisan editors "destitute at once of the urbanity of gentlemen, the information of scholars, and the principles of virtue."[17] Thomas blamed American press problems on partisanism. Devoting three pages to a minister's press criticisms, Thomas wrote that "the selfish principle prompts men to defame personal and political enemies; and where the supposed provocations . . . are numerous, . . . an inundation of filth and calumny must be expected."[18]

More directly on the issue of impartiality, a letter in a Vermont newspaper in 1798 said that since several powerful newspapers represented either party, people reading only one paper had no access to the truth if that paper was partisan. Readers would inevitably take on the prejudice they were constantly exposed to. The writer believed, however, that "dispassion" was possible and could be achieved if editors would suppress their own political opinions, read at least one outstanding paper of each party, and publish equal amounts—in quantity and quality—of thoughtful, decent articles from both sides, avoiding "squibs, and . . . rancorous party trash. . . ." The letter writer concluded this would "certainly be highly serviceable to the public."[19]

Motivations for the rare criticisms of journalistic officeholding or other political involvement often seemed based more on political strategy than conviction. An Edenton, North Carolina, printer, smarting from criticism for "publication of Mr. Jefferson's character" in his first issue in 1800, wrote:

I never intended, by commencing *Editor* of a *newspaper,* to commence *politician* at the same time. —I never have been able to discover any natural connection between the *two.* I know an opposite idea has got into the minds of a number of our *printers,* but when I read their opinions, views and representations of things, so contradictory, that they do not appear to me to understand . . . *politics* any better than myself, who would wish to let it alone altogether.[20]

His prospectus warned, "Scurrility, glancing at character, and every fulsome stuff, with which most of the public prints are frequently crouded [*sic*], are not to be admitted," and continued in another paragraph, "No production to find a passage, but that which comes forward, with the gentility and liberality of the gentleman, and man of sense."[21] Yet the article on "Jefferson's character" seems to have engaged in the very activities the printer condemned. One writer in 1858, quoting a promise of fairness and impartiality in a newspaper prospectus from 1800, noted that never was such a promise so often offered and so seldom kept as in the early nineteenth century.[22] That failure was no doubt linked to the press's perceived role.

Those out of power criticized incumbents for appointing journalists to political office or granting them government printing contracts, yet when they gained power, they followed the same practice. In 1826, for example, Duff Green, the editor of the *United States Telegraph,* a paper established to help elect Andrew Jackson as president, wrote:

We refer to that which operates on the press, and which tends to convert this sentinel of freedom into a spy of power . . . it is in vain to talk of a free press, when the *favor of power* is essential to the support of editors, and the money of the people, by passing through the hands of the Executive, is made to operate as a bribe against liberty. It is a most solemn truth, and should be deeply impressed on every mind, that if liberty shall ever expire in our country, it will die of the poisonous draught of corrupt patronage.[23]

Green was notoriously partisan, however, and in the campaign for Jackson used his newspaper to raise every possible issue against the Adams administration. Introduction of a patronage bill by Henry Clay, a member of Adams's administration, seems to have prompted this outburst, so Green's conviction about the injury of partisanism to liberty seems shallow at best.[24] The historian Culver Smith says two fears generated editors' criticisms of patronage: that the government did not distribute printing contracts equitably, thus creating or denying economic advantages for journalists, and that those granting contracts would keep themselves in power through manipulating patronage.[25]

After 1800 little discussion was found of impartiality or the possible conflict of interest in partisan journalism until President Andrew Jackson's unprecedented use of the press and appointments of editors in the 1830s. Having grown distrustful of Green, Jackson, after winning the election, established a new Washington paper to support his administration, and its editor soon received printing contracts.[26] Furthermore, Jackson appointed more journalists to political office than perhaps any other president in history. Pollard cites the *National Journal*'s listing in 1829 of forty journalists appointed by Jackson, adding the list was thought to be incomplete.[27] The *National Intelligencer* in 1832 published a list of fifty-seven journalists Jackson had appointed to federal positions.[28] Although some raised questions about conflicts of interest, the practice was hardly considered improper.

James Madison, whose efforts during the Alien and Sedition Acts controversy marked him as one who profoundly understood the meaning of the press in a free society,[29] did not seem to consider partisanism improper, although he deplored the resulting distortion of ideas in the polity at large. The year of Andrew Jackson's first election to the presidency, Madison, in a letter to a friend, implied that he saw the press's political role as legitimate. He called impractical the only solution he could think of to a "biased" press—allowing each party to present views on the same issues in the same newspapers—because it would require new arrangements every time parties changed and would bring worse problems than having newspapers that supported only one party while distorting information about all others. Madison wrote:

There is but too much truth in the picture of newspapers sketched in the letter to the Philadelphia printer. But the effect of their falsehood and slanders must always be controuled in a certain degree by contradictions in rival or hostile papers, where the press is free. The complaint nevertheless applies with much force to the one-sided publications which may happen to predominate at particular periods or under particular circumstances. It is then that the minds best disposed may be filled with the most gross and injurious untruths. Those who see erroneous statements . . . without any exposure to their fallacies, will, of course, be generally under the delusions so strongly painted by Mr. Jefferson. It has been said, that any country might be governed at the will of one who had the exclusive privilege of furnishing its popular songs. The result would be far more certain from a monopoly of the politics of the press. Could it be so arranged that every newspaper, when printed on one side, should be handed over to the press of the adversary, to be printed on the other, thus presenting to every reader both sides of every question, truth would always have a fair chance. But such a remedy is ideal; and if reducible to practice, continual changes in the arrangement would be required by the successive revolutions in the state of parties, and their effect on the relative opinions and views of the same editors. . . .[30]

Andrew Jackson surrounded himself with journalists and was closer to the press than perhaps any other U.S. president. Some have said he was the only president to run the country via the newspaper press. For these reasons, and because he appointed so many journalists to office, his views of journalistic conduct are important. As criticism heightened against his appointments of journalists, he defended them vigorously, and one can glean from his writings several arguments supporting the journalist-politician role:[31]

1. Jackson was only doing what prior presidents had done.
2. The appointments were only for the public good.
3. He would not exclude his friends from public office just because they were friends.
4. Before condemning his actions, people should wait to see the results of the appointments.
5. Editors were motivated by the same patriotism as others.
6. Why should editors be excluded from office to which people no more patriotic or qualified aspired?
7. Denying editors opportunities for political appointments would soon mean that people of good character would no longer seek to be journalists.
8. Excluding editors from rewards available to other professions degraded the press.
9. All citizens wanted to see the press elevated and made a vehicle of truth and useful knowledge. (Presumably, this suggested that editors would not dare to abuse the press through their political position.)
10. To take from the press those who aspire to higher aims than being mere agents for advancing others is subversive of this aim.
11. Finally, Jackson said, "I refuse to consider the editorial calling as unfit to offer a candidate to office. . . ."[32]

One of the first attacks on Jackson's appointments of journalists came from an ardent supporter, Thomas Ritchie, editor of the Richmond, Virginia, *Enquirer*. Because Ritchie supported Jackson's election (and because his words ring true), one wishes to believe his motives were pure. But in 1844, Ritchie was brought to Washington to publish a newspaper on behalf of the new administration of James K. Polk. Powerful in Virginia politics, he had used the *Enquirer* aggressively in Jackson's campaign,[33] and at least one editor saw his criticism in 1829 as hypocrisy. (The editor of the *National Journal* asked, "Why has not the Editor expressed the wish at an earlier period?")[34] James Pollard has mined Jackson's published correspondence, and the following owes a great debt to his book *The Presidents and the Press*, which identifies sections of the correspondence illuminating Jackson's position. Of Jackson's appointments after the 1828 election, Ritchie wrote in the *Enquirer*:

> We wish the Executive would let the Press alone. We cannot any more approve of the appointment of so many of its conductors to office, although they be required to give up their papers, than we approved of the great pains which were taken by Mr. Clay to turn obnoxious Editors out . . . and to put in his devoted Partizans. —We know that General Jackson solemnly disclaims all intentions to *reward* his supporters or to bribe the Press to support his measures. And we believe him—we know also, the reasons by which he justifies these appointments. . . . But we are better satisfied with his *motive* than his *reasons*—with the integrity than with the expediency of the appointment.[35]

Ritchie also protested to Vice President Martin Van Buren about "so many of the Editorial Corps favored with the patronage of the Administration," arguing that the appointments mishandled the press, brought its freedom into contempt, and endangered people's rights:

> A single case would not have excited so much observation, but it really looks as if there were a systematic Effort to reward Editorial Partizans, which will have the effect of bringing the vaunted Liberty of the Press into a sort of Contempt. I make allowance for the situation of these Gentlemen . . . I allow for all these things, and still the truth cannot be disguised, that the press, which shrinks like the sensitive plant from the touch of Executive Power, has been heedlessly handled. Invade the freedom of the Press and the freedom of Election, by showering patronage too much on Editors of newspapers and on Members of Congress, and the rights of the people themselves are exposed to imminent danger. I know that this was not the *motive* of such appointments; but I argue about *effects*. . . .[36]

Possibly Ritchie had expected an appointment as a reward for his help in electing Jackson, and his criticism may have come from disappointment and anger. However, no evidence was found to confirm this.

Jackson defended the appointments to Van Buren, saying he had "only followed the examples of my illustrious predecessors, Washington and

Jefferson," and called on Van Buren to give Ritchie a good "dressing down":

I would advise the answering of mr Richie's letter; and, in the most delicate manner, to put him on his guard with respect to letter writers from washington. . . .
You may assure Mr. Richie that his washington correspondent knows nothing
of what will be the course of the President in appointments, or he would have
known that the President has not, nor will he ever, make an appointment but
with a view, to the public good. . . . I cannot suppose mr Richie would have me
proscribe my friends, merely because they are so. . . . I have drawn your attention
to these facts because I apprehend that our friend mr Richie has not reflected
upon the subject, or he would not have suffered himself to be so easily alarmed.
I have, I assure you, none of thsoe fears, and forebodings, which appears to disturb the repose of mr Richie, and his Washington Correspondent. . . . Say to
him, before he condemns the Tree, he ought to wait and see its fruit. . . .[37]

T. L. Miller also complained in 1829 about appointments of editors,
and Jackson replied that editors "were actuated by the same generous and
patriotic impulse that the people were," asking, "Why should this class
of citizens be excluded from offices to which others, not more patriotic,
nor presenting stronger claims as to qualification may aspire?"[38] Jackson
argued that proscribing newspaper editors would mean "men of uncom-
promising and sterling integrity will no longer be found in the ranks of
those who edit our public journals." He continued:

relative to the appointment of Editors to office, I am constrained to disagree
with you. It is true as suggested, that the press being an important essential
in the maintenance of our republican institutions, its freedom and purity can
not be too carefully guarded. . . . I agree with you, that considerations of no
sort, neither hopes nor fears, should be held out by Government to Editors of
papers, nor indeed to any description of men, to induce a course of conduct not
sanctioned by principle, and by their unbiassed judgment.[39]

Two years after the letter to Miller, Jackson's views had not changed,
although a letter to John Randolph in 1831 may have been prompted
by some concern that such an issue could damage his chances in the up-
coming election. The last sentence suggests that perhaps Randolph (or
others) had recommended removing some printers from the government
payroll, possibly to defuse the subject as a campaign issue. Jackson wrote:

I was never sensible of the justness of the exceptions stated to the employment
of Printers in the public service. The press is the Palladium of our liberties. Dis-
franchise those who conduct it: or what is the same thing make the calling of an

editor a disqualification for the possession of those rewards which are calculated
to enlarge the sphere of talent and merit, and which are accessible to other callings in life, and you necessarily degrade it. . . . it is the object of all who really
take an interest in the honor and welfare of our country to elevate the character
of the press and make it the vehicle of truth and useful knowledge. What scheme
can be more subversive of this object than one which virtually withdraws from
the service of the press those who aspire to some higher character in life than
that of mere agents for the advancement and distinction of others? . . . I refused
to consider the editorial calling as unfit to offer a candidate for office; and ac-
cordingly appointed them on a few occasions when they were deemed honest
and capable. . . . On the score of numbers the proportion of printers who have
been appointed will be found to warrant no such interference.[40]

So long as the press's political role dominated, discussions of journalistic conduct were couched in terms of that role. And, as noted above, the
meaning of impartiality derived at least partly from views of whether the
press should report both sides regarding parties. Excess in tone was expected and tolerated as the press primarily advocated one side or another
of political issues. Madison, for example, had asserted in 1799 that people
must have freedom to be zealots; anyone seriously defending a position
"must expect and *intend* to excite . . . unfavorable sentiments, so far as
they may be thought to be deserved," and to prohibit that intent violated
the principles of freedom of the press and of free government.[41] "Some
degree of abuse is inseparable from the proper use of everything," he maintained, "and in no instance is this more true, than in . . . the press."[42] The
information model, however, which emerged after 1830, rested on different assumptions and led inevitably to different kinds of criticisms and
suggestions of journalistic standards.

The Middle Years, 1830–1850

Whereas the political role of the press emphasized groups (for example,
parties or the business sector), the information or news role emphasized
the individual in its stress on providing the individual with information
useful in life's conduct, decision making, and participation in the political
system. Mott summarizes the penny press editors' view of their role as
fulfilling a duty to provide the news—not to serve a party or mercantile
class; to provide a realistic view of contemporary life, despite taboos; to

expose abuses wherever they were found; and to report items of human interest.[43]

This information role, emphasizing the individual rather than a group, had several natural consequences that led to criticism directly affecting standards. Suggested journalistic standards embedded in criticism of the "new" press differed from these implicit in earlier years, thus revealing that the press was undergoing redefinition in the public's perception. Statements increasingly stressed the press's information and news function over the partisan function, and the concept of responsibility emerged in discussions of journalistic conduct.

The consequences of the press's changing role included far-reaching implications for journalistic standards, which are discussed in the following sections.

The Watchdog Function and the Public's Right to Know

As the shift occurred, the emphasis on the press's "watchdog" function and the public's right to know inevitably grew. The latter did not abruptly emerge at this time, however, for its relevance to participatory government had highlighted it in earlier periods. The drive for access to the Senate and House of Representatives, for example, rested on the view that people must know what elected public servants did in order to participate effectively in the new form of government.[44] But the public's right to know took on an added dimension as the information model of the press emerged in the middle of the nineteenth century, with its growing focus on individual knowledge for protection from abuses by government and other institutions. Furthermore, beginning with the election reforms of the 1820s and the Jacksonian view that anyone could hold public office, the expansion of democratic principles to encompass the political abilities of all citizens implied greater public need for information for pursuing political interests. If the press was to serve individuals and protect them from the abuses of institutions, then it must watch institutions and expose abuses. Correlated with this function, the public had a right to know about such abuses in order to be able to correct them and protect individuals from powerful institutions.

Traces of an emerging information model highlighting the role of individuals are visible before the penny press era, as a libel trial in Massachusetts in 1822 illustrates. The defendant journalist, presenting his case to the jury, defined what has come to be called the watchdog role and implied, without using the phrase of today, the public's right to know:

I am an advocate for a "press free to discuss all subjects fit for the public eye —privileged to tell every truth, and every fact, which it concerns the *public to know.*" I contend for the freedom of the press which "gives to *individuals* the power of *exposing and punishing offences which no other power can reach,* and which every *individual* has an interest in suppressing"—such as "assaults upon our liberties by bad rulers"—frauds upon the public by corrupt and unprincipled agents —knaves, who dressed in a little brief authority, grow rich at the expense of honest men,—who hold the keys to the exchequer and rob its vaults. I contend for a press free to "expose all inroads upon public morals, by daring and ostentatious innovators—insults to common sense and good taste by bad authors," shameless quacks, and ignorant pretenders. These are crimes against the public, which no judicial tribunal can reach or punish. These are offences committed where civil authority has no jurisdiction. There is no domestic retreat so secure—there is no public sanctuary so holy, that it cannot be invaded by the unhallowed or lawless foot, or poisoned by the pestiferous breath of the hypocrite.[45] (emphasis added)

The attorney, summing up defense arguments, lauded a watchdog function also. "While it refrains from attacks on private vices or follies," he said,

Let the press continue . . . to
          "Brand the bold front of shameless guilty men."
Let it examine, fearlessly, but in dignified and decent language—public institutions, characters and transactions; and whether the subject of its scrutiny be the bench, or the legislature, the cloister or the conventicle, the monk or the fanatic, it will confer a public benefit. . . . I assert the right of full, uncontrolled, and animated discussion, and let those who think it . . . safe for them, attempt to restrain it.[46]

Press Responsibility

As the shift to the information model occurred, it was also natural that concerns about the press's responsibility in transmitting news should increase. When the press came to be viewed as providing information for the individual's use in improving his life, becoming more aware of and connecting with his community, nation, and the world, participating in government, and defending his rights, then whether that information was "accurate" and of a quality, tone, and nature to meet these ends became significant issues. Although excess and partiality, however mean-spirited and vigorous, were not incompatible with the process of political discussion that the party press had facilitated, as Madison's remarks quoted above maintained, they were inimical to the information role.

Assessment of Journalistic Conduct

A related and equally important consequence of the press's emerging role was that, as the public became inured to expecting information to meet specific needs, content that failed—for whatever reason—drew increasing criticism. For example, the long tradition of journalists' insulting each other through the newspaper came under attack during the middle decades.[47] In many respects, this issue represents the press's role in transition: so long as editors took verbal swipes at each other in the party press era, they were engaging in a by-product of the debate dominating those years. Although it may have been tasteless and poorly informed, their behavior correlated with the "personal" style of politics in the earliest years of the nation.[48] Furthermore, convincing readers of the correctness of one's own position on an issue often necessitated destroying the opponent's credibility, and examples of denigration abound. When the information model emerged, however, such behavior was superfluous and incongruous—and it wasted valuable news space. Readers criticized journalists for attacking each other, and more than one during the era urged them to end such behavior.[49]

Fairness

A fourth implication of the shift in role was that the press was obligated to present "all sides" of issues. As long as the press was tied to the party system, one rationale for partiality was that it served a higher purpose—that of advancing the "best" or "right" policies (in the printer's and his party's views). When that role no longer dominated, however, providing all sides of issues became important to facilitating the individual's knowledge as a citizen. Bovee notes Greeley's emphasis on this principle; David Nord stresses William Lloyd Garrison's unyielding assertion of it; and Jeffrey Rutenbeck notes William Cullen Bryant's fervent plea for it in his coverage of Elijah Lovejoy's death.[50] Bryant editorialized:

The right to discuss freely and openly, by speech, by the pen, by the press, all political questions, and to examine and animadvert upon all political institutions, is a right so clear and certain, so interwoven with our liberties, so necessary, in fact, to their existence, that without it we must fall at once into despotism or anarchy.[51]

In 1836 Russell Jarvis, editor of the Philadelphia *Public Ledger*, declared an editor's post to be one "of high responsibility" and denounced those who would "be frightened" from their duties "by the cry of '*stop my paper*,' or who would "withhold one stroke of the lash from the back that deserves it."[52]

Taste, Trivialization, and Invasion of Privacy

A fifth implication of the new model was that unsettling kinds of news began to appear, leading to confusion and anger because they countered traditional norms. Mott points out that through human interest and crime stories the penny papers recognized people previously ignored by the press.[53] As individuals received more attention, some naturally resented the press's intrusion, which led to criticisms of its invasion of privacy and demeaning of reputations. Furthermore, some saw this emphasis on "lowly" members of society as trivializing the news and the press's vast potential. Also, the greater variety of news now committed to print and all its permanence matters about society generally only whispered about in closed circles, and this led to criticism of the press as indecent and immoral. The moral war against James Gordon Bennett exemplifies the repugnance of such content, and many other examples could be cited.[54] The plaintiff's summation in the Massachusetts libel case cited earlier condemned invasion of privacy, although it did not use that expression. The plaintiff argued:

I object . . . to this sacrilegious tearing of the veil, which covers the affectionate intercourse of domestic society. I object that the altars of the household gods should be violated, that private and confidential intercourse which renders home happy, and brightens the family circle, should be exposed; that the playfulness of youth, the ingenuous matters of artlessness and innocence should be brought before the public eye, and that every unguarded act, which looks for its protection to the paternal roof of a father's power and a mother's kindness, should be stripped from its shelter and presented to the gloating eye of impertinent curiosity.[55]

Moreover, the new journalism committed to print the repellent or embarrassing ills of society, revealing too much about America's weaknesses while the nation was still working out an experiment intended as an example for the world. Hezekiah Niles, editor of the Baltimore *Niles' Weekly Register*, expressed such concern in explaining why he would not report all mob activities during the 1830s: "We cannot consent to hold up our country to contempt and scorn of the old world, and shall, therefore, generally suppress" any stories about riots and mobs.[56] But perhaps more important, a pervasive view that the reporting of evil actually generated it caused people to recoil at reports of life's seamier side. Many journalists, citing both reasons, criticized others who published crime news.[57] An editor in 1842, explaining how his newspaper would be conducted, suggested that he knew what kind of material should remain unreported:

We hold it, in nine cases out of ten, to be a better qualification for an editor to know what to keep out of his paper than to possess the rarest excellence in producing original matter to put in it; for the reputation gained by a whole season of successful intellectual labor may be lost by a single piece of mismanagement in admitting objectionable matter from any source.[58]

The consequence of the shift to the information model, and these attendant implications, was that responsibility began to take on a compelling meaning. In part, it meant withholding whatever was thought to lead to further ills (for some, this was news of crime or violence) and that did not elevate people and society (reporting the doings of base, ordinary, trivial, or "unimportant" people). It meant featuring whatever upheld "American" activities and values; it meant supporting and promoting individuals' interests through various functions, including dogging institutions, exposing corruption, and asserting the public's right to know. And it began to mean reporting all sides of an issue—a germ of the meaning that would eventually evolve. In short, it meant that journalists increasingly recognized the press's role in maintaining, advancing, and promoting society's goals. Press content had begun to meet a norm enunciated by the judge in the libel case noted above. Instructing the jury, the judge said that "in a country, in which piety, virtue and morality lie at the foundation of society, and are declared, by its constitution, to be its home and cement," "it can scarcely be said . . . that an exposure of crime, and vice, . . . and influence, are not within the fair scope of the liberty of the press." He asserted: "The press, in this country, is constitutionally free. It has the right of bringing government, magistracy, and individuals, to the bar of public opinion."[59] Indeed, the courts' use of a responsibility model in defamation trials was not unusual.[60]

Nevertheless, the far-reaching implications of the press's entrenched political role overshadowed the clear emergence of a pure information or news role. Statements during this period reveal that many observers felt overwhelmed by the press, especially because of its unprecedented growth, and were thus not only unable to distinguish between partisan and news functions (although the public increasingly demanded the latter over the former) but also believed that the press wielded immense power over public opinion.

The growth of the press during the century's first decades spurred concerns about press function that critics began to articulate after 1850. People noted the growth with awe and pondered what the press could and should do. In 1836, a secondary press criticism—the first to be found that was published in America—noted that "periodical literature has for many years been . . . rising . . . until it has . . . attained an influence of unspeakable value for either weal or wo," and that the "daily press . . . exercises the most potent influence."[61] A writer for the *Southern Quarterly Review* declared in 1842 that there was "no one institution of liberty . . . more important to truth, to virtue, to morality, to improvement, to private peace, to public order; no one in which the risen, and the rising generation, the several States of our confederacy, and the whole Union, are more deeply concerned, than in the establishment and maintenance of an able, just, liberal and high-toned Newspaper Press. . . ."[62]

Despite subtle changes in concepts of journalistic standards, ambiguity, ambivalence, and outright paradox marked discussion of partisanism. Although some argued against partisanism, established patterns favored journalists' continued political involvement. Observers often referred to partisanism in the same sentences in which they expressed "new" press values, thus fusing partisanism and information dispersal into one conception of the press's role. For example, the *Southern Quarterly Review* writer condemned partisanism in a tolerant tone:

Under the galleries and reaching around on either side to the Speaker's Chair, in the Representatives' Hall at Washington, are the tables of the Reporters and Letter-Writers, who constitute what is humorously called "the Fourth Estate,"— a class of individuals, who exercise a greater influence on popular opinion, than is generally understood by the people at large. The letter-Writers aim simply to catch and set forth, in their correspondence with the leading editors throughout the country, the spirit and general tone of whatever is said and done in the halls of Congress. They are usually partizans; and . . . their communication is in close keeping with the principles . . . aims and wishes of the party, to which . . . they are attached. . . . Their statement of facts, notorious and acknowledged, is not infrequently mixed up with their own speculations, surmises and prophecies, and by those who wish to ascertain the truth, and nothing but the truth, uncontaminated by party influences, is to be received with much caution. . . . It is affirmed . . . that these Letter-Writers . . . have been sometimes obliged to defend their bodies from the assaults of members, who have either fancied or discovered, that the spirit of the speeches they have delivered, has not been exactly reported, but misrepresented . . . and that pugilistic encounters have actually taken place on the floor of the house, in which the spirit-catchers, or sum-and-substance-men, have gotten the better of their antagonists, and that "the Fourth Estate" has risen, in consequence, to the position which it seems disposed to occupy, as a branch of the National Legislature,—a representation which, if correct, reflects little dignity, and certainly enhances nothing of the character for prowess of the Representative Body. We do not now allude to the Reporters, who occupy a most important and eminently useful position, in which fidelity and accuracy, when they are attained, entitle them to the highest praise and confidence. . . .[63]

The stress on "fidelity and accuracy" are noteworthy, but these values existed alongside continuing partisanism, and the writer's reference to the latter is typical. By mid-century, some critics argued more convincingly against partisanism, whereas others condemned it while simultaneously justifying a legitimate political role for the press. The familiar theme of partisanism creating unequal economic advantages remained strong, as many argued that it hurt the independent printer and stifled journalists' freedom of expression.

An item published in the *New York Sun*, America's first successful penny newspaper, in 1833 shows resentment of party editors' greater economic advantage. Referring to printers as "mechanics," a common term in the era, the editor wrote:

The term Printer is used as a title of distinction at Washington. The Congress of the U.S. appoint for their printer, a lawyer, a paltry politician, a "gentleman at large," in fact any body who may come to hand, but the mechanic himself. His business is to get their printing done—for which they order him well paid from the treasury of the nation. A man dubbed Printer to Congress may make his fortune in a few years, provided he does not "spree" or gamble away his income—whereas the real mechanic gets but a bare sustenance. We should suppose our 'great men' at the capitol could so embrace it, that when they pay a good price for their printing, the mechanic in preference to the politician, might be benefitted thereby.[64]

Although he firmly condemned combining politics and journalism as a conflict of interest, the editor of the *Chicago Tribune* may have been more concerned about the economic advantage of the appointees. Noting the appointment of an editor to the Post Office in 1841, he wrote:

> We have not exhausted our objections to the appointment of an editor of the *American* to the Chicago Post Office; but content ourselves for the present with this conclusion—that the appointment of an editor, publisher, or other person interested in a newspaper, is unjust and impolitic. . . .[65]

In 1842 an editor in Hannibal, Missouri, argued that newspapers should not support politicians who were not subscribers: "No newspaper ought to support any man for any office . . . unless he is a regular subscriber to it. The press has long enough been the drudge for the elevation of illiberal and selfish men."[66]

Horace Greeley was a thoroughgoing partisan who had edited two party papers by the early 1840s, and his statement in 1841 about his founding of the *New York Tribune* exemplifies the ambivalence about the press's political role. Greeley maintained that the press could legitimately serve parties:

> My leading idea was the establishment of a journal removed alike from servile partisanship on the one hand and from gagged, mincing neutrality on the other. Party spirit is so fierce and intolerant in this country that the editor of a non-partisan sheet is restrained from saying what he thinks and feels on the most vital, imminent topics; while, on the other hand, a Democratic [or] Whig . . . journal is generally expected to praise or blame, like or dislike, eulogize or condemn, in precise accordance with the views and interests of its party. I believed there was a happy medium between these extremes—a position from which a journalist might openly and heartily advocate the principles and commend the measures of that party to which his convictions allied him, yet frankly dissent from its course on a particular question, and even denounce its candidates if they were shown to be deficient in capacity or (far worse) in integrity.[67]

Despite Greeley's assertion that the paper would avoid partisanism, he expected Whig party support, and sought it less than a month later. He wrote to the "boss" of the party, Thurlow Weed, on May 10: "thus far I have not had $30 of advertising from Whigs . . . , though I expected more.

I don't want to beg any of it, but I shall have a hard fight to live through the summer without some help. . . ."[68]

In summary, the press's role was clearly and directly related to journalists' notions of standards, and although a different role was emerging, the partisan tradition dominated at mid-century. As individuals suggested or implied various functions and continued to espouse an independent versus a party press, partisanship began to take on a new definition that would ultimately be called bias. But in 1850, the so-called independent newspapers espoused ideals and promoted leaders of a favored party just as vehemently as had their predecessors. The publishers of these papers seemed to mean by independence only that their newspapers were not formally affiliated with a party. It would take time to work through intellectually the full implications of an independent press. The ambivalence toward, and the ambiguity and paradoxical fusion of, partisanism and news functions resulted from the embedded tradition of the party press, and that would take decades to weaken significantly. During this era, journalists' views of the press hardly differed from those of nonjournalists, to whose criticisms of the press in the first half of the nineteenth century we now turn.

Chapter Five

Press Criticism to 1850

I know too well the work Providence has committed to [the press]. Before this century shall run out journalism will be the whole Press—the whole human thought. Since that prodigious multiplication which art has given to speech —multiplication to be multiplied a thousand-fold yet—mankind will write their books day by day, hour by hour, page by page. Thought will be spread abroad in the world with the rapidity of light; *instantly conceived, instantly written, and instantly understood at the extremities of the earth— it will spread from pole to pole. Sudden, instant, burning with the fervor of soul which made it burst forth, it will be the reign of the human soul in all its plenitude. It will not have time to ripen—to accumulate in a book; the book will arrive too late. The only book possible from to-day is a newspaper.*
Alphonse de Lamartine, letter to the editor of the Revue Européane *(1831)*

An editorial . . . is a man addressing men, but the skilled . . . journalist, recording . . . the thing that has come to pass, is Providence speaking to men.
James Parton, Famous Americans of Recent Times *(1866)*

The early nineteenth century brought the first serious press criticism in England and America as writers began to ponder the press's effects on society. Vast changes expanded publishing and distribution facilities, and people were confronted with unprecedented issues: the pervasiveness of newspapers, what the press could and should do, and the implications for society. This chapter explores that early criticism, but it is important first to consider what the printed word meant to nineteenth-century minds, for perceptions of the press shaped expectations of it, and hence press criticism and notions of journalistic standards.

We of the twentieth century, bombarded daily with an "information implosion" from a plethora of media, are too far removed to realize how awesome the press was to those of the nineteenth century. The printed word, as one scholar of mid-nineteenth-century publishing put it, "reigned supreme."[1] This was in part owing, no doubt, to dramatic changes early in the century both in the press and in people's perceptions of it and its capabilities. Before the invention of printing with movable type in the fifteenth century, the tedious work of recording information confined printing to the absolutely essential; anything beyond was required to be of a nature that elevated and ennobled humankind. Time, labor, and materials were too scarce to squander on recording anything else in print. The invention of the movable-type press eased the burden of recording historical events and humankind's store of knowledge, and to some, the press was surely an instrument of Divine Providence to enable precisely the maintaining of that record and disseminating of God's word throughout the world. A predominant view saw the press as the keeper of the record of humankind and civilization's store of knowledge.

Because labor and materials remained scarce for four centuries after the press's appearance, such views of its uses were deeply entrenched as the nineteenth century began. Although the invention eased the burden of recording information, operating it was difficult and time-consuming, and paper was an expensive commodity. Even by the beginning of the nineteenth century, materials, labor, and press capabilities remained sufficiently limited to discourage their use on less-than-ennobling words. The broader issue of what the press should commit to print was hardly relevant as long as these conditions persisted—although criticisms were leveled at specific content, such as the name-calling that accompanied political debate in the new American nation, crime reporting, and sensationalism.

But early nineteenth-century developments eroded these long-standing traditions and views about the press just as traditional sociopolitical views were changing. New technology reduced the labor required to operate a press; materials became cheaper and more available; and means for distributing newspapers constantly expanded. The printed word began to convey much more than merely a record of essentials and that which elevated humankind. And this development raised squarely the issues of what the press should print and its effects on society, which in turn generated the first serious criticism of the press as an institution potentially influencing all of society.

This chapter surveys that criticism in secondary British and American sources during the first half of the nineteenth century. The intent was to discover what ideas about the press and journalistic standards were current in publications—regardless of who expressed them or what sector or profession they represented. The emphasis is on concepts or ideas—what people thought and wrote about the press and journalistic conduct—and not on who the critics were. The term *critic* here refers to anyone who criticized the press, journalism, and journalists and is not intended in the sense in which the term *press critic* is used today. (In fact, no body of press critics, as conceived today, has been identified for the nineteenth century.) To convey the nature and level of concepts, original phrases and terms have been retained. Despite extensive condensing and paraphrasing, preserving the original phraseology in which concepts were framed requires a liberal use of quotations in this and the next two chapters.

The term *secondary* refers to criticism published in sources other than newspapers. A few of these sources were books, but most were magazine articles published in England and America. The magazines, especially before the Civil War, were of a genre known as "reviews" or "literary reviews," which contained articles on a broad diversity of subjects and were remarkably important in early nineteenth-century English and American culture. A recent study by Walter Houghton holds that they met the needs of a growing middle class "that was eager to acquire the education it lacked." Contrasting the books and treatises "of a more laborious age" with modern writing, Houghton quotes Walter Bagehot's characterization in an article published in 1855: the essays published in such magazines were "exhausting nothing, yet really suggesting the lessons of a wider experience." Houghton says that the reviews "commanded an influence and prestige without parallel"; at one level they addressed the common reader and, at another (again quoting Bagehot), "the articulate classes, whose writing and conversation make opinion."[2] A writer in 1842 evaluated twenty-two such American periodicals and referred to others, calling them the "embodiment . . . of the national mind on all great questions, in which the interests of arts, sciences, letters and politics are involved"; they were products of "a high state of civilization," and the best evidence available of "intellectual advancement and of the prevalence of a pure and elevated philosophy."

Their aim is, to discuss subjects thoroughly, learnedly, profoundly,—in such a manner as to affect the whole social system, and to produce a broad, deep and permanent impression upon the character of a whole people, and upon the destinies of an entire age . . . to diffuse knowledge, not to foster prejudices; to create, direct and control, not to echo, opinion; to produce beneficial changes upon a large scale, not to perpetuate, or even tolerate, existing abuses.[3]

The *Edinburgh Review*, which published its first issue in 1802, was regarded as the model of all literary reviews of the period, and such periodicals proliferated throughout the nineteenth century.[4] Discussion of the press in the sources that were located were read with special attention to views of the press and of its functions and concepts of right and wrong journalistic conduct. (See the appendix for a description of these sources.)

Because examination of early press criticism leads through ideas current almost two centuries ago, a caution seems in order. All criticism must be read with appreciation for the ideas embedded in the culture producing it. Some of the earliest criticism may seem ultraconservative today, but it cannot be characterized according to late twentieth-century values. Ideas that we might easily label radically right- or left-wing were often in the cultural mainstream of previous periods. For example, arguments in the early nineteenth century against the notion that people are capable of governing themselves cannot simply be dismissed as archaic. They were dominant arguments in the eighteenth century, representing a set of values that was receding as the nineteenth century began. Yet they remained serious, viable arguments in both the United States and England, forming part of the intellectual framework for appraisals of journalistic conduct during the era. Furthermore, such arguments have special significance for press content and conduct, especially in America: the very ideas of self-government and public opinion as a restraint on power made the press central, if not crucial, to the form of government taking shape in America.[5]

The previous chapter considered journalists' statements about the press, particularly in relation to the press's role. But journalists seemed more likely to respond to specific issues as they were raised, such as impartiality and patronage, rather than to introduce them. Nonjournalists talked about the same issues, but their discussions ranged wider. In expressing fears about the deterioration of society and the destruction of general erudition, they revealed deep-seated values. As many saw it, the press forecast and abetted the deterioriation. Most critics directly charged the press with leading and directing what they were certain were downward trends, and they worried that sufficient thought was not given to this institution that threatened to overshadow all others—if in fact it had not already done so. Two Americans, for example, wrote in an article in 1836 that newspapers' "lightness and mobility" carried them "throughout the land . . . to the doors and firesides of even the humblest"; thus, everyone became "more or

less imbued with the principles and tastes" newspapers embodied, producing the danger of a superficial "sciolism" becoming the "prevailing fault of
our people." Revealing traditional values of the era, the article continued:

> But order and security being . . . the great value of every system of government,
> and the best constituents, too, of their vigour and health, we should see with a
> livelier satisfaction a state of things which held out the promise of more fondness
> for the cultivation of the intellect, greater reverence for institutions of learning,
> and more sacredness attendant upon the tenure of property.[6]

These Americans succinctly expressed the sentiments of British press critics of the era, although the latter were more pessimistic. American critics, continuing to fret about the press's great power at mid-century, were
more positive in identifying its contributions and more thoughtful about
possible solutions to abuses.

As we have noted, the earliest press criticism located was British. The
first located book devoted entirely to press criticism appeared in England
in 1811,[7] another English volume appeared in 1820,[8] and articles about
the press appeared in English magazines throughout the century. The extent to which British publications were available in America is unknown,
but evidence indicates that they did circulate in some circles—most likely
among journalists and booksellers. Moreover, because of the long tradition of collecting news from ships stemming from Americans' need to learn
news of England, Americans very likely continued to seek and read any
British publications they could get.[9] Because Americans often answered
British criticism, it was assumed that they knew what was published in
England and that it contributed to ideas published in America. Indeed,
writers often took pains to differentiate American from British journalism
—efforts that at times seemed to overreach real differences—and in doing
so revealed a growing intellectual separation from England.[10]

English sources were examined during the earliest decades for several
reasons. Secondary press criticism in the United States during this period
was scant, but sources from Britain help to fill the gap because although
the two nations were politically and physically separated, they shared a cultural heritage of similar values. Furthermore, much of the discussion dealt
with the press in general, and strikingly similar sentiments were expressed
in secondary British and American criticism. Finally, English sources were
assumed to be available in America and to influence American thought.
An American writing in 1842 said that the British reviews were readily

available; entering the homes of "our opulent citizens, or even of those who are in comfortable circumstances," one would see "English Reviews and English periodicals, cheap American editions of them, every where, and in the hands of every one, who makes the slightest pretensions to literature."[11] Indeed, it is clear that the ideas expressed in British sources were current in America; but it is also clear that Americans increasingly diverged from those ideas. The ideas represent competing sets of values, and over time, the sources reveal emerging versus receding values. This chapter first deals principally with British criticism into the 1830s because it forms a foundation for understanding American criticism as it unfolded across the century. The chapter's second part focuses on American criticisms up to 1850.

Press criticism throughout the nineteenth century is loosely classified as abstract or concrete. Abstract criticism, on the one hand, deals with the relationship of press and society; more generalizeable, it refers to the press's broadest consequences. Concrete criticism, on the other hand, addresses issues of specific conduct and procedures—implying standards that, for example, a particular journalist or newspaper could be pointed to as offending or excelling. The latter level of criticism has historically been fairly constant, and as noted earlier, may be more readily identified with moral principles than those that change with culture. Concrete criticism of procedures, however, does change over time, as we shall see in Chapter 7. These types do, of course, overlap because criticism at one level often merges into the other. Without ignoring this overlapping, however, criticism is organized according to whether its dominant thrust is abstract or concrete.

British Criticism

Since pre-nineteenth-century British criticism has been referred to, a brief sample begins this section to illustrate the nature of very early criticism and its recurring themes, and to set the stage for considering subsequent discussions of the press. All these first examples represent concrete criticisms and are emphasized because they reveal themes current virtually since journalism began: truth, profit seeking, and sensationalism. Abstract themes follow, beginning with an example of sensationalism that shows the merging of both levels. Next comes an example of crime reporting, discussion of which frequently merged concrete and abstract criticism but is here classified as abstract because of the critics' emphasis on harm to society. Additional themes are the press's effects on society's moral fabric—especially religious institutions, on general knowledge, on public opinion, and on youth and women; the influence of editors, and partisanship. The portion on British criticism concludes with implicit journalistic standards and remedies to press problems.

Concrete Criticism: Examples of the Earliest Themes

Truth

Foremost among recurring themes in press criticism was the complaint that journalists' reports lacked truthfulness. In a book about the *Grub-street Journal*, a paper published in England from 1730–1738, James T. Hillhouse notes that "the most fertile ground for attack on the papers lay in their inaccurate and misleading, not to say false, reporting." The author cites an eighteenth-century writer as maintaining that "it is a distinguishing mark of news writers to exceed their subject"; "their chief excellence . . . lies in fiction and they show great skill in working up the truth with embellishments and surprising circumstances." Another writer is cited as finding journalists' "untrustworthiness and irresponsibility" the most reprehensible, referring to their "dubious" style of beginning articles with "*We hear, We are informed, It is said,* and so forth," calling such phrases "useful in case of news which turns out later to be false or is known at the time to be false, but which the writer wishes the public to hear."[12]

Profit Seeking

Another recurrent theme was that journalists seek profit above all else. Although the basic accusation has remained relatively stable, the particular excesses attributed to the profit motive have changed over time. One such excess was news stealing in England in the eighteenth century, when journalists paid for a significant portion of what was published. Some of newspaper journalists' bitterest complaints reveal how widespread the practice was as they accused magazine journalists of stealing material they had to pay for. The *Grub-street Journal* printers, for example, according to Hillhouse, saw the *Gentleman's* and *London* magazines as "subsisting almost altogether on stolen goods."[13] In the seventeenth and eighteenth centuries, the first journalists to publish advertisements were also criticized for putting profit motives above journalistic responsibilities.[14]

Sensationalism

Another theme concerns what came to be called sensationalism—that is, too much attention to violence, crime, sex, and gossip about the socially prominent. Hillhouse notes that the "bulk of the news . . . consisted . . . of murders, suicides, and other crimes of violence reported with as many horrible details as the writer could discover or imagine, and . . . of the activities of the socially great presented in minute detail and with the most deferential formality." Of the latter category, Hillhouse summarizes one *Grub-street Journal* issue's satirical analysis that calls to mind present-day criticism of media attention to celebrities:

First . . . come the doings of the royal family, whether they are dining at home or abroad, whether they walk, ride, or go on the water. Such news is valuable since it informs the public that the royal family is in health, and also since it gives entertainment to those of low station. Second come the activities of the nobility; their entertainments, births, deaths, and comings to town. At first glance such matter may not seem important, but it is very useful to tradesmen, who thus know the proper time to solicit custom or the payment of bills. In the third place . . . one finds preferments in church and state. Thus the public sees how well the younger sons of gentry and nobility are provided for, as well as the dependents of some few great men, and learns of the elevation of great parts, never heard of before.[15]

Hillhouse notes that "all the details of horrible accidents, suicides, and crimes" were "spread abroad for the edification of the public," and all the dailies presented crude horror in reporting many. As an example, he cites a story about a surgeon who had "opened a vein in what was thought to be a dead body, and, having carelessly left it open, 'The next day he (the corpse) was found really dead, but with his legs drawn up, and a cold sweat on his face, with a large quantity of blood in his coffin.'"[16]

In the early 1800s Massachusetts representative Fisher Ames echoed these British complaints, merging the abstract and concrete as he criticized newspapers in 1800 for too much attention to sensationalism.

Are oddities only to be hunted? Pray tell us, men of ink, if our free presses are to diffuse information, and the ignorant people can get it in no other way than by newspapers, what knowledge are we to glean from the blundering lies, or tiresome truths, of bullies that fight till one or the other gets his eyes closed —or how a drunken fellow, in reeling home at one in the morning, fell into the gutter! or how Angelina, in reading while in bed that instructive novel, "the Brigand's Bride," fell asleep and came within a hair's space of setting the bedclothes on fire! [17]

Although these examples represent concrete criticism in that any newspaper or journalist might be cited, complaints that sensationalism harmed the larger society represent abstract criticism. And Ames's clearly espoused this view.

Abstract Criticism: The Press's Effects on Society

Ames went further than many critics of his era in defining the great harm he believed sensational reporting would bring. Questioning the value to general knowledge of such information, he condemned it for numbing the senses, generating imitation, diverting the mind from healthy reading, and ultimately tending to the brutalization of society.

Every horrid story in a newspaper produces a shock! but after some time that shock lessens. At length such stories are so far from giving pain that they raise curiosity; and we desire nothing so much as the particulars of tragedies and crimes. Now what instruction is there in these endless wonders? Who is the happier or wiser for reading about them? On the contrary, do they not shock tender minds, and addle shallow brains? Worse than this, some eccentric minds are turned to mischief by such accounts. The spirit of imitation is contagious. Boys are bent on doing what men do. When the men attempted to fly from the steeple of the North Church, at Boston, every unlucky boy thought of nothing else but flying from a signpost! [18]

Crime Reporting

Concrete and abstract criticism merged most often in discussions of crime reporting. Ames also condemned crime news as corrupting public morals and inuring minds to attend only to reading that shocks the senses:

Is the history of Newgate the only one worth publishing? . . . On the whole, we may insist, that the increasing passion for printing wonderful tales of crimes (unless accompanied by a proper moral) is worse than ridiculous. It corrupts both the public morals and the public taste. It multiplies fables, prodigious monsters, and crimes, and thus makes shocking things familiar; while it withdraws all popular attention from familiar truth, because it is *not* shocking.[19]

Other criticism during the first half of the century in England and America echoed Ames's concern that the press was in effect corrupting public taste and morals.

Effects on Morality

Two very strong themes at the abstract level—the power of the press and moralism—framed all criticism until after the publication of Darwin's *Origin of Species*. The earliest press criticism, and the bulk published before 1850, was steeped in moralism, which overlay a view of the press as almost omnipotent. Critics lamented the damage done by the press to society's moral fiber and religious and social institutions, such as the church, the family, and education. British criticism especially reflected a fear of the press's harm to political institutions and traditions. British critics deplored, for example, the "democratic" press's "leveling" influence, concluding that society's "better elements" were so far outnumbered by the "mass press" that they could not get their messages heard, and that "wealth" was powerless to stem the trend toward social breakdown brought on by the "radical" press. Fears about destruction of deference and ruin of society's highest values permeate the criticism. Although most Americans' writing during this era did not reflect the values underlying the British criticism, moralism and awe of the press's power also dominated the first American criticism in the 1830s.

Published anonymously ("by a layman") in England in 1820, *Observations upon Sunday Newspapers* epitomized the moralism, although its viewpoint may be more conservative and permeated with more religious orthodoxy than most.[20] The author expressed views supporting the maintenance of social deference and of class distinctions and hostile to the notion that people were capable of self-government through, for example, democratic political systems. He advocated seditious libel laws, arguing that governments (that is, rulers) should not be criticized and characterizing any such criticism as sedition.

Views like these were not uncommon in America at the time, but they represented receding values.[21] Still, although the British author's views did not reflect the mainstream of American thought, several factors suggest that those regarding religious instruction—the book's focus—must have struck responsive chords. First, the early nineteenth century was one of the most important eras in the religious history of the United States as the mass revival movement of the Second Great Awakening swept from the eastern seaboard to the western frontier and from north to south.[22] Second, there were only four regular Sunday newspapers published in the country prior to the Civil War because organized opposition impeded their development. Third, Americans' slowness in sustaining regular Sunday newspapers resulted from the same views as expressed by the author. They objected to newspapers' taking people's minds off spiritual matters, to work being conducted on the Sabbath, and to noisy hawking of papers on a day meant for serenity and worship.[23] Finally, discussions of the press as a rival to the pulpit, although rare during the early decades, continued in press criticism until the end of the century. Indeed, American articles in the 1880s and 1890s virtually duplicate sentiments about the Sunday press expressed in *Observations upon Sunday Newspapers*.[24]

Because this British book's ideas form an important point of departure for considering American criticism of the nineteenth century, they are treated here at some length. Its long third chapter, "Sunday Newspapers considered in reference to their religious and national Evils," asserted that even the most "superficial observer" could see that "the principles of infidelity and irreligion . . . of disloyalty and sedition" had been "generally and successfully diffused throughout the nation," and maintained that nothing had had "so obvious and powerful an effect in extending the violation of the Sabbath as the whole system of Sunday newspapers."[25]

Among specific condemnations, the author argued that everyone employed with Sunday newspapers "flagrantly" breached "the day of rest" and that all such traffic was "eminently calculated to interfere with religious instruction." Both those employed by the newspapers and those who read them were lured away from public worship, and the "irreligious and secular spirit . . . excited and formented" by perusing the papers weakened the effect of religious instruction even for those who did attend. The delivery of the newspapers was generally too late to leave time for those employed by the papers to get to morning service; and many who took the papers, including their children, were absorbed by the newspaper and stayed away altogether or occasionally from church.[26]

The Sabbath's purpose was to transport minds from earthly to spiritual matters, and the author argued that the papers instead withdrew them from God to associate Sunday "with the perishing objects of time and sense, and to chain it down to tastes and pursuits . . . material, sensual, and temporal. . . ." Even those who continued outward appearances of piety and attended church carried "there an unprepared and worldly mind" if their imaginations were

> to be first filled with the news of the week, the state of the markets, the price of stocks, the bankrupts of the preceding night, and all the still more offensive matter of criminal trials, police examinations, criticisms of the theatre, and disquisitions upon politics—prepared, for the most part, by obscure and mercenary writers, who are utterly ignorant of the first principles of a science upon which they speak with such an unmeasured and unseemly confidence.[27]

The writer argued that Sunday newspaper editors catered to the "worst passions of the multitude" because it was in their interest to do so, and truth was "neither the object of their pursuit, nor of their attachment." Moreover, Sunday newspapers fomented rebellion: they "openly promulgate such doctrines as are inimical to the existence of all lawful authority; tend to excite resistance to such authority in every shape; and propagate, without reserve, the principles of disloyalty and sedition. . . ."[28]

Factors connected with the sale of Sunday papers, such as advertising, further impeded keeping the Sabbath, the author continued. Many shops opened on Sundays only to sell the papers; and those that had added newspaper sales to their businesses—such as hairdressers, greengrocers, pastry cooks, and so on—"would not be open at all on the Sabbath merely for . . . their own trade." Furthermore, posting bills and placards announcing the papers provided "such detail of the contents . . . as shall excite curiosity, and whet the appetite for the papers," written in such "brief, but pithy and forcible, comments" as to give "the same spirit as appears in the journal itself." The placard thus had the "double effect of inducing a purchase" by many who would not otherwise want or even think of a paper and of "producing extensive mischief upon those" unable to buy one because of "finances, or other circumstances." Finally, the *"blowing of horns* and the *public crying of the newspapers"* constituted a great offense to anyone wishing to keep the Sabbath.[29] Although the British writer wrote only of Sunday newspapers, the book suggests that he saw little if any value in newspapers in general.

An article published in 1831 in the English *Fraser's Magazine for Town and Country* also discussed the press's damage to public morals, particularly through its publicity of "all the details of vice, crime, and infamy" that could "be collected in police offices and . . . courts." The author called such reporting a far greater danger than any defamation of "private character," which he called a "minor evil" in the "catalogue" of the press's "sins," largely because it served as a "corrective" of, rather than "stimulant" to, personal slander. The press's "inroads . . . into domestic affairs" were no more than the "concretions of public rumors," he wrote, "the extension and circulation of party and club-room whispers, rendered tangible by being printed . . . converted into a morning repast for common-councilmen, the small scandal-mongers of beer-shops and libraries, the young *lady* behind the bar and the old women before it. . . ." But such publicity was the "best corrective of defamation" because it militated "against the credibility and respectability" of newspapers, excited "disgust in the many," and led journalists ultimately to "a higher respect for truth and decorum" because that was better for business.[30]

Distinguishing between two kinds of press influence—attacks on private character and contamination via "promiscuous reports"—the author called the latter the far graver danger because newspapers offered no corrective and had no remedy for them. To remedy the former required "a simple denial, an act of justice to the injured party, demanded and exacted by himself"; but the latter was an "offence against society," for which there was "no party to demand redress, or in a condition to enforce it."[31]

Stressing the gravity of newspapers' "influence on public morals," he condemned the appeal to mass taste as spreading the lowest tastes and most corrupt morals throughout society:

They make every reader as familiar with the lowest scenes of debauchery in the brothel, drunkenness in the tap-room, knavery in the gaming-house, and bold-faced villainy in the den of burglars, as are the victims of these vices themselves, with whom they too often sympathise. They introduce the language of Newgate and the police courts into our kitchens; and the slang of the pickpocket, the blackleg, and the prizefighter, the corrected and amended vocabulary of Petticoat Lane, into our clubs and drawing rooms. They render the details of prostitution a source of amusement and gain. They make Ikey Solomons a hero of romance, and John Thurtell, who was hanged for a cruel murder, a martyr to gallantry. Adultery is made a subject of interest to every girl in her teens; an elopement, a matter of jest; profligacy, in cases of seduction, a sort of patriotism in the rake, at which the gentle nursery maid laughs, and the staid matron, behind her counter, deprecates for the sake of example, but still reads with avidity. The frailty of a poor wretch, prevented from committing suicide from the . . . Waterloo Bridge, provides incidents sufficient for a fashionable novel—fiction being impressed to give colour to infidelity, and misfortune made an excuse for inebriety and a life of licentiousness.[32]

Such, the author concluded, formed much of newspapers' content—or "agreeable light reading," he sarcastically called it.[33]

Effects on General Knowledge

The author of the *Fraser's Magazine* article sounded another common theme—the press's damage to general erudition. Saying that the press debased language, destroyed interest in higher arts, and spread vice and discontentment, he decried newspapers' role in bringing about the change in language and "sentiment." "Public taste has undergone a change," and the wit of such authors as Beaumont and Fletcher—whose plays, he lamented, were no longer produced—was "considered repugnant to what is called the spirit of the age." This had occurred because "the terms and subjects of ridicule" had changed completely.

The people do not now choose to have their vices and their follies censured in the same language as they were a few centuries ago. Not that they are more moral; on the contrary, they are less so; but they are more fastidious with respect to phraseology. A lie is not now a lie—it passes by some other name. A fraud is not now called a fraud. A *liaison* by an actress is a mere error in sentiment—an excusable breach of morality under peculiar and unavoidable circumstances.[34]

Conceding that language might have become "less gross, or more pure," the author declared that, without question, "ideas of morality" had "retrograded." Having contributed to "this revolution in sentiment," newspapers were "responsible for the deterioration in national morality"; to illustrate, he cited "one of those festivals of blackguardism and brutality called a prize-fight." A prize fight attracted "all the worst characters of the metropolis," he wrote: the "housebreaker . . . , swindler . . . professional bully, and his friend, who keeps a house of ill-fame . . . my lord the patron . . . and a pickpocket on a stolen horse—in short, the whole . . . ragamuffinry of the town." The fight itself did little harm, he wrote, and could do little even if half the spectators knocked out the "eyes or the brains of the other." But the battle was "fought over again next morning in all the newspapers

—every round described with most felicitous and pugnacious accuracy—
every blow struck . . . and where it fell . . . every word . . . each blackguard
said to the other. . . ." The effect, he argued, especially on young men and
apprentices, was "a strong desire to mix in the next affray":

> The organs of combativeness are excited—the details of the fight are perused
> by thousands, who, but for the newspapers, never would have heard of it; and
> the abominable slang, the lingua-franca of thieves and prostitutes, instantly and
> henceforward becomes the favourite language of the lower orders.
>   For this, at least the newspapers are answerable. . . .[35]

The newspaper—what could be "the best possible public instructor"—
was the "*only* instructor" for certain classes, and the "very worst" that could
have been invented. It was the only source of information for the "middle
orders," the "mechanics and operatives of large towns, the smoking interest of the beer houses"; and its "natural and unavoidable consequence" was
initiating them "into all the vices of London society" and making them
"discontented."[36]

Considering whether newspapers created "this appetite for vice" or
simply, to use a contemporary phrase, gave the public what it wanted, the
author concluded the latter. Newspapers carefully followed and fed on the
public's "capricious" taste; it was only natural that they should "minister
to this depraved taste, and adopt the slang of the blackguard, and . . . activity of the partisan" to gratify their readers, extend their popularity, and
augment their profits.

> If the public taste inclines towards private scandal, the exhibitions of connubial
> infidelity, the gross scenes of a London watchhouse, the feats of inebriety and
> street outrage, the intrigues of profligacy, the debaucheries of a green-room, or
> the indelicacies of a poor idiot under a commission *de lunatico inquirendo*—who
> can blame the newspapers, whose existence and profits depend on the public
> will . . . ?[37]

An entire article published in *Blackwood's Edinburgh Magazine* in 1834
addressed the issue of the press's injury to society, albeit from a distinctly partisan viewpoint. Labeling the press's "grand characteristics" as
its "democratic character," "licentious tendency," and "paramount ascendency over the influence of property and education," the author said these
also constituted its greatest danger: "Its democratic character shakes the
foundations of government; its licentious tendency saps the bulwarks of

morals; its ascendency over property gives it the victory over all institutions of society."[38]

Daily becoming more licentious, the press's "strong and vivid pictures addressed to the passions and the imagination" incited "sensual indulgence," and "that fatal union of genius with voluptuousness . . . the well-known sign of a declining age," had "become prevalent." Despite the existence of numerous other publications, the "immense circulation" of those that stimulated political or "private passions" proved that they "fall in with the spirit of the age."[39]

Society's bonds were being rapidly dissolved "under the influence of an unrestrained discussion of public affairs," and property and education could not "counteract or check this downward progress" because of the peculiar form in which knowledge was transmitted, which had been given little attention except by the press. To illustrate, the writer said, wealth, education, or virtue could not "encourage" the daily press—"from which nine-tenths of mankind implicitly adopt their opinions"—in any way proportionate to their resources or importance. The "lower orders'" greater number gave them power over "all the better classes"; because "ten radicals, subscribing together," took as many newspapers as a nobleman and five times as many as the "Great Unknown," this meant that "ten persons on the democratic side, whose united income is probably not £500 a year, neutralize one Conservative whose income is two hundred times as great as all theirs. . . ." No one could read more than one or two newspapers a day—and a "seaver or coalheaver" could do this as well as "a prince or philosopher," he contended, holding that this "simple principle . . . ever must give, an overwhelming superiority to numbers over property in determining the character of the public press. . . ."[40]

Arguing that it was against human nature for "ignorance to resist flattery, or ambition the possession of power," the author blamed the press's "democratic character" entirely on the seductiveness of flattery. "The majority of mankind, totally incapable . . . of taking any useful part in public affairs, like nothing so much as to be told that they are perfectly qualified to take the lead"; the "immense multitude of the middling and lower orders . . . brood incessantly over the democratic press—over those who laud their wisdom, and magnify their capacity, and flatter their vanity— who tell them, that their opinion cannot err, and that, in the increase of their influence, is to be found the only effectual antidote to all the evils of society. . . ." The person who had studied history or politics for twenty years, he wrote, would find difficulty in deciding many current issues and "willingly withdraw from . . . responsibility . . . in directing public affairs"; but a "ten-pounder, who has read the Radical journals for a few months," would not hesitate to decide on "the weightiest interests of society, without any other instructors but his favourite political flatterers."[41]

Effects on Public Opinion

An intensifying theme across the century was the press's role with respect to public opinion, and these earliest discussions centered on whether the press created or followed it. The critic writing in *Blackwood's Edinburgh Magazine* in 1834 cited Madame de Stael on the French Revolution to argue that ideas in print had more effect than those that were spoken. Madame de Stael had written that "hired writers introduce into public opinion much more depravity than could arise . . . by speech" wherein "judgment could be formed only upon facts." But journalists inflated facts, the critic implied, adding that "when opinions concerning every circumstance, every work, every individual, are subject to a Journalist's word of command . . . the art of printing becomes, in its abuse, a most formidable engine of evil."[42]

Addressing whether newspapers were sources or "merely channels" of public opinion, the writer in *Fraser's Magazine* concluded that newspapers simply followed public opinion—because they must to thrive. "Not one of these papers dare array itself against this low *caste* of what is called 'public opinion' in any way whatever," he declared. "Their whole study is to watch and reflect the prevailing bias, or the ascendant excitement."[43]

Effects on Youth and Women

Another theme was the press's harm to young people. After citing several newspaper excerpts exemplifying the "low taste" of which he complained, the English author of *Observations upon Sunday Newspapers* argued that adults "voluntarily" deceived by newspapers had "no right to complain that falsehood is presented to them," but that youth should be protected. Inexperienced and uncorrupted, the young deserved better "than to fall into the hands of such venal and profligate scribblers." He called it painful to think of the "widespreading mischief"—"among thousands who have yet their principles to form"—presented in the "most subtle and palatable shape, and on a day when so much more leisure is left for its full operation."[44]

Critics usually classed women with children as detrimentally affected by newspaper contents. The writer in *Fraser's Magazine* complained that

Women are made familiar with descriptions of brutal outrages, and of acts of obscenity—with the minutest details of lust, and of nameless crimes—with the ornate representations of low vice in the police courts—with, in fact, scenes that should be veiled from the eyes of youth and innocence, and which, in the times of their grandmothers, would have raised a blush on every female cheek.[45]

Exposure of women to newspaper reports about sex was of particular concern. The same critic wrote that a shopkeeper's wife, picking up the morning paper, would first read the Bow Street reports or perhaps those of proceedings in the sheriff's court, "where . . . an action of any criminal convict occupies three or four columns." Her attention might be attracted by a report of a murder, "but if there should be a paragraph" about "Mr. Peter Giles's wife . . . caught emerging from the chambers of a barrister of the Temple, her husband being on the watch, and the paramour bearing her arm," the woman's whole attention would fix on that. "The scene . . . is . . . of the most revolting nature; but it makes a deep impression, and continues to be the theme of gossip, till it merges in some affair of deeper interest and more astounding guilt."[46]

Some even seemed to suggest that women's exposure to news reports of violence and sex was at the root of most social ills. The writer in *Fraser's Magazine*, for example, contended that such familiarity with vice could have only a pernicious effect, as attested by the "enormous increase in crime—the fearfully corrupt state of morals in the metropolis—the profligacy and dishonesty of the lower classes—the exhibitions of female indelicacy in the streets—and the openly avowed disregard of religion and decorum."[47]

The Influence of Editors

The *Fraser's Magazine* author sounded another recurring theme—that of the influence of editors over those who write for newspapers. By the 1870s this concern would evolve in America into a sophisticated articulation of subtle pressures on reporters to shape the news to editors' views, but in 1831 the English writer spelled out the core issue:

Whoever writes for that paper must prostitute himself to the prevailing bias, otherwise his contributions are valueless and inadmissible. No matter how transcendent may be his talents . . . the interest of the proprietors is an unsuperable bar to his genius or his correct views, and he *must* flatter every vulgar demagogue, and advocate the most servile and obnoxious principles, deal out perdition to his dearest friends, and place in the most favourable light sentiments which he abhors, or—his occupation's gone![48]

Partisanism

The issue of partisanism, although not overt in the discussions cited above, permeated British criticism of the early nineteenth century. British critics did not, however, see the partisan press as bad in itself, even though they often criticized newspapers' excesses in denigrating the opposition. Rather, they were preoccupied with finding some way of balancing the press's representation of parties—while at the same time most wanted that balance tipped in favor of their own party. Their remedies therefore sought this end as several adamantly argued for government regulation.

Remedies and Journalistic Standards

By the 1830s, critical writing conveyed a sense of individuals overwhelmed by a phenomenon they did not begin to understand. Such was their bewilderment that they emphasized basically two kinds of remedies for press abuses—government regulation and "buying off" journalists. And they appealed to "better minds" to consider the press. The critic writing in *Blackwood's Edinburgh Magazine* in 1834, for example, considering possible remedies, repeated astonishment that serious thought had not been given to such an important issue as the power of the press. Calling it a "matter of universal observation" that the press's influence was chiefly responsible for the "great changes of recent times," he wrote that everyone endowed with "foresight or historical information" knew the press's influence and deplored "its present pernicious tendency." Why, then, he wondered, had so little serious attention been given to its governing principles?

Every wise man trembles at the perilous ascendancy of democratic ambition which the extension of political reading . . . to the lower orders has given, and every good man laments the ruinous vigour with which the depraved principles of our nature have shot up under its fostering influence; but no one thinks of considering how this new and terrible power is to be mastered, and the dissolving principles with which it is invested, again brought under the dominion of virtue and religion.[49]

As a remedy, this writer rjected both regulation and the marketplace theory in favor of "buying off" journalists. Such solutions as censorship, prosecution, or "measures of coercion" were "brutal remedies, fit only for a savage age, and in the end totally inadequate." The theory of the marketplace of ideas promised no corrective either:

> Men . . . are not judges of what is true; on the contrary, if left to themselves, they will in general select what is false, because falsehood always wears a specious guise, and truth a homely aspect. They are not judges of what is for the good of society; on the contrary, when left to themselves, they will in general select what is likely to prove ultimately prejudicial, because it always wears the seductive garb under which error conceals the ashes of the whited sepulchre. For these reasons, the principles of free competition are permanently inapplicable to morals, politics, and religion. . . .[50]

The solution, he suggested, lay in capitalizing on journalists' interest in earning a living. Journalists, he asserted, were not generally inclined "from conviction, or a sense of public duty, to revolutionary principles," but were driven by a desire for profit. They espoused democratic politics or licentious morals because these were most popular, "and because they would rather sell thousands of their papers . . . than hundreds." Most looked on their work "merely as a livelihood, and would as willingly take a retaining fee on the one side as the other." Numbers were on the side of democracy, but the "weight of property" could be used to sway journalists to the other side. The way many editors "abandon their principles, and veer about with all the almost daily fluctuations . . . of public opinion, sufficiently demonstrates" that many "would be perfectly willing, for adequate consideration," to lend the newspaper to "any other purposes which might present a more inviting aspect." Thus the "only effective way of combating the evil" of the democratic press was "to provide as great encouragement for Conservative" as was "afforded to Revolutionary ability. . . ."[51]

British critics offered hardly tenable solutions to the many problems they delineated; reflecting traditional values that emphasized wealth, property, and deference, they suggested simple remedies in keeping with these: regulation or coercion that would maintain elite power. Yet they dwelt —almost brooded—on what they saw as press abuses, projecting a very dismal view of what the rapidly spreading newspaper press meant to society. Nevertheless, these early British writers reflected the foundation of

ideas about the press that Americans departed from at the beginning of
the nineteenth century. Increasingly, however, differences between British
and American views were becoming clear—even in this early period—as
the next section reveals.

American Criticism

The first located secondary press criticism published in America, an article
by E. L. Bulwer and Sergeant Talfourd, appeared in the *American Quarterly Review* in 1836, just as the penny press had begun to succeed in New
York and when the information model of the press's role oriented to the
individual was becoming apparent.[52] This and subsequent American articles were more optimistic than previous English ones had been, although
Bulwer and Talfourd reflected sentiments closer to those in English criticism than did later American critics. American writers referred to the same
kinds of press abuses, but they saw problems as more complex, and elusive
of simple solutions; and, instead of dwelling on problems, they emphasized the press's contributions, marveled at its growth, and defended its
difficult tasks. They made a big issue—self-consciously so—of the unique
freedom the American press enjoyed, the distinctive institutions of the
United States, and the differences between England and America as they
affected journalism. As did the English, the American articles implicitly addressed the press's great power and its partisanism as overriding issues, but
they often identified specific powers and praised the press's manifold positive influences. Bulwer and Talfourd's criticism paralleled the British view
of the press as a threat to orderly society, and it proposed similar solutions,
indicating shared concepts of journalistic conduct and standards.

As was true of the English critics, American discussions reveal tensions between competing values—those of democracy versus elitism, social
deference versus class "leveling," agrarianism versus controlled economic
direction. "With a press corrupted and enslaved, the purest and most
enlightened citizens shrinking or driven from the contest, unprincipled
demagogues grasping all the fruits of possession, and instigating the worst
passions of the mob . . . to further their own selfish designs," Bulwer and
Talfourd asked, "what has our country not to fear?" They answered that
"she has to fear disorder, agrarianism, the reign of ignorance and of terror, the destruction of fondly cherished hopes, and the dread reality of
anarchy."[53]

This article indeed reveals shared American and British views. But it also represents a point of departure; succeeding American articles were not so steeped in these values, and despite the similarities, the article represents a subtle divergence from sentiments expressed in the British articles in that it praised the press's contributions to society. The divergence increased throughout the ensuing discussion.

Themes of American criticism are identified and the same headings (in the same order) as in the previous section used to highlight the degree of shared concern, divergence from British views, and early evolving values in this era. Two issues not found in the British discussions are added: freedom of the press and the defense of journalism. (Discussion of editors' influence on reporters, not found in American articles during this period, became important later in the century, as Chapter 7 illustrates.) An outline of American critics' proposed solutions and suggested journalistic standards concludes this chapter.

The Press's Effects on Society

Three features distinguished American from British criticism. First, noteworthy throughout was an underlying emphasis—often explicit—on the press as an instrument imparting knowledge in service to the individual and the public good. These early American discussions, taken together, in effect conceptualized the information model of the press's role as they accompanied its emergence. They also marked the contours of issues that continued as trends associated with that model developed through ensuing decades. Second, American critics proposed concrete approaches to problems of the press and suggested journalistic standards. Third and perhaps most important, whereas the British dwelt on what they saw as press abuses, Americans set the stage for increasingly serious consideration of the press and society. In fact, all American discussions of the middle decades of the nineteenth century tended toward the abstract level of criticism, and so all topics below are subsumed under the broad heading of the press's general effects on society.

Crime Reporting

Less concern about the reporting of crime appears in American than in British articles, although the same assumption of its harm is apparent. That is, people believed such news appealed to the lowest tastes, dulled the senses, and seemed not only to sanction crime by the very reporting of it, but to glorify it. In 1842, for example, the *Southern Quarterly Review* writer, noting that newspapers gratified the "lover of the marvelous and horrible" with accounts "of the last duel . . . the latest murder or suicide, with perhaps the dying confession of the felon, and a minute account of all that took place at the time of the execution," said editors might accompany such reports with "some judicious remarks . . . against . . . public executions, as having a tendency to increase, rather than prevent . . . crimes, by the pomp and consequence it attaches to the victim of the violated laws." Notwithstanding such "sage opinion," however, the editor continued "to feed the depraved appetite of his readers with all such items . . . seeming to forget, that the publicity . . . he . . . thus gives to crime, renders it more interesting and less odious. . . ."[54]

Effects on Morality

American critics did worry about the press's impact on public morality, but none expressed that concern as dismally as had the British. Some in fact argued that the press aided public morality. Far from corrupting public morals, one writer called urban America's morning newspaper "as important an article of daily food for the moral man, as bread is for the physical."[55] And in sharp contrast to British critics' fears about the harm to religion, an American minister, in a lengthy article published in 1844, extolled the press as indispensable to the spread of religious instruction, repeatedly avowing that "Divine Providence" had brought the invention about especially for this purpose. Noting that the thirteenth-century English laborer had to pay the equivalent of sixteen years' labor to purchase a Bible, he marveled that "an agency had been discovered which could multiply copies of books with astonishing facility and cheapness, and to a boundless extent."[56]

Effects on General Knowledge

Another divergence was that American critics gave less attention to the press's damage to general erudition; some in fact denied it. The *Southern Quarterly Review* writer proclaimed, "The Newspaper is the greatest agent in promoting civilization known to modern times"; its influence on "popular opinion" and its diffusion of information "through all classes

. . . upon subjects of vital interest, political, commercial, statistical, literary and religious" were "great beyond calculation." Summarizing the press's historical development, the author recounted that printing brought books, including the Bible and "classical works of antiquity, . . . ponderous tomes of divines and schoolmen, and . . . works of science and literature," to those who "entertained a proper appreciation of the value of knowledge"—thus providing "durability and almost immortality to the works of genius, including the speculations, researches, and discoveries of the learned in various fields of inquiry."[57]

Ranking the newspaper's value second to health, the author recounted an anecdote of a missionary speaking in the American interior of the death of Jesus Christ. A woman, asking when he died, apologized for her ignorance because, she said, her husband did not take the newspaper, although she had "frequently insisted upon his doing so. . . ." The writer asserted:

How dull and stupid a city or a village must be, where there is no newspaper!
We can scarcely conceive, in our day of any community being in so forlorn a
condition,—of none certainly that lays much claim to advancement. What would
life be worth, in an enlightened age, and in a country full of plans and projects,
reforms and changes . . . where facts and information of prime importance must
be speedily known, in order to be promptly acted upon, without some such
organ of intelligence, regularly published, on whose statements the people might
rely with perfect confidence?[58]

In defining the newspaper's value in increasing individuals' knowledge, this writer summarized the emerging conception of the information model: the newspaper was a "vehicle of news,—of intelligence,—of knowledge," a shrinker of boundaries, without which human affairs could not be conducted. Not the least of the value of newspapers was that they brought knowledge *to* people; that is, they reduced the effort needed to pursue knowledge and made attaining it a simple, easy, and pleasant experience.

Newspapers are what the ancients used to call a *microcosm*,—a little world
in miniature, where, without going out of the house or mingling with the
mass . . . , a man may look on quietly and without interruption, and see whatever of interest is passing or being transacted in the gay, bright and busy world
around him, not only at home in his own neighborhood, but abroad in Europe,
. . . in fact, throughout the whole world, wherever any thing of striking and
startling interest has occurred that requires to be known and recorded.[59]

Effects on Public Opinion

Early American critics did not differ substantially from the English in their
interest in the press's role in forming or following public opinion. Bulwer
and Talfourd distinguished among types of periodicals, saying that the
"daily press . . . exercises the most potent influence" on "popular taste and
feeling," and monthlies and quarterlies were more effective in "correcting
and checking" newspapers' "excesses" and "in holding out the promise of
a higher tribunal, by which to be judged and to which to appeal." Still,
the authors concluded that the American press was "content to follow . . .
popular opinion at the moment, without seeking to direct its progress in
the ways of justice and reason."[60]

A writer in the *Southern Quarterly Review* in 1843 said the press did not
"represent public opinion" but "the opinion of a party," adding that parties
consisted "of cliques and factions" controlled by "a few master spirits"—
or one person, whose goals were often his own interests "rather than the
public weal." On the other hand, the press "may often be nothing more
than the expression of the mere opinion of an Editor, which so far from
reflecting the popular voice or the truth, may only give vent to his personal
enmities or antipathies, or the spite or malice entertained by his friends
against individuals of worth, character and influence." In such cases the
press did not represent public opinion, "although, in the hands of talented
men," it might "do extensive injury to individuals, and, through them, to
the public, by creating false impressions."[61]

A large portion of the article published in the same review the year before, however, dealth with "whether the Newspaper Press creates, or . . .
only follows and represents" public opinion. Calling the effect on popular opinion "great beyond calculation," the author argued that the press
could reflect and create public opinion—and sometimes did both. The
press created opinion when it was "under the control of men of commanding powers of mind and genius, and great experience and sagacity." Every
community had such men "who lead and direct, to a considerable extent,"
people's opinions; and if they were managers of a free press, they could
exert incalculable influence on public sentiment in an "age of light and
inquiry." The writer called public opinion "usually nothing more than private opinion . . . first conceived in some master mind," then made public
and ultimately "incorporated into the popular creed" simply because its

truth had been "brought home forcibly" to people's understanding. When it became current, everyone could "claim a common property" in it: it could be used "at second hand, by the conductors of the press, as well as by all other persons"; it could be "employed advantageously for the common purposes of life and business" by those not "particularly inventive"; and it could "minister to the appetite for novelty," pervading the world "by striking out, new, bold, and original views of things," which when published were "seized on with avidity" and became, "in their turn, popular opinions."[62]

The "most independent thinkers," he continued, were "liable to be borne down" by party influence, particularly during "times of political excitement." People were "so constituted, and society so organized, that in great emergencies, and even in the ordinary course of affairs," they rely heavily on each other for their opinions. "Mind acts on mind, and, in its turn, is reacted upon; principles are thus elicited and established." Emphasizing that America's "maxim" was "measures, not men," he wrote that "measures do not create themselves"; rather, "they are first suggested . . . introduced to public notice . . . supported by men, and men claim the honor . . . as no slight distinction, that, they have been instrumental in originating plans . . . subsequently acted on by a whole party, or by the government . . . and . . . finally incorporated into the settled policy of the country."[63]

Additionally, the press created public opinion when editors were "men of strong mind and inventive intellect" who had long "studied the science of government with care, and witnessed the progress of affairs at home and abroad, with a view to public interests." The press created public opinion when such editors asserted leadership in crises "by strong appeals to the good sense of the community," instigated reforms and introduced "changes in popular opinion, and the action of whole masses, whose influence is sensibly felt throughout the entire . . . society, even by rulers and legislators."[64]

But the writer maintained that, in most cases, newspapers simply supported the opinions of statesmen who had achieved their positions because of moral and mental superiority and extensive influence. The press often did little more than echo the views of these men, who "must be heard . . . in the State legislatures and halls of Congress." It used their arguments and enforced their favorite measures, "which, being always the measures

of the party . . . the press . . . becomes the agent . . . of a party, in maintaining a certain set of political opinions or principles in preference to
another. . . ."[65]

Effects on Youth and Women

The fear of harm to youth and women, so profoundly expressed in the
British articles, was also less marked in the earliest American discussions.
This can be seen, along with the positive tone of American criticism, in the
1842 *Southern Quarterly Review* writer's summary of a newspaper issue's
use. The passage calls to mind the English critic who wrote of the London "shopkeeper's wife" scandalized by newspaper content and of fears for
youth exposed to the press. Notably lacking in such sentiment, it reflects a
very different perspective and is quoted at length because it provides rare
insights about newspaper circulation. The author wrote of the "morning
print, in our commercial cities":

Observe, how it goes the rounds. It is called for first by the master of the family,
and after its ample sheet is expanded and dried before the fire, he devours its
contents with an eagerness that shows how deeply his whole soul is in it. It
then passes into the hands of the good lady of the house, who is usually satisfied with a perusal of . . . the poet's corner, with the interesting items . . . in the
hymeneal or obituary departments, with the strictures, light and graceful, upon
the last published novel, or with the laughable anecdotes with which its page is
usually enlivened. The daughters next claim . . . the paper with the view to the
on dits of the day or place, the latest fashions, the next concert or assembly, or,
if among the patrons of the stage, the play or opera for the evening entertainment. Thus the important visitant passes from hand to hand, till every member
of the family has gratified his . . . curiosity, down to the little children, who ask
permission to look at the ships, the houses, or the pictures of wild beasts that are
for exhibition in the menagerie. After . . . this accustomed circuit of the home,
some little urchin from a neighbor, who is too poor or too covetous to patronize
the press, comes with the modest request, of "a loan of the morning paper only
for a few minutes, as mistress wishes to know at what hour the furniture auc-
tion takes place today." He is scarcely gone, when a messenger from some other
neighbor comes running at . . . top . . . speed and all out of breath, with a "pray,
sir, father says, as how he will be much obliged to you for a sight of the morning
paper, just to look at the ship news half a minute." And so it circulates from one
to another, till the numerous thumbprints upon the margin bear evidence of as

faithful service, as grandmother Cloe's big Bible, which has been in the family for three generations;—a practice of borrowing and lending, which is apt to provoke some severe animadversions from the editor, when the time of paying his compositors and pressmen comes round, but which provides one thing, and that not a little flattering to his vanity,—how very important newspapers are, every where, and to every body.[66]

Partisanism

Partisanism permeated all American criticism in this era, but unlike the British, Americans ridiculed it. British critics seemed to accept partisanism as a characteristic of journalism, but by the 1840s some Americans suggested that it tainted journalism. The British argued that partisanism should be more balanced in the press; the Americans groped to express a more fundamental dissatisfaction with it. But by the middle of the century neither the British nor Americans had confronted forthrightly whether journalism should, or could, be totally separated from partisanism.

An American writer in the *Southern Quarterly Review* in 1843 saw partisanism as the press's greatest problem in that "bad men" controlled too much of the nation's press: "Bad men, however able, are not fit instructors of a free people in the principles of government, in manners, morals, in religion, in literature. . . ." "Our best editors," he continued, "are, unfortunately, partisans, and party spirit, selfish, overreaching, monopolizing, regardless of means and of consequences, is the bane of our institutions—a foul blot upon our liberty, discreditable alike to our assumed intelligence and our virtue."[67]

Although some during this period questioned whether journalists should be partisan, the writing of journalists themselves leaves an impression that perhaps debunking partisanism was popular. It may have been so much rhetoric, for seldom did anyone go beyond generalization to specify the ills of partisanism; only after the middle of the century did writers begin to deal with the issue in depth.

Americans gave considerable attention to two subjects not considered in the British discussions: freedom of the press and the defense of journalism. Very self-conscious of press freedom, Americans extolled its uniqueness and its value to the nation. British discussions of freedom of the press generally focused on what it did not mean—licentiousness and unrestrained reporting of whatever might occur to an editor. The other issue, the defense of journalists and journalism, received much attention—but not equivalent to that given to criticism of the press.

Freedom of the Press

Every American critic paid tribute to freedom of the press, often taking pains to note that it was unique to America, and especially contrasting American and British journalism in this regard. Clearly, British criticism of American journalism was partly responsible for prompting the preoccupation with differences between the English and the American press. For example, the author of the article in the *Southern Quarterly Review* in 1842 wrote:

No people can be free, whose press is not free; no country can be said to enjoy liberty, where leading and influential men, who give tone to opinion and character to the masses, are not permitted to act freely and without restraint on the popular mind; and in this country, such, we are confident, is emphatically the case. The Press in America is Constitutionally free; our fellow citizens, who conduct it, are born freemen, and live and die such; and its broad impress everywhere bears upon it the deep and indelible stamp of the free American mind . . . a representative government.[68]

Comparing America and England, the critic enumerated newspapers in England for the years 1795, 1809, and 1837, including the aggregate circulation for the last-named year. Assuming eight readers an issue—a conservative estimate, considering that "one newspaper answers for all the members of a family, and that borrowers . . . in large cities, usually exceed the actual patrons"—he remarked on the "vast number of human beings" touched by newspapers. Remarking that there was no "means of ascertaining" the number published in the United States, he wrote:

We are altogether a freer people; individuals . . . masses are freer; freer to pursue their own interests . . . to better their own condition. Human nature is more respected among us; and the artificial distinctions of an imperfect social organization, which minister to the pride of a few, while they occasion mortification to the majority, do not exist in America. . . . the leading questions arising out of our peculiar condition and circumstances, are essentially different from those that occupy the minds of Englishmen; our thoughts run in altogether different channels; the machinery of government which we are called upon to sustain by popular opinion is . . . quite different; the wants and interests of the people are different; the evils . . . to be guarded against are so; the reforms that, from time to time, are essential to the health of the body politic, and the improvements . . . introduced into various branches of legislation, are all diverse from those which either mark progress, or indicate the decay or weakness, of an ancient monarchy. . . . Our duties are peculiarly American, and, in their proper performance, we require not the assistance of foreigners, nor are we disposed to tolerate patiently their interference.[69]

Furthermore, the American press compared favorably with the British press "as an engine of party opinion, and a vehicle of intelligence, not only in the amount, variety and character of its matter, but in the good sense, sound principles, and high, manly and generous tone . . . ; in the tact, information and literary qualifications of its editors, in their respect for religion, for truth, for moral principle, for liberty, for the rights of man."[70]

Certainly, press liberty had "been no more abused in the United States," and probably not as much, as "in other civilized nations"; defamation prosecutions were fewer than "in Great Britain during the last half century," and the American press's discussions, suggested by the nature and functioning of America's "free institutions," had been "usually of a more manly character, than those of the British Press." The American press's goal had been to "elevate the masses to their proper position in society," and they had "more distinctly espoused and more ably sustained the cause of truth, justice, equity, and human rights." Furthermore, the American citizenry was permeated with such a "tone of thought," feeling, and "moral delicacy" that it recoiled "with instinctive disgust" from whatever was "false, low, mean, ungenerous and unjust"; journalists were "obliged, for very shame . . . to join in the general acclaim of virtuous indignation against these things, wherever they exist. . . ." The English press was no freer of partisanship and personal bitterness than the American press. The American press was in fact "a purer organ, equally dignified, and less hemmed in by ancient prejudices and prescriptive errors."[71]

Another critic, responding in 1843 to British criticism of the American press, said that if the American press was corrupt, then the British press was "equally or more so"; but "even the British revilers admitted that some American newspapers were respectable." Asserting that the press "on both sides of the Atlantic" stood "greatly in need of reform," he wrote that America's primary business was "reform at home."[72]

Defense of Journalism

No critic called the American press perfect, but some praised it, ratio-
nalized its faults, and defended journalists as having virtually impossible
tasks. The *Southern Quarterly Review* writer in 1842 called America's "leading journals . . . published at the seats of government, and in our large
commercial emporiums," ably conducted. "Their editors," he wrote, were
"often men of fine talents and extensive information, capable of exerting
a decided influence," and he classed them among the "leading and most
influential minds in the country" "when any subject of exciting interest
is before the public." He also defended journalistic faults: "The press has
generally been lawfully employed . . . in the exercise of its true vocation,
and an elevated vocation . . . it is"; but, he argued, it was unreasonable to
expect a flawless press;

The Newspaper Press . . . is like the Tree of Knowledge of Good and Evil. If we
would have the good, it seems to be the lot of humanity . . . to take the evil . . .
and we can no more separate these . . . in the present condition of the world,
than we can divide light from darkness at the point where day ends and night
begins. . . . When we look at . . . the advantages . . . the Newspaper has con-
ferred on society and the age; the evils it has corrected, the good it has done,
the reforms it has achieved, the light and information it has shed everywhere, we
are ready to pronounce it a blessing to the world and to our country; but when
. . . we contemplate the various offences it has committed against truth, justice
and decorum, against good institutions, against the peace of society, and the
stability of governments, we are ready to deprecate it as a curse; we are disposed
to think that the common rumor is no fable,—that a real devil,—a veritable imp
of hell, is certainly attached to a printing office, and that Lucifer himself could
not have devised a more fitting instrument, than the press . . . to aid . . . in his
wicked efforts to banish right and justice from the earth, to unsettle principles,
to demoralize and disgrace our race. At one moment, we are prepared to declare,
that the press has been employed to promote its legitimate ends, the cause of
truth, virtue and humanity; at the next we exclaim, that it has been perverted
and abused and prostituted to the vilest uses. Both . . . opinions are true beyond
a question.[73]

Many faults were the result simply of people's zealousness in supporting strong views and, the writer seemed to imply, were therefore understandable. If the press might sometimes be charged with being lacking in
courtesy and emphasizing partisanism and personal bitterness, these were

only faults in human nature "under such circumstances." These belonged "to the race of men, when engaged in the maintenance and support of favorite views and theories, which they deem all important, and which are contradicted and opposed, as they think, without reason, and in an unceremonious manner." Some newspapers were certainly better conducted than others, and what some lacked "in racy and original speculation" was often made up for by a "more sacred regard to truth and principle, by greater industry in seeking out and obtaining correct information, and by the general prevalence of a better and less erratic judgment of men."[74]

The author gave much attention to journalists' work pressures, defending them for shortcomings stemming from lack of space or time and repeated interruptions on the job, and expressing wonder at what they did accomplish. Newspaper articles were so hastily prepared and under such pressure that time was insufficient for thorough inquiry, research, and investigation. The speed with which journalists wrote thus frequently resulted in their making "rash and ill-advised assertions" when "extreme . . . caution" was needed; articles were often, unfortunately, characterized by "loosely drawn and inadmissible conclusions from altogether hypothetical premises, . . . careless disregard or utter omission of weighty objections, and by a hurried, indifferent, and quite unfinished style of composition."[75]

The author referred here to the incapacity of newspapers to inform about literature and science—a frequent criticism then and later. But he excused journalists, asserting that "a single sheet, crowded with advertisements, shipping news and various items of intelligence, . . . laws, and sketches of legislative proceedings" had too little space for "full and thorough discussion of any subject." Even though articles might continue from day to day "till an argument is completed," the whole subject could not "be presented to the mind in one connected train of reasoning"; the "leading ideas and whole links of argument" were "often lost to the reader, and . . . nothing" could "supply the defect, but frequent and tedious repetitions." Furthermore, he argued, editors were too frequently interrupted to have time for "calm reflection" and "deep meditation on the important subjects . . . constantly arising . . . in the present age, and for the preparation of thorough, able and well studied articles, suited to the tastes of the learned, fastidious, critical reader, or even of the less scrupulous scholar, and man of plain sense" who could clearly and fully understand facts and arguments, but without the embellishments "a more cultivated mind, studious of reputation" might give them. Although correspondents might be better able to do such work, motivated as they were only by patriotism or reputation, they were unlikely to "perform a serious duty under a pledge of pecuniary recompense" and were unreliable for substantial or continued effort. The editor was "the responsible party, . . . the person to whom his patrons" looked for discussion and embellishment of subjects "with all the lights of science and the graces of literature." An editor who lacked these inclinations or abilities—as was often the case, the author noted—made up for it by "invective, declamation, unmannerly abuse or party slang"; and then the press became "prostituted, the taste of readers debased, and the worst passions of human nature . . . excited and indulged."[76]

Remedies and Suggested Journalistic Standards

What notions of appropriate and inappropriate conduct emerge from American press criticism? Generally, early writers jumped from broad criticisms to proposing broader solutions, seeming to assume that everyone knew the problems, and their suggestions typically encompassed altering the press as a whole. It is clear that those espousing receding values sought to turn back time. In their view the press needed to be brought under control in order to prevent further deterioration of established sociopolitical structures and values. Those American critics who were more in tune with competing (that is, emerging) values defended the press, and it is noteworthy that expressions like *the individual, knowledge,* and the *public good* figured prominently in their discussions. The critics' solutions to the problems they identified ranged widely. Suggestions included "buying" a "good" press—giving a different twist to the British suggestion of "buying off" journalists; ensuring that only "good" people controlled the press; reducing the number of newspapers so that quality could be improved in those remaining; getting journalists to agree to eliminate infighting; and writing a solid history of the press to provide perspective, point out sources of problems, and show the degree to which the press had stayed within constitutional bounds. American critics emphasized responsibility more than the British, and some believed that the press—untampered with —would ultimately correct its own problems.

Proposed American solutions to press abuse did not include legal regulation, as had the British. Still, some British themes appear in Americans' solutions. The emphasis by Bulwer and Talfourd on the propertied, educated classes as the press's salvation paralleled that in earlier English criticism. Because "disorganizing factions" rarely included people "blessed with a large share of this world's goods," they usually failed for lack of financial support; thus, the "mass of revolutionists . . . the mob . . . can be governed in but two ways: by the terror of force . . . or by the milder process of enlightening and improving them." The authors called the latter "the nobler remedy," adding, "*and it may be effectually offered through the press*" (emphasis in original). Echoing the recommendation offered by the author of the article in *Blackwood's Edinburgh Magazine* in 1834, that the "better sort" must gain control of the press, Bulwer and Talfourd maintained that the "wealthy, . . . educated, . . . refined, and . . . intellectual classes in the United States" had more to do than they realized in the country's growth, and they could "operate through" the daily press on "the people at large." Even if they could not avoid party strife, they could influence the shape and power of the press: "*They can withhold their patronage from those papers which minister to the bad passions of the populace, and they can accord it to those publications whose tendency is to encourage security, repose, and rational freedom*" (emphasis in original). The authors continued to spell out their views of appropriate journalistic conduct:

Newspapers should be made the vehicles of sound political doctrine, and of correct religious principle—the advocates of the purest morality, and the undeviating, unflinching supporters of order and justice. Their editors should aim . . . at cultivating the literary taste of their readers; and endeavour to sustain the real dignity of their calling. They should be alive to the great responsibilities of their station.[77]

The writers advocated patronage for such journalists, urging that it be given by "those who have the means" to "secure the services of men whose high talents could not be better employed than in improving the condition of their country."[78]

Bulwer and Talfourd seemed to credit the press with infinite power over the nation's institutions, particularly government. If "good" people were in charge of the press, the nation would flourish in education, science, and the arts, and society as a whole would triumph:

With such a press . . . enlightened, regulated, and free, and with the best talents of her best sons enlisted in her service, what has America to fear? Her high offices would be filled by men worthy to fill them. Literature, the arts and sciences, education . . . in a word, the best interests of the country, and not the mere benefit of any particular party, would be fostered and promoted, and in the far future, the second sight of even the most croaking prophet would spy nothing to dread.[79]

In such a country, "where the laws and constitution prohibit any other check," the only recourse was to warn of the danger and so enlighten "the mass that they may fully comprehend and knowingly meet the emergency." If the press should be "undeviatingly on the side of order and true liberty," society would be secure. Foes would then "batter the walls of the social edifice in vain." The press's "firm foundations" would "resist all their impotent efforts at destruction."[80]

The critic writing in the *Southern Quarterly Review* in 1843 also suggested that "good and able men . . . be entrusted with the control of the Press" because "none other can command the confidence of the people —who, in the main, are honest and respect principle,—and none other should be invested with such formidable power."[81] The year before, the *Southern Quarterly Review* author whose article has extensively illuminated the dimensions of American press criticism in the early nineteenth century, wrote that the nation's "immense" number of newspapers was far more than necessary, and suggested encouraging fewer of higher quality: "if the same amount . . . now expended in supporting a multitude of indifferent newspapers, were employed in improving the appearance, and in imparting additional value and interest, in a literary, as well as political point of view, to a few leading journals . . . in our large cities, it would be much better for . . . the whole country." He concluded that it was obviously in any country's best interest "to have a few good newspapers, edited with spirit and ability and extensively patronized, than many poor ones, feebly edited and miserably supported."[82]

One critic in 1843, particularly weary of the bickering among journalists, proposed as a beginning solution a convention of the nation's "leading Editors" to meet in Baltimore, "upon the rising of the one for the nomination of president." And "then and there," he recommended, they should "enter into mutual pledges, in the most solemn manner, each with each, and each with all the rest, to abandon, henceforth and forever, the miserable and contemptible practice of vilifying public functionaries, and candidates for public offices, and abusing each other as knaves, fools and pickpockets." They should "form a virtuous resolution, that they will hereafter control their passions, moderate their language, pursue the truth for the sake of the truth, and maintain it with decency and decorum." The writer believed that people would joyfully hail such a move and, if unanimously adopted and strictly followed, "it would not lessen an iota the chances of any one of the rival candidates for the Presidency, or of the candidates for any other office, and would contribute, not a little to the respectability of the Press of the nation."[83]

The writer publishing in the *Southern Quarterly Review* in 1842 suggested a history of how well the American press had remained within "just and Constitutional limits" since the nation began; saying that such a history would be that of human nature, he implied that the press can never be better than the varied individuals who conduct it. The history of the press in America would be a history of men "displaying, according to their character and principles . . . , the best or the worst features" of their race.[84]

There was still "great, very great room for improvement" in the press, the writer stressed, but human nature had to improve to "elevate its tone" and "make it what it ought to be, as an organ of light and intelligence for a free people." People had to "learn to act on correct principles"; "pure morals must prevail; education must be cherished; arts and sciences must be cultivated; the truth must be loved for itself alone; and society, in all its leading characteristics, must be greatly reformed and regenerated." Journalists must help accomplish these ends, and they had the ability; they must only "put their own shoulders to the wheel and exert all their strength. . . ."[85]

Nearly all American critics sounded the theme of responsibility that accompanied the emerging information model. The *Southern Quarterly Review* author in 1842 argued that the press was "a powerful instrument for good or . . . evil," and those who "assume the responsibility of it" should aim to "disseminate the truth and the truth only, free from passion, . . . prejudice . . . , influence of party spirit, as far as such exemption from injurious influences, is attainable by man in the present condition of the world."[86]

Some invoked responsibility when grappling with how to control inappropriate press conduct, and others emphasized it in connection with press freedom in court cases of the era. The *Southern Quarterly Review* writer in 1842 argued that press freedom did not mean "the liberty to print . . . any thing and every thing, . . . whether the motive, that prompts the publication, be innocent or mischievous":

Man has no liberty to do wrong wilfully, to propagate error voluntarily, and to employ a free press for this purpose. The liberty of the press is as much violated by this intentional mischief, as the liberty of speech . . . is violated by base and malicious slander. . . . The very idea of control denotes dependence somewhere; and on whom and on what does the press lean for support? On man, the free agent, and it is no more and no less free, not a jot, than its master is. . . . The press is the instrument, the agent, the representative, so to speak, by means of which the free agent, man, develops his powers and accomplishes his purposes.[87]

The journalist was free to a certain extent "and no further," because a person holds freedom "under . . . the bonds of good behavior" and "cannot break these bonds with impunity."[88] Editors were "bound by law," and the law they must follow was "THE TRUTH . . . in every thing"—the law by which "a free moral agent, a politician, a philosopher, a man of letters, is to govern his conduct, and be governed in it." And this—"nothing more than this"—constituted freedom of the press and freedom of speech—"the liberty to speak, . . . to write and to publish the truth, and all kinds of it, for the benefit of individuals and of society at large."[89]

Efforts to define responsibility permeate the Massachusetts libel trial cited earlier. Analyzing truth as a defense in libel cases, the justice first defined press liberty, and in doing so, described the press as "an instrument of great moral and intellectual efficacy." "The liberty of the press . . . is nothing more than the liberty of a moral and intellectual being . . . to use that particular instrument . . ."; and, he asserted, "the liberty of a moral agent to use any instrument, depends upon the motive and end he has in using it":

For a good motive and a justifiable end, he has a right to use it;—that is, he has a liberty to use it.

For a bad motive and an unjustifiable end he has no right to use it;—that is—he has no such liberty;—in other words such use of it is licentiousness.

Liberty is, in relation to every other instrument, characterized by, and coextensive with, the nature of its justifiable use. And this depends upon the quality of the motive and of the end.[90]

Some American critics seemed to believe the press's "evil" would ultimately "cure itself." Those conducting the press, a critic wrote in 1843, would, "from severe experience of the miserable consequences . . . to themselves and to others from their mutual disputes and indulgence of violent and unreasonable passions and prejudices," be "led finally to abandon the practice of crimination and abuse, so discreditable to high-minded and sensible men, as a measure not less of honor, than of personal peace and security."[91] The writer for the *Southern Quarterly Review* in 1842 argued that press improvements would "keep pace with advances of individuals, and of society, in arts, in science, in morals, in religion, in a knowledge of the principles of government, in literary attainments, and in whatever can adorn life and elevate the tone of thought, of feeling and of action." He mused that this would probably follow "in . . . a few years, when the States will be everywhere intersected with rail-roads, and the intercourse between town and country . . . more free, rapid and direct," as had already occurred in England, "as is evident from their newspaper statistics during the last quarter of a century, showing a gradual falling off in the number [of newspapers] published . . . , but by no means a diminution in the number of readers."[92]

Concrete suggestions of specific standards were sparse in this era, but a few critics, in delineating undesirable journalistic conduct, stated some fairly clearly. Bulwer and Talfourd, for example, posing several questions in 1836 and remarking that they feared for the press's credit should "an up-right and independent man" answer them, criticized the press as being too dependent and timid, pandering to base taste, and failing to take a stand against threats to the public good. At the same time, they revealed their view of standards that journalists should aspire to. The press should be independent, fearless, and forthright in expression on any topic; it should boldly state views and be able to withstand the consequences, leaving read-ers to make up their own minds. Editors should be above mass "prejudices or passions":

Is the press in the United States sufficiently independent? Is a fearless expression of opinion in either politics, morals, or literature, sustained by that of the pub-lic, evinced in an unhesitating and decided way? Does the press boldly avow its sentiments, conscious of their integrity and leave the result to the good sense of the community, careless of the consequences? Or is a dictum upon any topic weighed and measured by what is supposed to be consonant to the views and in-terests of the mass of subscribers? Does an editor ever, for the purpose of sailing along with a prosperous wind and tide, fall in with the prejudices or passions of the mass? or does he boldly and invariably stem the current when it sets counter to reason, religion, morality, and the public good?[93]

The *Southern Quarterly Review* essayist in 1842 followed a similar pat-tern. The reverse of what he stressed as improper journalistic conduct is taken to be what he considered appropriate conduct. He insisted that improper journalistic conduct consisted of publishing any untruths (a "mischievous" tendency)—circulating false statements and "erroneous opinions, on any subject, knowing them to be so, the withholding of the truth, by partial representations of acknowledged facts, and the addition . . . of false and extraneous matter, not true"; and using the truth to disturb the public peace. For such abuses, those spreading opinions via the press were "responsible to . . . conscience, . . . God, and . . . country."[94]

American criticism of the first half of the nineteenth century reveals divergence from British values, which supported deference, authoritarian attitudes about what reading matter should be popularly available, fear of the printed word, and a view of the press's purpose as primarily to serve the interests of the elite classes. Although these themes were present in the earliest American discussions, by mid-century press criticism increasingly reflected competing values that rejected deference, assumed worth in everyone, lauded the popular availability of all reading matter, and saw the press as serving both individuals and the wider society.

Divergence appeared also in perspectives. If British criticism erred on the side of pessimism, American criticism erred on the side of optimism, for views of the press as the salvation of the human race permeated much of the latter. Although the British were consternated by the press, Americans were overawed. In their criticism, however, Americans tended more toward specifics and were closer to delineating "appropriate" journalistic practices than the British.

Although hardly precise, some notions of journalistic standards emerge from these discussions. Consisting largely of generalities in both American and British discussions, they represent significant progress: these early critics began to consider press-society issues seriously, and discussions of public opinion represented a peak of thought and debate for both British and American criticism during the era. They raised important issues that critics during the century's second half would continue to discuss. In short, they laid the foundation for discussion of issues throughout the century. Based on this precedent, later critics would become increasingly specific, ultimately relating journalistic procedures to press functions.

Chapter Six

Criticism, 1850–1889: Press Functions and General Problems

Ques. *The purchasers of the daily papers must consist of a different class from those in England—mechanics must purchase them?*
Ans. *Every mechanic takes a paper, or nearly every one.*

. . .

Ques. *Then the working class receive their papers regularly through the carrier in the morning?*
Ans. *Yes.*
Ques. *What time are they delivered . . . ?*
Ans. *Between six and seven, as a rule.*
Ques. *Do these people generally get them before they leave home for their work?*
Ans. *Yes, and you are complained of if you do not furnish a man with his newspaper at his breakfast. . . .*
Ques. *Then a shipbuilder, or a cooper, or a joiner, takes in his daily paper in the morning, and reads it at his breakfast time?*
Ans. *Yes, and he may take it with him to read at his dinner, between twelve and one; but the rule is that he wants his paper at his breakfast.*

From Horace Greeley's testimony before a House of Commons committee on the press, September 16, 1851

By 1850, a shift in values from those of the 1820s and 1830s is apparent in comments about the press's positive influence on society and other social institutions. Indeed, the view of the press as an aid to the individual had expanded to that of aid to the world. During the 1840s and 1850s, a period some historians have characterized as the "Sentimental Years,"[1] discussions endowed the press with an aura of infinite beneficence, almost personifying it as they claimed it could achieve humankind's most desired goals, such as universal education and world peace.

Another indication of changing values is that press criticism after 1850 —and especially after the Civil War—differed markedly from that of earlier decades. Frequency of discussion increased, quickening especially after the war, until approximately one hundred magazine articles appeared in the last decade alone. (Because space did not permit dealing with the last decade's abundant material, the study of press criticism ends with 1889, when the first article using the word *ethics* in its title was published.) More important than frequency, however, criticism of the second half of the century—again, especially after the Civil War—differed from earlier criticism in nearly all respects. One striking difference is a clearer, more precise and direct writing style that incorporated better-reasoned arguments and well-drawn examples. The impact can hardly be overstated. Compared to earlier writing, in which one sentence often ran pages in length, ideas were expressed concisely. Pre-Civil War criticism consisted largely of generalizations; writers attempted in single articles to deal with the entire phenomenon of the press; and press conduct was generally condemned in wholesale terms. Articles after 1850, however, increasingly emphasized single problems and specific practices.

But more important differences included deliberate examination of press functions. Critics began to use the term *function* after the war and, in grappling with many issues, initiated a line of thought toward what might be called press theory—at least as they understood it. To highlight this development, this chapter focuses on critics' definitions of press functions and on the more abstract press criticism from 1850 to 1889.

Notable in discussions after the middle of the century are attempts to explain how the press operated and to justify and defend journalistic conduct. Early nineteenth-century discussions of the press gave virtually no insights about how it operated. But the elementary state of newspapers' business structure provided little to discuss. By 1850, however, numerous positions had become commonplace on both the news and business sides —and examining their activities became preliminary to understanding the press. Discussions began to dissect the "profession," explicating and distinguishing among the press's various functions and tasks and explaining the differing roles of reporters and editors, and how the press in general—and its different departments in particular—went about its work.[2] Journalists, or those with journalistic experience although not necessarily identifying themselves as journalists, dominated these efforts as they increasingly wrote about the press and its functions, benefits, and problems. The earliest to produce a series of such articles was Samuel Bowles III, editor of the *Springfield* (Massachusetts) *Republican*. Edwin Godkin, founder of *The Nation* in 1865, also wrote frequently of journalism.[3] Earlier critics only occasionally defended journalism, but especially during the last three decades of the century, journalists increasingly defended the profession against specific charges.

Such a shift from generalities to specific abuses and conduct is not surprising. With little press structure and very simple operations to discuss, critics in the early part of the century reiterated journalism history and referred broadly to how the press influenced language and taste, "flattering" ordinary people and abetting the discontent of the "lower orders." Criticism of Sunday newspapers and prize fight news and the scattered oblique references to crime reports were rare instances in which critics specified what they saw as journalistic conduct that caused problems. But critics after the Civil War related abuses to journalistic practices and often examined larger detrimental effects on society in terms of press functions. They increasingly discussed what the press could and could not do as opposed to what it ought, but was failing, to do. Indeed, as journalism historian Thomas Connery and others have noted, it was as if Americans had lost their innocence—and, surely, the Civil War represented figuratively, if not literally, that turning point.[4] Much rhetoric, however, still glorified the press.

General Functions

Although the wistful view of the press as providing an almost magical solution to such social problems as illiteracy, coarseness, and strife dwindled, it remained strong in the years just preceding the Civil War. Through the 1850s, when the United States was torn by growing sectional strife, discussions at times hailed the press as peacemaker between warring nations. People called it a current uniting minds across the world, a near-instantaneous transmitter of history-changing ideas, a defender of nations, a vehicle of peace, a companion, and an opinion molder. Such views of the press's general capacities are presented below, followed by discussions of its role in public opinion. The chapter then focuses on discussions differentiating press functions, and the concluding section sets forth general criticisms, emphasizing evolution from earlier decades.

Press Functions: Great Expectations

Among the more glorified functions attributed to the press were those of educator (a constant view across the century); symbol and propellor of progress and civilization; universal reformer; protector of the peace, liberties, and general moral health; the "brain" of communities; individuals' and humankind's moral guide; an instrument of peace; and a "companion." In an 1858 editorial, Bowles wrote that the press had become "the instructor, the corrector and the stimulator of the age, and its high mission . . . more and more elevated" as it "more perfectly" fulfilled "its world." It provided the great "incentives to progress and beneficent exertion," and stimulated people to effort by publicizing their deeds.[5]

Six years later, in 1864, Charles Holden, a former editor addressing the first meeting of the Maine Press Association, called the press a lever for moving the world, a "great reformer" of immeasurable power. An ounce of lead made into a bullet used in a rifle would "fly a mile or two, and do its errand efficiently, if it meet no obstacle. But that ounce of lead made into types, and put upon one of the swift presses of the day, will go thousands of miles, and do its errand with truest aim . . . on millions, . . . though oceans, rivers, and mountains intervene." The press had "invested the public speaker with greatness, whether . . . clerical, or political or moral," Holden continued. In ancient Athens, where "there were no reporters or telegraphs," Demosthenes could reach at most six to seven thousand of the fourteen thousand inhabitants; but a member of Congress, speaking before a few hundred in 1864, addressed "a million in a few hours," "uttering words which the next day shook the nation."[6] James Parton wrote in 1866 that the newspaper connected "each individual with the general life of mankind," making the one "part and parcel of the whole"; those who didn't read newspapers, or talk with people who did, could hardly be called "members of the human *family*." "They are beyond the pale; they have no hold of the electric chain," he wrote.[7]

In 1869, in the first article dealing almost exclusively with journalistic standards, Richard Grant White called journalism the "cheapest defence of nations"; "the surest safeguard of liberty, the most certain antidote against corruption"; the "brain of a community, the organ of its collective thought"; "the chief among the active visible forces of modern civilization"; a "constant guide, a daily counsellor"; an informer and educator that expanded "the horizon of men's thoughts and sympathies" while increasing "their means of attaining for themselves and their families comforts and luxuries." Like a train's headlight, he wrote, journalism was a "moving beacon . . . of warning and . . . promise, casting its light . . . forward upon the way that must be followed" and not over the path already traveled.[8]

By the 1880s, definitions of function had shifted subtly from the press as a vehicle of moral and intellectual growth to more pragmatic versions. A writer in 1884, calling the press a "great power for distributing intelligence of all kinds," wrote that it was a "vast popular educator, in science, the useful arts, taste for literature, music, painting, sculpture, in all that belong to human existence in this world." And this power continually increased, becoming "more and more beneficent." When travel was difficult and infrequent, he wrote, "papers were of necessity local . . . , limited in their circulation, restricted in their horizon," and "the Wide, Wide World was a child's look over a fence." But the great newspaper had become a vehicle of news from "every part of the planet. . . ."9 A writer in 1889 called the newspaper "the daily history of the world and record of the doings of mankind, political, commercial, social, artistic, accompanied by editorial comments on the subjects of passing interest." It was "a vehicle . . . whereby" community needs were "interchanged" through advertisement.10

Rare references defined the press as a companion—a kind of function recognized in recent years. In 1856 George Lunt implicitly defined the newspaper for the first time as something beyond a simple provider of information and opinion. Calling it a "miscellaneous text-book of popular literature," "an object of daily interest, common as the air, the companion of our firesides and of all our resorts to business or pleasure," he said that it was "suited, in its multiplied manifestations" to "tastes," "habits," "pursuits," "recreations—in fact, to all the diversified elements of the human mind; and become, at last, an absolute necessity of life." Newspapers carried people "along with them, abreast of the rapid flood of passing events," gave them their "morning subjects of discussion," wiped "the misty cobwebs of dreamland" from "opening eyes" and provided the "materials" for "evening solace," until being dropped with the "final yawn" at night. After being read, papers were flung "aside with indifference," but "in truth, we should miss them absent. . . ."11 In 1866 Parton echoed this sentiment when he referred to the "gloom" on the two holidays when no newspaper published: "A shadow appears to rest on the world . . . as when there is an eclipse of the sun. We are separated from our brethren, cut off, lost, alone. . . ."12

References to the press as an instrument of peace, common before the Civil War, reveal the subtle shift from moralism. The earliest such references seemed to be based on an assumption that spreading God's word

throughout the world was prerequisite to achieving peace. But later references seemed to be based more on the assumption that the prerequisites of
peace were the spread of knowledge and the capability of communicating
ideas across the world. Bowles's words in 1851 merged both assumptions
but tended to adopt the latter, subtly presaging the shift from moralism
to secularism. Defining the press as a nurturer of minds and shrinker of
boundaries, Bowles called it a vehicle for peace. Writing that the press was
"destined, more than any other agency, to melt and mould the jarring and
contending nations of the world into that one great brotherhood which,
through long centuries," had been "the ideal of the Christian and philan-
thropist," he called the newspaper then and for the future "the high priest
of History, the vitalizer of Society, the world's great informer, the earth's
high censor, the medium of public thought and opinion," "the circulating life blood of the whole human mind," "the great enemy of tyrants,"
and "the right arm of liberty." Speculating that the newspaper's "mission"
might never be "perfectly understood," Bowles predicted that in a few
years "a great thought uttered within sight of the Atlantic" would "rise
with the morrow's sun and shine upon millions of minds by the side of the
Pacific"; that the "murmur of Asia's multitudes" would be "heard at our
doors"; and the newspaper, "laden with the fruit of all human thought and
action," would "be in every abode, the daily nourishment of every mind."[13]
Similar expressions accompanied what was thought to be the successful
completion of the transatlantic cable in 1858, when the editor of the *New
York Herald* devoted much space to acclaiming this accomplishment as the
means to international peace and brotherhood.[14]

The glorified functions appeared after the war only in occasional passing
sentences tinged with praise of the press as a symbol of freedom. A writer
in 1887, for example, wrote that the modern newspaper was born in the
American and French revolutions, when "that powerful organization," the
press, "became a tribune of the people, more potent for the sustenance of
law and order than any courts of justice or military force."[15] George T.
Rider, however, writing in 1882, more nearly epitomized the evolution of
press theory beyond glorification; his words nevertheless show that journalism's larger function still confounded those who tried to define it. Using
the common phrase "the fourth estate" in referring to the press, Rider
held that journalism stood "beside, if not above, the ancient three" estates.
Journalism had a "short root, no accumulations, and no treasury in the
past." It was without "traditions," "precedents," "organization or corpo-

rate relations," "prescience," or "clearly ascertained heirship for the future." It lived, moved, and had "its being outside the unfolding drama of growing civilization." Journalism was only "impersonal voice—comment," and its "illumination" was "cold, auroral, spectral." Journalism, he wrote, multiplied "its offices to keep pace with the demands of a civilization all the while branching . . . among its subsidiaries." Following a lengthy praise of journalism, Rider defined it as "nothing unless . . . immediate"; it was "quick as a wink" in its methods "and bristling with ultimate decisions, cut and dried, and warranted specific for any emergency. . . ."[16]

Although statements glorifying the press's functions virtually disappeared during the 1870s, deep concern about journalistic power continued, and expectations of what the press could do often remained unrealistically high. Implicit in all such discussions was the belief that the press shaped public opinion, debate of which represented the peak of earlier critics' thought as they pondered whether the press created, shaped, led, or simply reflected public opinion. After 1850 the focus shifted subtly from whether the press shaped public opinion toward how it did so, the importance attached to the press by the public, and implications; by the late 1880s, another theme was its declining influence and predictions that the "newspaper age" was ending.[17] Because this issue stood out across the century and intensified after 1850, it merits separate treatment here.

Function: The Press as Molder of Public Opinion

Belief that the press molded and controlled public opinion continued in a virtually straight line from earlier critics' views. Godkin in 1868 proclaimed the press's essential role in forming public opinion, especially since the legislatures had "abandoned all pretence of influencing public opinion through . . . debates." In an editorial prompted by letters protesting the "impolicy or injudiciousness of opposing the recent measures of Congress," he stressed the cruciality of such policy debate. Because the legislature rushed through laws "conceived in secret committees," without "reference to . . . popular feeling and . . . thought . . . , or their probable effect," the "formation of public opinion" was "left entirely to the press," and people had to learn from newspapers everything they needed to know "to make up their mind about every question."[18] A year and a half later, in 1869, Godkin asserted that dailies could "mould public opinion completely" by "their mode of reporting." Newspapers colored the "light" through which readers saw the world "and really almost" determined, "by the extent" to which they helped build up or denigrate "the reputations of legislators and other public officers," whether a community's laws would be "nullified or enforced."[19]

By the late 1880s, attitudes about the press's power over public opinion were more studied. In a thoughtful analysis, editor Charles Dana said in 1888 that, unless people read newspapers critically, the press could impose opinion. The press's power was great: it took people when their information was incomplete, their reasoning not yet worked out, their opinions not fixed, and it suggested, intimated, and insinuated opinion and judgment that readers then often accepted as "established and concluded" unless they had "great intelligence and force of character." The press exercised this power over people's minds "often without any knowledge or any criticism on the part of the person" subject to it.[20]

Whereas the century's earliest critics seemed to view the press as an extension of other institutions, by the 1880s critics were defining the press, particularly the newspaper, as unique, with functions unlike those of the academy, church, or arts. Discussion of individual press roles and functions further underscores this evolution in concepts of the press.

Differentiated Functions

Journalists dealt in abstractions less often than nonjournalist critics, and they almost always reduced newspaper functions to news, opinion, and as the century progressed, advertising. The first to articulate the news function clearly, Samuel Bowles, after becoming editor of the *Springfield Republican* in 1851, wrote that news, "to which all other things [in a newspaper] must bend," would be the paper's first aim, followed by "politics, morals, religion, physics" and anything else editors might discuss.[21] In a later editorial in 1855, Bowles also became the first to attempt to dissect the press's tasks. Declaring the newspaper's primary purpose as "to give the news," he distinguished among news of fact, opinion, incident, event, policies, administration of public affairs, men and personal character, society, social movements, and life. Journalistic developments of the previous decade had "made this qualitative analysis of news one of the most rigid necessities of the profession."[22]

Fifteen years later, Godkin in 1870 continued this dissection, trying to articulate editorial and reportorial functions. Prompted by a statement that newspapers would be better if confined to their "proper function of collecting and distributing the news" and had no editorials, he noted arguments that editors' and reporters' functions were incompatible because the reporter's interest was scientific, whereas the editor's was purely practical. Attempting to distinguish and justify each (albeit with some sarcasm regarding the editorial role), Godkin wrote that the reporter's or correspondent's "business" was "simply . . . minute and . . . comprehensive enquiry"; the editor's was usually advancement of some "scheme—such as the extinction of slavery, the extension of the suffrage, the acquisition of territory, the depression or advance of shares in the capital stock of 'some great national enterprise,' located in the neighborhood of the editor's native town."[23]

In 1886 another writer attempted to explain and justify "Editorial and Reportorial" functions. Both must interest, attract attention, and present products that acted "as an appetizing tonic." Editorials must take decided positions—and do so with the "fewest words," the "greatest vigor," and always with such a tone as to "forbid the suspicion" that opposing arguments existed. Reporting, however, was supposed to be the "great device by which modern civilization" transmitted to posterity "a plain, unvarnished, and veracious account of itself," and this required factuality.[24]

Definitions of functions ranged from the simple to the complex. In one of the simplest statements, Parton in 1866 wrote that "journalism brings the events of the time to bear upon the instruction of the time." "The word *newspaper* is the exact and complete description of the thing which the true journalist aims to produce. The news is his work. . . ."[25] White in 1869 offered a more complex view, defining two levels of press functions and attempting to distinguish where morality entered. Implicitly he argued that journalists must take responsibility for the direction of human progress and civilization, and it was this that brought morality into journalistic work. Journalism's "true function, even in its lowest stage," White wrote, was "to inform, to enlighten, to place within the knowledge of men the facts which concern their most important interests, ignorance of which may expose them to loss," "perplexing error," and "suffering." From this "level" he continued, journalism rose to "the position of a counsellor and a prophet" to whom "statesmen must listen," and a judge "from whose sentence" even "autocrats" had "no appeal." Journalism's first and most legitimate function was purely "mercantile and clerical"—gathering information, "bringing it to market," and recording events; its ultimate function, however, was that of teacher ("one of the highest offices man can assume") when it made "those events the subject of comment and discourse." In the latter, journalism rose "from the material plane to that of morals."[26] In defining a journalist's function in 1870, White emphasized the public's right to know. The newspaper was primarily a record of the day's events, and a journalist's function, besides collecting news, was to try to "improve the world and to bring about a better state of things." Readers had a "right to expect" journalism to be a "guide in public affairs—not absolutely infallible," because that was beyond human capacity, "but trustworthy . . . according to the abilities and opportunities of . . . editors."[27]

Melville Stone, writing in his autobiography in 1923 of the founding of the *Chicago Daily News* in 1876, said that his newspaper's "first intent" was "collection and presentation of the world's news." He divided and ranked editorial department functions; to print the news, to try to "guide public opinion aright," and to provide entertainment; it was a "business mistake to invert this order and to make entertainment . . . of first importance."[28]

The author of an article published in 1884 held that the press's primary function was to "convey enlightenment to the multitude." The press was part of a triad of "sources of power"; all other social agencies were only "variations on the themes" proposed by the press, theater, and pulpit. The stage's purpose was to entertain, cultivate, refine, and elevate, the church's to "inspire the human soul," and the press's to "impart a complete information." The writer described broad news processes in his defense of journalism. The cost was "something fabulous" to maintain "correspondents, charged with . . . reporting deeds and transactions" in "every chief center, in every great city." The necessary "energy," "enterprise," and "disciplined skill" were "fairly beyond computation," and the "brain-work of the editor in chief"—and "of the subordinates—must be prodigious, and . . . unceasing." After news was gathered came the process of explaining, accounting for, and interpreting "the external facts"—disclosing their meaning, indicating their "tendency," foreshadowing their "consequence." All this required "comment by experienced minds" who had studied the subject; the "best statisticians, critics, historians, financiers, scholars, must be employed to reduce to reason the crude material."[29]

Dion Boucicault, writing three years later, in 1887, of the press's decline and fall, defined three functions: "First—the collection and circulation of useful and important news. Secondly—The perception of the subjects . . . agitating the public mind, and the opinion of thoughtful minds thereupon." The third function was advertising, without which, he wrote, expenses covering the first two functions could not be met.[30]

In a lecture delivered in 1888, Dana called the newspaper's main function to "give the news"—to tell the world's events "of all sorts, political, scientific, and nonsensical"; but he also emphasized a larger sociopolitical function. An editor's first task was to "look for news," and that meant "everything" that occurred, "everything . . . of human interest, and . . . of sufficient importance to arrest and absorb" the public's attention "or any considerable" part of it. But the press's power of "speaking out the sentiment of the people, the voice of justice, the inspiration of wisdom, the determination of patriotism, the heart of the whole people" was much more important. If the press erred, as did those "on the other side" in the Civil War, "their power" amounted to nothing. The function Dana stressed as "more momentous" by far, however, was that of safeguarding the Constitution. "When every other bulwark is gone, the free press will remain to preserve the liberties that we mean shall be handed down to our children, and to maintain . . . the republic in all its majesty and glory for ever and ever. . . ."[31]

The emphasis on the broadest contours reflected in these discussions resulted from concern about the press's effects on society. Earlier critics' preoccupations with morality and public opinion were extended, and their meanings became more diverse. Although more general than specific, other criticisms suggest the evolution of thought as critics moved toward a more narrow focus on separate aspects of the press.

After 1850, the themes emphasized in the criticism of the early nineteenth century shifted. Some receded as time passed; others, latent or barely visible in earlier discussions, gained strength, and new ones emerged. Themes that recurred throughout the century reflected subtle changes. For example, concerns about the press's great capacity for both good and evil and about newspapers' detrimental impact on literature were voiced throughout the century; but emphasis shifted from moralism in the former, and the latter declined as people increasingly defined the newspaper's function as unique among those of society's institutions. The complaint that learned thinkers had given so little attention to the press also received sporadic expression. In 1851, Bowles expressed wonder that the "moralist and the philosopher" had not begun to consider the implications of the "new state of things"—what he described as an era of communications brought about by increased "facilities" for news "transmission." The railroad, steamboat, and telegraph had shrunk the world, making "neighborhood among widely dissevered States," bringing the "Eastern Continent" closer and the "whole civilized world into contact." Newspapers had "liberalized" the world, making nations and individuals "immediately responsible" to world opinion, universalizing interests, and putting behind "petty interests, feuds, gossip and strifes of families and neighborhoods."[32] Introducing a lyceum lecture in 1856, George Lunt, former U.S. attorney for the District of Massachusetts, said he knew of no "philosophical lecture" that had focused on the press, although people should be profoundly interested in "an honest investigation of the characteristics," "merits," "deficiencies," "powers," and "obligations" of the institution on which they so depended.[33] An article published in 1890 expressed a similar sentiment, but by that time a spate of articles had given serious attention to the press.

Among more abstract themes that gained strength with succeeding decades were those of the press's partisanship and corruption and journalists' excessive power. The relatively mild and rare references to the influence of editors in earlier criticism evolved into charges that they exercised power over people, public opinion, policy, and issues; that they shaped news through subtle pressures on reporters; and that journalists (especially editors) held such power in part because of anonymous writing or use of the "editorial we," through which they in turn escaped responsibility.[34] Receding themes included the press's impact on morality, youth, women, and erudition. Because the later expressions of criticisms that preoccupied critics in the first half of the century are important in tracing the evolution of underlying concepts, the next section emphasizes that evolution in abstract themes, beginning with a discussion of America's first book-length work of press criticism.

Criticism: The Press's General Effect on Society

The first American book devoted entirely to press criticism appeared in 1860. Lambert Wilmer's *Our Press Gang* marks a turning point, echoing earlier complaints and projecting future ones. Neglected by historians—perhaps because its caustic tone makes its contents suspect—it was published when press criticism remained general and before concerted efforts to explain how the press did its work. Yet the book foreshadowed virtually every criticism, and itself introduced many, that dominated discussions following the Civil War, and its anger set the stage for the often shrill denunciations of the press after 1880. Although more clearly written and more focused on specific examples supporting or clarifying criticisms than earlier writing, its style remained closer to pre- than to post–Civil War criticism. Because the book thus stands apart, in bold relief as it were, its criticisms are summarized at length as a preface to remaining criticisms during the last half of the nineteenth century.

The First Book-Length Work of Press Criticism

Wilmer's attack on the press was scathing. Prefacing his criticisms by "I charge the American newspaper press with . . ." or "I assert that the American newspaper is . . ." and using strong language, Wilmer listed fourteen complaints—generally devoting a chapter to each and multiple chapters to some, and referring to six additional complaints that space did not permit him to include.[35] Writing the book after thirty-five years of journalistic experience, he took pains to deny any grudge against the press, but his bitter criticisms must be read with knowledge that frequent bad luck had marked his editing career.[36] Still, Wilmer's criticisms cannot be lightly dismissed. He was articulate and thoughtful; he wrote for some of the outstanding publications of his time, held considerable status, was respected for his literary talent—was invited, in fact, by Edgar Allan Poe to become his partner in a literary magazine.[37] His forceful descriptions of events and questionable newspaper activities have the ring of truth, and when viewed in the context of press criticism throughout the nineteenth century, his statements become pivotal. Abstract and concrete themes overlap in Wilmer's criticisms, but he predominantly attributed general problems to the press.

In one area, Wilmer was behind—or at least at one with—the times. During the growing abolition controversy in the 1830s, the press was commonly charged with provoking, aiding, and abetting violent outbreaks.[38] Writing in 1859, Wilmer echoed this criticism when he charged the press with "a systematic and continuous effort to mislead the judgment of the public in relation to matters of the greatest national importance." Devoting three chapters to this issue, he focused one on the "Negro Question."[39] Accusing the press of exciting "rebellion, urging the . . . rabble" of cities to "revolutionary movements, and offering encouragement and protection to rebels and traitors, especially to those of foreign birth," he cited numerous riots and mob incidents.[40] In what would seem a related charge, he asserted that newspapers provoked "ruffianly individuals and the excitable classes" to violate laws, "causing many sanguinary duels, many disgraceful cases of assault and battery, and terrible popular commotions," which often led to "bloodshed and the destruction of much valuable property." Here, however, Wilmer focused on antagonisms among editors, with two chapters about editors' duels.[41] Although such criticisms continued until the Civil War, they virtually vanished after.

Wilmer offered another criticism reminiscent of the 1830s (although also stated by earlier critics) that was not found in works after his. Maintaining that the press was "controlled and directed" largely by "MEN OF FOREIGN BIRTH" and that many of the "most influential public journals were "Anti-American," he listed 129 foreign publications according to the ethnic background of the publisher—a list not including all those that made "*no secret* of their foreign proclivities."[42] Wilmer here echoed the general ideology associated with antiforeignism and the American Nativist movement of the 1840s.[43]

Except for the antiforeign overtones, Wilmer's elaboration on what he saw as the press's subservience to corrupt and moneyed interests parallels criticism that emerged with strength during the 1880s as the press increasingly industrialized. Charging the press with "practical hostility" to the American form of "republican government and to all free institutions," he called it the "zealous advocate and interested colleague of every form of villainy and imposture . . . , the abettor and confederate of all who defraud and plunder the people"; it enabled "such cheats and despoilers" to expand "their operations, and to carry them on with facility and impunity."[44]

Wilmer echoed a consistent theme across the century in saying that the press debased literature and retarded "the diffusion of useful knowledge" by withdrawing people's attention from "useful, salutary, and legitimate objects of study." A related concern—one rarely expressed by others—was that the press made the "intellectual character of the American people much less respectable" than it merited "in the eyes of other nations."[45] And voicing another theme, more common before 1860 than after, Wilmer said that the press fostered "immorality and vice" and was "instrumental in producing that want of sterling integrity" prevailing "among all classes."[46]

Like earlier critics who were concerned about the press's mysterious, seemingly unlimited power, and foreshadowing later discussions of abuses of that power, Wilmer charged the press with tyrannically exercising power and authority to which it had "no just pretensions," calling "its usurpation . . . a daring infringement on the rights and liberties of the American people."[47] A related criticism, which lay just below the surface in earlier discussions and rose to the fore in later decades, concerned journalists' abuse of their position. Wilmer asserted that the almost "supernatural powers attributed" to newspapers caused "much awe and apprehension among the unfortunate," who felt compelled to "submit" to all the press's requirements, "knowing or believing that an offended editor could ruin . . . their business" and reputation "merely by throwing some scandalous hint in his next issue."[48]

An important criticism not found earlier but which emerged in the 1880s and intensified over ensuing decades was that newspapers "unwarrantably" interfered "with the administration of public justice" and made it "impossible for any man charged with a criminal offense to have a fair trial."[49] Although later criticism remained confined to what became known as the free press/fair trial issue, Wilmer went much further, holding that the press had "often caused the most desperate offenders to be acquitted and turned loose on society" while, by "unwise or malicious meddling," it brought to "condemnation and punishment" many innocent persons. "Many guiltless victims of journalistic folly, prejudice, or ill-will," he wrote, were "enduring unimaginable torments of body and mind" in prisons, and "many others (more fortunate, perhaps)" had been "brought by the same detestable agencies to a shameful and agonizing death."[50]

In condemning the press's encroachment on privacy, Wilmer's expansion on a familiar theme foreshadowed the dominant postwar criticism. Linked with the issue of privacy was Wilmer's condemnation of what later became formulated as violations of taste and good judgment. The press invaded "the sanctuary of private life," disturbed the "peace of families," extensively circulated "groundless and malicious slanders," calumniated the "worthiest and most honorable men and the purest and most innocent women," drove many to "phrenzy and desperation," and made them "in reality as vile and worthless" as represented "by their malignant and remorseless slanderers."[51]

In two areas Wilmer was ahead of his time, charging the press with purveying fraudulent and questionable advertising, and with accepting what came to be called "junkets" and "freebees." These criticisms, rare before the publication of Wilmer's book, received little attention until the turn of the century. The press was "accessory to thousands of murders every year," Wilmer wrote, "by assisting quack doctors or 'patent-medicine men' to make extensive sales of their pernicious compounds."[52] Regarding junkets and freebees, he likened journalists to a monarchy with special "prerogatives"; the "newspaper sovereigns" had "free admission to all the theatres, opera houses, hippodromes, monkey-shows, picture galleries, dioramas, living crocodile exhibitions, etc. free passages over railroads and in steamboats, free access to the bars and hotels, wine and liquor stores and lager-beer saloons, and untaxed admission to the tables of sixpenny coffee-houses and shilling refectories. . . ."[53]

Emphasized differently by later critics, Wilmer's views of partisanism paralleled more nearly those of his predecessors—although none had stated them as he did. He charged that the press encouraged and promoted "official corruption and malfeasance"; used its "influence to secure the election or appointment of bad and irresponsible men to important political stations"; persuaded people to submit quietly to the extortions and oppressions . . . incidental to all governments . . . administered by agents without honesty or responsibility."[54]

Other Critics' Views

Other critics of this era generalized less about the harm done to society by the press than had earlier critics, but when they did discuss it, the familiar themes of lowered social morality and danger to women and youth recurred. And some expanded this theme to say that the press lessened the ability to reason. But increasingly, critics emphasized partisanism, journalistic corruption, and editors' powers. These general criticisms directly link the highest-level abstractions—as reflected in the above views of press functions—to the specific press abuses discussed in the next chapter.

Effects on Morality (or the Social Fabric)

As the older assumption of the press's influence gradually evolved from moralism to secularism, the older criticism of the press as detrimental to morality evolved into a view of the press as detrimental to the "social fabric." And the same concepts that underlay criticism of the press's harm to morality underlay later condemnations of the press for sensationalism, trivialization, and bad taste.

In his lyceum lecture in 1856, Lunt castigated the press in the general terms of earlier criticism, although his statements often read like those of Wilmer and implied criticisms that had not yet fully emerged. A portion of the press was, he declared, responsible for "vast mischiefs"; it had fanned "feverish excitements . . . leading to daily disorders in the body politic and social," poisoned the "minds of the young," destroyed "the peace of families," polluted "the purity of life," sent currents of "a flippant, mocking, disbelieving spirit" through the community, and "set at naught" the "authority of wisdom, virtue and experience." Newspapers did not "meet the . . . demands . . . of the times" if they were intended to be read "as mere matters of amusement, . . . to occupy only . . . idle hours"—if indeed there were idle hours in "this modern, busy, bustling world of ever-existing and constantly-growing responsibilities."[55]

Effects on Youth and Women

Criticism of the press for corrupting youth and women continued until the end of the century. In 1864, Holden also seemed closer to earlier than to later critics as he dwelt on crime reporting and its effect on women and youth, emphasizing the "multiplied capacity" for harm in newspapers' vast increase. "These winged messengers light down in every nook and thoroughfare, by-way and high-way—read and reread, by youth and age, matron and maiden, the innocent and the impure! . . . How are the young instructed and brutalized, till their modesty and purity are clean gone forever!" The young were vulnerable, and the press had power to channel that vulnerability. Youth had a strong desire for "the light and frivolous" instead of "the more solid and useful," and the press had significant power to control these "false and hurtful tastes." Youth, "whose culture" had been "neglected," who congregated "mainly in cities or large towns" and lived "only for the present," formed a "great inflammable mass" that was "set on fire by the licentious pictures of seducers and bravos, and pirates,—if they but be dressed in that splendid setting, whose forte" it was "for some so winningly to do."[56]

Concern about the press's effect on youth and women received less expression as the years passed, although the theme was revived in the 1870s and 1880s, coinciding with a surge of sentiment identified with the Victorian era. But as perceptions of press functions evolved, such criticisms increasingly met arguments about the press's positive effects on youth and women. W. T. Harris, for example, responding to the fear that "evil communications corrupt" and "descriptions of sin and crime" would "harden the heart and blunt sensibilities," argued that young people should not be shielded from newspaper content. "They must be gradually inured to contact with the world," and under "no conceivable circumstances" could "the young girl learn to know" the real world "in a safer mode than through . . . the daily newspaper." "The girl or the boy that grows up in our day and generation without free access to the newspapers certainly will miss the most important instrumentality for self-knowledge and for knowledge of mankind."[57]

Crime Reporting

Holden also criticized news of crimes in a manner similar to that of his predecessors. Whereas earlier critics rarely specified the "evils" crime news brought, however, Holden maintained that it pandered to low taste, deterred people from reading better material, created sympathy for criminals, and inspired imitators. Readers' curiosity about the "wonderful and marvelous," their "thirst for the terrible in some shape," was "partly an acquired appetite," and they read "particulars of a trial for *murder*" much more avidly than "all the great things" written about their country that they needed to understand to "become worthy [of] the exalted privileges" they were "striving to preserve!" All communities had people who shunned crime because it was disgraceful, but they also had many vulnerable "creatures of imitation." When crime was made familiar to them, its "odium" taken away and "its perpetrator" made into a "hero," "this class of imitators" was "well on the downward road," Holden argued, adding, "The tenderness of the human heart should never be allowed to exercise its sympathies to render the law inefficient."[58]

After the war, some who discussed crime coverage emphasized the distorted view it gave readers rather than that it generated crime; still others defended it. Augustus Levey argued in 1886 that the "daily diet of detailed accounts of all crimes" produced false views of morality and social obligations and an effect equivalent to that created should an editor devote space to "detailed narratives of every case of hydrophobia . . . in the world." Readers would find it "extremely difficult," he wrote, "to escape the conclusion that this was one of the most frequent occurrences. . . ." Any inferences based on "these collections of abnormal and exaggerated instances . . . naturally" tended to "involve readers in repeated errors of insufficient generalization. . . ."[59]

Although a few defended crime reporting in isolated instances before 1850, the criticisms far outweighed the defenses until after the Civil War.[60] In 1866 Parton argued that publicity was the best means of combating crime and other social ills, and by 1888 a fairly sustained defense of crime news was perhaps best epitomized by Dana's statement that he was "not too proud to report" "whatever the Divine Providence permitted to occur."[61]

Effects on General Knowledge

Another criticism of the press's effect on society was that it retarded the growth of knowledge. The press, Lunt argued in 1856, lowered "the standard of human knowledge" through "a constant and frittering process of intellectual amalgamation" in which "the relations . . . become . . . confused between the half-thinker or shallow thinker" and the gifted and inspired mind. As a result, "charlatans, sciolists and smatterers" gained "mastery of affairs," and "vain and empty pretension" became "the rule and standard. . . ."[62]

Lunt especially emphasized that the press lowered thinking ability. Bad newspapers, he said, had corrupted "the popular mind," demeaned public sentiment, diluted public taste, weakened public judgment, and substituted "themselves . . . for higher and better sources of knowledge," conditioning people to "rely on the crude, . . . flimsy, . . . irresponsible speculations of a veiled, . . . mysteriously effective agency" instead of the "old, sound, manly sense of the individual" who investigated and reflected on facts and arrived at conclusions through "a process of hard thought." What person would "take the trouble of thinking," he asked, when newspaper editors were "paid for doing this tedious business in his behalf?" Thus, Lunt argued, the individual was lured from the "exercise of his own powers." He learned "to distrust a judgment" he did not use and became "the puppet of others"—probably no more qualified than he—who played with his opinions, loosened "the hold of his social and personal obligations," generally modified his thoughts, molded "his sentiments," formed his character, and left him an unthinking, "artificial and superficial man." Too often, newspapers converted a reader into "one of those feeble and wavering creatures" who were "swayed by the weakest impulses and . . . in-

sensible to the highest duties of manhood and citizenship and religion. . . ."
He continued:

If we rely upon newspapers instead of thinking for ourselves, we have really
constituted a numerous body of public instructors, leading public sentiment,
moulding public morals, formerly public and private character, effecting great
changes in our social condition, working to some end, . . . undermining . . . if
. . . not strengthening, the foundations of our civil rights.[63]

Lunt called "the busiest men . . . who read all the newspapers" an "inter-
mingled mass of eager, moving, wavering, puzzled beings . . . of unsettled
thoughts and indecisive minds" who lived in a "blaze" that only dazzled
and bewildered them; they learned little of "true and sober knowledge";
rather, they drank "intoxicating draughts from every shallow rivulet" that
trickled or stagnated "on their way." For his part he would rather rely on
"the plain, thinking, self-schooled philosophic nature" of people who lived
where the daily press scarcely shed "its pervading beams." Although he
did not believe that the human mind had "absolutely dwindled," as the
"criterion of the newspapers" might lead people to believe, he asserted
that a "false and vicious standard of things" had "tended very much to the
obscurity of . . . mental vision. . . ."[64]

Although attributing to the press a long-term effect of lowering reasoning abilities, Lunt argued that its immediate effect in transmitting
knowledge was transitory. Reading newspapers "for casual and tempo-
rary amusement" seldom produced anything that remained in the mind.
The contents made "but a very slight impression," and one would "be
at a loss" after a moment to recall anything read. Furthermore, what a
reader had learned "towards the advancement of his intellectual and moral
nature" might be little more than a blank. What "distinct idea" remained,
Lunt asked, "of that rapid succession of incident, and of those intermit-
tent flashes of speculation, which played rather upon the eye, than ranged
. . . intelligently before his understanding?" "The interest" was "transient,
and . . . gone"; what results were there today and tomorrow of "this eager
inquiry after knowledge?"[65]

Thirty years later some writers agreed with Lunt, suggesting little change
in this issue over three decades. Levey wrote in 1886 of the effect of
newspaper reading as "infinitely more detrimental in its permanent" than
immediate results because it created an "indisposition and distaste." The
newspaper-reading habit had become "nearly fatal" to the acquisition of "a

correct literary taste or the formation of sound habits of thought." Levey argued that the "mental inertia caused by continued supplies of ready-made opinions" deprived the mind of "essential material" because the brain became merely a "depository" where nothing valuable was put.[66]

By the late 1880s the common concern about partisanism had merged with that of the press's detrimental effect on knowledge; for readers' reliance on editors' views stemmed, at least in part, from seeking to learn a favored party's positions. Obviously, however, concern about partisanism comprised both concrete and abstract issues. On a general level, critics deplored the press's poor performance, when directed by partisan interests, of an essential role in democracy; on a more specific level, they assailed its lack of truth and accuracy so long as it served parties.

Partisanism

This concern about partisanism permeated criticism until the issues of privacy and sensationalism overshadowed it late in the century. Critics in the first half of the century had suggested that a partisan press could not serve the public as well as a nonpartisan one—and, indeed, the penny press stands as testament to this belief. After 1850, individuals increasingly grappled with the meaning of an independent versus a political press. But steeped in the partisan tradition, they struggled to conceive of a press divorced from politics. Some argued that newspapers should be free of political affiliation; others later held that they should be free of *any* affiliation. In the meantime, various writers debated the opinion versus news functions of journalism, with some arguing that editorials should be eliminated whereas others, believing that newspapers had to be political, tried to justify that role.

Bowles, a leading advocate of an independent press, wrote in 1855 that it was "fast supplanting the merely partisan press," and that a "merely party organ" had become "a thing despised and condemned" and could "never take rank as a first class public journal. . . ." He vowed that the *Springfield Republican* would not be a party organ, "blindly following the will of the party," because it had "its principles and purposes."[67] The partisan press existed on unsound premises, and he believed that widespread education would end it. In an editorial published in 1858 pronouncing that the partisan press was "happily" vanishing in America "in proportion to the increase of popular intelligence," Bowles predicted a time when "these instrumentalities of a partial and one-sided civilization" would be unknown. People were rapidly realizing that the partisan paper could not be honest: "under the stress of a constant temptation to suppress" facts unflattering to its party and to exaggerate those favoring it, a paper might adequately report "the small news . . . —the murders, fires and accidents" —but everyone expected it to distort, falsify, invent, or color reports of political events; thus, even a party newspaper's "partial truth" had "the effect of falsehood." Unable to survive on people's support, the partisan press relied on government, a dependence Bowles called "dishonorable in itself and bad in its influence." Such a newspaper was "no more expected to give a true account of political affairs" than an attorney was "expected to give the jury a truthful and just exposition of the facts. . . ." A special plea, "for a consideration," was made in both cases, and the only basis for success was "the ignorance of a portion of the jury."[68]

But partisanism did not die. In editorials in 1868, 1869, 1870, and 1880, Godkin especially harped on it. In 1868, stressing the necessity of public debate and the press's crucial role in it, he wrote of partisanism's harm to the polity:

If . . . newspapers only present . . . one side . . . , a "snap judgment" may be taken, and an appearance of popular approval be secured for the time being for anything the "leaders" like to bring forward. But the public does not remain long content with this half-knowledge. The question is gradually turned round, and the other side is revealed . . . by reflection, . . . fresh light or . . . experiment in legislation. Then come distrust, dissatisfaction, disgust, and reaction.[69]

Continuing this argument in 1880, Godkin asserted that "traditions of party fealty and advocacy"—"too strong to be overthrown"—still dominated newspapers. Considering the public's growing dependence on newspapers for everything it knew, this was "a very serious state of things." Newspapers provided no intelligent person with information necessary for forming "a rational judgment" about, for example, political feeling in the North or the "prospects of the opposing Presidential candidates." A foreigner reading the papers would "never imagine that the collection of news— . . . the description of facts just as they occur"—was one of the nation's largest businesses, that "tens of millions of capital were invested in it, and probably more ardent, unremitting industry ostensibly devoted to it than to any other money-making calling."[70]

Newspapers fulfilled "the function of newsgathering fairly enough" when reporting nonpolitical events—murders, fires, collisions, boat-races,

elopements, floods, pestilence, or foreign war—but they failed in informing the public about issues. All newspapers, Godkin wrote, reported hard
news pretty much in the same way, with differences only in degree of accuracy or literary quality. But he worried about issues the public must
consider to arrive at decisions. Community opinion about nonpolitical
events prompted no organized action and thus had little significance. Error
"based on sheer delusion," however, would be far-reaching, he warned,
when half the nation, having reached some understanding about politics
based on knowledge of legislation and social conditions, decided on some
course of action.[71] Bowles too believed that the press's subservience to
parties deterred it from issues. In a letter to a friend during post–Civil War
reform efforts, he touched a theme that grew stronger in the next decade:

The press really seems to be the best, if the only instrument, with which honest
men can fight these enemies of order and integrity in government. . . . American journalism is now but in its infancy; but we have more to fear at present
from its good nature, . . . its subserviency, . . . its indifference, . . . its fear to
encounter prosecution and loss of patronage by the exposure of the wrong and
the exposition of the right.[72]

In 1886 Levey contended that, because of partisanism, no controversy
could be "readily discussed in newspapers." "Editorial polemics," he wrote,
"always distort and exaggerate" and lead to opinions divided into "those
who think as we and our newspaper do—the true believers"—and "those
who think as does the newspaper we do not read—the heretics." But it
was the public that was primarily at fault because it expected newspapers
to agree with it. The editor produced, "at the worst," "exaggerated expressions," illiberality, and "*ex-cathedra* assumptions of infallibility." Because
people read only those newspapers with whose editorial views they agreed,
their conversations revealed "the weak filtering through a feeble brain of
the recollections of the contents of a favorite journal." And this effect of
"education by newspaper" showed "the secret of the superficial dogmatism
of the age," for those "respectable, dull, worthy people" gave "modern
society its tone."[73]

Despite arguments against partisanism, many critics nevertheless betrayed beliefs that it inhered in press functions. Those who did not forthrightly condemn partisanism as incompatible with journalism tried either
to justify it or to explain how a partisan editor could be a moral journalist.
O. B. Frothingham, who in 1884 attempted to defend a political press,
stressed that political discussion was essential in a democracy and that

newspapers had to take positions on issues to assure debate. "Informing the general mind about [politics,] scrutinizing candidates, testing questions, and estimating issues" was of utmost importance. Major discussions were continual, with the merits and demerits of causes portrayed, proportions of phenomena ascertained, and absolute principles brought out "in the course of debate." These discussions affected the higher education of the general community, and every "considerable paper" was "obliged to have political sympathies" and "undertake political advocacy." The constant political debate served to enlighten the public mind, purify the "general conscience," and raise the "standard of equity" and the "level of truth," and journalists were largely responsible for all this.[74]

Conceding, however, that the "necessity of paying attention to local politics" jeopardized journalistic morality, Frothingham distinguished between "the ideal and the more practical profession." The ideal, he wrote, stood upon principle, whereas the practical profession stood upon policy. He seemed to place journalism in the "practical" (policy) category and asserted that any "calling," as soon as it left "principle for policy," risked "moral depreciation."[75]

Critics simply did not resolve the partisanism issue, and numerous instances reveal the ambiguities of thought about it. Addressing the Minnesota Editorial Association in 1888 on principles of ethics, George Lanphere, editor of the *Moorhead News*, said, "The fact is, a newspaper does not amount to anything politically unless it is partisan," but he added that not every editor need be partisan.[76] A college lecture by Dana in 1893 suggests that the line between political and news functions remained blurred. Dana called Horace Greeley—a thoroughgoing partisan—his "great exemplar in journalism" and told those seeking a career in journalism that "to be of importance" in world affairs in the newspaper profession, "you must be a politician, and you must know not merely the theories and doctrines of parties, not merely the recondite part of politics, but you must know practical politics, . . . the individuals, their ideas, their purposes, and their deeds. . . ."[77]

Press Corruption and Editors' Powers

In the 1880s, criticism turned to journalistic corruption beyond partisanism—newspapers serving political machines and monopolies, for example—although critics believed journalists had ridden into these on party coattails. In 1869, Richard Grant White foreshadowed this shift, revealing what some seemed to think had been journalism's path into subjection to "moneyed" interests.

White asked whether the effusive homage paid an editor was not more because of "a desire to use or to placate the paper" than a respect for the man. He cited instances in which editors had been appointed to committees or positions so that either their papers would not attack or their influence might be gained in promoting "some business or project." This reflected a "certain ruffianism," he maintained, referring to journalists who said by deeds, if not by words:

Serve me, work with me, and I praise you; know me, treat me with consideration, and I compliment you. Oppose me, refuse me your advertisement, or the support of your name for this or that office, and I denounce you; keep aloof from me and fail to treat me with consideration, and I sneer and scoff at you and do all I can to drag you down to my level.[78]

A dozen years later, in 1882, George Rider contended that party organizations had shifted from "principles and measures" to "men and spoils." Journalism, he wrote, had become the "voice and echo of party—the veriest slave of the Ring" (what he called "that leprous excrescence of modern municipalities"), so that it no longer provided "patient, lucid discussion of underlying principles." People could no longer find "direction in the tangled issues of the day" because of the press's growing "insincerity and duplicity." In "subjection to cliques of traders and manufacturers, and rings of stock-gamblers and monopolists," journalism could not "rise higher than its fountain-springs of subsistence." How, he asked, could journalism, while remaining "lawful thrall and property of 'ring,' clique, 'corner,' or monopolist," "expose and denounce the sly tricks of spoliation of directors and monopolist-officials, in the plunder and dilution of stocks" that were the people's property; in "the perversion and defiance of legislation, in the violation of characters, in the unsettling and destruction of values by 'corners' and 'combinations'—ghoull-like tampering with food and fuel between producer and consumer?"[79]

Clearly, Rider argued, a greater power than the press had "thrust a golden ring through its nose" and was leading it, "exclusive of chattel and creature." What could it then say "bravely, or worthily, or trustfully, about anything" as long as it remained "manacled and branded as private property, or in bondage to its advertisers . . . ?" No longer dependable "as a

guide and monitor," journalism would be "shorn of all its moral dignity"
—left only with a "languishing and spasmodic influence"—until it broke
"loose from all equivocal and venal affiliations."[80]

Generally, editors were blamed for such corruption, and some said that
they had destroyed the credibility of newspapers. But critics fulminated
most forcefully about editors' power over policy, issues, and reporters.
Discussions of public opinion often fixed on journalists' power rather than
on the press per se. In 1869, for example, White wrote that the editor
of a high-circulation newspaper held one of the most influential positions
"known to modern society," for he had the public's ear; taking ten or
fifty thousand people "quietly aside in their brightest, most impressionable
mood, refreshed by rest and before they have committed themselves" to
the day's business, he could "in a quarter of an hour give their minds a
bias from which they may never recover"—a feat no other person could
accomplish. Furthermore, the editor could repeat this daily until he accomplished his purpose, in which, if he was persistent, he rarely failed,
because the power of repetition was, White insisted, supreme in journalism. To dispute with such an editor was as "indiscreet as . . . to dispute with
the commander of ten legions," for unless one had at command "other ten
legions," which meant "another leading newspaper," he would "be crushed
to earth"; although the truth he fought for might "rise again," he himself
would not. The editor, "or even the principal writers of the editorial staff
of a great paper," could "make and unmake reputations, and set men on
the road to wealth as well as to high position. . . ."[81] In the same year
Godkin also voiced this theme: editors had the "making of men's reputations in their hands," and "public happiness largely" depended "on men's
reputations."[82] In 1888 Dana said that the journalist could take a person's
mind and, without his knowing it, direct it, sending him "along a road"
he did not know and, very often, which the journalist did not know.[83]

Godkin particularly lambasted editors for being too ready to play "priest
or soothsayer for the Congressional gods," for serving the party "by treating the people as imbeciles or children," and for having no "faith in the
people." Such editors, although they professed to respect people's "decisions as conclusive," would question one's sanity for suggesting that they
"tell people the whole truth, presenting all sides, before asking for their
decision." An editor thus devoted himself to "deceiving and humbugging,"
carefully concealing facts he thought might depress readers while making
the "most of all facts . . . likely to elate them"; he pretended high spirits

when defeat was certain, prated "incessantly about 'justice' and 'the rights of man'" when law was at issue, and stood firmly on "the letter of the law" when morals were at issue. "Perhaps, most degrading of all offences" was editors' extolling favorite leaders when they made a speech or introduced a bill. In a sarcastic tone, Godkin wrote that nothing else created such an "uproar" among the "'moulders of public opinion' in this the most advanced political community in the world."[84]

In an article published in 1870, Godkin declared that the "meanest intellect" could see that an editor's interest would likely "work sad havoc among the facts scientifically collated and presented by his reporter." When presented with a careful, fact-based story pointing to conclusions contrary to his views, the editor would publish an editorial to deter people from those conclusions. The reporter then took "his cue" from the editorial and afterward would "paint in much more glowing colors the condition and prospects" of anything he saw as his editor's interest; and so it went "perpetually," with the truth irretrievably lost in efforts to make "facts and the journal's perception of them agree."[85] Godkin next raised an issue that gained increasing attention and, a century later, became the focus of a classic study in newsroom controls on what gets published.[86] Editorial opinion, he wrote, had "sudden and irresistible power" over a reporter's sensitive nature, and the latter soon learned "instinctively what to disclose, what to hide away, when to report broadly, when to hint a doubt, where openly to deny"—until he was "no longer a reporter, but a retained attorney for the prosecution of the editor's pet schemes."[87]

A paper's attitude toward politics was "settled by the editor," and reporters then either colored all news so that it supported the editor's view or collected only that which did. Calling the "Southern question" the most "striking illustration," Godkin held that Democratic editors never saw "outrages or any ballot-stuffing at the South," while Republican editors had seen these as Southern whites' "principal occupation and amusement" since the war. An editor sustained "an unanswerable argument for putting or keeping his own party in power," and a reporter sent South "to discover the real state" of affairs always found the facts that "exactly" agreed with his editor's views. Every conspicuous person "on the opposite side" was described "either as a drivelling idiot or a great scoundrel," and his speeches were either unreported or reported in a way that made them seem "an outburst of . . . wickedness or folly." The opposition's meetings were "described as wretched failures" because of poor turnout or as "a huge assembly of the criminal class, drawn together by a brass band and calcium lights and addressed in the intervals of disorder and tumult by notorious political profligates."[88]

The critics of the forty years after 1850 discussed the same basic issues as had their predecessors, but conceptions of these issues changed. Some dwindled in emphasis or evolved into others while new ones emerged, and critics in the second half of the century added greater clarity to the discussion. Critics before the Civil War glorified the press with hyperbole and awesome expectations, whereas critics after the war examined press function and how it could fulfill its "mission." This focus led them to define the uniqueness of the press, separating its functions from those of other social institutions.

Struggling to understand and define the press, they often used the words *theory* and *function,* and their discussions were dominated by press analysis. In attempting to define the functions and operation of the press, critics after 1850 also began to analyze what these meant in the press's overall effect on society. They were thus beginning to articulate the rudiments of a theory of the press. Increasingly, they also linked specific journalistic procedures with press abuses and offered solutions that had implications for journalistic standards then and later. Although they did not resolve the issue of partisanism, by the end of the 1880s there was a consensus that news and editorial views ought not to be mixed; that reporting crime served positive ends; and that editors must recognize and judiciously use their power in society's best interests. Some critics were ill at ease with newspapers that all looked alike as standardization increased. They struggled to distinguish between an unquestioned press function—providing what the public needed and had a right to know—and what some saw as the dubious function of entertainment. Newspapers more and more often manifested the latter in content that was amusing, exciting, and even thrilling to readers. Those who acknowledged entertainment as a legitimate function could not decide on an appropriate limit—that is, to what degree the press should entertain, and what were proper subjects for entertainment. That to fulfill this function the press seemed to abandon good taste, decorum, propriety, and even individual feeling complicated the issue, as will be seen in the next chapter, in which we consider the more concrete criticisms and solutions during the last half of the century.

Chapter Seven

Criticism, 1850–1889:
Specific Journalistic Conduct,
Remedies, and Standards

There is a man here named Barnard, on . . . the Supreme Court. . . . He is unscrupulous, audacious, barefaced, and corrupt to the last degree. He not only takes bribes, but he does not even wait for them to be offered him. He sends for suitors . . . and asks for the money as the price of his judgments. . . . A more unprincipled scoundrel does not breathe. Yet the press and bar are muzzled . . . and this injurious scoundrel has actually got possession of the highest court in the State. . . .

    If I were satisfied that, if the public knew all this, it would lie down under it, I would hand the Nation *over to its creditors and take myself and my children out of the community. I will not believe that yet. I am about to say all I dare say . . . in the* Nation *to-morrow. Barnard is capable of ruining us . . . and could of course imprison me for contempt . . . and I should have no redress. . . . Moreover, I have no desire either for notoriety or martyrdom, and am in various ways not well fitted to take a stand against rascality on such a scale as this. But this I do think, that it is the duty of every honest man to do something. Barnard has now got possession of the courts, and if he can silence the press also, where is reform to come from?*

    Edwin Godkin to Charles Eliot Norton, April 23, 1867

Press criticism, especially during the 1870s and 1880s, charted significant directions. The era reveals lively discussion of press conduct that at times rose to the level of debate (that is, argument of differing positions on single issues). As noted in the last chapter, critics also began to confront forthrightly the meaning of the press in society, beginning a process of thought, discussion, and activity that culminated in numerous changes in journalistic practices during the early twentieth century.[1] Implicit in the discussions were efforts to relate journalistic techniques and goals to press problems, the need for education for journalists, and (first stated by George Lunt in 1856) the need for ethics training or a code of conduct.[2] This chapter examines the themes of concrete criticism and implied journalistic standards from 1850 to 1889.

The bulk of nineteenth-century press discussion came after the Civil War. Because the press had expanded in dimension and capacities, becoming ever more pervasive, critics groped to find their way in making sense of it. While the Civil War transfixed Americans' attention, the press was transformed. Postwar discussions give the impression that people were caught off guard—as if, while they had been looking the other way, the press mushroomed into a social institution of a complexity and potency beyond the reach of conventional discourse and understanding. During the war, the U.S. economy shifted completely from an agrarian to an industrial base, and Americans' collective views of the world, their place in it, and their relationships to community, nation, and government changed. The press, too, changed dramatically. It permeated daily life, and its expanded capacities and techniques permitted it to reach far beyond any previous levels of information gathering and dispersal. Clearly, those writing of the press after the war recognized changing directions. Clearly, too, they saw an urgent need to examine and somehow bring this suddenly overgrown institution within understanding. As they struggled to fathom the press in this "new age," they wrestled with what might be appropriate boundaries of conduct. In doing so, they identified various problems—many of which remain issues today.

Themes that gained strength with succeeding decades were profit seeking, serving advertising over news functions, invasion of privacy, sensationalism, and overemphasizing the trivial or unimportant. Criticism of the profit-seeking motive coincided with the industrialization of the press. In an era that stressed business goals, and during which the press increasingly took on a corporate structure, discussions defined journalism as a business first and foremost. Terms such as "manufacturing," "product," and "commodity" in reference to news gathering and news permeated even those discussions that did not address the profit motive. The issue, however, often subtly turned from condemnation of profit seeking per se to the fact that the press *was* a business and served society as such. This led to increasing concern about advertising abuses and charges that journalists were guided primarily by profit motives. The privacy issue, latent to barely expressed in earlier criticism, took on greater clarity over earlier generalizations about the press's encroachment on firesides and came to dominate criticism during the 1880s. From the beginning, however, it was entangled with issues of sensationalism and taste. Complaints about sensationalism—a term that emerged by 1870 and was common throughout the remainder of the century—were apparent in earlier broad condemnations of the press for reporting crime, sex, violence, and gossip, and competed with the privacy issue for dominance in the criticism of the 1880s. Charges of trivialization, or that the press overemphasized the unimportant, grew out of the information model's efforts to serve the individual and inform on all aspects of life. It received strongest expression in the 1850s and evolved into charges that the press trafficked in gossip and merged, by the 1880s, with criticisms of sensationalism. Accusations that the press violated good taste, emphasized "personal journalism," and reported unnewsworthy phenomena were all part of the criticism of sensationalism. (*Personal journalism*, another term that emerged by 1870—but used differently than it is today—also became a common criticism for a time.) [3] A new criticism was that the press violated the right of the accused to a fair trial; and although not emphasized in the sources studied, charges that journalists accepted "freebees" and "junkets" also seems to have emerged after 1850. [4]

But as had their predecessors, these critics raised rather than resolved issues. They did not resolve even the oldest issue, that of partisanism—in part, perhaps, because others seemed more pressing. Among these, many of which continue to perplex media critics, were issues generally thought to have arisen later. Invasion of privacy, for example, has been dated from Samuel Warren and Louis Brandeis's article "The Right to Privacy," which was published in 1890. [5] Sensationalism has been dated—with bows to previous occasional outbursts—from William Randolph Hearst's and Joseph Pulitzer's circulation battles in the Spanish-American War era of the 1890s. [6] Post–Civil War criticism, however, reveals that concern about these issues began to build after the war and reached a near fever pitch before 1890.

Concerns about journalistic conduct in this era show that trends begun in the 1830s had reached unprecedented bounds. Expanded press capacities and journalistic techniques enabled a seemingly infinite production of what during the war had been discovered as an eminently salable commodity. The press was compelled by new drives: new sources and seemingly infinite means of news gathering produced a new level of aggressiveness in news-publishing. But ironically, the same features that had habituated people to the press also made it ever more intrusive as it capitalized on the means of reporting on lives, slices of life, and individual activities. Trends begun by the individual-oriented press of the 1830s and 1840s had, in some critics' view, gone too far. And as they grappled to understand and perhaps control the press, they mingled criticisms in the abstract with assaults on specific journalistic conduct. Throughout the latter half of the century, an array of criticisms addressed specific journalistic conduct, although often as part of treatments of the press's general effects on society. One of the oldest criticisms, the profit motive, for example, almost always moved into generalities. Newer issues, such as sensationalism, invasion of privacy, and trivialization, all of which received increasing attention after the war, were at times treated as causing society's deterioration as well as more particular harm.

The last chapter dealt primarily with the perceived functions of the press and its general effects on society. Study of press criticism of the last half of the century, however, led to classification of several issues as more specific and concrete; the profit motive, trivialization, invasion of privacy, journalists' abilities, journalistic practices and techniques, sensationalism, and free press/fair trial. The following focuses first on these; the second section considers standards emerging from the criticism; and the final section addresses remedies specified or implied by critics.

The Profit Motive

George Lunt in 1856 and Edwin Godkin in 1869 condemned the profit motive as ultimately injurious to the whole society. Although repeatedly vowing that many good newspapers existed, Lunt wrote that a "mighty swarm" was "issued solely upon the selfish consideration of pecuniary advantage,—ready to tamper with any principle,—prompt to listen to any scandal, glad to sell mischief and abuse by the square,—eager to bargain, either to apply or withhold a venal praise." He primarily blamed public toleration, but argued that

nothing can be so effectual, as a corrupt and subservient press, to foster its unspiritual habitudes, and to pander profitably to appetites, which grow by what they feed on,—until the unwholesome leaven has finally worked itself into all the constituent elements of the incorporated mass,—and cause and consequence begin to act interchangeably . . . , and the things which once were real become . . . little better than shadows, and those which we once sought for our blessings are now our bane, and the names of former glory are but a mockery and a reproach, and virtue, truth, honor and religion,—the dignity of learning and the incitements to manly enterprise,—the grace, the charm and the ornament of life,—the aims, the ends and the means of knowledge,—all sink together into one common abyss of degradation, ignominy and ruin.[7]

Thirteen years later, Godkin wrote that if people of "other callings" operated as did some newspeople, "solely with reference to profits," "civilized society could not hold together." What maintained human progress and made the world "fit for intelligent beings" was that most people recognized that they owed their country, their "kind," and themselves something; that they had "not done their whole duty" by making a fortune; that civilization was entitled to their contribution, and the smallest an individual could make was "to be a better, honester, and more high-minded and scrupulous man than the criminal code" required—or his "pecuniary interest" alone would tempt him to be.[8] The same year, Richard Grant White wrote that journalism seemed to "have its full share of the gross, loose, money-seeking spirit of the day" that had "corrupted . . . legislative bodies and . . . courts." Journalists too often spoke "not from conviction, but for a consideration," which might be an office, an advertisement, the "bringing of a certain interest into the clientage of the paper," "gratifying an ancient grudge," "creation of a profitable sensation, or the desire, praiseworthy in itself, to help a friend." But whatever it might be, the result was "a violation . . . of good faith, a taint . . . of professional dishonor." Accepting money for a newspaper's influence was "the lowest . . . of editorial degradations," "a coarse and grovelling form of corruption."[9]

The earlier defense that newspapers had to cater to low taste to succeed was very common by the 1880s, but critics after 1850 increasingly challenged it. Joseph Bishop, responding in 1885 to the claim that editors simply gave readers what they wanted, argued that if journalism was only publishing whatever paid, the profession had become "the lowest of human callings—lower than brothel-keeping or liquor-selling" because these didn't presume to respectability, whereas journalists posed as guides and teachers of the public. "If a newspaper can do anything that pays, then journalism becomes . . . the only [profession] whose members, tacitly at least, admit that in their professional conduct they are not 'governed by the same principles . . . a gentleman follows in his personal conduct.'" The journalist who peddled "moral precepts with one hand and scandal, vulgar gossip, and family secrets with the other" presented a "most revolting" "spectacle." To argue that one must sell such news because people wanted it was the same justification for selling obscene books and pictures—and laws governed those.[10]

Charges that advertising heightened and fed the profit motive became common after the war. White called the advertisement desk "the most insidious to the fair fame of journalism." Newspapers had adopted the system of selling too cheaply to profit from circulation, "which, from a business point of view," had value only in making the paper a "more desirable medium of advertising," to which publishers looked for profit. Advertising's influence resulted in great corruption of journalism, but journalists alone were not to blame. If people advertised on condition that editors publish favorable comments about their wares, or if they withdrew advertising because they disapproved of the paper's position on an issue, they could only expect "their demand" to "cause a supply" of the kind of journalist whose opinions and endorsements might not be trustworthy or disinterested.[11] Eighteen years later, in 1887, Dion Boucicault also saw advertising as the chief source of press problems:

When it was apparent that the revenue arising from this source was enormous, the newspaper attracted the attention of capital as an important investment, and it soon became a commercial enterprise to which all other considerations were subordinated. The only business of the newspaper proprietor was to increase its circulations by any means, for on its circulation depended the value and number of its advertisements. In this sordid struggle the editor and his staff were instructed by the proprietor to pander to the degraded appetites of the reader. The most unsavory details of crime and domestic misfortunes were paraded in conspicuous fashion; the literary and moral standard was hauled down to give place to these flags of abomination. Its emissaries were sent into the houses of private citizens to obtain the offal of society—the filthier the better. It became a ragpicker when the nation was engaged in any great political struggle. The journal shielding itself behind its impersonality and the cry of 'the liberty of the press' would hurl accusations of the most infamous character against its opponents, to the sacrifice of all dignity, conscience, and truth. It carried the craft of misrepresentation to the level of a fine art. This was the work of the commercial proprietor of the newspaper. . . . The journalist became his hired scribe, who waited on his will.[12]

Trivialization

One of the penny press's achievements, some historians have argued, was recognition of ordinary people. As noted earlier, Mott has said that it gave attention to people who were interesting merely as human beings.[13] Although Bowles lauded this development as a great social benefit because it spurred people to improvement and brought progress, many critics after 1850 argued that the press squandered its efforts on trivialities.[14]

Calling the press a "self-constituted image-maker" that daily set up objects of "brass and clay" for adoration, Lunt enumerated a veritable catalog of the sins of trivialized news. He asserted that the press was "too ready" to "lavish printed praises" on people unfit for public distinction; it made heroes and geniuses of ordinary people, creating so many wonders as to reverse human nature, and insulting society by suggesting that such average individuals were its rarities; journalists sought in everyday activities things to exalt, publicly flattering people for nothing more than fulfilling the responsibilities of their jobs. Such journalism only fostered "idle vanity"; stimulated "ill-founded ambition," "petty jealousies," and "bad blood"; discouraged good sense; injured unpretentious effort; perverted truth; undermined praise by making it common; created a petty standard of public estimation; and blurred distinctions between excellence and mediocrity. At the same time, a spirit of detraction led the "press flippantly to arraign and improvidently to misjudge men of more than common mark,—to undervalue their abilities, . . . slur over their virtues, . . . gloat at . . . their failings, . . . molest their lives and despoil even their graves of the . . . sanctity of repose."[15]

Godkin branded the "sedulous and persistent puffing and exaltation of feeble, ignorant, or worthless and naturally obscure persons" as "just as great an offence against the common-weal as the persistent villifying and belittling of really able and good men." To bestow praise on "unworthy objects" defrauded the public because it enabled people of "no ability or character" to appear fit for and attain "places of honor and emolument"; it endowed their opinions and wishes with a respect—or their wares with a demand—they didn't deserve; and it perverted popular judgment and deprived people "of real value of their proper place in the public estimation."[16]

Six months after Godkin's article appeared in 1869, White singled out the press's bringing "unimportant persons to public notice" as harmful to both the community and the profession, for this misled most people—who would know such persons only through the newspapers—into thinking them important. White condemned this perversion of journalism, the use of the power of the press to reverse its "proper influence"; newspaper mention of someone "in connection with public affairs" lent a "certain importance" or "notoriety"—which a person could seek out and use to further his own ulterior aims.[17]

By the 1880s, such criticism evolved into charges that the press indulged in trivial incidents and "gossip." White again had earlier epitomized the shift, emphasizing that journalism, without decency, descended "into a kind of intellectual debauchery," stimulating and gratifying "a prurient curiosity by giving the dignity and permanence of print" to what was at best the "idle gossip of the hour, or at worst its stinging . . . or . . . injurious slander."[18] Little more than a decade later, George Rider condemned journalists for "an inordinate hunger and thirst for gossip" that threatened to create "a nation of gossips."

Trifles, trivialities, and tattle, like the plague of locusts and grasshoppers, swarm through the columns . . . and the more commanding and lordly the journal, the stronger and steadier the pressure of gossip. . . . the insufferable particulars of back-doors and farm-yards, the monstrous calf, the inevitable coming and going of the innumerable nobodies, the raiding of a melon-patch or a dozen silver spoons—all are industriously woven into the diurnal web of "local items" . . . and served up to the omnivorous people.[19]

Such gossip filled "a full third" of all America's newspapers, Rider noted, lamenting the waste and frustration for busy people who had to hunt through it to find useful, legitimate news.[20]

Invasion of Privacy

After the Civil War the issue of violating private life often became muddled with concerns about distortions and what came to be called sensationalism. Struggling to articulate what should not be published, critics tried to state what it was the public's business to know. Hence, in defining the public's business, they often lumped together all that was not, without distinguishing between what they saw as too private, too offensive, or too insignificant or trivial for publication. Lunt's criticism typifies the generalizations about protecting family and fireside that prevailed through the earliest decades. By contrast, Godkin's remarks are more concrete, exemplifying criticism style and the tendency to run various complaints together in the later decades.

Newspapers exposed too much of people's lives, Lunt argued in 1856, so that people lived "abroad, instead of at home"—which he called "the sole fountainhead of all reliable virtue." The "privacy of life" became "converted into an open spectacle," with details unfit for firesides and "malicious discussions of character, such as no private assembly of respectable men and women would countenance," printed daily "for the amusement and to the peril of the injudicious and unthinking."[21]

Fourteen years later, Godkin emphasized that journalists must have "perspective" to know the difference between public and nonpublic business, mixing the issue of what was considered too offensive to good taste for news coverage with those of the invasion of privacy and distortion. Some journalists, Godkin said, seemed to consider distortion of perspective "their charter of success," citing the trial of one man for assault and battery after he pulled another's nose during an argument on a train. The press made a "*cause célèbre*" of a "strictly private affair" of no concern to the public. The "journalistic instructors of mankind" painted the "trivial affair" as "another episode in the long battle between tyranny and liberty." Prosecution became a "manly blow struck for the right," the victim became a martyr, and the nose-puller's assault—because he was "a Beacon Street aristocrat"—became an attempt to "establish caste." Reading the Boston papers, Godkin wrote, would lead one to believe that "New England was on the eve of a social uprising." A worse distortion of news perspective, however, concerned a Mrs. McFarland-Richardson, who "was plunged in the deepest affliction by events of which everybody had been informed." A reporter who failed when sent to see her to report "her condition and feelings" sought others to interview instead. Remembering stories of "matrimonial difficulties" between a Mr. Fisk, who lived in New York, "and Mrs. Fisk, who lived in Boston," the reporter interviewed Mrs. Fisk "on her relations with her husband"—and next day, "as usual, the public" was "regaled with full particulars. . . ."[22]

But the "most astounding illustration" of a lack of "sense of moral and intellectual perspective in the very class whose business" was to report the day's events "in their true relations to other events" concerned an "obscure" Methodist minister who had left his wife and family to elope with an "unknown school-girl." "A case can hardly be imagined in which the public have as little interest as this, to say nothing of the exquisite cruelty to the families involved in publicity." But the story was "raked out in all its disgusting details," the minister's history was given, the causes that "led to his sin" were analyzed, and the country was "scoured for *memoires pour servir*." The minister publicized his position and assaulted an editor; the reporter interviewed his wife "about *her* feelings. . . ." Thus, a "petty scandal swells to . . . a public calamity." Godkin concluded, "What an odd condition the editorial eye must be in when metropolitan papers have come to this!"[23]

The 1880s brought a spate of articles condemning the press for invasion of privacy. Although more clearly stated than it had been, this criticism remained integrated with denunciation of what came to be called sensationalism. Criticism of newspaper coverage of, for example, President Garfield's illness, funerals, and "hanging days" included as many (or more) references to outright sensationalism as invasions of privacy.

In 1882, Rider criticized the "hungry eyes" of journalists, which peered "into private houses," studied "banquets, halls, teas," read the "tempting *menus* by this great caterer," criticized the "decorations by that crack florist," noted the "brands of champagne," and audited the "very sum-total of the outlay. . . ." He condemned the press for its "insolence and dogmatism" while President Garfield's life was "in hourly suspense." Journalism

crept into the sick man's chamber, . . . the memorable Long Branch train, . . . the seaside cottage, . . . the councils of attending surgeons; buttonholed nurses, servants, apothecaries; followed probings, incisions, dressings and prescriptions, with oracular comment and unabashed dogmatism, until it almost came to appear that journalism . . . , under different conditions, might have rescued the heroic sufferer.[24]

Journalism "kept at its effrontery and pretension" until the end—ignoring renowned surgeons and science—with "perpetual diagnosis and prognosis, . . . bulletins and decisions—a long drawn-out torment and aggravation to the suffering people, a scandal and offense to the medical profession at home and abroad."[25]

Four years later, William H. Bushnell's words seemed much like those of critics before 1850, except that Bushnell gave examples of what he considered matters too private to be addressed by journalists. He nostalgically recalled a time when the "hearth of home was hedged about with as much of divinity as ever mythically surrounded a king"; when young love could "breathe vows unmolested"; when only moon, star, and breeze knew "the blushes of modesty"; when marriage was not "fulsomely paraded in type"; when death was viewed with "awe and regarded as holy from outside inter-meddling"; when "curious . . . prying eyes were not turned upon tearful faces, sobbing breasts and broken hearts."

But such "tenderness and respect" had been "sadly outlived."[26] De-nouncing "the audacity of news gatherers" for bribing servants to "worm out family secrets," Bushnell wrote that "engagements between young people" were viewed as "public property," and that the bride's wardrobe "might as well be aired to the public gaze on a clothes line in the open street." Newspapers described and criticized even "the most concealed of her garments": "the number of tucks" was counted, "the lace patterned," and "to the fraction the size of her corset, and length, color, fineness and cost of her hose" assessed. Wedding bells were "made to proclaim, as from housetops, every phase of the ceremony and a messenger, swift as Mer-cury, and with eyes as sharp as one of the Furies," followed "from church to hotel" and could "scarcely be shut out from the bedchamber." Funer-als were turned into "gala occasions"; "corpse, shroud, flowers, mourn-ers" were treated as "legitimate plunder," and the "procession dogged, inspected and described" up to the instant that dirt covered the coffin.[27]

"The law, as laid down by Sir Edward Coke," that a man's home was his castle, had become a "mockery," Bushnell wrote, as "morbid curiosity" and "eager and impertinent desire" intruded on table and fireside. The en-terprising journalist pried out the "most minute skeleton hidden in closet or . . . beneath hearthstone" and hung it up to public gaze. Walls of houses seemed to have been "turned into telephones" with bells connected to newspaper offices. "One might about as well live with open doors and windows, or have repeating speaking tubes leading from every room into the street," for nothing escaped the "ubiquitous reporter," and his "fertile imagination" magnified "the most minute and innocent mole-hills into the most lofty and disreputable of mountains." Bushnell asserted that "stealing one's good name" was "as much, aye, more of robbery, than the felonious abstracting of his purse from his pocket," and "breaking into his private chamber for personal gossip a more nefarious burglary than plundering money drawer or iron chest." The "dearest of all earthly treasures" were the "fair name, reputation and virtue of wife and daughter"—which, "once tarnished," could "never be restored."[28]

Also in 1886, Joseph Bishop, after giving several examples of what he labeled equally "flagrant" intrusions on private rights, attacked the "extraordinary course" of newspapers regarding coverage of President Grover Cleveland's recent marriage. Calling attention to the "intolerable lengths" of "the modern system of newspaper espionage," Bishop asserted that the "subject of newspaper conduct" had never been "more pressing." This kind of surveillance was "the supreme demonstration of the resources of a system" that had "been growing steadily" over several years and which saw the president's marriage as "an opportunity to lift itself into national prominence."[29]

After failing to confirm weeks-old rumors that the president intended to marry, reporters pursued his—and his "suspected *fiancée*'s"—relatives, "scouring the country to find them and using every effort to get them to talk." After the fiancée was identified and located in Paris, "spies" were hired via cable to "discover everything . . . possible about her and her plans and daily occupations." When these efforts failed, false stories about her activities and "every bit of gossip, however trivial or impertinent, which could be found or invented about the lady and her family, or about her relations with the President," were "eagerly published." News of her intended return roused "the detective instinct of the press" to "unprecedented activity." One newspaper "distanced all others . . . by interviewing the steward or some other employee of the steamer . . . , obtaining a minute account of everything she had done or said in public upon every day of her voyage"; no smile "or even nod of the head was missed." The press then set up watch at her hotel, publishing every fact—including when the lights went out in her room, how the president greeted her when he visited, and the precise time of his arrivals and departures from her hotel room. "Press detectives" followed the bride to Washington for her wedding, subjecting her and the president's sister "to personal descriptions," some of which, Bishop charged, surpassed in "vulgar impertinence" anything ever published, and outdid any "previous detective exertions."[30]

Although Cleveland had announced that the wedding ceremony would be private because of a death in the bride's family, reporters "insisted upon treating the request for privacy as an incentive for increased activity,"

Bishop complained. Especially distasteful was journalists' pursuit of the honeymooning couple. Bishop included an excerpt from one account that proudly described how reporters had thwarted efforts to keep the honeymoon site secret:

Rumors of the President's intention to leave Washington with his bride were sifted so thoroughly on the wedding-day that before the ceremony . . . probably a dozen reporters . . . believed he was to go to Deer Park. . . . From early . . . evening . . . the White House grounds were picketed, and pickets were employed . . . on the streets, avenues, and roads for half a mile or more beyond the grounds. The President couldn't have escaped undetected, and there was a small troop of saddle-horses and carriages at the call of the pickets, to follow wherever he might lead. In the afternoon men were seen working on an awning and steps at the rear of the White House. This indicated the means of exit for the bridal pair. . . . [T]wo reporters saw the President's carriage leave the grounds . . . and followed . . . over a devious route, to . . . the special train. . . . They had previously learned from what point it would start, although that was really a railroad secret.[31]

Bishop noted that other reporters soon learned of the route. "Fifty minutes after the bridal pair had started," six reporters followed via express train and, after a hard night, were "at their posts in the shrubbery under the windows of the President's cottage before daylight. . . ." He quoted another reporter:

When President Cleveland rose at ten o'clock this morning and looked from the front windows of his cheerful little domicile upon the handsome vista of glade and green that stretched out before him, among the objects which met his astounded gaze was a small pavilion standing in the midst of a handsome cluster of trees, and in and around this pavilion lounged the flower of Washington journalism, somewhat battered by lack of sleep and a midnight wrestle with country telegraph operators, but still experiencing a lively interest in the Chief Executive and his whereabouts.[32]

The journalists' mission, Bishop wrote, was to "stand in the trees and shrubbery" three hundred yards away and watch the newly married couple. There they stood, observing the house all day, noting the time the president first appeared at the windows, examining dishes when meals were sent to the couple; "they distended their ears to catch every scrap of conversation which floated from the piazza" when the pair went outside, "took notes" of their clothing as well as "every nod and look and smile"; "they stood in the bushes until the lights in the cottage were put out," recording the time carefully. Reporters continued "this persecution" for six days, and when the newlyweds cut short their stay and returned to Washington, they followed close behind.[33]

Journalists' Abilities

Discussions of journalists' abilities escalated during the last half of the century, generally emphasizing incompetencies. Some critics addressed areas in which journalists lacked education and training. Others referred to journalistic practices that militated against competent work. And still others argued that the low state of journalism deterred the best young people from entering the profession.

The area most often pointed to as beyond journalists' capabilities was criticism of literature and the arts. Most argued that journalists did not know enough about literature to qualify as critics and made fools of themselves when they wrote reviews. Some blamed the press for what they saw as the decline in drama, saying that journalists wrote incompetent reviews, served as image-makers for actors, and traded in favors rather than attempting serious diffusion of literary knowledge.

Lunt, for example, stated all the usual complaints. Among all their other failings, journalists had "converted . . . the republic of letters into an unwholesome wilderness of worthless and noxious weeds" because they were "really disqualified" to be "literary critics." The "lavish and indiscriminant praise" newspapers bestowed on "worthless and sometimes really pernicious writings" showed "either a blindness of judgment . . . or a willingness to tamper with the best interests of society. . . ." He protested the press's "degrading practice" of sacrificing impartiality in opinion—"the sole test of its independence, and the only basis of its utility"—thus betraying public confidence by "selling literary judgment" and "permitting its sheets to become the mere vehicles" of people "whose only object" was "pecuniary gain. . . ." "As if it were not enough for the press" to appeal to public sympathy, or—in trying to increase circulation—"to have substituted . . . for the solid food of the mind, lucubrations" that provided only a "very unsatisfactory repast for the hungry mind," good literature, "the very elements of . . . mental growth, the guides of . . . youth, the refreshment of . . . manhood, the solace of . . . age, the material of . . . reflection, and the inspiration of . . . progress," was no longer sought. "As if this were not quite enough to disorder the faculties . . . of the general mind," many still had to indulge in "popular deception"; and if they did not "dress up false-hood," they allowed it to appear as truth, so that ultimately an editor could not be expected to mean what he said nor anyone expected to believe him. Such newspapers seemed to assume that "truth and excellence" could "take care themselves," but a literary reputation thus gained was worthless.[34]

Lunt called editors' "absolute ignorance" about "common topics of intellectual society" a "culpable offence," because it "implied presumption" and prejudiced the "cause of human improvement." Readers readily saw through editors who treated "commonplaces of literature" as new dis-coveries of their own and who, seeming not to "know how often a good story" or joke had been published, attributed to "the sailor or the Hiber-nian of today" tales "such as the Greeks and Romans laughed at" centuries ago and which readers had known since childhood.[35]

More than two decades later, Rider wrote that journalism was "deeply in default" as "conservator of language and literature," that it ran "to coarse-ness and slang" and daily spread "farther and wider its corrupt, mongrel vocabulary," with "words and phrases . . . in editorials and the honor-places of the foremost 'dailies' which no liberality of scholarship" could "excuse or tolerate." He lamented that "recklessness of statement, exag-geration, contortion, distortion, and chronic hysteria" had "come to mar the fair beauty and symmetry of idiom and construction."[36]

Dion Boucicault wrote in 1889 that drama began to decline when news-papers started reviewing plays in the 1830s and 1840s. People began to read newspaper reviews before deciding whether they had enjoyed a play or an artist; they "lost their sense of appreciation from lack of exercising their powers of judgment," he argued, and leading actors neglected their art to "cultivate their social and press influences." Actors and actresses be-came products of the press, with their success depending on newspaper type size. Newspapers had assumed functions art lovers once fulfilled. The public had transferred its confidence from such dilettanti to press critics, and critics had betrayed that trust "from sordid motive."[37]

Parton in 1874 found the "little knowledge" journalists had of the "human mind" and "arts by which good work can be continuously got . . . without impairing their working powers" as the most surprising aspect of the press. But Parton and others defended it and tried to explain its work. Although not condoning journalism's faults, he asked readers to consider "this most difficult, most exacting, and least developed of all liberal professions." Reminding them that before the telegraph, "news was written as fast as the pen could be driven over the paper," he recounted how Greeley wrote an editorial column in an hour and often "kept at this furious rate so long" that he had to wrap his arm in wet bandages "to reduce the swelling and ache to the bearable point." And although modern methods had greatly eased journalists' burdens, the work they attempted was "among the most difficult that man ever undertook; being no less than the gathering, writing, and publishing of the history of the world for one day *in* one day," a task requiring the cooperation of hundreds "scattered widely over the earth, many of them far beyond the reach of supervision."[38]

Over time, critics increasingly advocated education (discussed below) as a solution to many journalistic inadequacies. But by the late 1880s they also seemed to define newspaper functions as separate from literary ones.

Journalistic Practices and Procedures

Critics increasingly dwelled on journalistic practices they saw as encouraging or permitting abuses. As Rider wrote in 1882, the issue was not "journalism itself"; rather, "its failures and abuses alone are in question." Rider stressed the growing belief that there were "fundamental failures in journalism, . . . portentous and perilous abuses of function and misconception of duty, . . . infringements and intrusions, both insolent and incendiary, . . . with pretensions that threaten private right and public well-being."[39] Responding to a suggestion that newspapers abandon editorials, Godkin remarked that this would not solve press problems or make newspapers more truthful because so few journalists were competent in the very difficult work of news selection. And worse, "the tendency of all newspaper training" seemed to be "to take away whatever natural fitness" journalists might have.[40]

Increasingly, critics targeted journalistic practices as problems. According to the demands of the times, news reports were to be "spicy," "saucy," "smart," "interesting," exciting. Reporters were to exhibit "enterprise"— that is, be aggressively resourceful in getting interesting stories, and be "lively" writers. In speeches given between 1888 and 1893, for example, Dana said that the newspaper's "invariable law" was to be interesting. Telling the truth boringly did little good because it did not stay in the mind, and no one thought better of a journalist because he "told . . . the truth tediously." "The telling must be vivid and animating," the story must be conveyed so that readers feel "its qualities and events" and are "interested in them." A report "enlivened with imagination, . . . feeling, or . . . humor" resulted in "a literary product that no one need be ashamed of." If a reporter, in stating facts accurately, could "state with a little degree of life, a little approach to eloquence, or a little humor," Dana said, "his report will be perfect."[41]

But many believed that such goals diverted reporters from accuracy, precluded the development of good reporters, and subverted journalism's true purposes. Godkin, for example, wrote that the number of "honest, painstaking, scrupulous, and accurate men employed as reporters and correspondents" was "far smaller than it should be" because such people were "systematically not encouraged for their honesty and accuracy." Such qualities, instead of being treated as "essential to professional success," were treated as "far inferior to smartness, 'spiciness,' and enterprise." In other words, he wrote, reporters were required first to "supply at least as much news" as other papers, and second, to "supply as much more as possible." Anyone not wanting to "telegraph or write" what he saw as "a sensational falsehood"—although it would put his paper in demand—preferring to "discriminate between facts and rumors" or to "remain silent," would likely find "his prospects grow dim." But the "busy and unblushing collector of all the rubbish" he could find too often grew "rapidly in the profession" —and "all the more rapidly" if he made his news the "means of damning political or other opponents."[42]

Because of this, reporting was "about as demoralizing a business as a young man" could enter, Godkin wrote, and "not a good place for scrupulous men." Some of the profession's best known loved "notoriety more than anything else," and "chuckle[d] over a well-told lie, or successfully defamed character, as an artist over a good picture or statue." Although few in number, such persons usually did "four times as much work as their betters" and won most of the profession's prizes. Consequently, many talented, qualified young people avoided journalism because they didn't want to be "detailed to listen behind doors or under sofas, to steal private confidential correspondence, . . . to dress up sensational blatherskite, . . . blackguard respectable men old enough to be their grandfathers . . . or . . . to have to associate with . . . those who do these things."[43] After almost twenty years of intensifying press criticism, Bishop asked in 1886 what kind of young people would be attracted to a profession where "this meddling, prying style" was the rule.[44]

White criticized the principle advanced by "the founder of a very successful newspaper," that whatever would interest "any one hundred people" merited "report and comment." This meant, White charged, that nothing was "too vile" or "too trivial" for coverage in the daily newspaper. General adoption of this rule, which had been facilitated by the telegraph and by many papers' hiring the same reporters (making "all the leading papers so nearly alike"), had cost "all the great papers" in the character of their news departments. Although all boasted about the value of their news, the only difference among them was in the nature of comments. "The mere sending out of reporters to discover and record occurrences, and publishing the reports" might be termed "mechanical work only," if it incorporated the "skill and contrivance that go even to good work of that kind." But it was "rather like sending carts out for loads of soil and rubbish to dump them all in a heap."[45]

White cited many examples of bad journalistic conduct, dwelling especially on invasion of privacy and the "personal journalist," whom he called "the pest of the period." Known through many generations, the personal journalist in earlier times would mostly "sting or terrify his victims," trusting "for his reward to the delight some people" found in others' pain. Although continuing this pattern, he had added over the years "a sweeter tone" and "more decorous form of speech," so that he lived "chiefly by fawning, by feeding vanity, and by pandering to petty curiosity." His "sting," still occasionally used "with all his old wantonness and venom," had become hidden as he had learned he could "vilify the few, and be tolerated, and even applauded" if he would "but flatter the many."[46]

Many newspapers depended on the personal journalist, and few were "free from the contamination of his touch." He tainted "the social atmosphere" and developed "a moral disease" in everyone because the curiosity he nurtured was "but a monstrous and distorted form of the desire of knowledge, a perversion of the humanity supposed to be expressed in Terence's famous line, 'I am a man, and regard nothing as foreign to me'" —a line, White wrote, that had become the "excuse for prying into others' affairs." The personal journalist made it "his business to do for gain what the gossip, scandal-monger and quidnunc" did "single-handed and under protest," and he told to "thousands and tens of thousands" what they told only to individuals. Decency did not restrain the "enterprise" carrying him "beyond the limits of privacy for the satisfaction of curiosity." Personal journalism had "voided man's life, and woman's too, of all semblance of privacy." The personal journalist regarded it as a first duty "to excite and gratify" curiosity "at whatever cost," and the printed gossip often circulated "false rumors" that placed "ladies . . . before the whole newspaper-reading public in the position most shocking to a woman of any delicacy."[47]

Interviewing was increasingly relied on as a source of news after the Civil War, and because it was a procedure for revealing personalities and reporting on what might today be called "celebrities," many saw it as a cause of poor journalistic conduct. Rider blamed most of journalism's problems on interviewing, which he called a "latter-day nuisance" with "its indelicate and offensive parading of personalities, of appearance, presence, and conversation." It caused violence to even the "sanctities of domestic life and marriage" and made "profane eyes" as "familiar with bridal trousseaux as the ladies' maids themselves."[48]

The accelerated emphasis on news gathering after the war put pressure on reporters to come up with a story. Aggressiveness and resourcefulness became significant prerequisites for reporting—qualities that were labeled "enterprise" on the part of the journalist. But some saw this aggressiveness as costly, risking truth, facts, taste, privacy, and moral conduct generally to "show off" the traits that were in demand.

Bushnell in 1886 condemned "enterprise in journalism" for "simply converting the columns of a paper into scandal and gossipmongers." Enterprise was a "very poor cover and lame excuse for violating all the sacredness of social and, particularly, home life," and it opened the door for "the widest abuse, to the washing of extremely soiled and noisome family linen, the pandering to most vitiated and base appetites, the debauchery of public minds, and the creating in young minds of a taste fatal to all the ethics of purity and honor." All the "sanctities of life" were "ruthlessly violated," with "the only justification" being "enterprise, the gathering of news, the desire to place before the public everything of interest or importance." Calling the "theory" unsound, with "false premises based upon the most sordid of motives and wanton disregard of all the amenities" that made "life pleasant and worth the living," he wrote that such a justification, the "put money in thy purse" doctrine, completely disregarded "the feelings or rights of others to truth, manhood, honor or common decency." Finally, he called enterprise "simply the abuse of a questionable custom," the "overstraining of a self-made law" that was "monstrous in the conception," "infamous in its workings and deadly in its results."[49]

In the same year, Levey argued that journalistic procedures precluded truthfulness. The need for "embellishment, . . . arising from that fundamental requirement" of journalism—"interest, *i.e.* excitement"—resulted in a "uniform . . . divergence from facts," even allowing for "individual idiosyncrasies of observation." "If all events must be made to appear interesting . . . , then, truth must necessarily be sacrificed; for the most momentous occurrences of history have occurred most prosaically." Sudden historical effects were usually superficial; causes running "deep down into the roots of future events" produced the most serious effects only slowly and became "part of the familiar order of things" before the changes they produced were noticed. Even then, cursory observers often did not see them as connected with the cause. People "whose store of facts" came "exclusively from newspapers" had to live in "an atmosphere of fictitious existence." Led to believe that facts that didn't excite didn't affect them, newspaper readers had learned "to measure the importance of events" by headline size. They were led to believe that newspapers presented "a miniature history of the world" when in fact they presented only a "collation of heterogeneous incidents selected by the 'night editor'" for their ability to "tickle the jaded palates of the great public."[50]

Sensationalism

The earliest located reference to "sensational" journalism occurred in one of Godkin's editorials published in 1869. Thereafter the word was common, appearing in journal article titles during the 1890s.[51] Godkin attacked publishers of "very cheap" papers, questioning whether they must be "as wildly sensational, vulgar, and slangy" as they said they must; he blamed the *New York Herald* for setting a bad example that "begot" the "lively writer" who had become "the great bane of the press." Although that paper succeeded primarily because of its news qualities and its innovations over its "ponderous and dull predecessors," its "most striking feature was . . . its telescopic mode of treating everybody and everything"—on the one hand magnifying "all men and all subjects . . . to more than mortal dimensions," while belittling them "infinitesimally" and acting as if it was all a "good joke" on the other. Although it labeled everything "grave or thorough," "old fogy" or "fossil," and "treated religion and wisdom and morality and knowledge and discretion and everything else" that made "individuals or states in the slightest degree respectable, as funny but transparent humbugs," the paper "took"; it "found a market, . . . increased its circulation enormously, . . . indeed, founded a school of journalism." But the worst in the press, Godkin wrote, came from the *Herald*'s "immense pecuniary success" as a "buffoon." Imitators "improved greatly on its morality, . . . retained many of its methods and some of its spirit, and justified themselves as it did, by alleging that they gave the public what it wanted"—and as a result their sales were growing.[52]

Rider wrote that "hanging days" brought out the worst of journalism as it followed the "condemned, from the setting of the grim death-watch, with sleepless eyes and vampire persistency, at meal-time, catching every chance or privileged word, intruding upon the closing solemnities of religion, and winding up at the foot of the gallows with the last convulsion of the dangling victim before the ghastly business is over." Certainly justice should not be secret, nor "the terrors of the law be shorn of their fierceness." But he argued that, at such "late date," the world hardly needed "to learn the paralyzing sequences of all brutal exhibitions on the general conscience. . . ."[53]

Journalism's attitude toward "public morality" was an especially grave concern, for it had dropped "all distinctions between wholesome, necessary intelligence" and that which corrupted and contaminated; it had lost the "old sensitiveness and reserve concerning sex" and had become "habitually guilty of indecent exposure of transactions and behavior from which healthy souls shrink in disgust and abhorrence." Calling dailies "rarely fit for home-reading without thorough expurgation," Rider wrote that the "minute and filthy reports of scandalous trials alone" constituted a "flagrant and unpardonable offense against public morality, and should be made indictable and subject to sharp and severe penalties." Having become "propagandist of all manner of indecency, unnamable outrages and crimes of most shameful sort, that breed from the very telling," journalism tore "off the roof," pulled down "the walls and sheltering partitions," and "wantonly" exposed "all defilement and consuming lust of poor human nature, as if it were . . . a beneficent and philanthropic duty"; journalism had become "a perpetual stimulant to pruriency and vice," "degrading and seductive" in "its very essence." Rider asked what journalism was doing for groups trying to aid the city's needy through "midnight missions" and "houses of mercy," while filling "column after column" with "all the multiplied abominations of the prize ring."[54]

According to Levey, when "sensationalism requires that solid facts be misshapen or distorted, the result is a system in absolute hostility to truth."[55] Rider especially attacked the Sunday press. Reiterating themes in *Observations upon Sunday Newspapers*, published in England more than sixty years earlier, he argued that journalism encroached on the Sabbath; Sunday newspapers were "avowedly and offensively secular," a "direct and deliberate bid for the popular eye and ear in competition with the pulpit." "Sunday journalism creeps into houses before breakfast, and spins well its web of thrall and glamour before morning service." The makeup of the Sunday newspaper was itself "the triumph of seductive art. Memorable verses, brilliant tales and novelettes, racy gossip, with salacious flavorings of mischief and scandal in high and low life, sea-flittings and watering-place delights, oddities and outlandish provincialisms, provide a whet and stimulant in every column. . . ." More than "half a million of these anti-church emissaries" were "peddled from the metropolis alone every Sunday." And although taverns and theaters remained closed on Sundays, journalism alone was left to "resist the unanimous conclusions of Christian people and profane the Lord's day in its greed of gain. . . ."[56]

Bushnell noted that a "class of papers" was "above such vile intermeddling, such 'ear at the keyhole' baseness, such despoiling of moral graves, such lowering, debasing and making merchandise of the most holy of our nature." But the base practice had "enlarged" like a "circle in the water," until it affected the whole "social fabric" and shocked the "very nerve centers of the human heart, alarm[ing] religion and threaten[ing] the body politic." Because it had been tolerated out of "lax indifference, the evil" had grown "monstrous," "overstepped all the bounds of decency, trampled under foot every particle of restraint, . . . leaving its serpent slime upon everything clean and pure. . . ." "Aided by the most execrable of wood-cuts and abortions of electros," it had become "worse than intrusive"; it had become "brutal." "Such journalism" was a "cancerous ulcer . . . eating its way to the very heart" of all that was "noble, refining, exalting"; it was "moral leprosy" that was infecting all of the press. The "contamination" was "continually spreading," the "foul disease" was "contagious" and becoming "epidemic."[57]

Bishop proposed a test of journalistic conduct: to consider the reaction if "private persons" indulged in such behavior as journalists exhibited in covering President Cleveland's wedding. Maintaining that people would have seen anyone behaving in that manner as a "blackguard," he wrote, "No other kind of people, in private life, pry about their neighbors' houses, peer into their windows, listen at their keyholes, and try in other ways to penetrate the sanctities of their homes." And if such censure applied to individuals who snooped just to be able to delight friends with gossip, what of a newspaper—with all its "resources and power"—that published such information to the whole world?[58]

As critics increasingly questioned, and often ridiculed, the claim that editors merely gave readers what they wanted, Rider equated the common defense that if "people insist upon gossip, the papers must supply it, or go to the wall" with "corner-dram-shop logic": "It is a pretty circle, to wit: the papers promote and feed gossip-hunger, therefore they must provide for it!"[59]

Free Press/Fair Trial

In 1882, Rider charged journalism with stepping "boldly into the halls of justice," sitting "beside the 'enthroned majesty of the law,' tampering with testimony and procedure," muddling and inflaming public opinion, and "sometimes unsettling the stability of jurisprudence by its own antagonistic verdict, even converting the criminal into a martyr, or robbing the innocent of due vindication." When "critical cases involving weighty issues" were in "adjudication in the various courts," a "double trial" occurred— "one before the constitutional authorities, and another before the juries of journalism."[60]

Five years later, Roger Foster warned that trial by newspaper was superseding trial by jury, especially in some cases. Newspapers had been indispensable to the public good in helping detect criminals and bringing prosecution, and they excelled in the role of detective or historian. Indeed, without the press's aid, no judge could secure justice for the accused. But noting three kinds of contempt named by Lord Hardwicke—"scandalizing the Court itself, abusing persons . . . concerned in causes" before the court, and "prejudicing mankind against persons before the cause is heard," Foster claimed that newspapers exceeded proper boundaries when they undertook "to try causes pending in the courts."[61]

Standards

Critics during the last half of the century who stated or implied specific recommendations were "all over the board," so to speak. Some directed suggestions at very specific, narrow changes; some took broader views; some listed attributes of a "good" newspaper; and others used a favorite newspaper as representing standards for others to imitate. All critics in the latter half of the century emphasized press responsibility. They simply did not clearly articulate what that meant. The result was much ambivalence, often an appearance of "hand-wringing," and some defensiveness. Thus, although discussion intensified after the Civil War and became heated during the 1880s, it reflected little agreement on specific issues or recommendations by 1890. Only one presumption was consistent throughout: there could be no legal restraint on the press. As irresponsible as the press might be, critics, although they often argued among themselves about the good of some externally imposed restraint, ended up opposing restrictions. What critics viewed as "right" journalistic conduct during the last half of the nineteenth century is outlined below.

Responsibility

The concept of responsibility, which had begun to emerge in earlier discussions, came into sharp focus after 1850. A consistent view, always stated broadly before the Civil War, held that journalists must be responsible. Lunt averred that they should be more capable than legislators, and he and Bowles said that the world's increasing complexity made that responsiblity graver. Charles Holden emphasized editors' great responsibility, especially during the war then raging.[62] Editor Melville Stone, stressing that limitations on journalists were "infinitely greater than those of other businesses," held that "in the conduct of so important an educational force as the daily newspaper, the editor was chargeable with a very high duty . . .—a duty he could not escape." He asserted flatly, "There must always be a sense of responsibility."[63]

White wrote that journalism offered "one of the most terrible moral powers" that could be possessed. An editor could attack a party, cause, person, opinion "at his pleasure" and "inflict as many wounds to reputation and feeling" as he desired so long as he remained "within the limits of . . . libel." He could refuse to publish a reply, or publish one only to make it "the occasion of an onslaught worse than the first." A journalist could, and usually did, have the last word, and his view was left with readers. Having such power "tempts to cruelty," White maintained, and because human nature led people to seek victory rather than truth in discussions, journalists—who were only human—could not all be expected to resist that temptation. Journalists' sense of responsibility should therefore be all the greater, and they should be held all the more accountable for a power they acquired neither by birth nor legislation—"their abuse of which their very humanity makes probable."[64]

White called a newspaper that couldn't be trusted worse than "no newspaper at all," and one that might be "either right or wrong" as "fitted only to create apprehension and excite alarm, or at the least to awaken curiosity" it didn't satisfy. By publishing as fact what was untrue, the journalist could do "great injury, and even . . . bring ruin not only upon individuals, but upon whole classes," because his "wares" were "not like those of other vendors," in which worth concerned only "one purchaser of each article." He continued that "one spurious utterance wrongs thousands . . . and . . . not merely by palming off on them a worthless thing, but by giving them false premises from which no wisdom or suttley [*sic*] of reasoning" could "draw sound conclusions, and by subjecting them to the influence" of a misleading "assertion or . . . thought"—"the consequence of trusting to which" would likely "be misfortune more or less embarrassing in the present, and possibly not without evil consequences that embitters a whole life."[65] Addressing the Maine Press Association in 1876, William H. Sampson, editor of the Belfast *Republican Journal,* asserted, "Of course there are limits of decent propriety and respect due to individual right and feeling, which every editor understands are not to be passed—and within which he is bound, by moral sense no less than by the strong motive of self-interest."[66]

Eleven years later O. B. Frothingham declared, "There is an ethics of the press." "Behind every fact lies a moral no less than an intellectual cause," and the "antecedents are often exceedingly subtle"; but, he insisted, "phenomena are subject to law; they implicate conscience; they are connected with the inner history of mankind," and these "relations must be indicated." The editorial writer, then, must be conscientious and "must tell about the right and wrong of movements." Frothingham seemed to think aloud, writing that "men exercised in the knowledge of moral questions are employed" to "meet this requirement," but it is unclear whether he was stating a fact or what should be. He equivocated about the degree to which any journalist could be a moral leader, because a newspaper must stay abreast of community morals—and this prevented journalists from being able to provide ethical leadership. Concerning what those "men exercised in the knowledge of moral questions" might accomplish, he wrote, "Of course, the moralizing is more or less conventional"; it "appeals to the general conscience," and the "paper assumes the average moral sentiment of the community,—the highest average sentiment . . . ,—and is compelled to be . . . commonplace." The paper could not "diverge far from accepted principle," for then it would be "unfaithful to its leading purpose," which was "to enlighten the minds of its contemporaries, not directly to elevate their consciences." A newspaper took "existing laws of duty for granted," followed tradition, and "however fresh and forcible" its "expression," abided by "conceded examples." An editor might occasionally venture "on original theses," indulge in "speculative lucubrations," or propound "ethical theories beyond his calling," but essentially he was an "interpreter," not a "prophet."[67]

Catering to Public Tastes

Frothingham indirectly addressed the greatest issue in the debate, especially during the 1880s—that newspaper content, however unseemly to some, or however trivial or unworthy, had to provide readers what they wanted for the newspaper to succeed. All critics dealt with this problem in one way or another. Perhaps the best statement of the argument was made by Dana, who said that a newspaper "must be founded upon human nature . . . must correspond to the wants of people," and couldn't succeed if it didn't "furnish that sort of information which the people demand." To the argument that "certain kinds of news ought not be published," he said he was not "prepared to maintain any abstract proposition in that line," having always believed that he "was not too proud to report" "whatever the Divine Providence permitted to occur."[68] When criticized for sensationalism in reporting about aggressive post–Civil War reform movements, Bowles wrote that "the topics of daily journalism are by no means matters of its own choice, nor, to a great extent even, is the manner of their treatment," and it had no right to "suppress discreditable things by ignoring them," even if it could. A newspaper had to tell the good and the bad; it existed "mainly to describe what is . . . whether it be cholera, murder, abortion, tornado, revival, Jim Fisk, Tweed . . . ," Bowles said, adding that there was no other law of journalism but "faithful reporting, faithful comment."[69] Sampson pointed to failures of newspapers founded on notions that some kinds of news did a "public wrong," and that the "editor should sift his news," publishing only what was "highly moral, and therefore fit and proper to read." His description of failed newspapers reveals what sort of news some called unfit for publication:

From these expurgated sheets everything that carried . . . suggestions that vice and immorality existed . . . was carefully excluded. If a woman was murdered in a place of resort for the vicious, it was not suffered to be an offence to the city news. If a man was hung, no unpleasant spectacle of the gallows disfigured its columns. Theatres were condemned as sources of immorality, and so no announcement of actors or plays found place.[70]

But the public, "naturally indignant at being treated like children, said 'give us . . . all the news, and we will select what we desire to read.' "[71]

Frothingham stated the issue more broadly, attempting to explain why journalism could not be as "moral" as some might wish and must provide what the public wanted. He saw the "most important limitation" of the press—and what differentiated it from the pulpit—as editors' lack of power to originate moral forces, which resulted from the press's status as a "great business" and, therefore, its subjection to business rules. With "enormous" expenses, the press was "a venture, conducted on the principle of every pecuniary investment." If a paper's worth—and some, he noted, represented more than a million dollars—derived from subscriptions, "the public taste must be consulted," and if from advertising, the "business community must be accommodated." Advertisements depended on circulation, which depended on popular approval, creating "an unavoidable peril," financial and moral, "for the public mind" was nowhere "remarkably high-toned." Management might "regret this necessity of pleasing a fickle public," might "rebel against it," might "suggest, teach, remonstrate, inculcate, enjoin"; but, Frothingham asked, wasn't this a circumstance beyond control? Even when the "multitude" became "infatuated, possessed, maddened" by some "strange prejudice," some "unwarrantable persuasion," must not journalists still "be careful how they run counter to the tide?" No paper could "afford to defy the world, or become so independent" that it put "itself in opposition to all opinion." A newspaper was "dependent on its very independence," and an editor who ignored people's judgment dashed his business like a "vessel on a rock."[72]

Stone, however, wrote that his staff in the mid-1870s was involved in more than "a mere business enterprise" to "provide anything and everything that the public might crave."[73] White followed the common reasoning at the time—that accumulating wealth and enhancing one's life-style were less virtuous than gentility in one's work-style. He anticipated that his criticisms would draw the response that journalists' "employer"—the public that "pays . . . so much quicker and better for the . . . personal news than for public"—would deter journalistic improvement. But, he argued, it would be better to live modestly than to "wear purple and fine linen and fare sumptuously . . . by the prying, gossipping, tattling, fawning, scandal-mongering trade of personal journalism."[74]

By the mid-1880s, the claim that newspapers' success depended on such news shifted to a questioning of the demand for such journalism and whether it was, indeed, profitable. Bishop, for example, wrote that he had seen no newspaper show greater prosperity with than without "improper" journalism. Conceding that some readers wanted such news, he asked whether newspapers should peddle "scandal and impertinence" just because some of the public wanted to read it. This kind of journalism would ultimately weaken a newspaper's editorial influence because the "functions of scandal-monger and moral guide" could not be made to work "successfully together." And who would continue to buy a paper he could not leave where the family might see it? Such journalism would not become the rule, he believed, because too many editors abhorred and protested against it, and the American public would not tolerate it. "They will insist . . . that the newspaper has some other purpose . . . than to amuse and entertain the thoughtless and the vicious; they will insist that the duty of selecting goes hand in hand with the duty of collecting the news. . . ."[75]

Accuracy, Truthfulness, and Unbiased News

Critics often focused on what might be done to assure accurate, truthful, unbiased news coverage. This concern led to recommendations for eradicating partisanship and other nonnews affiliations. Some believed that either separating editorial and reportorial departments, or eliminating editorials, would solve all problems. Others, unable to conceive of a press divorced from politics, expounded on how to make partisan journalism ethical.

White wrote in 1869 that it might be understood by readers that the journalist was "the advocate of a party," and that he would "support . . . that party by the strongest argument" he could make; "but it is not, or it should not be, understood" that he was "at liberty to make intentionally a single erroneous assertion, or to warp a single fact." His party loyalty did not "absolve him from one line of his obligation to truth," nor "justify or palliate a violation of public decency by attacks on personal reputation or an invasion of the private life of an opponent." An editor could give "all the weight of his journal's influence" to the party he advocated or to "any scheme or project . . . before the public"; and although this was perilous, he could do so "without the slightest taint of dishonor, without in the least perverting journalism to base uses, or disregarding the great responsibility" he had assumed—if he did so "without any other motive . . . than a conviction of the truth." If, however, he expressed an opinion for his own or his friends' interests that he would not otherwise have expressed, he "violated his good faith and sacrificed his honor. . . ."[76] Godkin wrote in the same year that one of the press's first duties was "not . . . to publish no false news,"—for that was impossible, "but to do its utmost to get accurate news, and . . . not to color it to suit the editorial taste or necessities."[77] Dana said a news report "must be accurate . . . free from affection, . . . well set forth," so that it left no doubt about any detail.[78]

Virtually all who argued thus ultimately became mired in how to assure accuracy and trailed off in ambiguity or ambivalence, or into calling news indefinable and dependent on individual character. Godkin did all this in describing news as "an impalpable thing—an airy abstraction" that someone had to "collect," "condense," "clothe in language" to make a "ponderable, merchantable commodity"—and in relegating it to the category of an individual matter whose whole value depended on the character of those who performed these tasks.[79] White, too, maintained that it was unreasonable to demand impartiality of journalists. "For what is the journalist responsible to the public?" he asked, and answered that the "highest conceivable attainment in journalism" would be "absolute impartiality." A newspaper that gave "an absolutely faithful report of all the day's events, uncolored by party bias or personal feeling," that sought no other end than truth, "regardless of consequences to parties, to schools, to corporations, to individuals, and . . . to the interests of the editors and owners of the paper itself" would be "a second sun." But this would not solve the problem because, although people would buy such a paper, everyone would still buy "the other paper," the one that "pampered" their wishes, cheered their hopes, respected their prejudices, and gratified their hates. "Like Poins with his two shirts," people should have one paper for "super-fluity and the other for use," but they would naturally "love the superfluous more than the useful" one. Thus the independence of newspapers that called themselves independent—if they survived—"came to mean merely that they held themselves free to favor this cause today, that to-morrow, and the other the day after. . . ."[80]

Stone's solution was to divorce the newspaper from all affiliations. An independent paper's only masters were its readers: the paper itself was its sole ambition and "in no sense the means to some other end"; it was un-connected to a political or "any other selfish interest" and had only two sources of revenue—"sale of papers and advertising." The business depart-ment in one sense must "have no influence . . . , and yet in a larger sense it must have everything to do with" publishing a newspaper.[81]

Among those who believed that the chief problem of journalism lay in editorializing, Godkin advocated separating news and "expository" de-partments. "It would be hard to think of any new agency which would contribute so much to the rational decision of great political issues, and to the encouragement of talent and integrity among public men, as the application of the rules of conduct" which made it "infamous for a man to sell watered milk, or sanded sugar or fill life preservers with hay." But he concluded that such an advance would probably have to wait for a new generation of "newspaper pioneers."[82] Boucicault argued that opinions should be "subsidiary" and probably not included among a newspaper's essential functions. As had been "frequently and clearly shown," people had come to disregard this part of a paper, and most readers might wel-come "a simple sheet of pure news, unadulterated with opinions," because they had "little time to wade through the bulky mass that encumbers . . . attention and interferes with easy digestion."[83]

Possible Solutions

Critics struggled to define what newspapers should not contain and what journalists should not do. They usually began by condemning sensationalism but generally lumped this issue with those of invasion of privacy, bad taste, and trivialization. Rarely precise about improper journalistic conduct, they often gave examples that suggest definitions and tried to specify what journalists should do.

Addressing sensationalism and poor taste broadly, White wrote that although "tastes will be depraved," this was no "defence for the journalist who not only panders to but propagates them." Journalists were duty-bound to "check such vanity" and "to check and do away with any other evil." The extent to which journalists could free themselves from personal influence remained a problem, but every "worthy career" posed the same difficulty, and an honest, kind journalist could "find words . . . to tell the truth tenderly in a way that ought not to alienate even his dearest friend."[84] It was reasonable, White asserted, to demand "candor, good faith, and decency"—a decency that respected individual personality and the community's "moral tone." The journalist's candor and good faith "should be absolute, undarkened by the lightest shadow of personal motive, without an iota of swerving."[85] About the same time, Bowles wrote that it was "no part of a newspaper's legitimate business to go around digging up social scandals"; "no newspaper" had "the right to print scandal . . . for scandal's sake, to make its columns 'spicy.' . . ." A newspaper was "bound to take care" as far as possible "that the public interest" was not damaged.[86] Godkin asserted that a journalist without a "sense of perspective" had "no right to exist." A journalist must "be able to distinguish between the important and unimportant, true and false," what deserved publishing and what didn't. A journalist had to "survey an immense field of fact, rumor, and fancy" in composing a report, "throwing into relief" what touched, "or ought to touch" the public most and eliminating the doubtful, irrelevant, or private.[87]

Rider wrote that journalism had "no immunity from general laws of modesty and purity," and no one could "rightly print and publish" what "he would not tell his wife and children face to face." He warned that "before journalism" could stand "unchallenged as a supplemental fourth estate, working out the great problems of a regenerated society in harmony with the family, the church, and the state," there would have to be a "radical paring away of many hurtful, jarring elements of misdirection, and a wiser recognition of its responsibilities to the permanent interests of civilization." But he believed such change was inevitable. A time would come when journalism would "not lure men to evil, but shine full and fairly on all highways to better, nobler living." He predicted, "in the spirit of blind optimism," a time when, without "partisan political bondage," newspapers would represent "great truth and fearlessness of utterance," "duty and dignity," and they would shine "star-like in their exaltation above the foul handling of ring, corner, or monopolist," with "an unswerving conscience of paramount fidelity to the people in the promotion of culture, purity, and true manliness."[88]

It was "time for something more than merely indignant protest," Bushnell asserted in 1886. He beseeched "every publication having the least claims to respectability to raise their voices in severe condemnation, and use their columns as a lash to scare the scullions and bandits of journalism . . . back into . . . decency and a just regard for the rights of others." "Every lover of good order, fair dealing and the sanctity of life should rise in rebellion and wage an unceasing warfare" against "such a villainous prostitution of journalism." But the "longer the delay," he warned, the harder the task; "the knife should be used unsparingly and unflinchingly, and the eradicating mixture administered with a liberal hand."[89]

Among all the problems of the press that were identified, critics tried hardest to define private rights and find ways to prevent their infringement. In the controversy over Bowles's imprisonment after he had published articles about James Fisk, Fisk's attorney contended that his work as a lawyer was private and therefore inappropriate for news coverage. Bowles responded that he could not accept such limitations on journalism, asserting that "the conduct of public men is the legitimate subject of its discussion."[90] Critics thereafter struggled to spell out the boundaries of privacy. But White, the first to attempt it, set the tone in 1869.

Decent journalism required a clear, easily followed rule for respecting private life "absolutely," White wrote. Whatever brought a person into "relations with the public"—his "public course," speech, book, picture, suit at law, breach of the public peace, contract with the government—constituted a "proper subject" for journalism. But no one had the right to bring before the public anyone's "personal affairs, relations with family, his friends, acquaintances, clients and customers." This was a "breach of good taste which an editor should not permit," except in the form of paid advertisement. White argued that it should be libelous for a journalist to invade privacy, "whether to praise or to blame"—suit for which would be at the discretion of the person "whose privacy was invaded."[91]

On the same theme, Bushnell wrote in 1886 that "public life, actions and utterances become by their very nature public property, and are proper subjects for comment, for trial . . . within reasonable grounds." But "private conversations, acts, credit, and affairs of the heart are not, never should be; and the line of demarkation should be sternly and deeply drawn" and "strictly respected, or the penalty . . . be severe in the extreme." He conceded that reports giving "vivid descriptions of death upon the scaffold, the last dying speech and confession, the contortions of agony and the choking out of breath" might "be possibly defended upon the ground of public policy and police regulations," but "matters of home life" could not "by any stretch of imagination."[92]

Before 1890, few critics dealt directly with the free press/fair trial issue, but one writer devoted an entire article to it in 1887. Although Roger Foster favored legal control, he was unwilling to demand it; but he nevertheless emphasized that the growing problem required a remedy and appealed to the press to "stand off and confine" its "strength to the enforcement of fair play" while cases were in process. Press controls inherited from England had long been overthrown, but it was perhaps time to consider whether some should be restored. Then, calling it unwise to bring back the full powers of English chancellors, he asked whether comments "other than a fair report upon proceedings pending in the courts" might not be made an indictable offense.[93]

One of the thorniest problems for these critics was advertising. Critics of the first half of the century occasionally grumbled about the subversion of news to advertising, but they were not surrounded by advertising as were post–Civil War critics. While the press per se expanded phenomenally from 1850 to 1880, total advertising sales rose from approximately $1 million in 1850 to $27.5 million in 1880 and mushroomed to more than $95 million by 1900.[94] Perplexed by the obvious fact that advertising enhanced business and press capabilities at the same time that it seemed to intrude on news functions, critics dealt guardedly with it. White, for example, argued that eliminating advertisements would enhance the "honor and independence of journalism," but he said that advertising must appear in newspapers. The only "safe course," therefore, was an absolute rule that editorial columns would contain nothing in the interests of the advertiser. "It should be understood . . . that payment for advertising . . . secures the advertisement, and nothing more," he asserted.[95] Discussing several problems stemming from advertising, Sampson focused on the editor's responsibility to the public. He condemned mixing advertising with other content and "teasers"—announcements inserted after a "thrilling story's" beginning that the remainder was in another publication. (In such cases, readers had trusted the editor at "a bribe of ten cents per line.") But worse were husbands' notices about absent wives, which he called "a relic of barbarism" that pained a "defenceless class" and was almost always "instigated by mean revenge." Wives usually left husbands to escape cruelty, he said, recommending that editors publish facts about the husband alongside such ads. Finally, he condemned publishing "puffs"—editorial notices about an advertised item—gratis. Editors profited less than other professionals, who made one "pay roundly" for any assistance, so why should they be asked to write notices of someone's "business, his improvements, his inventions, his ship, or anything whereby he is to profit . . . ?"[96]

Occasionally, critics revealed their notions of correct journalistic standards by listing what a paper should contain or describing a favorite newspaper. Bowles said a newspaper should provide "the highest class of news, most intelligently discriminated and wisely set forth" and cultivate readers' taste for such. A good newspaper had "positive opinions and a positive way of stating them," belonged to itself, without fear of "politician, caucus, or convention"; it did not pretend to be infallible; it claimed an honest purpose, sought no favor and knew no fear in "discussing public measures and public men"; it sought to "speak the exact truth," regardless of the party that might benefit, and to "do justice though the political heavens fall. . . ." Duty was no less because it happened to be painful. Publishing all the news and giving each side a fair hearing would bewilder at times. Seeing opposing statements, assertions and contradictions, charges and countercharges, and conflicts "of plausible arguments" in the same paper, the reader might not know which version to believe or what to think. But, Bowles suggested, such a reader might be consoled to know that journalists often experienced the same confusion—and that, he noted, exemplified independent journalism's "embarrassment of riches."[97] Summing up what he called "the philosophy of independent journalism in a nut-shell," he wrote:

> But it is better than to hear only one side,—than to be daily lied to, and hoodwinked, and made a fool of. The honest reader may take our opinion on trust, if he chooses. But if he prefers, as he ought, to compare and weigh and strike the balance for himself, we are bound to furnish him the raw material.[98]

In another editorial, Bowles summarized the growth of journalism during his lifetime, concluding:

The Independence, which has been held and despised as Indifference, and the Impersonality, which was denounced as irresponsibility, are now seen in their higher and broader character. . . . henceforth American Journalism . . . will exhibit its outgrowth both of Partyism and Personalism. It will become a profession, not a stepping-stone; and a great journal will not longer be the victim of caprice and passion, or the instrument of the merely personal ambition. . . . instead of a man, called to direct and contribute to its columns, importing himself to it, the paper will import itself to him.[99]

Some critics implied standards of conduct in advising editors how certain problems might be handled. Sampson held that editors must not exclude opinions they disagreed with because such a practice always amounted to "a confession of error or an acknowledgement of weakness" that readers' sense of fairness readily recognized and condemned. Readers' sympathy then went to the person "deprived of a fair chance in the controversy." Admitting journalists' susceptibility to pressure groups, he said that there would always be "certain touchy people in every community" ready to complain and to see anything the newspaper did as "a disparaging allusion to themselves, their party, their friends, their church, or some other tender spot." But an editor should treat such people with "distinguished consideration . . . , regret the injustice . . . done, and tender full reparation," inviting complainants to write a correction, which should be published in "a conspicuous place." Editors must avoid being influenced by pressure groups—those who wished to use the paper's columns "to fire upon people" or whatever they disliked, who wanted to "lie in safe ambush and send poison shafts. . . ." But worse than these were people who wished to publish items anonymously, or who inundated editors with unsolicited literary efforts—which he advised against publishing.[100]

Obituaries were especially sensitive, Sampson noted, because the bereaved were "scarcely willing to believe that the great world hurries on. . . ." Journalists must treat those people with sensitivity. An unsolved problem was whether to charge for publishing tributes. Marriage notices presented no difficulty because "the parties" were "usually so wrapped up in their own supreme bliss" that they did not care "what the papers say or fail to say"; divorce notices, however, brought criticism whether published or not.[101]

All critics implicitly urged that journalists be well educated, and the issue of journalism education, rarely discussed in the 1850s, became overt in the 1870s. At that time controversy flared about whether journalism education could offer any better preparation than experience. Lunt, who recommended education for journalists in 1856, seemed to suggest a code of ethics. "I am sure, I should be glad to see a college, or a commission established, to settle upon a firmer and fairer basis the theory of editorial qualifications . . . to raise the standard of instruction, in ethics, as well as in learning, amongst those, whose duty and whose privilege it is to teach"; he then asked why those "who are to educate the people" should not be educated "for the public service, upon the public responsibility." The benefits to the journalist were clear:

> For education . . . does tend to the enlargement of his faculties and the elevation of his soul—so that they, who come from the select company of those, who, in all ages, have dignified and glorified the condition of manhood, are less susceptible of mean views,—less liable to petty temptations,—less easily controlled and led away, by the madness of the populace demanding infamous compliances.[102]

A year later, Congressman Justin Smith Morrill of Vermont introduced a bill emphasizing practical education which K. T. Wulfemeyer says helped make vocational, technical, and professional training part of higher education and college training accessible to people of diverse backgrounds and interests. Twelve years later, in 1869, Washington College offered the first journalism course plus scholarships for young men who wanted "to make practical printing and journalism their business life" and would work an hour a day in a college printing plant. In 1873, the Kansas State College of Agriculture and Applied Science established a printing course; in 1878, David McAnally of the University of Missouri School of English offered a journalism history course and required students to summarize his lectures with the "reporting method"; in 1884, he added a "materials of journalism" course. In 1888, Eugene Camp of the Philadelphia *Times* found that most respondents to a survey of leading professionals favored a broad, general education for journalists—including economics, law, politics, oral and written communication, and history. In the meantime, during the 1870s, the president of Cornell designed a journalism curriculum, and the university offered special journalism lectures until 1888, when it began offering journalism courses.[103]

Although some advocated broad education for journalists, critics of journalism education abounded. In 1872, *New York Tribune* editor Whitelaw Reid advocated the study of history, law, language, politics, logic, and economics as appropriate preparation for a career in journalism. But Henry Waterson of the Louisville *Courier-Journal* said in 1875 that the only school of journalism was in a "well-conducted newspaper office"; a journalist could not "be made to order." Frederic Hudson, editor of the *New York Tribune*, asked in the same year: "Who are to be the teachers? The only place where one can learn to be a journalist is in a great newspaper office. . . . College training is good in its way, but something more is needed for journalism."[104] In 1887, E. J. Carpenter argued against schools of journalism, insisting that journalism was not a theory "but wholly practice," and that it was absurd to think that college classrooms could turn out finished journalists. Journalism and teaching had in recent years been added to the "three learned professions of law, theology and medicine"; journalism had achieved that status because the times demanded an educated person in the journalist's role. Nevertheless, he argued, journalism could not be learned except by the "hard, unwearying labor" of experience, and he wondered if those suggesting otherwise could possibly be serious.[105] Dana, who advocated a "universal education" for journalists, said in 1888, "I do not see how a college instruction in journalism can be of any adequate practical use." In his judgment, no "special school" could "give [the aspiring journalist] much valuable instruction in the duties and labors of his future professional life. . . ." He too emphasized that "there is only one school for that purpose, and that is the newspaper office. . . ."[106]

The word *ethics* appeared in discussions by 1850, but it remained rare through the 1880s. Writers generally used the word *moral* when referring to desired journalistic conduct. Nevertheless, a trend toward formulating some guidelines was clear.

Although Horace Greeley and George Childs had rules of conduct for journalists working on their papers, and others likely did also, Stone may have proposed the first somewhat systematic principles in the 1870s, application of which was, as newspapers were then conducted, "practically revolutionary." Among Stone's rules were the following: (1) there could be "no pandering to the vitiated taste of the unthinking" and "no publishing of so-called sensational and exaggerated or scandalous material" to achieve sales, or of anything a "worthy young gentlewoman could not read aloud in . . . mixed company"; (2) "every man's activities" in relation to the public "were a proper subject for attention," but "in his domestic relations he was entitled to privacy which no newspaper was privileged to invade"; (3) every effort must be made to be accurate and impartial, and "a fair, frank, and open acknowledgement and apology" must follow any errors; (4) the paper's owners were not permitted to hold stock in any public utility corporation; (5) advertising must not "encroach" on news space; (6) "puffs" calling attention to advertisements were not to be published; and (7) "good plays were called good and bad ones called bad."[107]

The instructions of James Gordon Bennett, Jr., to an employee in 1882 emphasized the money-making drive of the business-oriented press of the late nineteenth century. "First of all I wish you to particularly consult economy," he said, and urged "judicious condensing so as to get all the points of the day's news without the verbiage." He asked that the "City News" department provide "enterprising, lively," "thoroughly condensed" items ("excepting the 'features'"), "edited carefully down to the smallest items," and that "particular attention" be paid to Wall Street. . . ." He wanted a daily local feature ("the chief topic of the town" and "not a mere flimsy sensation worked up out of whole cloth"), "thoroughly well written and edited so as to make it fresh, lively, and readable." From the "General Domestic News" department, he sought "the fullest and best account" of any "important piece of news," and admonished that "expense or space" never be spared "when the news justifies it." Journalists must know to let "a thing drop the moment public interest in it begins to flag," he maintained, emphasizing, "The instant you see a sensation is dead, drop it and start in on something new." Ship news should never be omitted, and theater notices should be "brief, lively, and always frank and fearless." Good reviewers were to be rotated "to avoid having a regular 'critic,'" something Bennett considered "a mischievous and bad system. . . ."[108]

Dana remarked that although doctors and lawyers had a "system" or "code" of ethics, he knew of no "maxims or professional rules" to guide journalists. He thus proceeded to offer his own, which he called "pretty general" but which seemed to "cover the case very well":

I. Get the news, get all the news, and nothing but the news.
II. Copy nothing from another publication without perfect credit.
III. Never print an interview without the knowledge and consent of the party interviewed.
IV. Never print a paid advertisement as news matter. Let every advertisement appear as an advertisement; no sailing under false colors.
V. Never attack the weak or the defenceless, either by argument, by invective, or by riducule, unless there is some absolute public necessity for doing so.
VI. Fight for your opinions, but do not believe that they contain the whole truth or the only truth.

VII. Support your party. . . . But do not think all the good men are in it and all the bad ones outside of it.

VIII. Above all, know and believe that humanity is advancing; and there is progress in human life and human affairs; and that, as sure as God lives, the future will be greater and better than the present or the past.[109]

Critics after 1850 struggled to define appropriate journalistic conduct and were more specific than their predecessors in citing abuses and corrections. But by 1890 they were still groping with what had become an immense social institution of overwhelming capabilities. Some trends are clear, however. First, critics confronted bias in news coverage and pretty much agreed that opinion and news must be separated. Second, they were unanimous that care beyond the profit principle must be exercised in news selection. Although they did not agree on what was trivial, they agreed that trivialities squandered a newspaper's space and readers' time—and, many suggested, presented a distorted view of the world. Especially before the Civil War, vestiges of the value system emphasizing deference are apparent in arguments that covering "ordinary" people trivialized news. After the war, critics called "gossip" trivial and began to merge the issue with that of invasion of privacy as they focused on the impropriety of publishing detailed accounts of weddings and other aspects of people's lives.

Third, material that violated good taste and judgment had no place in newspapers. A problem, however, remained in defining what crossed over the bounds of acceptable taste: some believed crime news did; others argued it did not and, indeed, that the press had a responsibility to report such news. Some argued that coverage of executions and funerals violated good taste.

Fourth, a culmination of emphasis on such issues charted directions regarding the matter of invasion of privacy, for this debate, and the journalistic conduct that generated it, no doubt motivated two jurists' development of the article on privacy published in 1890 that set the course for legally recognizing rights to privacy.

Fifth, critics saw separation of news and business functions as essential, but they were more subdued on this issue than on any other. Most critics blamed the press's business nature for its problems, but they were ambivalent about how to deal with it. The issue underlying every criticism was whether newspapers' success, or even survival, depended on publishing

the kind of content critics so objected to. In an era that elevated the role
of business in society, some were timid in coming to grips with this consideration. But they charted an important direction with such suggestions
as assuring that advertisements were labeled as such and recommending
that editors refuse to "puff" an advertiser's wares and prohibit advertisers
from influencing news policies in other ways.

Sixth, critics defined journalism as difficult, demanding work requiring
intellectual and moral ability. Critics were concerned about the kind of
talent the press attracted and whether systematic training for journalists
should be established. Although few endorsed specialized education for
journalists, all advocated training through college education and practice.
And increasingly the word *ethics* cropped up in discussions, indicating a
trend toward some code of conduct. Indeed, the kind of emphasis on these
two concerns seemed to define the next stage of discussion.

Seventh, these discussions, especially after the Civil War, laid the foundation for the development after the turn of the century of journalism education, professional organizations, and other means of monitoring journalistic conduct. Rudiments of codes of conduct articulated by individuals
of this era paved the way for further definition of appropriate journalistic
conduct and development of codes of ethics in the early twentieth century.

With the sets of "rules" proposed by editors during the late 1870s and
1880s, press criticism seems to have reached a turning point of sorts.
The demands for improvement surely influenced the formulation of these
rules, thus demonstrating that critical discussions did indeed affect the
press over time. But to a great extent the rules represent how far the discussions still needed to go. Stone's "principles" deny and defy partisanism,
whereas Dana's "maxims" include how to be "ethically" partisan, signifying that the issue was far from resolved. Bennett's rules epitomize the
"industrialized" press on its way to corporate structure and the making of
"media barons" in an era that raised still other issues. Finally, the guidelines
reflect the relationship of standards to the press's role as it was perceived
and as it operated within the polity. What, then, are the implications for
current journalistic standards and the debate of media ethics today?

Chapter Eight

Implications of Historical Study of Journalistic Standards

Shall telegraphs yet be made to work by dispensing with wires and using wholly the earth as a conductor, so that the editor of the future shall have a private line, free of tolls, with stations everywhere? Shall he dispense with the joint toil of brain and hand in preparing editorials, and record his thoughts by delicate and subtle machinery that shall spare his nerve force and double his capacity for labor? Will he be trebly blest in some curious invention that will rapidly set the unerring types of his columns, and be the uncomplaining slave that shall never ask an increase of wages, or join in strikes? Is there coming a mechanical genius who shall construct a perfect press, and evoke from the hidden forces of nature some inexpensive motor, and chain it to the wheel? . . .

Gentlemen, if a prophet shall arise and tell us that all this is to be the advance of another century, I think the conclusion would be that we all had been born a hundred years too soon.

William H. Sampson, editor of the Republican Journal, *Belfast, Maine*

The nineteenth century was a time of dramatic changes in the press and of examination of the press's role in American society. The press changed in response both to the shifts in society and to its own needs, emphatically demonstrating press-society interaction. During the century, critics and journalists tried to come to grips with questions that go to the very heart of democracy, questions that continue to beset thinkers about the press: What can the press do? How can it do it? What should it not do? What are its faults and excesses? And what are their implications? Much of what the present day takes for granted about the press's capability and responsibility evolved in the middle and late years of the last century. Although changes occurred after 1900, the foundation was laid during those nineteenth-century decades, particularly after the Civil War.

Tracing the evolution of concepts of journalistic standards over the course of the nineteenth century reveals the interaction between press and society in many ways. Cultural changes altered the press as a social institution, which in turn led to changes in journalistic goals, procedures, and rules defining its work. As a social institution, the nineteenth-century American press changed variously with the nation's shifting political and economic structures, ideologies, and cultural trends. The press's own capabilities and journalistic procedures and goals changed dramatically as production and distribution technologies developed, as literacy rates increased, and as demographic, economic, political, and value structures shifted. The press evolved from essentially a one- or two-person, small-shop operation of precarious stability to a corporate structure engaging thousands and irreversibly interlocked with society. Procedures evolved from simple recording to complex reporting—from reprinting items as received to physically pursuing news across communities, nation, and world, to "dressing up" information to entice readers, to "manufacturing" news to retain them.

Over time, discussions of the press reflected cultural changes—particularly shifts in values; but more important, they revealed changing perceptions of the press's roles, purposes, and functions. Directly related to journalistic standards, discussions also revealed changing expectations of the press, demonstrating the relationship to shifting values. In effect, these discussions crystallized the interaction between press and society, showing how people perceived of and thought about the press, how they saw it as comporting or not with social needs.

The press's role also showed this interaction. As a cultural artifact, the press's role changed with culture. The social institutional role (defined as the confluence of the press's place in the larger social structure, people's perceptions of it, and its actual functions) is never static, although patterns of change may be imperceptible in the short term. The role depends on society's intentions and value structure and on the press's capabilities. As American society changed, press capabilities also changed, effecting changed perceptions of its role; at the same time, social changes shifted the press's purpose and functions; and changed press capacities also altered its role.

Examination of the social institutional role throughout the century revealed a political press role in the earliest years giving way by mid-century to an information model, which, by the 1890s, merged into a business model. Press criticism across the century and newspaper content in the decades 1800–1810, 1850–1860, and 1890–1900 confirmed these models.

Finally, the very notion of appropriate and inappropriate journalistic conduct reflected the press-society interaction. As cultural trends, press capabilities, and press role changed, concepts of journalistic standards— determined by press role, press capabilities, and value structures—also changed. As suggested in Chapter 1, notions of what may be right or wrong about journalistic conduct flow from society's value structure, from what people perceive the press to be capable of doing, and from what the press does. Study shows that, as values changed during the century, press role and standards changed also.

Research sought to discover the development of concepts of journalistic standards, and several findings defined that development. Of singular importance, there was an awakening in America to the press's potency, reflected by both critics' discussions and the press's response, especially after the Civil War. In effect, the press's role in society was essentially rethought and readjusted by the postwar generation.

General Awakening to Press-Society Issues

Clearly, after the Civil War, Americans recognized that the importance of the printed word had changed. It no longer represented merely a "safe" record of political debates, historical events, or erudite lore—relatively impersonal and apart from people's everyday lives. It dealt with one's friends, neighbors, employer, with the inner dealings of one's party or business. The printed word was no longer a receptacle of information that people could read and store with detachment on a shelf. It intruded into their lives and involved readers—provoked feelings, represented something used in daily life (information about the next-door neighbor, the business project altering a community, commodities, entertainment). Undercurrents of these changes are visible before 1860, but it is a general American recognition of them that makes the post–Civil War era significant. Perceiving new reaches of the press, Americans at the same time began to try to understand the newspaper press in society and the implications of the changes. That was a tall order, for it signified a revolution in views about the importance of the printed word.

In addition to maintaining humankind's store of knowledge, the printed word was suddenly recognized as a medium for communicating nonreligious, nonliterary ideas, attitudes, events, issues, views, rationales, and perspectives on the world, nation, government, community, groups, individuals, and behavior. As press critics showed they were keenly aware, the printed word represented a record not only for posterity but also for one nation's view of others, and increasingly, for one individual's view of another. By mid-century in America, the press made such information available to everyone. It was natural that profound questions should then be raised: What, generally, was the effect of newspaper content on people's thinking and opinions? Might some parts of society be affected negatively by certain content? And how could the vulnerable be defined and protected, if necessary?

During most of the century, Americans learned new lessons daily about what the press was capable of exposing; it may not be overstatement to say that each day's newspaper revealed a new capability and exposed a previously unreported facet of life. After the 1830s, especially, the new content exposed details of daily lives and life's seamier side. People raised serious questions about whether such information should be printed. After all, how did it elevate the soul or ennoble minds? By the 1880s, newspaper content exposed corrupt practices (especially in government) and intruded on private affairs, as for example in the episode of journalists accompanying the president of the United States on his honeymoon. Such revelations shocked the public, and they also unquestionably provoked thought about the propriety of their being in print at all. A person reading in the morning paper that his mother kicked her dog the previous day when he has never before seen such information printed (about his or anyone else's mother) would be jolted. Critics seem to confirm that nineteenth-century newspapers (especially in the middle decades) frequently startled readers. Most people would have to think through several issues if they fully considered the sudden appearance of this new kind of "news": they would have to internalize that such information had been printed before considering what might be its implications, and for whom; whether a newspaper should contain such information; what material was appropriate newspaper content; what limits might be reasonable on a "free" press, and so on. Of course, most did not follow these issues through to a conclusion, especially when posing them was in itself a new experience. Whether horrified or nervously amused, most stopped at the realization that such information had been committed to print, for it did not fit prevailing notions of the printed word's function.

One result of the traditional view of the printed word was that the press received little attention until after the Civil War. But other reasons for lack of attention to the press also loom large. Early nineteenth-century Americans' short experience with newspapers provided little basis from which to give them considered attention. However, that short-term experience was rapidly overwhelmed by a glut of experience as the press grew phenomenally during the century. But the growth occurred while Americans' attention was necessarily focused on more compelling issues. There simply was little compulsion—or perhaps time—to study the press. The vast amount of literature on the press during the century's last decade seems very revealing from this perspective. By that time, having forged a new government, established a viable multi-party system, fought a civil war (among others), tried to restore the resultant damage, and settled a continent, Americans finally had the luxury of being able to look closely at institutions such as the press. Or, one might say, considering the shrill concern expressed in the 1880s, they concluded that the press demanded attention. In any case, during all those years of nation building, the press had grown by monstrous proportions. By 1870, it was overgrown but not mature.

Study of press criticism confirms the relationship between the press's role and journalistic standards. Critics' concerns—and the language of criticism—changed, revealing patterns that correlate to the differing models in the three eras. The earliest model is clearest. The middle decades appear significantly transitional, for partisan traditions overlay an emerging information model intended to serve the individual and the good of the "whole" public. Nothing in history is ever static, and any era or trend, depending on how narrow the focus, can be seen as transitional; but the middle decades reflect a milieu that was not conducive to clarity by those considering the press. Critics in these decades seemed overwhelmed, overawed, confused, and uncertain about the press. Indeed, they clearly recognized and agreed on only two aspects—its phenomenal growth and its powers (to them unfathomable but real) over both public opinion and social structure. Although mid-century criticism possessed little clarity about the nature of the press and how it should be used, the recognition of the newly emerged information model is clear, and important issues were raised. By their nature, transitions create confusion, and critics cannot fairly be faulted for not comprehending the press. They were, after all, pioneers in studying it, although by 1830 the press had existed in America for two centuries. They might be blamed only if they had not considered at all a social institution that was so rapidly becoming integrated with everyday life.

Nineteenth-century press critics' concern about how information was selected, gathered, and committed to print cannot, therefore, be taken lightly. They were struggling to understand what to them represented a phenomenal advance in civilization—a phenomenon enabling the sharing of thoughts across physical boundaries and the revelation of events and activities in the world's farthest reaches, as well as allowing infinite possibilities for looking in on people's behavior—that which had always been public as well as that which had been considered intimate and private. That all this could be committed to print portended something awesome, although critics were not sure exactly what. Truly, these possibilities represented unprecedented powers, and those discussing the press were exercising the greatest sense of responsibility as they considered them. Regardless of how limited their abilities or visions were, they cannot be judged by present-day values, for their views were as important in their time as are those of today to the present. Their views may not be invalidated because they are disagreeable today any more than views of today may be invalidated by future generations. Furthermore, critics' views before 1860 related to a press that, compared to today's, was primitive, and to a world far less complex. And their vision emanated from a store of knowledge less voluminous.

Press Response

The response of the press to society occurred on several levels. Press capacities expanded in response to social changes, affecting the gathering, selection, and presentation of news—and, indeed, its very definition. Such changes directly affected journalistic standards, altering journalistic goals, procedures, and conduct. As such changes became visible, critics reacted, noting such goals, procedures, and conduct they believed to be inappropriate. And the press responded to the issues raised. Critics' overriding concern in the first decades was partisanism; by mid-century, it was trivialization of news; by the 1890s, sensationalism and invasions of privacy (both infused with concerns about taste) were compelling issues.

Study of newspaper content confirms the relationship of journalistic standards to the role of the press—another dimension of the press's response to society. But newspaper content also yielded some unexpected findings, showing both significant changes and continuities across the century. Content evolved from being idea-centered in the earliest decade to event-centered by mid-century, and to a diversity dominated by the "story" in the 1890s. The idea as the reason for newspaper items diminished steadily from being dominant in the earliest decade to virtual nonexistence by the 1890s. A continuity followed, however, in that ideas—the basis for most of the earliest news pages—were relegated by the 1890s to a special editorial page. It is notable, however, that many (if not most) editorials were prompted by actions, groups, and organizations rather than ideas; although ideas underlay editorials, they were submerged.

A noteworthy related change affected the theme of balance, or reporting all sides of issues. Although the early press emphasized ideas, a newspaper presented only one side of issues addressed, and the press's role virtually precluded any notion of balance. To learn the "other side's" position required reading another newspaper. This circumstance began to change as the information model emerged in the 1830s, and for a time in the middle decades, journalists did not seem shy of controversy. But by the 1890s, although journalists claimed to present different sides or viewpoints on issues, they increasingly seemed to avoid controversy—most likely because it might alienate readers. The business model, based on achieving high circulation, was aimed at pleasing everyone; hence, not only had the place of ideas in newspapers diminished by the 1890s, but controversial ideas that might offend and cost readership were fewer. It is ironic that, while critics lambasted sensationalism, journalists countered that it "sold" papers; hence, "offensiveness" sold, but controversial ideas were treated as unsalable "commodities."

Another change involved treatment of persons. The earliest papers rarely dealt with unimportant individuals. By mid-century, although interest continued in statesmen and officials and expanded especially to performing artists, content emphasized "ordinary" people, their milieu and lives. Important people again dominated in the 1890s—but now were the kind of people who are today called celebrities: business leaders and the very rich received much attention. Ordinary people figured in the news only because of drama in events associated with them. Critics made trivialization of news a big issue after the press's attention turned to the "ordinary," but journalists after the 1830s discovered that this focus provided an important link between papers and readers. Although by the 1890s they

gave little space to that kind of news, they mined the discovery by including personals columns (which, however, tended to emphasize notable
persons).[1]

It is also noteworthy that nineteenth-century critics' concern about diversity contrasts with today's concerns. The issue of diversity was most
discussed in the period of the fewest newspapers, during the political press
era, but it was unrelated to the number of papers in existence. Critics
often deplored the fact that a single newspaper provided no diversity of
views, meaning the positions of different parties. Later, however, concern about diversity was infrequently expressed. Horace Greeley, William
Cullen Bryant, and William Lloyd Garrison advocated the press as a forum
for diverse views, but no ground swell championing this view appeared.
After the 1830s, journalists increasingly sought diversity of *content*, and the
1890s newspapers reflect such diversity to a startling degree. But concern
about diversity of ideas was not evident. At the beginning of the twentieth
century, with the snowballing trend toward concentration of ownership
and reduced numbers of daily newspapers, the concern about diversity re-
emerged with some urgency. An irony, however, is that the concern then
related more to numbers of newspapers than to the substance of single
papers as it had a century earlier, and it arose at a time when idea-centered
newspaper content had virtually disappeared.

Finally, journalists' and other critics' views of the press began to diverge
in the 1880s. In daily contact with the press and all it did from the "inside,"
journalists worked with a social institution grown so complex by 1890
that even they had difficulty understanding it. Because they were on the
inside, however, they knew how it worked and had more basis for insights
about both its capacities and its limitations. What 1880s journalists knew
of the press from experience was far more than their predecessors of a generation before had known—largely because there was far more to know.
Even by the 1880s, those on the outside had far less knowledge about the
press than had critics of the previous generation, simply because the press
had grown so complex. Journalists were thus becoming something of a
separate class, a separateness indicated by increasing numbers of articles
and lectures by journalists intended to explain how the press worked. Journalism had become a specialized realm that those unassociated with the
press would not otherwise know about. That such specialization had developed is also evident in the discussion of appropriate training for aspiring
journalists.

Another divergence is reflected in the definition of news. After the Civil War, journalists increasingly defined news all-inclusively, arguing that items must not be omitted from newspapers purely because they related society's problems or its seamier side. As Dana asserted, journalism aimed to print "whatever the Divine Providence permitted to occur." Nonjournalists generally were not as clear or positive about what merited press attention.

Most journalists, however, seemed less clear than nonjournalists on the issue of partisanism. Although they defined news as separate from party obligations and independent newspapers as superior to partisan newspapers—and although partisanism had diminished by 1880—they often fused news and political obligations in the same press function. But the confusion is understandable when viewed against the background of press development throughout the century. Those journalists who were in their middle and later years in the 1880s had grown up on party newspapers and schooled themselves in politics. It is not surprising that they should have difficulty separating partisanism from a newspaper's role.

The divergence between the views of nonjournalists and journalists should not be overstated, but there is reason to believe that study of criticism through the 1890s would reveal growing divergence. After programs of journalism education emerged and professional organizations solidified, even greater divergence could be expected.

Nineteenth-century press critics no doubt had some short-term effects on reducing the amount of "trivial" news that was published, lessening partisanism, and in other areas that would become clear only with closer, more narrowly focused study. The longest-standing issue of partisanism was unresolved at century's end, although blatant subservience to parties had diminished remarkably. Still, Joseph Pulitzer served in Congress in the 1880s, and other notable journalists ran for and held elective office in the early twentieth century. Another irony is that until the last decades of the nineteenth-century Americans could not conceive of a press without partisanism and apparently saw no conflict of interest; one hundred years later, the opposite view prevails. Present-day journalists and critics cannot conceive of condoning a press largely intended to advance the positions of political parties, except for specialized publications that exist for that purpose alone. A further irony is that, although the present generation frowns on political involvements by journalists, the press's political effect is one of the most discussed and perhaps least understood issues today.

Nineteenth-century critics' inability to resolve the problem of the press's proper political role and the present-day confusion about its political effect are part of the legacy of the origins of the nation's press. Like the early nineteenth-century press, overgrown before thoughtful attention focused on it, the press's political role had become so embedded in society before attention turned to it that it may forever elude understanding.

Enduring Questions

As is often true of historical studies, research that began from a few simple questions necessarily dealt with many complex ones and raised numerous others. This is especially true of an exploratory work that ventures into uncharted territory. At the end, the questions raised seem to preclude definitive summary. And some of the most perplexing questions at the outset remain unsettled.

One basic question prompting the research was, Did journalists or press critics talk about truth during the nineteenth century, when journalistic conduct often seemed to belie all present-day notions of ethical behavior? This is a simple inquiry, but for several reasons it will not recede quickly after one attempt to explore it. First, the question begs an answer based on presumptions about ethics as understood today; although this research sought to find what critics discussed and whether truth figured prominently, journalistic ethics in history was not studied here. Second, one can perceive in the criticism—by the 1870s, certainly—underlying concerns with ethical issues (such as White's and Godkin's interest in traits of human behavior that should be enhanced); and by the mid-1880s, the term ethics itself began to appear in discussions. But in the main, critics worried about the press's effect on society and about particular content. Third, related to these points, the subject requires many explorations—some broad and many narrowly focused—from diverse perspectives before enough knowledge can be accumulated to allow any kind of conclusive answer. Fourth, this research makes clear that the question has no simple answer—and this bears further comment. One approach is to consider truth in the larger sense of knowledge and in the narrower definition of accuracy.

Conceptualizations of truth in the nineteenth century differ from those of today, so it is erroneous to impose present-day judgments without exploring historical meanings. With that caveat, one may observe that truth (in its broadest meaning) and its importance to newspaper content under-lay every journalistic issue. Even underlying the issue of whether crime should be reported was a concern about whether this was the "truth"—in large terms about society—and whether it was a "fit" truth to tell (that is, appropriate to commit to the record of humankind). People discussed accuracy of details—truth on one level very much as that journalistic stan-dard is understood today—but very seldom. Such a standard had little relevance to the press's political role and became significant only when the information model emerged after 1830. Hence, to expect nineteenth-century Americans to have dealth with journalistic truth in all its dimen-sions as understood today oversteps their limits and those of their press.

As the century progressed, people drew increasingly nearer to discussing ethics and the issue of truth. The approach to truth then may be identi-fiable only because by that time the conceptualization was closer to that of today. In any event, in answer to another question raised at the outset —whether discussions of journalistic standards affected the press—some debate, beginning in the 1870s and expanding especially in the 1880s, was part of post–Civil War trends that culminated in several significant changes by 1925. Newspapers established codes of ethics; journalism courses, de-partments, and schools were founded; textbooks were written; and asso-ciations were formed to provide at least a form of social control over press conduct and practices.

In addition to these observations, Chapters 2 and 3 (which delineated press roles across the century) and Chapters 4 through 7 (which revealed perceptions of press roles) show the relationship of the press and journal-istic standards to values—a much-neglected phenomenon. Just as views were delimited by critics' short experience with the press, they were created by values that determined how people saw the press's role and appropriate journalistic conduct.

This relationship highlights the critical role of values as determinants of the press's role and standards, which brings us to consider the implica-tions of historical analysis of standards for present-day debate about media ethics. At the outset, several observations may be made about values.

As noted in Chapter 1, the press reflects society's values. But values are not static, and as societies evolve, "traditional" values recede in the face of "new," emerging values—which over time themselves become traditional and are ultimately also outdistanced or overthrown. And so the cycle con-tinues. Press content, the most immediate harbinger of changing values, generates criticism when it counters familiar, traditional values. Those un-willing to abandon the receding values see only deterioration and believe the press is diffusing harm to society's moral fabric; rather than the prov-erbial messenger, they wish to kill the *message* that diminishes or degrades what they cherish. But in a sense they do also wish to kill the messenger—that is, eradicate the kind of press they identify with the disturbing form or content. And their notions of press conduct—were they alone imple-mented—would accomplish just that. Consider the critics of the "radical" press in the 1830s, or the Federalists who sought renewal of the Alien and Sedition Acts. They wanted controls that would eradicate the radical press—which, as is clear in hindsight, was the press of the future. Press criticism is, of course, generated by more concrete journalistic conduct. Publishing a photo of an auto accident that depicts a mangled body, for example, pains members of the deceased's family regardless of society's value structure. And a critic justifiably asks whether this is necessary.

It appears, therefore, that some analysis of media issues raised by the ethics debate might productively separate the concrete from those dictated by value structure. Such a task can't be easy and may be impossible, given the general lack of consciousness about the immediate value structure. Per-haps values structuring one's own society can be discerned only from the distance of time. But this can't be known until the attempt is made, and study of value structure in relation to media criticism seems worthwhile.

Historical analysis of journalistic standards also points up the degree to which discussion of journalistic ethics proceeds from theories. Some underlying assumptions can be ascertained, but explicit larger theories and attention to media role are generally lacking. For example, basic premises underlying today's debate are that journalistic performance needs improve-ment; that journalism and media can be improved; that improvement in journalistic performance is important for the good of society; and that journalists can learn or be taught to achieve an improved journalism and a better society through moral reasoning. Emphasizing moral reasoning, the debate stresses considering alternative actions and weighing consequences in working toward journalistic ends. The ultimate purpose is to assure that journalists will accomplish both the best journalistic goal and adhere to the highest moral principles at the same time. And the assumption is that strengthening journalists' sensitivity to ethics and instilling in them habits of moral reasoning will assure better journalism in the long term. Obvi-ously, this is good, but what are the larger purposes? What are the desired standards? And why? What is to be served in society at large?

In other words, contemporary discussions proceed from the practical and are focused on the everyday activities of journalists; in many respects, they cover different territory than did the nineteenth-century critics. The immediate concern today is the degree of morality inherent in journalistic decision making and conduct. Nineteenth-century critics through the 1880s never quite got to the point of focusing on decision making in relation to journalistic practices. They were moving in that direction, but their vision remained on the broader effects of the press. Present-day interest in decision-making processes leads to an emphasis on the concrete, the realm of standards, and confusion of standards with the higher-level abstraction of ethics—at the expense of studying ethics in the larger social context.

Historical analysis suggests a need to stand back, so to speak, and examine larger contexts and their relevance, asking some obvious questions. For example, why does concern about journalistic practices exist? What predominant interests does the concern address? What theory or theories, and about what, inhere in those predominant interests? That is, do the interests represent certain theories about society, social organization, social change, human behavior, journalistic organization? And do the theories represent the most appropriate approaches to solving problems of journalistic ethics? To paraphrase historian Lee Benson's summary of Karl Marx's answer to why history should be studied, Marx sought to determine why social conflict exists in human society, and what can be done to abolish it permanently. Marx's dominant interests, addressing economic and class elements, represented a theory of social organization based on conflict.[2] For a century and a half a great bulk of scholarship has in one way or another addressed whether Marxist theories are the most appropriate for determining why social conflict exists and how it can be eradicated. Others answer the question by saying that history is studied to discover how change occurs—to learn, perhaps, how to direct change more responsibly. This aim, too, like that of Marx, is driven by an underlying desire to achieve a better-ordered society.

For generations a line of historical inquiry has answered the question of how change occurs with a theory that in large part makes change the result of individual action. Called the "great person" theory, or "rational actor" model, this view emphasizes individuals as primary agents of change, focusing on the genius of a few individuals in any given era as responsible for shaping history. Thus far, the direction and assumptions underlying the journalism ethics debate are parallel. The debate emphasizes what the individual does or does not do as part of media work, without reference to context, agents of change, theories, or the scope of journalism as a social institution.

This is not to suggest that the debate is not driven by larger concerns. Clearly, a consciousness if not a clear conceptualization of the press as a social institution underlies the debate. Although much media criticism dwells on what would seem to be limited spheres related to individuals or small segments of society—for example, insensitive reporting surrounding tragedies, invasions of privacy, or excessive emphasis on certain themes— it is based on concern about the cumulative effect of such deeds on the whole society. But that concern is rarely confronted squarely and seems, in fact, submerged and secondary. A definite conceptualization of the role of the media in society may be more productive. To illustrate, a more deliberate attempt to define the dimensions of the effect of the media on society might lead to specifying or generating useful theories regarding the media, their present social role, and conduct and ethics in relation to that role. And it might reveal that theories, or at the least, assumptions guiding the debate—implicitly if not explicitly—merit closer scrutiny. Individuals are important—and some will always be better or worse at what is required —but considering nineteenth-century standards in the larger context of value structure and press role rather than individual actions makes them more understandable.

At a very basic level, historical analysis points up the overwhelming variety of media forms in today's world. During the nineteenth century, those discussing the press meant books, pamphlets, magazines, and newspapers—but primarily they meant newspapers. When they did refer to all of these, even though they were inexperienced in this kind of debate and often overwhelmed and confused, their discussions could proceed with more clarity than may be possible in the current debate, for media then had more similarities than differences. Today's media forms are far more diverse (radio, television, film, for example), with greater differences from one to another. Particular tasks among the media differ, methods and procedures differ, and consequently, standards or criteria governing procedures differ. However, blanket statements today often refer to all media as if they were identical on all dimensions. Careful analysis of media differences would seem productive: especially the different demands and constraints each form puts on the process of gathering, presenting, and disseminating information; their various capabilities and functions; and the distinctions among performance standards that might be most appropriate for each. Judging their performance against standards befitting each would likely advance the cause of achieving greater ethical conduct among all media.

Differences among contemporary media rest in the technological developments that have shaped them, and it is worth noting that historical analysis casts technological developments in a different perspective than that emphasized in current research. The latter tends to emphasize technology as an entity unto itself, to the exclusion of larger contexts of its development. Technological change represents cultural change at the broadest level; at a lesser level, it signifies alterations in social institutions over time. In journalism, this has meant changes in ways of conducting tasks, which in turn have led to changes in standards. It is worth noting, too, that historical analysis reveals a lack of awareness of the implications of new technologies as they emerged. Nineteenth-century discussions, for example, indicate unrealistic expectations about technological advances bringing about great and noble ends, such as world peace and solutions to other timeless problems. And as technical innovations were adapted to routine work, little thought seems to have attended their use as tools affecting society. In general, issues about the moral implications of technologies were raised only after a considerable lag—decades after their use had become part of routine procedures. When a "new" technology, or practices it brought into being, was seen as intruding on people's lives or society's welfare in some way, then the moral questions arose. The kinds of intrusions, however, were not anticipated. Again, possibly these can't be anticipated, but they are worth thought regarding the relationship of technology to society, directions its uses might take, and its implications. Not yet confronted with diminishing resources, overpopulation, and atomic bombs, nineteenth-century minds equated technological advances with advances in civilization: the former could only improve the latter. We in the twentieth century are not so sanguine, but the effects of technology on society remain under-studied.

Historical analysis also forces examination of meanings to enable exploration of any subject over time, which in this research highlights differences between moral principles and standards. Although the definitions used here may be flawed or disagreeable to some, the point nevertheless underscores the need for clear distinctions for the sake of discourse—and this, too, has relevance for the debate of media ethics.

The current debate has rarely distinguished, for example, between ethics and standards—that is, between basic moral principles as abstract ideals (such as telling the truth) and the standards journalists use at the more concrete level to govern and evaluate how they do their work. The debate seems to interchange moral principles (abstract constructs) with procedures (tangible processes of conducting one's work). Truth as a philosophical construct, for example, becomes intermixed with the issue of truth as accurate reporting of a fact—a name, an address. The moral principle (telling the truth) and the standard (accurate reporting of a fact) represent different levels of abstraction. The latter lies in the realm of practical, daily existence and can be easily understood and demonstrated; the former lies in the realm of philosophy and is not readily subject to proof. The distinctions between standards and moral principles are very fine at some levels; indeed, they overlap in some situations, and differences are not easy to discern or articulate. As a result, it is not surprising that moral principles (abstracts) and standards (tangible evidence pertaining to conduct and quality of work) become confused in discussions.

Moral principles are fairly universal and differ relatively little over time; standards, on the other hand, are linked with the procedures for conducting activities and hence represent products of culture more than do moral principles. As cultural shifts occur in a given society, standards change. Whereas standards, then, are connected with everyday practical procedures, moral principles are constructs, ideals, that are equally incumbent on all professions (all human activity, even); but like members of most professions, journalists are not routinely compelled to wax philosophical —that is, to think about or be involved with philosophical precepts on a constant basis.

This by no means suggests that the reponsible journalist is not constantly concerned about deeper issues associated with journalistic work. But the pace of few professions permits the luxury of deep, soul-searching thought on a regular basis, even when the instances creating moral dilemmas are infrequent and relatively similar. The pace of journalistic work perhaps permits less such time than most professions; and yet, the situations creating moral dilemmas for journalists vary greatly and may range from none to many on any given day. The responsible journalist is ever conscious of ominous responsibilities at several levels. At a broad level, in gathering and presenting information that tells what of significance is happening, the journalist is also informing society as a whole of its state of well-being. At other levels, the necessity to include individuals and painful aspects of events in such information presents the journalist with responsibilities for individuals' reputations, privacy, pain. Trying to serve all such ends under the pressure of deadlines leaves little time, indeed, for philosophical analysis as part of the routine.

Moral principles may be readily stated—truth, fairness, compassion; they are relatively few and can be set forth with little dispute about their desirability as part of any human activity. Identifying moral principles in action, however, is not easy. Many criteria for accomplishing one's tasks also are not readily identifiable, especially because different journalistic tasks prompt different procedures. News breaks unexpectedly, for example; events are never the same, never occur in identical ways, and thus it would seem impossible to create uniform procedures applicable to every journalistic eventuality—except perhaps in such broad dimensions as to be relatively meaningless. Furthermore, criteria are multiple and many-faceted; they are not static and are subject to debate as to which in a given situation is appropriate for proceeding. Criteria change from situation to situation, individual to individual, profession to profession—and they change over time. On the other hand, basic moral principles remain relatively static over time.

Criteria for accomplishing a journalistic goal may or may not incorporate the process of moral reasoning, which the ethics debate emphasizes, through no fault of the journalist. Some criteria are independent, neutral, as it were, in relation to the larger ethical issues. Responsible contemporary journalists are always concerned with accuracy in reporting, and accuracy is, of course, an essential dimension of the larger truth. But deciding to attend a city council meeting instead of interviewing each member and the mayor on separate occasions may be the most efficient way to get most information about city business. The issue of truth as a larger moral principle is unlikely to enter into the process—beyond the intent and effort to report accurately (adhere to the standard) what transpires— until the reporter begins to interpret what transpired. The reporter uses certain criteria (which may be private, based on her own judgment, training, and experience) for determining the meaning—the truth—and for selecting what shall be reported and how. This may or may not necessarily, however, involve the moral reasoning process referred to in the ethics debate. The goal is to report events accurately, and journalists follow certain criteria for accomplishing that end, including criteria for determining what is the best story. The primary and dominant intent is gathering and disseminating information to the public.

While focusing on the concrete, the ethics debate emphasizes the moral ideal, the construct that, although easily stated and undisputed as to desirability, lies at the highest level of abstraction. But complex processes and influences in work procedures impinge on, both facilitating and impeding, its accomplishment. And the moral ideal in any given journalistic situation may conflict with other moral ideals or with journalistic ends. The model, figure 8.1, depicts the processes. Journalistic performance, to some degree and in some form, proceeds through the steps listed on the left-hand side because they are part of daily work. But nothing compels a procession through the steps on the right-hand side, and the broken line on the left signifies that it is possible to bypass the moral reasoning stage altogether because it is not a built-in part of every task. The ethics debate has dealt with standards only as ingredients in the process of moral reasoning, which may account for what seems to be a confusion of standards and moral principles. Some dimensions are thus obscured and, in turn, understanding is impeded, creating difficulties that often become stumbling blocks to advancing the debate.

Lack of agreed-upon standards, for example, often becomes such a stumbling block. Existing codes of ethics are guidelines for achieving certain standards and do not spell out moral principles or how to practice and accomplish them. But there are no agreed-upon codes. The code of ethics published by the American Newspaper Publishers Association in 1923 comes closest, but it suggests a broad set of guidelines, about which the most that can be said with certainty is that they represent consensus only among the members of the group that initially developed and endorsed them and those who have since made the few changes in them since their establishment more than a half century ago. As guidelines they are not binding. Journalists generally hold the code in high regard, but any media organization may deal in any way with any employee's deviation from, or infraction of, any of the guidelines. One journalist might be severely reprimanded for infractions, whereas another might view such rules as incapable of being applied to every situation and cite dangers in rigid adherence to them for several compelling reasons: cases in which they have restricted the press's freedom to carry out legitimate journalistic work, in which they present conflicts among ethical goals, or in which strict adherence would prevent the publishing of a story of vital interest to the public and the national welfare. For example, when sources do not want information revealed—as in government matters requiring secrecy or in the Watergate events of the 1970s—strict compliance to the code could tie

Fig. 8.1. Journalistic Standards and Moral Principles

journalists' hands. Similarly, although no good journalist wishes to tarnish another's reputation, innumerable stories could not be told without doing so. If a city official has embezzled public funds, the public has a right to know about it; but the telling of the story certainly tarnishes the official's reputation. And since the official does not want exposure, the enterprising journalist may have to use unconventional methods to get the story—or let the public continue to be duped and defrauded. Thus beyond certain preliminary, basic tenets of practice, there is little consensus among journalists about what is right or wrong about methods of gathering, presenting, and distributing news.

Another problem is the centrality of moral principles to journalists' work. All would readily agree that journalists should tell the truth, but the same moral principle is equally incumbent on members of every profession. Yet for journalists the issue is central as in few professions, which heightens anxiety and aggravates debate about how to ensure truthfulness. Since the journalist's purpose is to convey information, truthfulness is an inherent issue; the degree of its presence or absence in the journalist's work is likely to be visible to (and perceived variously by) infinite numbers outside as well as in the profession. Journalists are therefore especially sensitive to the multiple dimensions and the tenuousness of truth. Disagreements arise about the meaning of truth, which truth, what portion of it to tell, which dimensions to emphasize, the appropriate method of gathering, selecting, and determining the truth, and whether one should intervene in any way for any reason—and if so, just what is appropriate—in conveying a source's version of it. Similarly, other basic moral principles —such as being fair and just—raise disagreement about what exactly they mean, for whom, the best method to accomplish them, and appropriate criteria governing ways of doing so.

The consequence of these difficulties is that standards exist largely in the private domain. Every journalist—and every media critic—has ideas of appropriate and inappropriate journalistic conduct. That is, most standards are derived from individual notions; they are as varied as journalists' views of appropriate and inappropriate procedures and can differ manifestly in practice across the profession. One model of behavior, situational ethics, sees journalists exercising judgment on the spot, on a situation-by-situation basis, as to what is right and wrong conduct. By its nature, much of a journalist's work consists of dealing with the unexpected— again, perhaps more than in most professions. Everyone who ever makes on-the-spot judgments knows the discomfort of the task, the tenuousness of the situation, and the fickleness of fate as to the efficacy of the decision. Leaving aside whether a society wants decisions about conduct in a pervasive and dominant profession (or any profession) guided principally by on-the-spot judgments, journalists who follow the model will decide and behave differently in similar situations. Each might see the other as deviating from appropriate standards, and the media critic would likely decide that at least one of two who behaved differently in similar situations deviated from acceptable standards. Journalists today, however, are closer than others to the daily problems of disseminating information, and their knowledge of these problems is much further removed from that of nonjournalists than it was a century ago. They are painfully aware of intricacies of ethical issues beyond nonjournalist's ken simply because of the constancy with which they face them.

Indeed, the differences between journalists' and nonjournalists' views of the press are far greater than they were at the turn of the century. At that time the press was just becoming specialized; today it is highly specialized, journalism education is regarded as essential for those entering the profession, and an additional body of media critics exists in the university scholars who study journalism as a full-time occupation. Hence, the specialized knowledge about the media that those outside the profession lack is far, far greater than it was a century ago. This does not minimize the importance of nonjournalists' insights, however. On one level, they represent the value structure that journalism reflects; on another, their lives are far more constantly touched by what journalists do. But it would seem that media criticism appropriately divides into varying levels, with journalists, nonjournalist consumers, and communications scholars each able to provide insights only at their own level. The views of all groups are essential for resolving issues of the relationship between society and the media and accomplishing the best functioning of the ever more significant media.

Nineteenth-century critics identified problems and abuses of the press in an age when both society and journalism itself were very different from those of today. Nevertheless, study of the press and their discussions of it suggests insights and distinctions that become apparent only through historical analysis. The critics of the last century can't provide those of today with solutions, for as this research makes clear, different value structures and press roles determined their concerns. But present-day critics may learn from them something about how to proceed, or not proceed;

what might work and what might not; and where criticism had effect—and why.

Those considering the press in the late nineteenth century had no clear idea of where it was heading. Some in the 1880s forecast the decline of the press, characterizing society as on the verge of revolution; one visionary in the 1870s articulated some future eventuality very like computer and satellite capacity. Generally, critics of the nineteenth century had no more insight about what the future press would be like than had the ordinary individual in 1860 about airplane travel. As imperfect humans, conscious that the press had changed and seeking to change it further, they struggled with difficult problems to which attention was long overdue. But with these givens, they cannot be faulted for lacking vision about the future. They had just begun to try to define the implications of the press in a society that differed radically from that in which they had been born. They could hardly define direction with certainty. Nevertheless, their discussions pointed the way: they set the stage for the next level of debate, for press reform in the early twentieth century, and for the development of education in journalism and mass communications; they laid the foundation for the way the press has been thought about since; and they are the forebears, the progenitors, of the present-day debate. As today's generation is indebted to the nation's first citizens for earnestly debating America's future course, so is it indebted to the press critics of the nineteenth century for beginning to consider the press and society.

Appendix
Notes
Bibliography
Index

Appendix

The brief descriptions below of sources of discussions about the press emphasize their nature for the time consulted. Because many ended and the remainder
changed with the times, no attempt is made to characterize those that have endured
into the twentieth century. Information about most comes from Frank Luther
Mott, *The History of American Magazines*.

American Historical Review. Founded in October 1895 with a fund to support
it for three years, after which the American Historical Association assumed control and included subscription fees in membership dues. The Association elected
editors. John Franklin Jameson, professor of history at Brown University, was
managing editor from 1895 to 1901; Andrew C. McLaughlin edited the *Review*
from 1901 to 1905, and Jameson resumed editorship in 1905, continuing until
1928. (Mott, 4: 138)

American Quarterly Register. July 1827–May 1843, Andover, New Hampshire.
Published by the American Education Society and edited by Bela B. Edwards and
others; intended to educate prospective ministers and missionaries, but included
general content. (Mott, 1: 491, 520)

Arena. December 1889–August 1909. Owner/editor: Bo Flower, founder
of Republican Temperance *Albion American Sentinel* (newspaper, 1880–1882).
Flower's primary interest was social reform; poverty, sweatshops, slum clearance,
unemployment, and child labor were important topics covered by the *Arena*, especially during the mid-1890s. One-fourth of the content of the first twenty volumes
was written by women. (Mott, 4: 401–416)

The Atlantic Monthly. Founded in November 1857 by Moses Dresser Phillips
of Phillips, Sampson & Company, publishers, in Boston, in consultation with the
firm's literary adviser, Francis H. Underwood. Edited by James Russell Lowell,
November 1857–June 1861; James T. Fields, July 1861–July 1871; William Dean
Howells, August 1871–January 1881; Thomas Bailey Aldrich, February 1881–
March 1890; Horace E. Scudder, April 1890–July 1898; Walter Hines Page, August 1898–July 1899; Bliss Perry, August 1899–July 1909. A literary publication
that remained New England oriented in outlook and content until the 1870s,
when it became more representative of America. Circulation declined from a peak
of 50,000 in 1869 to 20,000 in 1874 to 12,000 in 1881 and did not again reach
50,000 until after the turn of the century. (Mott, 2: 493–515)

Blackwood's Edinburgh Magazine. October 1818–. Literary monthly founded by
William Blackwood; edited by John Wilson and John Gibson Lockhart from 1817
to c. 1825, when Lockhart may have left to edit the *Quarterly Review* in London;
Wilson continued as editor at least until 1834, when Blackwood died, after which

the Blackwood sons and heirs continued the magazine. Strout quotes a twentieth-century scholar that the magazine's founding was "the most notable event in the history of English literature" and that no other British monthly could match its "array of contributors." Its first numbers were "brutal" in literary criticism; although it toned down somewhat after 1825, it remained a strong, conservative Tory publication. (Strout, *A Bibliography*, iv; Tredrey, *The House of Blackwood*)

Californian Illustrated Magazine. Monthly begun by Charles Frederick Holder in San Francisco in October 1891. Primarily literary, but included articles on science, politics, foreign affairs, and sports. Discontinued in 1894, after Holder became director of the Santa Catalina Zoological Station and sold the magazine to Edward J. Livernash. (Mott, 4: 105)

Catholic World. Begun in 1865 by Father Isaac T. Hecker as a general monthly magazine for Catholics. Published by Lawrence Kehoe, 1865–1867; Catholic Publishing Society, 1867–1868; Catholic World, 1888–; edited by Isaac T. Hecker, 1865–1888; A. F. Hewit, 1889–1897; Alexander P. Doyle, 1897–1904. A popular magazine of interest to the general reader, it also supported church doctrines and expressed Catholic views of literature, art, science, drama, education, and society. (Mott, 3: 329–330)

Century Illustrated Monthly Magazine. 1882–1929. (Continuation of *Scribner's Monthly: An Illustrated Magazine for the People*, 1870–1881.) Literary and general interest. Published by Scribner & Company, New York, 1870–1881; Century Company, New York, 1881–1930. Edited by Josiah Gilbert Holland, 1870–1881; Richard Watson Gilder, 1881–1909. Circulation began at 40,000, passed 100,000 by 1880 and 200,000 before 1890. (Mott, 3: 457–480)

The Chatauquan: A Monthly Magazine Devoted to the Promotion of True Culture, Organ of the Chautauquan Literary and Scientific Circle. September 1880–May 1914. General magazine published by Theodore L. Flood, Meadville, Pennsylvania, 1880–1889; Chatauqua Press, Cleveland, Ohio, 1899–1902; Springfield, Ohio, 1902–1904; Chautauqua, New York, 1904–1914. Edited by Theodore L. Flood, 1880–1899; Frank Chapin Bray, 1899–1914. (Mott, 3: 544–547)

Contemporary Review. English; issued from a New York publishing house established by Alexander Strahan of London and Edinburgh in 1865. (Mott, 3: 278)

Cornhill Magazine. 1860–1975. Literary monthly founded in London by George Smith in 1860 and published by Smith, Elder and Company. Henry James wrote in 1914 that the magazine's issues "were enrichments of life, they were *large* arrivals, these particular renewals of supply. . . ." Edited by W. M. Thackeray, January 1860–March 1862; G. H. Lewes, Frederick Greenwood, George Smith, and Dutton Cook, 1862–1871; Leslie Stephen, 1871–1882; James Payn, 1893–1896; St. Loe Strachey, 1896–1897; R. J. Smith and others, 1897–. (See Eddy, *The Founding of the "Cornhill Magazine"*.)

Cosmopolitan Magazine. Monthly general literary magazine founded by Paul J. Schlicht of Schlicht and Field, March 1886, Rochester, New York; published in New York, New York, from 1887. Edited by Frank P. Smith, 1886–1888; E. D. Walker, 1888; J. B. Walker, 1889–1905 (with William Dean Howells, 1890; Arthur Sherburne Hardy, 1893–1895). The magazine's circulation of 25,000 after the first year fell to 20,000 by 1889, then rose to 100,000 in 1892 and passed 300,000 in 1898. (Mott, 4: 480–505)

The Critic. January 1881–September 1906. Literary biweekly, 1881–1882; weekly, 1883–1898; monthly, 1898–1906. Published in New York, New York, by J. L. and J. B. Gilder, January–March 1881; the Critic Printing & Publishing Company, March 1881–January 1884; Good Literature Publishing Company, February–December 1884; the Critic Company, 1885–1898; G. P. Putnam & Co., 1899–1906. Edited by Jeanette L. Gilder, 1881–1906 (with Joseph B. Gilder, 1881–1901). Circulation approximately 5,000. (Mott, 3: 548–551)

The Dial. May 1880–July 1929. Monthly until August 1892; semi-monthly, September 1892–February 1915. Literary criticism; turned to public affairs after 1914. Mott calls it an intelligent, conservative, dignified periodical with high standards. Founded and edited (1880–1913) by Francis F. Brown. Published by Jansen, McClurg & Company, Chicago, 1880–1886; A. C. McClurg & Company, Chicago, 1886–1892; the Dial Company, Chicago, 1892–1914. Circulation 5,000 in 1893. (Mott, 3: 539–543)

The Eclectic Magazine of Foreign Literature, Science and Art. January 1844–June 1907. *The Eclectic Magazine and Monthly Edition of the Living Age.* 1899–1900. *The Eclectic Magazine of Foreign Literature.* 1901–1907. Published by Leavitt, Trow & Company, New York and Philadelphia, January 1844–August 1846; W. H. Bidwell, New York, September 1846–December 1868; E. R. Pelton, New York, January 1869–December 1898; The Living Age Company, Boston, January 1899–February 1905; Henry D. Noyes & Company, Boston, March–August 1905; Eclectic Magazine Printing and Publishing Company, New York, September 1905–June 1907. Edited by John Holmes Agnew, 1844–1846; Walter Hilliard Bidwell, 1846–1881; unknown, 1881–1907. (Mott, 1: 306–309)

The Edinburgh Review. October 10, 1802–. Moderate Whig quarterly that set a new standard in literary criticism. Founded by Francis Jeffrey, Sidney Smith, Henry Brougham; edited by Jeffrey, 1803–1829. According to Strout (p. 21), the "opinions expressed in the early numbers . . . permeated English criticism to an extent not commonly recognized." Others have called it high-spirited, aggressive, and the model all later reviews imitated. Circulation approximately 14,000 around 1820. (Strout, *John Bull's Letter,* 5–37)

The Forum. March 1886–January 1950. Monthly review devoted to debate of controversial issues, including political, economic, social, religious, scientific, and educational subjects. Published by Forum Publishing Company, New York, 1886–1910. Edited by Lorettus Sutton Metcalf, 1886–1891; Walter Hines Page, 1891–1895; Alfred Ernest Keet, 1895–1897; Joseph M. Rice, 1897–1907. (Mott, 4: 511–523)

Fraser's Magazine for Town and Country. February 1830–December 1882. Founded in London by Hugh Fraser and Billy Maginn; monthly literary journal that was Tory but independent in criticism and comment. Included a "spectacular array of contributors," such as Thomas Carlyle and William Makepeace Thackeray. Two historians of British periodicals say that *Fraser's* became in the 1830s what *Blackwood's* had been to the previous decade. It was "witty, capricious, and icono-

clastic" as *Blackwood's* was becoming "staid, dependable, and even reverential."
Thrall, holding that it contained the "best of Carlyle's and Thackeray's early work
and throws light on one of the most difficult decades of the nineteenth century"
when its editors "exposed the frailties and foibles of their generation with provoca-
tive comment rare at any period," called it "one of the most important organs of
progressive thought and open revolt in the Victorian age." Edited by Billy Maginn
until 1847; it was then edited by John W. Parker, 1847–?, who was succeeded
by J. A. Froude. The Longman publishing family bought *Fraser's* in 1863 and,
in 1882, changed its name to *Longman's Magazine*, which continued until 1905.
(Fader and Bornstein, *British Periodicals of the 18th and 19th Centuries*, 80–86;
Thrall, *Rebellious Fraser's*, i, 6)

The Galaxy. May 1866–January 1878. (Absorbed by the *Atlantic Monthly* in
1878.) Semimonthly, May 1866–April 1867; monthly, May 1867–January 1878.
Published by W. C. & F. P. Church, New York, 1866–1868; Sheldon & Company, New York, 1868–1878. Edited by William C. Church and Francis Pharcellus
Church. Founded to counter the *Atlantic Monthly's* emphasis on New England,
Mott says *The Galaxy* "touched popular life at more points and more directly than
most other important magazines have." Among those associated with the magazine
were Mark Twain, Henry James, Eugene Benson, Justin McCarthy, Richard Grant
White, Annie Edwards, Frederic Beecher Perkins, and Charles Astor Bristed. Circulation was 5,000 to 6,000 the first two years but rose to 23,000 in early 1871,
then fell to 7,000 in 1878. (Mott, 3: 361–381)

Harper's New Monthly Magazine. June 1850–. Literary monthly. Published by
Harper & Brothers, New York. Edited by Henry J. Raymond, 1850–1856; Alfred
H. Guernsey, 1856–1869; Henry Mills Alden, 1869–1919. Circulation began at
7,500, reaching 50,000 in six months and 200,000 by 1861. (Mott, 2: 383–405)

The Independent. December 7, 1848–October 13, 1928. Weekly religious "newspaper" established to espouse Congregationalism and oppose slavery. The first of
its four pages contained religious material, the second contained editorials and
news, the third carried news and advertising, and the fourth advertising. Mott
says that the religious newspaper genre flourished in America from the 1820s to
the 1880s. Although the *Independent* "printed denominational and other 'religious
intelligence,' its editorial discussions were . . . more important than its news."
During the Civil War, the journal's religious cast became submerged to a more
secular one and, during the 1870s, it became more literary, but it always took
strong stands on issues; throughout its life, it was one of very few of its kind
to maintain a general audience. Published by Henry Chandler Bowen, Theodore
McNamee, Jonathan Hunt, Seth B. Hunt, and Simeon Chittenden, New York,
1848–1896; Clarence W. Bowen, New York, 1896–1912; Independent Corporation, New York (Hamilton Holt, president, 1912–1914; Karl V. S. Howland,
president, 1914–1920; Wesley H. Ferrin, president, 1920–1921), 1913–1921;
Weekly Review Corporation, New York (Fabian Franklin, president), 1921–1924;
Independent Publications, Inc., Boston (owned by editors), 1924–1928. Edited
by Leonard Bacon, Joseph P. Thompson, and Richard S. Storrs, 1848–1861;
Henry Ward Beecher, 1861–1863; Theodore Tilton, 1863–1870; Henry Chandler

Bowen, 1870–1896; William Hayes Ward, 1896–1914; Hamilton Holt, 1914–1920; Harold DeWolf Fuller (with Fabian Franklin, October–December 1921), 1921–1924); Richard Ely Danielson and Christian A. Herter, 1924–1928. Circulation was 6,000 by 1850, when the magazine's stand against the fugitive slave law cost it 2,000 subscribers but brought it 5,000 new ones. Circulation continued to increase, to 10,000 by 1852, 25,000 by 1856, 35,000 by 1861, and 75,000 during the Civil War. After a peak in the early 1870s, circulation declined as scandal surrounded Beecher in the 1870s and heresy trials marred the Congregational church in the 1880s. The journal remained strong, however, achieving a circulation of 60,000 in 1916, and was significant in generating public opinion in favor of the League of Nations. (Mott, 2: 367–379)

Inland Printer. A typographical journal founded in Chicago in 1883. Edited by H. H. Hill, 1883–1884; Andrew C. Cameron, 1884–1892; Albert H. McQuilkin, 1893–1917; Harry Hillman, 1917–1928. Dealt with information for printers about printing—especially history and biography—and apprentice training. Many printers' publications were mere advertising sheets, but Mott calls the *Inland Printer*'s range "encyclopedic." (Mott, 3: 131)

Journal of Social Science. 1869–1909. Founded in New York by the American Association for the Promotion of Social Science, which organized immediately after the Civil War. Edited by Frank B. Sanborn, 1874–1897. Irregularly issued, less frequently than quarterly. (Mott, 3: 313; 4: 192)

The Land We Love. May 1866–March 1869. Founded and edited by General Daniel H. Hill. Devoted to the South, the magazine presented the South's story of the Civil War and displayed hostility to the North; written mostly by Hill, the magazine had several contributors and included literary and travel articles along with agricultural items and much material on the Civil War. Claimed 12,000 subscribers but complained of nonpayment of subscriptions. Absorbed in 1869 by the *New Eclectic* of Baltimore. (Mott, 3: 46–47)

Leisure Hour. 1868–1870. Monthly miscellany; succeeded the *Pittsburgh Quarterly Magazine*, 1867–1868. Published and edited by William O'Dwyer in Pittsburgh. (Mott, 3: 31)

Lippincott's Magazine of Literature, Science and Education. January 1868–April 1916. (*Lippincott's Magazine of Popular Literature and Science*, 1871–1885; *Lippincott's Magazine: A Popular Journal of General Literature, Science and Politics*, 1886–1903; *Lippincott's Monthly Magazine: A Popular Journal of General Literature*, 1903–1914; *Lippincott's Magazine*, 1915. *McBride's Magazine*, 1915–1916.) Primarily literary monthly, including travel, art, politics, science, criticism, and book reviews. Would not divulge circulation figures. Published by J. B. Lippincott & Company, Philadelphia, 1868–1914; McBride, Nast & Company, New York, 1914–1916. Edited by John Foster Kirk, 1868–1884; J. Bird, 1885; William Shepherd Walsh, 1885–1889; Henry Stoddard, 1889–1896; Frederic M. Bird, 1896–1898; Harrison S. Morris, 1899–1905; J. Berg Esenwein, 1905–1914; Louise Bull, 1914; Edward Frank Allen, 1914–1916. (Mott, 3: 396–401)

The Nation. July 1865–. Weekly devoted to current affairs, foreign news, literature, and miscellany. Contributors during the nineteenth-century decades included the most prominent scholars of the time. Edited by Edwin L. Godkin until 1881; Wendell Phillips Garrison, 1881–1907. Circulation never exceeded 12,000 during those years, but the journal was regarded as powerful in politics and literature. (Mott, 3: 329–360)

The New-England Magazine. July 1831–December 1835. General magazine regarded by Mott as the most important in New England before the *Atlantic Monthly* appeared in 1857. Merged with the *American Monthly Magazine* of New York in 1835. Published in Boston by Joseph T. and Edwin Buckingham, July 1831–May 1833; Joseph T. Buckingham, June 1833–October 1834; E. R. Broaders, November 1834–December 1835. Edited by Joseph T. and Edwin Buckingham, July 1831–May 1833; Joseph T. Buckingham, June 1833–October 1834; Samuel G. Howe and John O. Sargent, November 1834–February 1835; Park Benjamin, March–December 1835. (Mott, 1: 599–603)

The North American Review. Founded in May 1815 in Boston. Bimonthly until September 1818, then quarterly until October 1876, when it was again bimonthly until December 1878, and then monthly until August 1906. The earliest issues were a cross between a review and a miscellany; contents emphasized New England writers, Boston publishers and learned societies, and Harvard. Harvard professors edited the journal for more than fifty years. In later years, subjects ranged more widely, and the *North American Review* became an "acknowledged power and influence in the country," read by national leaders and "available in all important reading rooms." Published by seventeen different Boston publishers until 1878, when D. Appleton & Company, New York, became the publisher; thereafter, it was published in New York by several publishers until the North American Review Corporation became the publisher in 1915. Edited by William Tudor, 1815–1817; Jared Sparks, 1817–1818; Edward Tyrrel Channing, 1818–1819; Edward Everett, 1820–1823; Jared Sparks, 1824–1830; Alexander Hill Everett, 1830–1835; John Gorham Palfrey, 1836–1842; Francis Bowen, 1843–1853; Andrew Preston Peabody, 1853–1863; James Russell Lowell, 1863–1872 (with Charles Eliot Norton, 1863–1868; E. W. Gurney, 1868–1870; Henry Adams, 1870–1872); Henry Adams, 1872–1876 (with Thomas Sergeant Perry, 1872–1873; Henry Cabot Lodge, 1873–1876); Allen Thorndike Rice, 1877–1889; Lloyd Bryce, 1889–1896; David A. Munro, 1896–1899; George B. M. Harvey, 1899–1926; Walter Butler Mahoney, 1926–1935; John H. G. Pell, 1935–. Circulation reached 3,200 in 1830 and remained at that level until after the Civil War, when the journal struggled with a circulation that had dropped to 1,200. It was bought in 1870 by Allen Thorndike Rice, who moved it to New York in 1878. In a short time the *Review*, now conducted by people who had never entered Harvard, became a forum for all kinds of controversy. Circulation rebounded to 17,000 by 1889 and peaked at 76,000 by 1891. Mott notes that its total file is "unmatched by that of any other magazine of American thought through nearly a century and a quarter of our national life." (Mott, 2: 219–261)

North British Review. 1844–1871. Founded by supporters of the Free Church of Scotland over the issue of the church's freedom to run its own affairs, independent of the state. Whig in politics, it emphasized social and economic issues in

Scotland. Published by William Pattison Kennedy, 1844–1863; David Douglas, 1863. Edited by David Welsh, professor of ecclesiastical history at Edinburgh who lost his position because of his support for the Free Church, 1844–1845; Edward Francis Maitland, 1845–1847; William Hanna, 1847–1850; Alexander Campbell Fraser, 1850–1857; Rev. John Duns, 1857–1860; W. G. Blaikie, 1860–1863 (or 1871?). The magazine became an organ of the Liberal Catholics in 1869 until 1871. Circulation began with 4,000, dropped to 2,000 in 1846, and stabilized at 1,650 in 1849. (Shattock and Wolff, *The Victorian Periodical Press*, 145–165)

Our Day: A Record and Review of Current Reform. Founded and edited in Boston by minister Joseph Cook. Begun in January 1888; moved to Chicago in 1892, where it was issued by the Temperance Publishing Association; merged briefly with the *Altruistic Review* in 1895, then resumed in 1896 as a bimonthly, edited by Frederick L. Chapman; merged with *World's Events* in 1908. Among those associated with the magazine in editorial capacities were Frances E. Willard, national president of the Women's Christian Temperance Union; Edmund J. James, professor at the University of Pennsylvania and an advocate of labor reform; Anthony Comstock, secretary of the New York Society for the Suppression of Vice; and evangelist G. F. Pentecost. Primarily religious, the journal criticized Mormonism, saloons, and desecration of the Sabbath and included articles on reform abroad, book reviews, and poetry. (Mott, 4: 52–53)

The Outlook. January 1867–June 1935. Began with emphasis on religious and moral matters but turned to sociological and political issues. Established by Henry E. Childs in New York in 1867 as a Baptist paper called the *Church Union*. Taken over by the publisher J. B. Ford & Company in September 1869, it became the *Christian Union* and was transformed from a specialized religious publication to a general family journal. New serial numbering began in 1870; weekly, 1870–1932. Name changed to *Outlook* in 1893, signifying it had become a journal of opinion. Published by J. B. Ford and Company, 1869–1875; Christian Union Publishing Company, 1875–1877; New York and Brooklyn Publishing Company, 1878–1881; Christian Union Company, 1881–1893; Outlook Company, 1893–1935. Edited by Henry Ward Beecher, 1870–1871; Lyman Abbott, 1881–1923. Circulation reached 35,000 by the fall of 1870 and rose to 132,000 in 1873— the largest ever attained by a religious periodical. Circulation dropped to 10,000 by 1877 in the wake of the Beecher-Tilton scandal; reorganization followed and circulation gained steadily to 30,000 by 1894 and to more than 100,000 by 1902, where it remained for two decades. (Mott, 3: 422–435)

Scribner's Magazine. January 1887–May 1939. General monthly magazine, competing with three similar "quality" magazines—*Harper's New Monthly* (circ. in 1887 of 185,000), the *Atlantic Monthly* (circ. 12,500), and *Century* (circ. 222,000). Aimed at upper-middle-class readers, *Scribner's* emphasized literary topics and art and contained sophisticated criticism of national life and culture. Published in New York by Charles Scribner's Sons, 1887–1937; Harlan Logan Associates, 1937–1939. Edited by Edward Livermore Burlingame, 1887–1914; Robert Bridges, 1914–1930; Alfred S. Dashiell, 1930–1936; Harlan de Baun Logan, 1936–1939. At 110,000 in 1891, circulation suffered in the mid-1890s, but ended the century at 165,000 and continued to rise to a peak of more than 200,000 by 1911. (Mott, 3: 457–479)

The Southern Literary Messenger (title varies). August 1834–June 1864. Founded by Thomas Willys White in Richmond, Virginia. Intended as a voice of Southern culture, the *Messenger* was primarily literary but increasingly contained articles on the issue of slavery, especially in the 1850s, and became ever more sectional despite the cosmopolitan tendencies of its early editors. During the Civil War it was strongly political, hostile to the North yet critical of Davis. The journal struggled throughout its life in a city whose population was under 20,000 when the journal began. A constant problem was lack of payment for subscriptions, and the war years forced the price to $15 a year. The journal ceased publication in June 1864, when its printers were called to help defend Richmond. Published by T. W. White, 1834–1843; B. B. Minor, 1843–1847; Macfarlane & Fergusson, 1847, 1853–1863; John R. Thompson, 1847–1852; Wedderburn & Alfriend, 1864. Edited by James E. Heath, August 1834–April 1835; Edward V. Sparhawk, May–July 1835; Thomas W. White, August–September 1835, February 1837–December 1839(?); Edgar Allan Poe, December 1835–January 1837; Thomas W. White and Matthew F. Maury, January 1840(?)–September 1842; Matthew F. Maury, October 1842–July 1843; Benjamin B. Minor, August 1843–October 1847; John R. Thompson, November 1847–May 1860; George W. Bagby, June 1860–January 1864; Frank H. Alfriend, February–June 1864. Circulation of 600 to 700 rose to 5,500 during Poe's editorship. (Mott, 1: 629–657)

Westminster Review. 1828–1914. Financers were Jeremy Bentham and T. P. Thompson, 1828–1836; Sir William Molesworth, 1836–1838; John Stuart Mill, 1838–1840; W. E. Hickson, 1840–1852; John Chapman, 1852–1894; Harriet Martineau, 1854–1858. Marian Evans edited for Chapman; it appears that John Stuart Mill served as editor for two years in the late 1830s; W. E. Hickson was editor during the 1840s. Contributors included Harriet Martineau, John Stuart Mill, W. E. Forster, G. H. Lewes, A. H. Huxley, and W. B. Donne. Highest circulation reached was 1,620. (Sheila Rosenberg, "The Financing of Radical Opinion: John Chapman and the *Westminster Review*," in Shattock and Wolff, eds., *The Victorian Periodical Press*, 167–192)

Writer. Founded in Boston in 1887 by William H. Hills, local newspaper editor and director (via correspondence) of the Writer's School of Journalism and Literary Training. Most important of journals intended to help beginning writers, the *Writer* was a monthly containing news and notes about authors, speeches by well-known writers, and advice to writers. (Mott, 4: 142)

Notes

Chapter One: Journalistic Standards in History

1. Some recent books are, for example, Conrad C. Fink, *Media Ethics: In the Newsroom and Beyond* (New York: McGraw-Hill, 1987); Philip Meyer, *Ethical Journalism* (New York: Longman, 1987); Edmund B. Lambeth, *Committed Journalism: An Ethic for the Profession* (Bloomington: Indiana University Press, 1986); Frank McCulloch, ed., *Drawing the Line* (Washington, D.C.: American Society of Newspaper Editors, 1984); Robert Schmuhl, ed., *The Responsibilities of Journalists* (Notre Dame, Ind.: University of Notre Dame Press, 1984); Clifford G. Christians, Kim B. Rotzoll, and Mark Fackler, *Media Ethics: Cases and Moral Reasoning* (New York: Longman, 1983); Eugene H. Godwin, *Groping for Ethics in Journalism* (Ames: Iowa State University Press, 1983); Richard L. Johannesen, *Ethics in Human Communication*, 2nd ed. (Prospect Heights, Ill.: Waveland Press, 1983); John C. Merrill and Jack S. Odell, *Philosophy and Journalism* (New York: Longman, 1983); Philip Meyer, *Editors, Publishers and Newspaper Ethics* (Washington, D.C.: American Society of Newspaper Editors, 1983); Clifford G. Christians and Gudmund Gjelsten, *Media Ethics and the Church* (Kristiansand, Norway: International Mass Media Institute, 1981); John L. Hulteng, *Playing It Straight: A Practical Discussion of the Ethical Principles of ASNE* (Chester, Conn.: Globe Pequot Press, 1981); Clifford G. Christians and Catherine L. Covert, *Teaching Ethics in Journalism Education* (Hastings-on-Hudson, N.Y.: Hastings Center, 1980); John M. Phelan, *Disenchantment: Meaning and Morality in the Media* (New York: Hastings House, 1980); Lee Thayer, ed., *Ethics, Morality and the Media* (New York: Hastings House, 1980); Anne Vander Mirden, ed., *Ethics and Mass Communication* (Utrecht, the Netherlands: State University of Utrecht, 1980). The 1986 International Communication Association journal, *Communique*, lists eight centers as resources for media ethics.

2. Douglas Cater, "The Survival of Human Values," *Journal of Communication* 31 (Winter 1981): 190, notes, "Information processing—to use a term which embraces everything from accounting to entertainment—has become the dominant activity of an economy which once devoted its principal energies to the tilling of soil and then to the manufacture of products." See also Fritz Machlup, *The Production and Distribution of Knowledge in the United States* (Princeton: Princeton University Press, 1962).

3. In 1939, the journalism historian Frank Luther Mott and the communications theorist Ralph Casey co-authored a collection of statements made primarily by journalists throughout the nineteenth century that aimed to present views of the role and function of journalism historically. Although not always focused on these subjects, the published thoughts from various sources about many aspects of

journalism provided important initial insights, as did Edmond Coblentz's *Newsmen Speak: Journalists on Their Craft.* More recently, the British journalism historian Anthony Smith, in a chapter called "News Values and the Ethic of Journalism— A View of the Western Tradition," focused on influences shaping news definition, whereas Bernard Roshco, in a chapter surveying journalism history, touched on the evolving concern with truth in relation to journalistic practices. Frank Luther Mott and Ralph D. Casey, eds., *Interpretations of Journalism* (New York: F. S. Crofts, 1937); Edmond D. Coblentz, ed., *Newsmen Speak: Journalists on Their Craft* (Berkeley: University of California Press, 1954); Anthony Smith, *The Politics of Information* (London: Macmillan, 1978): 143–156; Bernard Roshco, *Newsmaking* (Chicago: University of Chicago Press, 1975): 22–37.

Several articles also contributed significantly, including one from the 1930s and another published recently that broached the subject more directly than most. In the former, Susan M. Kingsbury et al. related American newspaper ethics and criticism, concluding that "along with the denunciations [of the press over time] have gone increasingly definite formulations of the ethics of journalism." In an article published in 1982, C. Edward Wilson did not explicitly relate early press criticism to journalistic standards, but he added significantly to that work, as did Warren Bovee in an article that appeared in 1986, on Horace Greeley's views about the press as an open forum. Ted Smythe, in an article published in 1980 about reporters' working conditions in the 1880s and 1890s, dealt with effects on news practices; and *Journalism History* devoted an issue in 1985 to sensationalism, tracing it through press history, although without directly emphasizing its relationship to standards. Jean Folkerts's thoughtful article about reform press functions in the late nineteenth century had particular relevance. Of special importance, also, were Margaret Blanchard's article linking press criticism and reforms in the early twentieth century and Ronald Shilen's dissertation on objectivity in American journalism history. Susan M. Kingsbury et al., "Measuring the Ethics of American Newspapers: A Spectrum Analysis of Newspaper Sensationalism," *Journalism Quarterly* 10 (June 1933): 93–108; C. Edward Wilson, "Egregious Lies from Idle Brains: Critical Views of Early Journalism," *Journalism Quarterly* 59 (Summer 1982): 260–264; Warren G. Bovee, "Horace Greeley and Social Responsibility," *Journalism Quarterly* 63 (Summer 1986): 251–259; Ted Curtis Smythe, "The Reporter, 1880–1900: Working Conditions and Their Influence on the News," *Journalism History* 7 (Spring 1980): 1–10; "Special Issue on Sensationalism!!" *Journalism History* 12 (Autumn–Winter 1985); Jean Folkerts, "Functions of the Reform Press," *Journalism History* 12 (Spring 1985): 22–25; Margaret A. Blanchard, "Press Criticism and National Reform Movements: The Progressive Era and the New Deal," *Journalism History* 5 (Summer 1978): 33–37, 54–55; Ronald Shilen, "The Concept of Objectivity in Journalism in the United States," Ph.D. diss., New York University, 1956.

4. Donald H. Stewart, *The Opposition Press of the Federalist Period* (Albany: State University of New York Press, 1969); James E. Pollard, *The Presidents and the Press* (New York: Macmillan, 1947).

5. See, for example, "Some of the More Significant Attacks on Journals and Journalists Between 1625 and 1632," Appendix A in Joseph Frank, *The Beginnings of the English Newspaper, 1620–1660* (Cambridge: Harvard University Press, 1961): 275ff.; James T. Hillhouse, *The Grub-Street Journal* (Durham, N.C.: Duke University Press, 1928; rpt. New York: Benjamin Blom, 1967); Robert L. Haig, *The Gazetteer, 1735–1797: A Study in the Eighteenth-Century English Newspaper* (Carbondale: Southern Illinois University Press, 1960): 16ff.; Jeremy Black, *The English Press in the Eighteenth Century* (Philadelphia: University of Pennsylvania Press, 1987); Willard G. Bleyer, *Main Currents in the History of American Journalism* (Boston: Houghton Mifflin, 1927): 28–42.

6. Charles Tilly, *Big Structures, Large Processes, Huge Comparisons* (New York: Russell Sage Foundation, 1984). Only the conception of journalism as a "big structure" and "large process" relates to Tilly's book—which makes a plea for new (non-nineteenth-century) research models.

7. Referring to excluding "objectional" material from the paper, the *St. Louis Reveille* editor noted in the prospectus, "It is long since we marked down this point as a first rule in *our editorial code of ethics,* and under all circumstances we shall adhere to it most strictly . . ." (emphasis added); May 14, 1844.

8. "The Influence of the Press," *Blackwood's Edinburgh Magazine* 36 (September 1834): 373.

9. Aline Gorren, "The Ethics of Modern Journalism," *Scribner's Magazine* 19 (April 1896): 507.

10. W. S. Lilly, "The Ethics of Journalism," *The Forum* 4 (July 1889): 503–512.

11. George C. Childs had twenty-four rules at the *Public Ledger* during the Civil War; George Lanphere listed six ethical principles for journalists in a paper presented to the Minnesota Editorial Association in 1888. Charles Dana outlined his set of "maxims" in a lecture in 1888 (see Chapter 7). And C. C. Bonney, speaking on the "duties and privileges of the public press" to the Chicago Sunset Club in 1890, listed eight rules. Childs's rules appear in George Henry Payne, *History of Journalism in the United States* (New York: D. Appleton, 1925): 251–253; Lanphere's appear in the *Minnesota Newspaper Association Confidential Bulletin*, no. 20 (May 17, 1988): 4–5 (cited with permission of the Minnesota Newspaper Association, Minneapolis); Dana's statement appears in Dana, *The Art of Newspaper Making* (New York: D. Appleton, 1895): 19–20, and in Mott and Casey, eds., *Interpretations of Journalism*, 162. Bonney's speech is published as "The Duties and Privileges of the Public Press," in *Echoes of the Sunset Club*, comp. W. W. Catlin (Chicago: Sunset Club, 1891): 16. The rules set by James Gordon Bennett, Jr., for an employee in 1880 must also be noted, although they emphasized maximizing profit rather than establishing standards. In 1911, Will Irwin listed four areas of rules under his "Code of Ethics," which appeared in "The American Newspaper: A Study of Journalism in Its Relation to the Public," the eighth in a series of articles by Irwin published in *Collier's Magazine* in 1911; the articles are reprinted in Clifford F. Weigle and David G. Clark, eds., *The American Newspaper by Will Irwin* (Ames: Iowa State University Press, 1969); see also Robert V. Hudson,

"Will Irwin's Pioneering Criticism of the Press," *Journalism Quarterly* 47 (Summer 1970): 263–271.

12. According to Bovee, "Horace Greeley and Social Responsibility," 256–258, Greeley, trying to assure "all sides" an airing in the newspaper, set certain conditions for contributors, disallowing material "merely 'applauding our course'"; declining material that repeated something already published in the paper; requiring written material to be of reasonable length; excluding certain topics—spiritualism, revival of the African slave trade, "immoral" material, and "personal attacks" (but making a distinction between private persons, who must be protected, and public figures, who could not expect protection); and insisting that names be signed to all contributions. Childs's managing editor, William V. McKean, established the *Public Ledger* rules, which emphasized fairness and accuracy. See Payne, *History of Journalism in the United States*, 251–253.

13. Associated Ohio Dailies, *Proceedings* of the Eighth Annual Meeting (Springfield, Ohio: Hosterman, 1893): 43–44. I am indebted to Professor Gerald Baldasty, University of Washington, for data about the Associated Ohio Dailies.

14. See Sissela Bok, *Lying: Moral Choice in Public and Private Life* (New York: Vantage Books, 1979).

15. Smythe, "The Reporter, 1880–1900," 6.

16. *London Daily Courant*, March 11, 1702; cited in Harold Herd, *The March of Journalism* (London: George Allen and Unwin, 1952): 39–40; Bleyer, *Main Currents*, 16; Shilen, 16–17, cites passages that Samuel Buckley, after becoming editor a month later, spelled out the same procedures more clearly.

17. Bleyer, *Main Currents*, 24, 26. F. Knight Hunt, *The Fourth Estate*, 2 vols. (London: N.p., 1850), 1: 167ff., relates persecutions of several printers and writers, including Tutchin (Hunt's spelling), after the first daily newspaper began. See also *The Press and the Public Service*, "By a Distinguished Writer" (London: G. Routledge, 1857), especially Chap. 6 and 7. For more information about freedom of the press in England, see Fredrick S. Siebert, *Freedom of the Press in England, 1476–1776* (Urbana: University of Illinois Press, 1952).

18. James Carey gave this description of the evolution of ideas in "Advertising: An Institutional Approach," in C. H. Sandage and Vernon Fryberger, eds., *The Role of Advertising* (Homewood, Ill.: Richard D. Irwin, 1960): 3–17.

19. Sources on Enlightenment values include Crane Brinton, *The Age of Reason Reader* (New York: Viking Press, 1956), and Henry Steele Commager, *Era of Reform: 1830–1860* (New York: Van Nostrand Reinhold, 1960), which provides a good summary. For discussions of values in the Jacksonian era, see Commager, *Era of Reform*; Edward Pessen, *Jacksonian America: Society, Personality, and Politics*, rev. ed. (New York: Dorsey Press, 1978), which provides an excellent bibliographic essay citing numerous sources on various aspects of the Jacksonian era; Arthur M. Schlesinger, Jr., *The Age of Jackson* (Boston: Little, Brown, 1945); Glyndon Van Deusen, *The Jacksonian Era: 1828–1848* (New York: Harper, and Brothers 1959); John William Ward, *Andrew Jackson: Symbol for an Age* (New York: Oxford University Press, 1955); Alice Felt Tyler, *Freedom's Ferment* (Minneapolis: University of Minnesota Press, 1944).

20. James A. Michener, *Kent State: What Happened and Why* (New York: Random House, 1971); I. F. Stone, *The Killings at Kent State: How Murder Went Unpunished* (New York: Vintage Books, 1970). See also Joseph Buttinger, *Vietnam: The Unforgettable Tragedy* (New York: Horizon Press, 1977); George C. Herring, *America's Longest War: The United States and Vietnam, 1950–1975* (New York: John Wiley and Sons, 1979); Anthony Lake, ed., *The Vietnam Legacy: The War, American Society and the Future of American Foreign Policy* (New York: New York University Press, 1976).

21. John Finnegan, Jr., "Defamation, Politics, and the Social Process of Law in New York State, 1776–1860" (Ph.D. diss., University of Minnesota, 1985): 80–81.

22. Finnegan, 83–88. Finnegan defines norms as the "expected" behavior, that is, "socially preferred means for accomplishing cultural ends," adding that as "rules alone, they embody both the ideal [values] and expected in the behavior they regulate." Norms may be examined, he says, "for changes in distribution (who is included in the rule; explicit or implicit recognition of the rule); enforcement (nature and frequency of sanctions); and conformity (who does or does not live up to the norm)."

23. For a discussion of values in transition in the early nineteenth century, see Vernon L. Parrington, *The Romantic Revolution in America*, vol. 2 of *Main Currents in American Thought* (New York: Harcourt, Brace, 1927): iii–x; for cultural changes in the era, see Gordon S. Wood, "The Significance of the Early Republic," *Journal of the Early Republic* 8 (Spring 1988): 1–20. Commager, *Era of Reform*, also has a valuable discussion of values, particularly of the relationship of Enlightenment values to the reform era. See also Ward, *Andrew Jackson*, and Pessen, *Jacksonian America*. Among the values Finnegan, "Defamation, Politics, and the Social Process of Law," 95–96, identifies as prevalent in the early nineteenth century are deference, distrust of the printed word, and distrust of conflict.

24. Most sources about slavery in antebellum America imply these competing values. See especially Russel B. Nye, *Fettered Freedom* (East Lansing: Michigan State University Press, 1963); Leonard I. Richards, *"Gentlemen of Property and Standing": Anti-Abolition Mobs in Jacksonian America* (New York: Oxford University Press, 1970); William L. Barney, *The Road to Secession: A New Perspective on the Old South* (New York: Praeger, 1972); Donald E. Reynolds, *Editors Make War: Southern Newspapers in the Secession Crisis* (Nashville, Tenn.: Vanderbilt University Press, 1970); Paul Finkelman, *An Imperfect Union: Slavery, Federalism, and Comity* (Chapel Hill: University of North Carolina Press, 1981); Tyler, *Freedom's Ferment*, 463ff.

25. Robert E. Park, "The Natural History of the Newspaper," *American Journal of Sociology* 29 (November 1923): 273–289; Roshco, *Newsmaking*.

26. Roshco, *Newsmaking*, 24.

27. Ibid.

28. Wilson, "Egregious Lies."

29. Some examples of these different perspectives are found in Gaye Tuchman, "Objectivity as Strategic Ritual," *American Journal of Sociology* 77 (January 1972):

660–679; Ken Macrorie, "Objectivity: Dead or Alive?" *Journalism Quarterly* 36 (Spring 1959): 145–150; David Manning White, "The 'Gatekeeper': A Case Study in the Selection of News," *Journalism Quarterly* 27 (Fall 1950): 383–390; E. Barbara Phillips, "Approaches to Objectivity: Journalistic and Social Science Perspectives," in Paul M. Hirsch et al., eds., *Strategies for Communication Research*, Sage Annual Reviews of Communication Research, vol. 6 (Beverly Hills: Sage, 1977): 63–77; Roshco, *Newsmaking*, 38–57; Smith, *The Politics of Information*, 177–198; Mark Fishman, *Manufacturing the News* (Austin: University of Texas Press, 1980); Pertti Hemanus, "Objectivity in News Transmission," *Journal of Communication* 26 (Autumn 1976): 102–107; Herbert J. Gans, *Deciding What's News* (New York: Vintage Books, 1979): 182–213; Leon V. Sigal, *Reporters and Officials: The Organization and Politics of Newsmaking* (Lexington, Mass.: D. C. Heath, 1973); Jack Newfield, "The 'Truth' About Objectivity and the New Journalism," in C. C. Flippen, ed., *Liberating the Media* (Washington, D.C.: Acropolis Books, 1974); Edward Jay Epstein, "Journalism and Truth," *Commentary* 57 (April 1974): 36–40.

30. Richard Kielbowicz, "Newsgathering by Printers' Exchanges Before the Telegraph," *Journalism History* 9 (Summer 1982): 42–48; Stewart, *The Opposition Press*, 25; Frederick W. Hamilton, *A Brief History of Printing in America* (Chicago: United Typothetae of America, 1918): 24–25; Victor Rosewater, *History of Co-operative News-Gathering in the United States* (New York: Appleton-Century-Crofts, 1930): 1–3.

31. Milton W. Hamilton, *The Country Printer, New York State, 1785–1830* (New York: Columbia University Press, 1936): 7–9; Arthur M. Schlesinger, *Prelude to Independence: The Newspaper War on Great Britain, 1774–1776* (New York: Alfred A. Knopf, 1958; rpt. Westport, Conn.: Greenwood Press, 1979): 58. The "laborious process" involved "a dozen separate manual operations" to produce only two hundred pages an hour. Schlesinger notes (p. 54) that by 1750 newspapers had circulations of 300 to 500, rising to 1,500 to 3,500 at the height of the American Revolution.

32. Frank Luther Mott, *American Journalism*, rev. ed. (New York: Macmillan, 1950): 194–195. Rosewater, *Cooperative Newsgathering*, 6ff.

33. Mott, *American Journalism*, 144–146; Rosewater, *Cooperative Newsgathering*, 21ff.

34. John Finnegan, Jr., "A Paradigm for Examining Reportorial Innovations: Boston Dailies and the Convent Riot of 1834" (paper presented to the Midwestern Regional History Conference of the Association for Education in Journalism, Minneapolis, April 1980). Rosewater, *Cooperative Newsgathering*, 13, cites William Durant that when he joined the *Boston Transcript* in 1834, the editor "made a daily call at Topliff's reading room, the insurance offices and public places, all conveniently located on or around State street; spending most of the day in the chair editorial. . . ." Robert E. Drechsel, *News Making in the Trial Courts* (New York: Longman, 1983): 35–77, in a chapter tracing early court reporting, discusses news gathering in courts in the 1830s. The Ben Jonson play cited in the chapter epigraph refers to "emissaries" sent to gather news at the court, St. Paul's, the Exchange,

and Westminster Hall in London; see Hunt, *The Fourth Estate* 1: 16–17. Hence, a concept of news gathering had long existed, but it was undeveloped in colonial and early America.

35. Both Isaac C. Pray, *Memoirs of James Gordon Bennett and His Times* (New York: Stringer and Townsend, 1852; rpt. Arno Press and the New York Times Company, 1970): 117–120; and Don C. Seitz, *The James Gordon Bennetts, Father and Son, Proprietors of the "New York Herald"* (Indianapolis: Bobbs-Merrill, 1928): 24–26, relate Bennett's trip to Massachusetts to cover a trial. The editor of the *St. Louis Reveille*, August 23, 1850, noted three trips to New Orleans in three months.

36. Nils Gunnar Nilsson, "The Origin of the Interview," *Journalism Quarterly* 48 (Winter 1971): 707–713; George S. Turnbull, "Some Notes on the History of the Interview," *Journalism Quarterly* 13 (September 1936): 272–279. Mott, *American Journalism*, 386, notes very early forerunners of the interview, but he and Turnbull locate the origin of the formal interview as a news story in Horace Greeley's story in the *New York Tribune*, August 20, 1859, based on a conversation with Brigham Young. Bleyer, *Main Currents*, 181, says that Bennett reported a "verbatim" interview with the woman who discovered the murdered Helen Jewett in 1836, but Mott says an official was present and Bennett's report seems to have been a deposition. Seitz, *The James Gordon Bennetts*, 65, notes Bennett's interview with President Martin Van Buren in 1839, but Turnbull claims this was not a true interview story. Evidence indicates that Anne Royall interviewed Van Buren earlier and, in fact, that she boasted of having interviewed every president from John Quincy Adams to Franklin Pierce. Madelon Golden Schilpp and Sharon M. Murphy, *Great Women of the Press* (Carbondale: Southern Illinois University Press, 1983): 22; Maurine Beasley, "The Curious Career of Anne Royall," *Journalism History* 3 (Winter 1976–77): 98–102, 136. According to Mott, the American interview model spread to other countries following Greeley's 1859 story. Defining the term *interview* broadly, Nilsson argues that it was established in the 1830s and that the court report's question-answer format (popular in England from the early 1820s) provided the model.

37. The story by Elizabeth Cochran ("Nelly Bly") about conditions in an asylum for the insane in 1887 is an example of undercover journalism; see "Inside the Madhouse," *New York World*, October 16, 1887. Cochran's work is described with reprinted articles in Barbara Belford, *Brilliant Bylines* (New York: Columbia University Press, 1986): 114–149. A good contemporary article about undercover investigative news gathering to expose grave robbing for medical school cadavers in the early 1880s is L. N. Megargee, "Newspaper Sensation," *Lippincott's Magazine* 52 (December 1893): 719–736.

38. Little study has been done of specialized reporting history.

39. Elizabeth Cochran's articles and the grave-robbing exposé are cases in point (see n. 38 above).

40. Carey, "Advertising," 4.

41. Historical studies of the press have seldom focused on it as a social institution or considered how people viewed it in any given era. Critical evaluations have applied to producers of media content as if individuals—apart from the institu-

tion and concepts of purpose behind it—carried out press functions, whether for good or ill. Since the press's perceived role has changed through history, the large questions concern its function as a whole in the larger society over time.

42. See Siebert, *Freedom of the Press in England*; Leonard W. Levy, *Freedom of Speech and Press in Early American History: Legacy of Suppression* (Cambridge: Harvard University Press, 1960; rpt. New York: Harper and Row, 1963).

43. Local issues at times engaged the press. See, for example, C. Edward Wilson, "The Boston Inoculation Controversy: A Revisionist Interpretation," *Journalism History* 7 (Spring 1980): 16–19; and Jim Allee Hart, *Views on the News: The Developing Editorial Syndrome* (Carbondale: Southern Illinois University Press, 1970): 97–101. Although the controversy over smallpox inoculation has often been considered in the context of the history of freedom of the press, Wilson argues that members of the Boston government shared the printers' views on the issue, agreeing with Hart's conclusion that Franklin conducted an editorial campaign.

44. Mott, *American Journalism*, 118–122, discusses broad political issues that engaged the press from 1783 to 1801. See also Schlesinger, *Prelude to Independence*; Bernard Bailyn and John B. Hench, eds., *The Press and the American Revolution* (Boston: Northeastern University Press, 1981); Philip Davidson, *Propaganda and the American Revolution* (Chapel Hill: University of North Carolina Press, 1941). For postrevolutionary press involvement in political issues, see Stewart, *The Opposition Press*; James Morton Smith, *Freedom's Fetters: The Alien and Sedition Laws and American Civil Liberties* (Ithaca: Cornell University Press, 1956); Linda Kerber, *Federalists in Dissent: Imagery and Ideology in Jeffersonian America* (Ithaca: Cornell University Press, 1970); Schlesinger, *The Age of Jackson*; Richards, *"Gentlemen of Property and Standing"*; Ward, *Andrew Jackson*; Tyler, *Freedom's Ferment*.

45. Tyler, *Freedom's Ferment*; Richards, *"Gentlemen of Property and Standing"*; Nye, *Fettered Freedom*.

46. Tyler, *Freedom's Ferment*; Ward, *Andrew Jackson*; Julius W. Pratt, "The Origin of 'Manifest Destiny,'" *American Historical Review* 32 (July 1927): 795–798; Pratt, "John L. O'Sullivan and Manifest Destiny," *New York History* 14 (July 1933): 213–234.

47. Martin E. Dann, *The Black Press, 1827–1890* (New York: G. P. Putnam's Sons, 1971); Penelope L. Bullock, *The Afro-American Periodical Press, 1838–1909* (Baton Rouge: Louisiana State University Press, 1981); David P. Forsyth, *The Business Press in America, 1750–1865* (Philadelphia: Chilton Books, 1964); Lionel C. Barrow, Jr., "'Our Own Cause': *Freedom's Journal* and the Beginnings of the Black Press," *Journalism History* 4 (Winter 1977–78): 18–22; Philip S. Foner and George E. Walker, eds., *Proceedings of the Black State Conventions, 1840–1865*, 2 vols. (Philadelphia: Temple University Press, 1979); Sam G. Riley, "The Short Unhappy Life of the First American Indian Newspaper," *Journalism Quarterly* 43 (Winter 1976): 666–671; Richard LaCourse, "An Indian Perspective—Native American Journalism: An Overview," *Journalism History* 6 (Summer 1979): 34–38; Schilpp and Murphy, *Great Women*; Beasley, "The Curious Career of Anne Royall," 98–102, 136; Alexander Saxton, "Problems of Class and Race in the

Origins of the Mass Circulation Press," *American Quarterly* 36 (Summer 1984): 211–234.

48. William A. Dill, *Growth of Newspapers in the United States*, Bulletin of the Department of Journalism, University of Kansas, 1928. The first successful newspaper in the American colonies began in 1704 in Boston and was the only newspaper in existence for several years; in 1720, there were three; by 1730, there were eight. Sources list different numbers by the time of the American Revolution: Schlesinger, *Prelude to Independence*, 296, for example, says there were thirty-eight in 1775; Dill (p. 11) notes forty-eight in 1775; Edwin Emery and Michael Emery, *The Press and America*, 6th ed. (Englewood Cliffs, N.J.: Prentice-Hall, 1988), 65, say there were 35, of which only 20 survived the war—and, of 35 begun during the war, enough survived so that 35 were publishing at war's end. By the time of the first census, taken in 1790, there were 106 (Dill, 10). See also Thomas G. Tanselle, "Some Statistics on American Printing, 1764–1783," in Bailyn and Hench, eds., *The Press and the American Revolution*, 315–363. Regarding literacy, see Carl F. Kaestle, "The History of Literacy and the History of Readers," *Review of Research in Education* 12 ed. (1985): 11–53; William J. Gilmore, *Elementary Literacy on the Eve of the Industrial Revolution: Trends in Rural New England, 1760–1830* (Worcester, Mass.: American Antiquarian Society, 1982); Kenneth A. Lockridge, *Literacy in Colonial New England: An Inquiry into the Social Context of Literacy in the Early Modern West* (New York: W. W. Norton, 1974).

49. David Hawke, *The Colonial Experience* (Indianapolis: Bobbs-Merrill, 1966), Chap. 3–6, discusses the colonies' different origins and structures.

50. Hawke, *The Colonial Experience*, 368, notes that "America's thirteen self-centered colonies were ripped apart regularly by internal dissension; they suspected the motives of their neighboring colonies and of Great Britain"; when called on to help with western defense against the French, "to all but Virginia, French activity west of the mountains seemed unrelated to the colonies' welfare." A congress of twenty-three delegates from seven colonies met at Albany, New York, in 1753 to plan the defense against the French. A committee developed a plan of colonial union, but it was not seriously discussed and never materialized.

51. Schlesinger, *Prelude to Independence*, 67–84.

52. Lauren Kessler, *The Dissident Press: Alternative Journalism in American History* (Beverly Hills: Sage, 1984): 21–23, 74–76, 154–159, discusses the problems of access for blacks, women, and other groups to the mainstream press.

53. Bleyer, *Main Currents*, 168–171, identifies two efforts by newspapers to address women in the 1830s. No issues of one of the papers survive, and the second failed in part because advertisers thought it too narrow. See also Tyler, *Freedom's Ferment*, 424–462; Jean E. Friedman and William G. Shade, eds., *Our American Sisters: Women in American Life and Thought*, 2nd ed. (Boston: Allyn and Bacon, 1976); Barbara Welter, "The Cult of True Womanhood, 1820–1860," *American Quarterly* 18 (Summer 1966): 151–174.

54. Figures on literacy were not collected before the 1840 census, and then reporting methods were poor. Hawke, *The Colonial Experience*, 294–297, notes

that studies of seventeenth-century deeds and petitions show that approximately 40 percent of women and 90 percent of men in New England states could write their names; 25 percent of women and 55 percent of men in Virginia could write their names. Education lagged throughout the seventeenth century, and literacy declined among first- and second-generation settlers. Census figures for 1840 show 22 percent illiteracy, but this figure may be too high because the 1860 census data —based on better reporting methods—give an illiteracy rate of 19.7 percent; U.S. Bureau of the Census, *The Statistical History of the United States from Colonial Times to the Present*, ed. Ben J. Wattenberg (New York: Basic Books, 1976): 365. See also Gilmore, *Elementary Literacy*; Kaestle, "The History of Literacy"; and Lockridge, *Literacy in Colonial New England*. Gilmore and Lockridge conclude that literacy rates in New England were high compared with those in other parts of the United States. Lockridge, for example, determines that women's literacy rates rose from below 20 percent in the early seventeenth century to around 50 percent by 1850. Gilmore concluded that 60 to 70 percent of Upper Valley New England men and 50 to 60 percent of women could read by 1800.

55. Hamilton, *The Country Printer*, 102, 113–114. When Henry Clay deprived Amos Kendall, who increasingly supported Andrew Jackson, of public printing in Kentucky in the 1820s, Kendall suffered severe financial losses; *Argus of Western America*, September 26, 1827.

56. Henry Lewis Bullen, "The Evolution of American Printing Presses from the Year of Independence, 1776, to the Present Year," *The American Printer* 83 (July 1926): 70–71; Hamilton, *The Country Printer*, 5–20. Hamilton, *A Brief History of Printing*, 29–30, discusses changes in printing technology without citing capabilities regarding numbers of pages produced; Bleyer, *Main Currents*, 392ff., discusses changes in press capacities.

57. Mott, *American Journalism*, 244–247; Henry L. Stoddard, *Horace Greeley: Printer, Editor, Crusader* (New York: G. Putnam's Sons, 1946): 66; Rosewater, *Cooperative Newsgathering*, 25–26.

58. Mott, *American Journalism*, 194; Rosewater, *Cooperative Newsgathering*, 27–33; Stoddard, *Horace Greeley*, 66.

59. Mott, *American Journalism*, 244–245; Rosewater, *Cooperative Newsgathering*, 34–56; J. Cutler Andrews, *The North Reports the Civil War* (Pittsburgh: University of Pittsburgh Press, 1955, 1985): 6ff. Daniel J. Czitrom, *Media and the American Mind: From Morse to McLuhan* (Chapel Hill: University of North Carolina Press, 1982): 1–29, discusses the impact of the telegraph; see also "An Evening with the Telegraph-Wires," *Atlantic Monthly* 2 (September 1858): 489–495.

60. Allan Nevins, *The Emergence of Modern America, 1865–1878* (New York: Macmillan, 1927; rpt. Chicago: Quadrangle Books, 1971): 56, 86; Alan Trachtenberg, *Democratic Vistas, 1860–1880* (New York: George Braziller, 1970): 3–4; Andrews, *The North Reports the Civil War*, 6–7.

61. Rosewater, *Cooperative Newsgathering*, 14ff. Although no formal association represented all journalists in the 1830s, local printers' organizations had existed since 1786 and periodically set up rules about fees for work. Philadelphia printers, organized as early as 1786, became a "society" in 1802—the same year the

New York society of printers tried to induce uniformity through organizations in Philadelphia, Albany, and Washington, D.C. See U.S. Department of Labor, Bureau of Labor Statistics, *History of Wages in the United States from Colonial Times to 1928*, Bulletin no. 604 (Washington, D.C.: Government Printing Office, 1929): 119–123, 491–521. Hamilton, *A Brief History of Printing*, 77, notes that national conventions of printers began in 1837. Editorial associations began to form in the 1820s to cooperate in news gathering, set advertising rates, and formulate other rules affecting the press's financial status; Rosewater, *Cooperative Newsgathering*, 14–15; Holtzheuter, J. O., "The Wisconsin Editors' and Publishers' Association, 1853–1877" (M.A. thesis, University of Wisconsin, 1965): 2. The *St. Louis Beacon*, October 24, 1829, and the *Missouri Courier*, April 4, 1850, refer to such local associations. And Washington correspondents "associated" in petitioning for access to the U.S. Senate in 1838; see also F. B. Marbut, "Early Washington Correspondents: Some Neglected Pioneers," *Journalism Quarterly* 25 (December 1948): 373.

62. Richard A. Schwarzlose, "Harbor News Association: Formal Origin of the AP," *Journalism Quarterly* 45 (Summer 1968); Rosewater, *Cooperative Newsgathering*, 57ff.

63. Rosewater, *Cooperative Newsgathering*, 8–9.

64. Ibid., 5ff; Mott, *American Journalism*, 194–195.

65. Mott, *American Journalism*, 196–197.

66. See Francis Brown, *Raymond of the "Times"* (New York: W. W. Norton, 1951): 105; Frank M. O'Brien, *The Story of "The Sun," New York, 1833–1928* (New York: D. Appleton, 1928): 109; and Frederic Hudson, *Journalism in the United States from 1690 to 1872* (New York: Harper and Brothers, 1872): 622–623, for descriptions of the rivalry between newspaper editors. When Horace Greeley began the *New York Tribune* in 1841, Moses Beach, editor of the *New York Sun*, sent men to intimidate *Tribune* carriers, and street fights ensued between carriers for the two papers. Greeley threatened *Tribune* carriers with loss of their jobs if they handled the *New York Times* after Raymond founded it in 1851. Rosewater, *Cooperative Newsgathering*, 18ff., discusses the rivalry as well as news stealing.

67. Mott, *American Journalism*, 243.

68. When a bill introduced in the Arkansas legislature called for forced disclosure of correspondents' names, an editor asked journalists to unite to repel this encroachment on press freedom; *New York Sun*, November 29, 1833. The *New York Sun* for December 27, 1833, reported that when a judge expelled one editor's reporters from a court-martial, the editor himself went to get the story in order to assert the press's rights and to ensure that "his reporter could take notes" on the proceedings.

69. Printers suffered especially after the 1830s as organizational power increasingly shifted to editors, who ignored organized printers' local wage scales; they hired nonlocal printers—lured by prospects of "good business"—and untrained boys and women, providing necessary training. According to the 1833 New York printers' society constitution of 1833,

The consequence was that while a few grew rich at the expense of the journeymen, old established printers . . . were obliged to reduce their charges . . . or lose much . . . business; and as their receipts were diminished, the wages of the journeymen were reduced by degrees until, instead of a uniform scale of prices, every man was compelled to work for what he could obtain. (U.S. Department of Labor, Bureau of Labor Statistics, *History of Wages*, 122–123)

Editors also undercut printers by ignoring the apprenticeship system. In Washington, D.C., for example, Duff Green "fought long-term apprenticeship and made a point of employing 'two-thirders' and runaway apprentices" as journeymen and proposed establishing a school himself to teach printing to two hundred boys annually. The result was that printers' wages were lower in 1831 than in 1815, and because of the new technology, the New York printers' society constitution stated that "many who had spent from five to seven years of the flower of their lives acquiring a knowledge of their profession were left without employment"; U.S. Department of Labor, Bureau of Labor Statistics, *History of Wages*, 119–123. See also Stephen Botein, "Printers and the American Revolution," in Bailyn and Hench, eds., *The Press and the American Revolution*, 50ff.

70. A sample of newspapers in the 1830s and 1840s revealed an assortment of positions: three kinds of correspondent, eleven kinds of editors, proofreader, manager, and publisher—in addition to pressmen, printer, journeymen, apprentices, and carriers. By 1838, James Gordon Bennett had established correspondents in six European capitals, in many U.S. cities, and in Texas, Mexico, and Canada. In 1839, he organized a corps of correspondents in Washington, D.C., with Robert Sutton as "bureau" editor; see Pray, *Memoirs of James Gordon Bennett*, 251–254.

The U.S. census for 1850 shows that nearly 1,400 people listed themselves as editors, 14,740 as printers, 138 as reporters, 209 as newsmen, and 355 as publishers.

71. W. A. Linn, *Horace Greeley* (New York: D. Appleton, 1912), cites a letter written by Horace Greeley in 1836 to B. F. Randolph that reveals plans for an organized business department:

I want you to take command . . . and reduce the whole business to a system. . . . Thus far our business department has been but half attended to, and the consequence is that we have lost a great deal by bad agents, runaway subscribers, etc. To remedy this it requires a man steadily at the publication office who not only knows what business is, but feels a deep interest in the prosperity of the concern. It needs someone who knows every agent and the state of his account, familiarly, and who can almost repeat the names of the subscribers from memory. To do this he must make all the entries in the books himself and keep the accounts. . . . (p. 30)

72. Mott, *American Journalism*, 224, 298–302.

73. Edward L. Carter, "The Revolution in Journalism During the Civil War," *Lincoln Herald* 73 (Winter 1971): 229–241.

Chapter Two: The Role of the Newspaper Press in Nineteenth-Century America

1. The responsibility model was formulated after the turn of the century and is therefore not dealt with in this book. For a discussion of the responsibility theory, see William L. Rivers, Wilbur Schramm, and Clifford G. Christians, *Responsibility in Mass Communication* (New York: Harper and Row, 1980): 43; and Fredrick S. Siebert, Theodore Peterson, and Wilbur Schramm, *Four Theories of the Press* (Urbana: University of Illinois Press, 1956): 73.

2. Emery and Emery, *The Press and America*, 69–114; Mott, *American Journalism*, 71–281; Bleyer, *Main Currents*, 100–153; Gerald J. Baldasty, "The Press and Politics in the Age of Jackson," *Journalism Monographs* 89 (August 1984): William Ames, *A History of the "National Intelligencer"* (Chapel Hill: University of North Carolina Press, 1972); Culver H. Smith, *The Press, Politics and Patronage* (Athens: University of Georgia Press, 1977).

3. Stewart, *The Opposition Press*, 4.

4. Stewart, *The Opposition Press*, 11–12; see chap. 1, n. 42 for the list. Dwight Mikkelson, "*Kentucky Gazette*, 1787–1848: The Herald of a Noisy World" (Ph.D. diss., University of Kentucky, 1963): 11ff., describes John Bradford's several political positions. Hamilton, *The Country Printer*, 126, n. 128, counts "eleven country printers" of New York who were members of the state Assembly before, and seven after, 1830. Hamilton identifies one elected state senator and one elected U.S. congressman before 1830; four became U.S. congressmen after 1830. Distinguishing printers from editors, he notes that four editors were elected to the state Assembly before 1830 and five after; two to the state Senate before 1830 and three after; three to the U.S. House of Representatives before 1830 and four after. One was elected U.S. senator.

5. Ames, *A History of the "National Intelligencer*," 282.

6. Stoddard, *Horace Greeley*, 70, 289, 305–316; Brown, *Raymond of the "Times*," 136–140, 186–188, 305–315; Emery and Emery, *The Press and America*, 176; Payne, *History of Journalism in the United States*, 286–292, 330–332. Stoddard, Emery and Emery, and Payne discuss Greeley's candidacy for president. Greeley served ninety days of an unexpired term in Congress from December 5, 1848, to March 4, 1849. In 1854, Thurlow Weed rejected his proposal to run for New York governor or lieutenant governor. Greeley, stung by the rebuff, ended his long association with the political machine he had operated with Weed and William Seward; Brown suggests that resentment motivated his actions, which cost Seward the 1860 Republican nomination. Stoddard also credits Greeley with the Republican convention's outcome without reference to the 1854 matter. Hudson, *Journalism in the United States*, 548–552, contains a copy of the long letter Greeley wrote to Seward after withdrawing from the Seward-Weed-Greeley firm.

7. Brown, *Raymond of the "Times*," 76, 79–82, 88–91, 137–138; 234–235, 240–242, 255, 265–268, 282.

8. Ibid., 3–4; Stoddard, *Horace Greeley*, 146–147, 162–169, 199, 203; Harriet A. Weed, *The Life of Thurlow Weed*, 2 vols. (Boston: Houghton Mifflin, 1883); William Ernest Smith, *The Francis Preston Blair Family in Politics*, 2 vols. (New

York: Macmillan, 1933); Elbert B. Smith, *Francis Preston Blair* (New York: Free Press, 1980). Study of the decade of the 1850s and the 1860 presidential campaign reveals expansive political activity by journalists. After the collapse of the Whig party and the introduction of the Kansas-Nebraska bill in Congress, Greeley advocated the formation of a new party, and some, on the basis of an editorial recommending "Republican" as the name, credit him with naming it. In an editorial of January 5, 1854, Greeley proclaimed that passage of the Kansas-Nebraska bill would "arouse and consolidate the most gigantic, determined and overwhelming party for freedom that the world has ever known . . ." (Stoddard, 162–163); in the editorial "Party Names and Public Duty" published on June 16, he wrote, "We should not care much whether those united were designated Whig, Free Soil Democrats or something else; though we think that some simple name like Republican would more fitly designate those who had united to restore our Union to its true mission . . ." (Stoddard, 167–169). Payne, *History of Journalism*, 334–335, credits the editor of the Chicago *Tribune*, Joseph Medill, and others. Medill wrote to Greeley that some were considering the name "Republican" and asked for his advice. Greeley responded favorably, and his editorial followed this exchange.

Following the formation of the Republican party, Henry Raymond sought to win public confidence in the new party by detailing its principles and aims in the *New York Times*. When the Whig and Republican parties merged in 1855, Greeley and Raymond were actively involved. Raymond wrote an address for the New York delegation to the Pittsburgh organizing convention in February 1856 and the "address to the people" for the Republican national convention in June (Stoddard, 146–147). Weed and Francis Preston Blair were also involved in those activities and in the 1860 campaign, in which many saw the work of Greeley, in particular, as decisive. Murat Halstead, editor of the Cincinnati *Commercial*, telegraphed the newspaper from the convention, "The principal lions are Horace Greeley and Francis P. Blair"; Raymond telegraphed the *New York Times*, "For the result Greeley labored harder and did tenfold more than the whole family of Blairs"; and George William Curtis telegraphed *Harper's Weekly*, "We need hardly seek deeper than Greeley for the cause of Seward's rejection. 'The Tribune' was the creator of the Republican party and is still its great organ and censor" (Stoddard, 199, 203).

9. O'Brien, *The Story of "The Sun*," 114.

10. Alfred H. Fenton, *Dana of "The Sun"* (New York: Farrar and Rinehart, 1941): 151ff.; Candace Stone, *Dana and the "Sun"* (New York: Dodd, Mead, 1938): Chap. 1.

11. Robin Fisher Larsen, "Cooper Union Speech: New York Media Launch a Candidate," *Media History Digest* 6 (Fall–Winter 1986): 2–3.

12. Patricia Dooley, "Minnesota Journalists as Elected Officials, 1923–1938: An Historical Study of an Ethical/Conflict of Interest Question" (M.A. thesis, University of Minnesota, 1985). Dooley has found that a significant number of Minnesota journalists held political office at state and national levels during the years studied. She also notes (p. 6) that among well-known journalists who sought high political office during the early twentieth century were William Randolph Hearst, William Allen White, and Warren G. Harding (publisher of the Marion,

Ohio, *Star*). A survey of present-day journalists in small Minnesota towns reflects some ambivalence about whether journalists' involvement in certain kinds of local, small-town politics constitutes a serious breach of ethics; Dooley, "Newspaper Professionals and Political and Community Involvement: Ignorance Is Bliss" (Department of Journalism, University of Minnesota, 1983; photocopy).

13. Emery and Emery, *The Press and America*, 45–114; Mott, *American Journalism*, 113–209; Hudson, *Journalism in the United States*, 141ff.; Smith, *The Press, Politics and Patronage*.

14. Henry Robert Plomer, *A Short History of English Printing: 1476–1900* (New York: Empire State Book Company, 1900): 157ff.; Fox Bourne, *English Newspapers*, 2 vols. (London: Chatto and Windus, 1887), 1: 11; Black, *The English Press*, Chap. 1–2.

15. Leonard W. Levy, ed., *Freedom of the Press from Zenger to Jefferson* (Indianapolis: Bobbs-Merrill, 1966): 3–82; Warren C. Price, "Reflections on the Trial of John Peter Zenger," *Journalism Quarterly* 32 (Spring 1955): 161; Schlesinger, *Prelude to Independence*, 64–65; Charles H. Levermore, "The Rise of Metropolitan Journalism, 1800–1840," *American Historical Review* 6 (April 1901): 446–465.

16. Siebert, *Freedom of the Press in England*, 32.

17. Bleyer, *Main Currents*, 44; R. T. Barton, ed., *The Reports by Sir John Randolph and by Edward Barradall of the General Court of Virginia, 1728–1741*, vol. 1 of *Virginia Colonial Decisions* (Boston: Boston Book Company, 1909): 137. Governor Berkeley of Virginia wrote his superiors in 1671: "But, I thank God, we have not free schools nor printing; and I hope we shall not have these hundred years. For learning has brought disobedience and heresy and sects into the world; and printing has divulged them and libels against the government. God keep us from both." Berkeley's statement also appears in Mott, *American Journalism*, 6; Levy, *Freedom of Speech and Press in Early American History*; 21ff., also quotes Berkeley in providing information about the suppression of colonial printers.

Some scholars have argued that economic incentives may have more significantly affected colonial newspaper content. See, for example, Mary Ann Yodelis, "Who Paid the Piper? Publishing Economics in Boston, 1763–1775," *Journalism Monographs* 38 (February 1975): Stephen Botein, "Printers and the American Revolution," in Bailyn and Hench, eds., *The Press and the American Revolution*, 22, suggests that trade incentives occasioned the bland, noncontroversial content.

18. Emery and Emery, *The Press and America*, 26–44; Mott, *American Journalism*, 6, 15–20; Levy, *Freedom of Speech and Press*, 20ff.

19. Levy, *Freedom of Speech and Press*, 19–20.

20. Mott, *American Journalism*, 37. Hamilton, defending Zenger, referred to "informations"—indicating that the mechanism continued to be recognized as a threat.

21. Levy, *Freedom of Speech and Press*; Harold L. Nelson, "Seditious Libel in Colonial America," *American Journal of Legal History* 3 (April 1959): 160–172.

22. Stewart, *The Opposition Press*, 3; Levermore, "The Rise of Metropolitan Journalism," 447.

23. Schlesinger, *Prelude to Independence*, 20–22.

24. Ibid.; Philip Davidson, *Propaganda and the American Revolution* (Chapel Hill: University of North Carolina Press, 1941); Homer L. Calkin, "Pamphlets and Public Opinion During the American Revolution," *Pennsylvania Magazine of History and Biography* 64 (January 1940): 22–42.

25. Levy, ed., *Freedom of the Press from Zenger to Jefferson*, lxxvi; James Russell Wiggins, "Afterword: The Legacy of the Press in the American Revolution," in Bailyn and Hench, eds., *The Press and the American Revolution*, 366. The reversal of this view meant the press must have access to government information that it had previously been denied by such measures as the one enacted by the Massachusetts Council in 1725 that "printers . . . be ordered upon their peril not to insert in their prints anything of public affairs . . . without the order of government." A statement by Samuel Adams in the Boston *Public Advertiser* reflects the new view: "Whoever acquaints us that we have no right to examine into the conduct of those who, though they derive their power from us to serve the common interests, make use of it to impoverish and ruin us, is in a degree a rebel—to the undoubted rights and liberties of the people" (Wiggins, 367).

26. Stewart, *The Opposition Press*, 457–458, 472–473, explicates the Jeffersonians' arguments for a free press; see also Levy, ed., *Freedom of the Press from Zenger to Jefferson*, lxxviff.

27. Kent R. Middleton, "Commercial Speech and the First Amendment" (Ph.D. diss., University of Minnesota, 1977): 23–37, traces evidence supporting this view. *Media and the First Amendment in a Free Society* reprinted from the *Georgetown Law Journal* for March 1972 (Amherst: University of Massachusetts Press, 1973): 1–63, argues differently.

28. Smith, *The Press, Politics and Patronage*; Baxter Ford Melton, Jr., "Amos Kendall in Kentucky, 1814–1829: The Journalistic Beginnings of the 'Master Mind' of Andrew Jackson's 'Kitchen Cabinet'" (Ph.D. diss., Southern Illinois University, 1978); J. D. Daniels, "Amos Kendall: Kentucky Journalist, 1815–1829," *The Filson Club History Quarterly* 52 (January 1978): 46–65; Smith, *The Francis Preston Blair Family*; Smith, *Francis Preston Blair*; Michael W. Singletary, "The New Editorial Voice of Andrew Jackson: Happenstance, or Plan?" *Journalism Quarterly* 53 (Winter 1976): 672–678.

29. Joseph T. Buckingham, *Personal Memoirs and Recollections of Editorial Life*, 2 vols. (Boston: Ticknor, Reed, and Fields, 1852; rpt. New York: Arno Press and the New York Times Company, 1970), 1:21.

30. Czitrom, *Media and the American Mind*, 6ff., notes similar awe about the early telegraph; see also "An Evening with the Telegraph-Wires," *Atlantic Monthly* 2 (September 1858): 489–495.

31. Emery and Emery, *The Press and America*, 115–116; Mott, *American Journalism*, 159, 216; Stewart, *The Opposition Press*, 15. The papers cost $6 to $10 a year by subscription—or six cents each.

32. Stewart, *The Opposition Press*, 5–7; Morton Borden, *Parties and Politics in the Early Republic, 1789–1815* (New York: Thomas Y. Crowell, 1967): 10–11; Richard Hofstadter, *The Idea of a Party System: The Rise of Legitimate Opposition in*

the United States, 1780–1840 (Berkeley and Los Angeles: University of California Press, 1970).

33. Letter of Thomas Jefferson to the President of the United States, July 31, 1793, in Paul Leicester Ford, ed., *The Writings of Thomas Jefferson*, vol. 6, *1792–1794* (New York: G. P. Putnam's Sons, 1895): 360–361; Stewart, *The Opposition Press*, 5–7; Hofstadter, *The Idea of a Party System*, 90ff. According to Hofstadter, at least thirty-five "Democratic Societies" appeared throughout the country in 1793, all "out-spokenly pro-French and pro-Republican, and in some cases act[ing] as pressure groups on particular issues" (p. 92). It must be noted that just when "factions" became parties is yet debated by historians, and that many leaders during the era opposed both factions and parties. See also Richard P. McCormick, *The Second American Party System: Party Formation in the Jacksonian Era* (Chapel Hill: University of North Carolina Press, 1966).

34. Emery and Emery, *The Press and America*, 74–79; Stewart, *Opposition Press*, 7–10, 622–623; Smith, *The Press, Politics and Patronage*, 1–22.

35. Carl E. Prince, "The Federalist Party and Creation of a Court Press, 1789–1801," *Journalism Quarterly* 53 (Summer 1976): 238–241.

36. Hamilton, *The Country Printer*, 51ff.; Gerald J. Baldasty, "The Political Press in the Second American Party System" (Ph.D. diss., University of Washington, 1978): 4; Linn, *Horace Greeley*, 28; Smith, *The Press, Politics and Patronage*. The Kentucky Court party controversy, and the founding of Anti-Masonic papers in the 1820s and American nativist papers in the 1840s are examples of newspapers emerging around issues. Horace Greeley's *Log Cabin* was established for the 1840 presidential election campaign and discontinued afterward. Regarding the Kentucky Court party controversy, see Smith, *The Francis Preston Blair Family in Politics* 1:21ff.; Smith, *Francis Preston Blair*, 11–25; and Bob Nowell, "Amos Kendall's Role in the Election of Andrew Jackson as President of the United States, 1828" (paper presented at a meeting of the Association for Education in Journalism, East Lansing, Michigan, August 1981). Nowell also cites Arndt M. Stickles, *The Critical Court Struggle in Kentucky, 1819–1829* (Bloomington: Indiana University Graduate Council, 1929).

37. Reynolds, *Editors Make War*, 78–79, comments that Stephen Douglas, who made two trips to the South in the 1860 campaign, was the first to break the precedent, and hostile editors castigated him for it.

38. Hofstadter, *The Idea of a Party System*; McCormick, *The Second American Party System*, 3–31; Donald B. Cole, *Martin Van Buren and the American Political System* (Princeton: Princeton University Press, 1984): 83–98; Schlesinger, *The Age of Jackson*, 47ff.

39. Schlesinger, *The Age of Jackson*, 67ff; Pessen, *Jacksonian America*, 154ff.

40. Cole, *Martin Van Buren*, 83–98. Van Buren regarded the press as essential: "Without a paper thus edited at Albany [i.e., the *Albany Argus*], we may hang our harps on the willows. With it the party can survive a thousand . . . convulsions" (Cole, 87).

41. Baldasty, "The Political Press," 25–30, 37, 108; Hamilton, *The Country*

272 Notes to Pages 38–40

Printer, 150–152. The Schenectady, New York, *Cabinet* editor complained in an item on March 28, 1821, that "the editor of The American . . . is a *lawyer*—the editor of the (Ulster Co.) Craftsman is a *lawyer*—the (Hudson) Bee . . . is now . . . edited by a *lawyer*—the Argus is edited by one lawyer . . . the editor of the Northern Budget is a lawyer—the Sandy Hill Times is edited by a *lawyer*—the editor of the Geneva Palladium . . . is a lawyer." Francis Preston Blair and Amos Kendall were both trained as lawyers and, because of their political leanings, were approached by party leaders to undertake newspaper work. See Daniels, "Amos Kendall: Kentucky Journalist"; Melton, "Amos Kendall"; Smith, *Francis Preston Blair*; Smith, *The Francis Preston Blair Family*.

42. Pessen, *Jacksonian America*, 311–312.

43. Emery and Emery, *The Press and America*, 110–112; Smith, *Francis Preston Blair*, 63–89; Singletary, "New Editorial Voice," 677–678; Cole, *Martin Van Buren*, 66–98; Mott, *American Journalism*, 179–180, 257. Charles R. Brown, *The Northern Confederacy: New England and the "Essex Junto," 1795–1814* (Princeton: Princeton University Press, 1915) describes the early development of such a junto.

44. Gerald J. Baldasty, "The Charleston, South Carolina, Press and National News, 1808–47," *Journalism Quarterly* 55 (Autumn 1978): 519–526, documents Charleston newspapers' reliance on the *National Intelligencer* for news into the 1830s; Nowell, "Amos Kendall's Role," 11–12, uses the term "network" and lists newspapers that were linked politically. Smith, *The Press, Politics and Patronage*, and Cole, *Martin Van Buren*, discuss the linkages and orchestrated coordination.

45. Stewart, *The Opposition Press*, 18; Hamilton, *The Country Printer*, 59–67; Clarence S. Brigham, *Journals and Journeymen* (Philadelphia: University of Pennsylvania Press, 1950): 23–26; William H. Hale, *Horace Greeley: Voice of the People* (New York: Harper and Brothers, 1950): 40–41.

46. Hamilton, *The Country Printer*, 60–67.

47. Prince, "Court Party"; Hamilton, *The Country Printer*, 72–83.

48. Ames, *A History of the "National Intelligencer,"* 111–112, 153, 281–283. Erik McKinley Eriksson, "President Jackson's Propaganda Agencies," *Pacific Historical Review* 6 (March 1937): 47–57; and Smith, *The Press, Politics and Patronage*, also discuss income from patronage.

49. Reynolds, *Editors Make War*, 5. In 1860, the eleven states that became the Confederacy published 844 of the 4,051 periodicals in the nation. According to Reynolds, 83 percent of the South's periodicals were political, compared with 74 percent of those in the North. According to the 1860 census, 80.02 percent (3,242) of the total 4,051 were political; Joseph C. G. Kennedy, Superintendent U.S. Bureau of the Census, Eighth Census, 1860, *Preliminary Report on the Eighth Census, 1860* (Washington, D.C.: Government Printing Office, 1862): 103.

50. Explanations for the penny press's emergence include technological determinism, economic determinism, and political arguments, among others. David P. Nord, "The Evangelical Origins of Mass Media in America, 1815–1835," *Journalism Monographs* 88 (May 1984): summarizes these briefly in introducing a thesis that well-organized efforts to disseminate religious information provided the model for the 1830s mass press.

51. Commager, *Era of Reform*.

52. Commager, *Era of Reform*; Mary Beth Norton et al., *A People and a Nation* (Boston: Houghton Mifflin, 1982): 220–335.

53. Loren Baritz, ed., *Sources of the American Mind*, 2 vols. (New York: John Wiley and Sons, 1966), 1: 325ff.; Alfred Kazin, "Where Would Emerson Find His Scholar Now?" *American Heritage* (December 1987): 93–96.

54. Mott, *American Journalism*, 215–238.

55. Mott, *American Journalism*, 222–224. The *New York Sun*'s police court reports dealt with trivial aspects of people's lives and often seemed to ridicule those involved.

56. Hamilton, *The Country Printer*, 150, notes that journalist J. T. Buckingham, speaking at a meeting in 1848, said the "innovation" of hiring an editor began in 1811 at the *Massachusetts Mercury*, and although in the early years a printer regarded it as a disgrace "not to edit his own paper," Buckingham believed himself to be the only person in Boston, or perhaps Massachusetts, still combining the work of editor and printer in 1848. More than one editor complained of the burden of work. James Gordon Bennett, announcing he had to hire help, wrote in the *New York Herald*, September 7, 1835: "Heretofore, I have done everything myself . . . written my own police reports . . . Wall Street reports . . . squibs, crackers, jeu d'esprit . . . been my own clerk and accountant, posted my own books, made out my own bills and generally attended to all business details in the office." At the end of 1836, Bennett hired Frederic Hudson, who became his managing editor. By 1837, Bennett referred to his staff as "all the editors, writers, printers, pressmen" working on a "fourth edition." Pray, *Memoirs of James Gordon Bennett*, 288; Seitz, *The James Gordon Bennetts*, 44, 64.

57. Until the 1820s the term *reporter* seemed to mean only (or primarily) those who transcribed and reported legislative proceedings. But James Gordon Bennett began to report on other than political affairs from Washington, D.C., in the 1820s and, in 1830, traveled to Massachusetts to report on a murder trial. Seitz, *The James Gordon Bennetts*, 15–37. Hudson wrote, "It was not till 1837, '38, '39, and '40 that reporters were introduced on the Daily Press" (p. 720). Newspaper content from the early 1830s reveals common use of the term *reporter* in much the same way as it is understood today. Hudson (pp. 561–565) discusses the importance of interviews, but dates their origin from 1859. As noted earlier (Ch. 1, n. 35), Anne Royall and James Gordon Bennett reported interviews in the 1830s. See also F. B. Marbut, "Early Washington Correspondents: Some Neglected Pioneers," *Journalism Quarterly* 25 (December 1948): 369–374, 400.

58. Mott, *American Journalism*, 224; Hudson, *Journalism in the United States*, 425–426.

59. Study of newspapers in the 1830s and 1840s to identify journalistic jobs yielded eleven kinds of editors, three kinds of correspondents, and police reporter, in addition to pressman, printer, journeyman, apprentice, carrier, proofreader, manager, and publisher. The 1840 census showed that 1,372 U.S. citizens listed themselves as editors, 14,740 as printers, 138 as reporters, 209 as newsmen, and 355 as publishers. Editors outnumbered professors 1,372 to 943; adding these

gives a total of 16,814 in the newspaper industry. For an undeveloped profession, the total was not far behind the number of clergymen (26,842), lawyers (23,030); and doctors (40,564). U.S. Bureau of the Census, Sixth Census, 1840, *Compendium of the Enumeration of the Inhabitants and Statistics of the United States* (Washington, D.C.: Thomas Allen, 1841).

60. "The Newspaper and Periodical Press," *Southern Quarterly Review* 1 (January 1842): 18. Writing a year after publication of the English philosopher Thomas Carlyle's book that popularized the term "fourth estate," the anonymous author used the same phrase in discussing "another branch of the intellectual machinery . . . of the Newspaper Press" (p. 19) in which America had followed Britain's lead —the reporters on congressional proceedings.

61. Hudson, *Journalism in the United States*, 425.

62. Dan Schiller, *Objectivity and the News: The Public and the Rise of Commercial Journalism* (Philadelphia: University of Pennsylvania Press, 1981): 8–11; Mott, *American Journalism*, 243ff.; Michael Schudson, *Discovering the News: A Social History of Newspapers* (New York: Basic Books, 1978): 14ff.

63. Schiller, *Objectivity and the News*, 10.

64. Mott, *American Journalism*, 243.

65. James Crouthamel, "The Newspaper Revolution in New York: 1830–1860," *New York History* 45 (April 1964): 94.

66. Seitz, *The James Gordon Bennetts*, 41.

67. Quoted in Bleyer, *Main Currents*, 187.

68. "The Newspaper Press," 6.

69. Seitz, *The James Gordon Bennetts*, 40.

70. "The Newspaper Press," 6–7.

71. *Springfield Republican*, September 30, 1858.

72. Schudson, *Discovering the News*, 71ff., and Thomas Connery, "Fusing Fictional Technique and Journalistic Fact: Literary Journalism in the 1890s Newspaper" (Ph.D. diss., Brown University, 1984), discuss realism as a phenomenon of American journalism in the 1880s and 1890s. Linda Patterson Miller, "Poe on the Beat: *Doings of Gotham* as Urban, Penny Press Journalism," *Journal of the Early Republic* 7 (Summer 1987): 154ff., and Schiller, *Objectivity*, 87ff., persuasively discuss realism in the reporting of the 1840s.

73. Brown, *Raymond of the "Times,"* 14ff.

74. Thomas Carlyle, *Heroes, Hero-Worship and the Heroic in History* (London: Chapman and Hall, 1840): 152–153.

75. Lambert Wilmer, *Our Press Gang* (Philadelphia: J. T. Lloyd, 1860): 63–65.

76. U.S. Bureau of the Census, Eighth Census, 1860, *Statistics of the United States* (Washington, D.C.: Government Printing Office, 1866): xiv.

77. Wilmer, *Our Press Gang*, 65.

78. Although he proclaimed his newspaper to be independent, Horace Greeley sought financial support from the Whig party less than a month after establishing the *New York Tribune*; Stoddard, *Horace Greeley*, 65. See also Chapter 4 of the present work.

79. See, for example, Richard Grant White, "The Morals and Manners of Journalism," *The Galaxy* 8 (December 1869): 844; and the anonymously published articles "The Casuistry of Journalism," *Cornhill Magazine* 28 (August 1873): 198–206; and "The Nature and Limit of the Obligation of the Newspaper to Its Party," *The Inland Printer* 7 (October 1889): 49.

80. "The Press and the Tories," *Fraser's Magazine* 8 (September 1833): 330.

81. "The Influence of the Press," *Blackwood's Edinburgh Magazine* 36 (September 1834): 373.

82. Rev. J. M. Peck, "The Power of the Press," *Christian Review* 9 (March 1844): 70–71.

83. "The Newspaper and Periodical Press," 6–7.

84. Ibid., 7.

85. Ibid., 18.

86. Edward L. Carter, "The Revolution in Journalism During the Civil War," *Lincoln Herald* 73 (Winter 1971): 229–241; Emery and Emery, *The Press and America*, 145–171; J. Cutler Andrews, *The North Reports the Civil War*, 33–34; Louis M. Starr, *Bohemian Brigade: Civil War Newsmen in Action* (New York: Alfred A. Knopf, 1954); Bernard A. Weisberger, *Reporters for the Union* (Boston: Little, Brown, 1953).

87. Samuel Bowles published editorials on the independent press's superiority over partisan newspapers throughout the 1850s; see chapters 6 and 7 for a discussion. See also Reynolds, *Editors Make War*.

88. Smith, *The Press, Politics and Patronage*, 219–234, says that President James Buchanan had decided to end the pattern of a political newspaper for his administration; see also Robert Harper, *Lincoln and the Press* (New York: McGraw-Hill, 1952); Harlan Hoyt Horner, *Lincoln and Greeley* (Urbana: University of Illinois Press, 1953); Pollard, *The Presidents and the Press*.

89. Emery and Emery, *The Press and America*, 176.

90. Carter, "The Revolution in Journalism," 230.

91. Andrews, *The North Reports the Civil War*, 31–34; Mott, *American Journalism*, 330ff.; Emery and Emery, *The Press and America*, 171.

92. Andrews, *The North Reports the Civil War*, 6, 33; Carter, "The Revoluiton in Journalism," 230–231; Emery and Emery, *The Press and America*, 171.

93. Bleyer, *Main Currents*, 252; see also Donald Shaw, "News Bias and the Telegraph: A Study of Historical Change," *Journalism Quarterly* 44 (Spring 1967): 3–12.

94. Emery and Emery, *The Press and America*, 170–171; Andrews, *The North Reports the Civil War*, (Pittsburgh: University of Pittsburgh Press, 1970; rpt. 1985): 516–517.

95. John Finnegan, Jr., "Effects of the American Civil War on the Press" (lecture given at the University of Minnesota, Minneapolis, November, 1986); Carter, "The Revolution in Journalism."

96. Schudson, *Discovering the News*, 66, 88–120.

97. Andrews, *The North Reports the Civil War*, 6.

98. Donald Shaw, "News About Slavery from 1830 to 1860 in Newspapers of the South, North and West," *Journalism Quarterly* 61 (Autumn 1984): 483–492. See also Shaw, "At the Crossroads: Change and Continuity in American Press News, 1820–1860," *Journalism History* 8 (Summer 1981): 38–53.

99. Joe Bensen, "Visual Reporting of the Civil War" (lecture given at the University of Minnesota, Minneapolis, November, 1986).

100. Andrews, *The North Reports the Civil War*, 67–69.

101. Ibid., 6ff.

102. Ibid., 15ff.

103. Ibid., 21.

104. Stoddard, *Horace Greeley*, 226.

105. Andrews, *The North Reports the Civil War*, 33–34.

106. Ibid., 14, 20.

107. Ibid., 24.

108. Ibid., 6.

109. Ibid., 32–33.

110. Stoddard, *Horace Greeley*, 226.

111. Andrews, *The North Reports the Civil War*, 7.

112. Brown, *Raymond of the "Times,"* 275–276.

113. Lincoln J. Steffens, "The Business of a Newspaper," *Scribner's Magazine* 22 (October 1897): 447–467.

114. Emery and Emery, *The Press and America*, 210–211, discussing Joseph Pulitzer, tell of Nellie Bly's trip around the world—one such stunt that generated daily news; W. A. Swanberg, *Citizen Hearst* (New York: Scribner's, 1961), discusses William Randolph Hearst's creation of events to generate news coverage.

115. Morton Keller, *Affairs of State: Public Life in Late Nineteenth Century America* (Cambridge: Harvard University Press, Belknap Press 1977): 285.

116. Charles Holden, [address to the Editors and Publishers' Association], *Proceedings of the Maine Press Association . . . for the Years 1864, 1865 and 1866* (Bar Harbor, Maine: Mount Desert, Publishing, 1884): 24.

117. Quintus Wilson, "The Confederate Press Association: A Pioneer News Agency," *Journalism Quarterly* 26 (June 1949): 160–166; Rosewater, *Cooperative Newsgathering*, 99–146.

118. Bruce Catton, *The Civil War* (New York: American Heritage Press, 1985): 101–113.

119. Lynn Masel-Walters, "'Their Rights and Nothing More': A History of the *Revolution*, 1868–1870," *Journalism Quarterly* 53 (Summer 1976): 242–251.

120. Roland E. Wolseley, *The Black Press, U.S.A.* (Ames: Iowa State University Press, 1971): 25; Dann, *The Black Press*, 1–30; Frederick G. Deitweiler, *The Negro Press in the United States* (Chicago: University of Chicago Press, 1922): 53–100.

121. Nevins, *The Emergence of Modern America*, 169–173; Mott, *American Journalism*, 512–513.

122. Mott, *American Journalism*, 443–444.

123. William I. Rivers, Theodore Peterson, and Jay W. Jensen, *The Mass Media and Modern Society*, 2nd ed. (San Francisco: Rinehart Press, 1971): 40; Sidney

Fine, *Laissez-Faire and the General Welfare State: A Study of Conflict in American Thought, 1865–1901* (Ann Arbor: University of Michigan Press, 1956, 1964): 3–25; Edward C. Kirkland, *Industry Comes of Age: Business, Labor and Public Policy, 1860–1897* (New York: Holt, Rinehart and Winston, 1961): 163–180; Bleyer, *Main Currents*, 389–429.

124. Kirkland, *Industry Comes of Age*, 195–215; Nevins, *The Emergence of Modern America*, 178ff.; Keller, *Affairs of State*, 335–337; Harvey Swados, ed., *Years of Conscience* (Cleveland: Meridian Books, 1962).

125. Keller, *Affairs of State*, 373–375; Edward C. Kirkland, *Business in the Gilded Age* (Madison: University of Wisconsin Press, 1952); Kirkland, *Dream and Thought in the Business Community, 1860–1900* (Ithaca: Cornell University Press, 1956); John Tipple, "Big Businessmen and a New Economy," in H. Wayne Morgan, ed., *The Gilded Age*, rev. ed. (Syracuse, N.Y.: Syracuse University Press, 1970): 13–30; Fine, *Laissez-Faire*, 96–125; Louis Filler, *Crusaders for American Liberalism* (New York: Harcourt, Brace, 1939; rpt. Yellow Springs, Ohio: Antioch Press, 1964): vii–viii; Daniel J. Boorstin, *The Americans: The National Experience* (New York: Vintage Books, 1965): 115–123.

126. Keller, *Affairs of State*, 370–380; Tipple, "Big Businessmen," in Morgan, *The Gilded Age*, 13ff.; Fine, *Laissez-Faire*, 96–125; Filler, *Crusaders for American Liberalism*, 12.

127. Paul V. Murphy, "Near v. Minnesota in the Context of Historical Developments," *Minnesota Law Review*, 66 (November 1981): 116.

128. Norton et al., *A People and A Nation: A History of the United States*, 478–479, 507–610; Keller, *Affairs of State*, 295–297, 409ff. Tipple, "Big Businessmen," in Morgan, ed., *The Gilded Age*, 24; Fine, *Laissez-Faire*, 101ff.; Richard Hofstadter, *Social Darwinism in American Thought* (1944; rpt. Boston: Beacon Press, 1955).

129. Robert H. Wiebe, *The Search for Order: 1877–1920* (New York: Hill and Wang, 1967): 133–163; Keller, *Affairs of State*, 295–297; Fine, *Laissez-Faire*, 169–197; Filler, *Crusaders for American Liberalism*, 9–28; Alan Trachtenberg, ed., *Democratic Vistas: 1860–1880* (New York: George Braziller, 1970).

130. Norton et al., *A People and a Nation*, 468–491, 550–571; Keller, *Affairs of State*, 394ff.; Filler, *Crusaders for American Liberalism*, 19ff.

131. Carter, "The Revolution in Journalism," 230.

132. Mott, *American Journalism*, 444–445.

133. E. J. Carpenter, "Journalism as a Profession," *Education* 7 (February 1887): 414–415.

134. Hamilton, *The Country Printer*, 11ff., details costs of press equipment and supplies up to 1850; Mott, *American Journalism*, 498, notes that the cost of a press in the 1872–1892 period ranged from $40,000 to $80,000; Hudson, *Journalism in the United States*, 566–567, lists the *New York Tribune*'s expenses for 1865 and 1866. In 1864, George W. Childs bought the *Public Ledger* for "slightly over one hundred and fifty thousand dollars"; Elwyn B. Robinson, "The *Public Ledger*: An Independent Newspaper," *Pennsylvania Magazine of History and Biography* 64 (January 1940): 52.

135. Dill, *Growth of Newspapers*, 37; Mott, *American Journalism*, 204, 314, 401–

402, 498. Paper cost $300 a ton in 1810. The cost dropped from 14 to 8 cents a pound between 1833 and 1860; after escalating during the Civil War to as much as 28 cents a pound, the cost was down to 8½ cents a pound in 1874, and it continued to decrease—to 6 cents in 1882 and 3 cents a pound by the end of 1892.

136. Brigham, *Journals and Journeymen*, 19–22; Stewart, *The Opposition Press*, 16–17; Mott, *American Journalism*, 159, 303, 402–404, 506–508, 546–547; Dill, *Growth of Newspapers*.

137. Mott, *American Journalism*, 385, 443–444, 488–489; Smythe, "The Reporter, 1880–1900." John Lesperance wrote in *Lippincott's Magazine* 8 (August 1871): 180, "For the majority of readers it is the reporter, and not the editor, who is the ruling genius of the newspaper."

138. Mott, *American Journalism*, 443–444; Hudson, *Journalism in the United States*, 536–538, 656–666, 703–704.

139. Carolyn Stewart Dyer, "Economic Dependence and Concentration of Ownership Among Antebellum Wisconsin Newspapers," *Journalism History* 7 (Summer 1980): 42–46; Mott, *American Journalism*, 462; Bleyer, *Main Currents*, 402ff.

140. Mott, *American Journalism*, 404, 411; Dill, *Growth of Newspapers*, 28–29; Emery and Emery, *The Press and America*, 231; Hudson, *Journalism*, 770ff. The U.S. census lists 4,051 periodicals in 1860 and 12,652 in 1890; Ayer's *American Newspaper Annual* lists 16, 152 in 1890; Dill's data (from U.S. census reports) show a total of 5,871 periodicals published in the United States in 1870 and 18,793 in 1899; in 1860, dailies numbered 387; in 1899, there were 2,226 dailies; total subscriptions were 13,663,409 in 1860, 20,842,475 in 1870 and 106,889,334 in 1899; subscriptions to dailies numbered 2,601,547 in 1870 and 15,102,156 in 1899.

141. Frank Presbry, *History and Development of Advertising* (New York: Doubleday, Doran, 1929): 210, 591.

142. Swanberg, *Citizen Hearst*; W. A. Swanberg, *Pulitzer* (New York: Scribner's, 1967); Don C. Seitz, *Joseph Pulitzer: His Life and Letters* (New York: Simon and Schuster, 1924); Emery and Emery, *The Press and America*, 253–278.

Chapter Three: Changes in News During the Nineteenth Century

1. An exception is the *New York Times*, which began in 1851.

2. The number of newspapers publishing continuously in the earliest years of the nation is difficult to calculate because of numerous name changes. Seventy-nine were counted, based on Clarence S. Brigham, *History and Bibliography of American Newspapers, 1690–1820* (Worcester, Mass.: American Antiquarian Society, 1947). The higest-circulation newspapers in 1890, according to Ayer's *Newspaper Annual*, were as follows:

1. *Chicago News*, 262,000
2. *Philadelphia Evening Item*, 207,460
3. *Philadelphia Record*, 186,387

4. *New York News*, 178,560
5. *Cincinnati Post*, 176,805
6. *Philadelphia Inquirer*, 157,552
7. *New York Sun*, 120,000
8. *Philadelphia Bulletin*, 117,281
9. *Chicago Tribune*, 110,000
10. *Boston Evening Record*, 109,516
11. *Cleveland Press*, 107,788
12. *Cincinnati Times-Star*, 103,405

Some newspapers were unavailable, so any six on the list were acceptable, but some substitutions were still necessary.

3. John Martin and Harold Nelson have developed a standard for measuring the accuracy of reports of one event (or series of events), but they concede that the problem of determining accuracy is difficult. L. John Martin and Harold L. Nelson, "The Historical Standard in Analyzing Press Performance," *Journalism Quarterly* 33 (Fall 1956): 456–466.

4. A very narrow study, focusing on a few or on just one category of stories, could perhaps accomplish what was not possible through this broader perspective.

5. Shilen, "The Concept of Objectivity," 38, quotes Mott's testimony before the Federal Communications Commission, January 22, 1942, that "indeed, one of these newspapers would be considered a traitor to its party and to its cause if it" printed news of the opposing party. See *Freedom of the Press* (New York: Newspaper-radio Committee, 1942): 24.

6. *New Hampshire Gazette*, June 2, 1801; published on Tuesdays by John Melcher, printer to the state of New Hampshire. Columns 1 and 2 of page 1 and all of page 4 were filled with advertisements.

7. *Boston Gazette*, January 22, 1801; published Mondays and Thursdays by John Russell and James Cutler.

8. *Hampshire Gazette*, June 24, 1801; published in Northampton, Massachusetts, on Wednesdays by William Butler; all of page 4 was advertising.

9. *Jenks' Portland Gazette*, February 2, 1801; published Mondays by Eleazer Alley Jenks, printer of the laws of the United States for the District of Maine. This issue was not in the sample, but was studied for reports of debates on renewing the Alien and Sedition Acts.

10. Ibid., June 22, 1801.

11. Ibid., December 14, 1801.

12. *The Spectator*, January 3, 1801; published in New York City on Wednesdays and Saturdays by E. Belden & Co., printers of the laws of the United States for the District of New York. Column 5 of page 3 and all of page 4 were typically all advertising in this newspaper.

13. *Jenks' Portland Gazette*, February 16, 1801.

14. *Centinel of Freedom*, June 30, 1801; published in Newark, New Jersey, on Tuesdays by Samuel Pennington and Stephen Gould. Typically, the paper had ads filling three columns on the front page, the fourth column of both inside pages, and all of page 4.

15. *Republican Star or Eastern Shore General Advertiser*, June 13, 1809; published in Easton, Maryland, on Tuesdays by Thomas Perrin Smith, printer of the laws of the United States.

16. Ibid., January 3, 1809.

17. *Mercantile Advertiser*, January 2, 1801; printed in New York City daily (except Sundays) by John Crookes "for the proprietor." Page 1, columns 1–2 of page 2, and pages 3 and 4 were all advertising; the paper sold for $8 a year.

18. Ibid.

19. *American Mercury*, January 15, 1801; published in Hartford, Connecticut, on Thursdays by Elisha Babcock.

20. *Maryland Herald and Hagers-town Weekly Advertiser*, June 7, 1809; published in Hagerstown, Maryland, by Thomas Grieves.

21. Ibid.

22. Ibid., June 14, 1809.

23. Ibid.

24. Ibid., June 21, 1809.

25. Ibid.

26. Ibid., June 28, 1809.

27. Ibid.

28. Ibid., December 13, 1809.

29. *Hampshire Gazette*, January 7, 1801; reprinted from the *Pittsburgh Gazette*.

30. Ibid.

31. Advertising generally filled two and one-fourth pages in a four-page paper and four pages in an eight-page paper.

32. For example, one issue's editorials discussed the national political conventions (of the Whig party in Baltimore, the Free Soil party in Cleveland, and the Liberty party in Buffalo), considered Franklin Pierce's candidacy, and summarized Pierce's voting record in Congress; *Springfield* (Massachusetts) *Republican*, June 8, 1852. Editorials in an issue of another paper commented on a new book by Genet, the approaching national elections, and the contributions of science to civilization; *Boston Transcript*, February 2, 1858. Still another newspaper editorialized on a specific court case, taking occasion to evaluate critically a rival paper's coverage, and assessed the agenda of the impending congressional session; *New York Daily News*, November 19, 1852.

33. *Springfield Republican*, August 31, 1852; the *Boston Transcript*, April 8, 1858, had only four international items, only one of which (about revolution in Venezuela) constituted significant news; another consisted of two lines datelined Halifax, Nova Scotia; another, headed "Siberia," was commentary prompted by publication of a journal of seven years' travel abroad; the fourth announced a local exhibit of British art.

34. Linda Patterson Miller, "Poe on the Beat: 'Doings of Gotham' as Urban, Penny Press Journalism," *Journal of the Early Republic* 7 (Summer 1987), 164.

35. *New York Herald*, August 30, 1852, p. 1, col. 4.

36. Ibid., October 25, 1852, p. 1, col. 3.

37. *Boston Transcript*, October 25, 1852.

38. *New York Times*, September 30, 1852.
39. *New York Herald*, February 26, 1852.
40. *Philadelphia Evening Bulletin*, July 6, 1891.
41. Ibid., April 10, 1891.
42. Ibid.
43. Ibid.
44. *Cincinnati Post*, January 5, 1891.
45. Ibid.
46. Ibid., March 10, 1891.
47. St. Paul, Minnesota, *Daily Pioneer Press*, April 18, 1891.
48. Ibid.
49. Ibid., June 19, 1891.
50. *Philadelphia Evening Bulletin*, January 23, 1899.
51. *New York Sun*, April 20, 1899.
52. *Philadelphia Evening Bulletin*, January 23, 1899.
53. Ibid.
54. Ibid., April 14, 1899.
55. Ibid., January 23, 1899.
56. *Cincinnati Post*, January 5, March 10, July 16, 1891; *Daily Pioneer Press*, January 16, April 18, June 19, 1891; *New York Sun*, January 3, 1891.

Chapter Four: Journalistic Standards and the Press's Role to 1850

1. F. B. Marbut, "Decline of the Official Press in Washington," *Journalism Quarterly* 33 (Summer 1956): 335–341; Mott, *American Journalism*, 256. In 1846 Congress adopted a rule that gave government printing contracts to the lowest bidder, thus undermining the practice of "rewarding" partisan editors. In 1860 the Government Printing Office was established, but Mott notes that after 1846 no administration newspaper in Washington had effective power.

2. Hezekiah Niles, asserting his own political opinions, tried to publish all sides of issues; see Norval Neil Luxon, *"Niles' Weekly Register"* (Baton Rouge: Louisiana State University Press, 1947): 38, 40.

3. Stewart, *The Opposition Press*, 12.

4. The party and visible leaders were not the only targets of criticism. Anti-Jackson journalists, in efforts to destroy Jackson's election chances, published vicious attacks and innuendos against Rachel Jackson. On the other side, the pro-Jackson editor Duff Green published that John Quincy Adams and his wife had engaged in premarital sex and otherwise aspersed Mrs. Adams's character (although without Jackson's consent). Gretchen Ewing, "Duff Green: Independent Editor of the Party Press," *Journalism Quarterly* 54 (Winter 1977): 733–739.

5. See Richards, *"Gentlemen of Property and Standing,"* for examples of journalists' involvement in suppression activities during the 1830s; Reynolds, *Editors Make War*; Nye, *Fettered Freedom*; Clement Eaton, *Freedom of Thought Struggle in the Old South* (Durham, N.C.: Duke University Press, 1940); Jeffrey B. Rutenbeck, "Partisan Press Coverage of Anti-Abolitionist Violence: A Case Study of Status

Quo Journalism" (paper presented at a meeting of the Association for Education in Journalism and Mass Communications, San Antonio, Texas, August 1987); Victoria Smith, "Newspapers and Freedom of Expression: Minnesota Press Reaction to Suppression During the World War I Era, 1912–1918" (M.A. thesis, University of Minnesota, 1985). Reviewing literature on journalistic response during social crises, Smith found a pattern of press support for suppression—tending to confirm the press's relationship to culture's prevailing value structure.

6. No nineteenth-century analysis of the concept of truth in terms of journalistic work was found. An article by Edward F. Adams, "Newspaper Work: Limitations of Truth-Telling," *Arena* 20 (November–December 1898): 604–614, is very general, emphasizing partisanship as limiting truth-telling. Although no thorough search of early twentieth-century discussion was made, the best "dissection" of truth for journalists found was Elmer Davis, "News and the Whole Truth," *Atlantic Monthly* 190 (August 1952): 32–38.

7. Harlan S. Stensaas, "The Rise of Objectivity in U.S. Daily Newspapers, 1865–1934" (paper presented at a meeting of the American Journalism Historians Association, St. Louis, October 1986): 5, cites C. G. Ross's use of the term "objective" as early as 1911: "News writing is objective to the last degree, in the sense that the writer is not allowed to 'editorialize'"; Charles G. Ross, *The Writing of News: A Handbook* (New York: Henry Holt, 1911): 20; see also Ross's news-writing rules (p. 18).

8. Smith, *The Politics of Information*, discussing eighteenth-century British newspapers' partisanship, notes the ridicule of one editor who "insisted on printing political speeches from both sides." Smith says impartiality then meant "that in the welter of propaganda and lies he [the journalist] was calling attention to the accuracy of a particular statement. It meant that he had not been paid to write something. . . . When a particular writer claimed to be being impartial he was claiming to have acquainted himself with all the factionalist material and to have reduced it to certain firm propositions, unpaid" (p. 147).

9. Schudson, *Discovering the News*, 183ff.

10. Stewart, *The Opposition Press*, 28, citing the Poughkeepsie, New York, *American Farmer*, October 29, 1799.

11. Ibid., 29, citing the *Newark Gazette*, September 4, 1798.

12. Ibid., citing the *Washington* (Kentucky) *Mirror*, July 17, 1799.

13. Ibid., citing the *Baltimore American*, May 16, 1797.

14. Ibid., citing the New York *American Citizen*, March 10, 1800.

15. Shilen, "The Concept of Objectivity," 38.

16. Kingsbury et al., "Measuring the Ethics of American Newspapers," 93.

17. Stewart, *The Opposition Press*, 30.

18. Isaiah Thomas, *The History of Printing* (New York: Weathervane Books, 1810): 19–21.

19. Stewart, *The Opposition Press*, 28, citing the Peacham, Vermont, *Green Mountain Patriot*, April 6, 1798.

20. *The Post-Angel or Universal Entertainment*, edited by Robert Archibald in Edenton, North Carolina, September 10, 1800.

21. Ibid., 1.

22. "The *National Intelligencer* and Its Editors," *Atlantic Monthly* 6 (October 1860): 477.

23. *United States Telegraph*, February 7, 1826; cited in Culver H. Smith, "Propaganda Technique in the Jackson Campaign of 1828," *East Tennessee Historical Society Publications* 6 (1934): 53.

24. For more about Green, see Ewing, "Duff Green"; Fletcher M. Green, "Duff Green: Industrial Promoter," *Journal of Southern History* 2 (February 1936): 29–42; Green, "Duff Green, Militant Journalist of the Old School," *American Historical Review* 52 (January 1947): 247–264.

25. Smith, "Propaganda Technique," 53–54.

26. William E. Smith, "Francis Preston Blair, Pen-Executive of Andrew Jackson," *Mississippi Valley Historical Review* 17 (March 1931): 543–556; published in Edwin H. Ford and Edwin Emery, *Highlights in the History of the American Press* (Minneapolis: University of Minnesota Press, 1954): 138–149; Smith, *The Press, Politics and Patronage*, 114–126.

27. Pollard, *The Presidents and the Press*, 161; the *National Journal* later revised the list, dropping one name and adding three.

28. Shilen, "The Concept of Objectivity," 39–40.

29. Levy, ed., *Freedom of the Press from Zenger to Jefferson*, 197ff.

30. Madison to N. P. Trist, dated Montpelier, Virginia, April 23, 1828; quoted in Mott and Casey, eds., *Interpretations of Journalism*, 113–114.

31. Dooley, "Minnesota Journalists as Elected Officials," 42, defines the journalist-politician as "any journalist who sought or held" any of several public offices. Here, however, the term is used to refer to those journalists who wielded political influence, whether they were officeholders or not.

32. Jackson to John Randolph, November 11, 1831, in J. S. Bassett, ed., *Correspondence of Andrew Jackson*, 7 vols. (Washington, D.C.: Carnegie Institution, 1929); 4: 371–372.

33. Mott, *American Journalism*, 188–189, 256; Charles H. Ambler, *Thomas Ritchie: A Study in Virginia Politics* (Richmond, Va.: Bell Book and Stationery Company, 1913).

34. *National Journal*, August 18, 1829; cited in Pollard, *The Presidents and the Press*, 161.

35. Ibid.

36. Thomas Ritchie to Martin Van Buren, March 27, 1829; in Bassett, ed., *Correspondence of Andrew Jackson* 4: 17.

37. Jackson to Van Buren, March 31, 1829, in Bassett, ed., *Correspondence of Andrew Jackson* 4: 19; spelling and grammar appear as in original.

38. Jackson to T. L. Miller, May 13, 1829, in Bassett, ed., *Corresponde.ce of Andrew Jackson* 4: 31; see also Pollard, *The Presidents and the Press*, 162–163.

39. See note 38 above.

40. Jackson to Randolph, November 11, 1831, in Bassett, ed., *Correspondence of Andrew Jackson* 4: 371–372.

41. Virginia General Assembly, House of Delegates, *The Virginia Report of*

1799–1800 Touching the Alien and Sedition Laws (New York: De Capo Press, 1970): 226–227.

42. Levy, ed., *Freedom of the Press from Zenger to Jefferson*, 216.

43. Mott, *American Journalism*, 242–243.

44. Gerald L. Grotta, "Philip Freneau's Crusades for Open Sessions of the U.S. Senate," *Journalism Quarterly* 48 (Winter 1971): 667–671. Ames, *A History of the "National Intelligencer,"* 23–30, describes Samuel Harrison Smith's defense of the press's right to report on the House of Representatives and Senate.

45. *Trial: Commonwealth vs. J. T. Buckingham, on an Indictment for a Libel, from the Municipal Court of the City of Boston* (Boston: New-England Galaxy, 1822): 21–22.

46. Ibid., 43.

47. Emery and Emery, *The Press and America*, 78–81; Mott, *American Journalism*, 174–175, 257. Mikkelson, *"Kentucky Gazette,"* 212ff., describes a series of duels among editors; Wilmer, *Our Press Gang*, devotes two chapters to editors' quarrels and duels; In addition to providing information throughout the book, Hudson, *Journalism in the United States*, also devotes a chapter to them. See also John R. Howe, "Republican Thought and the Political Violence of the 1790s," *American Quarterly* 19 (Summer 1967): 147–164.

48. Finnegan, "Defamation, Politics, and the Social Process of Law," 149ff., discusses the personal nature of politics during this era.

49. Pray, *Memoirs of James Gordon Bennett*, 203; "American and British Newspaper Press," *Southern Quarterly Review* 4 (July 1843): 238.

50. Bovee, "Horace Greeley and Social Responsibility"; David P. Nord, "Tocqueville, Garrison and the Perfection of Journalism," *Journalism History* 13 (Summer 1986): 56–63; Rutenbeck, "Partisan Press Coverage."

51. Rutenbeck, "Partisan Press Coverage," 14–15, citing the *New York Evening Post*, November 18, 1837.

52. Quoted in Shilen, "The Concept of Objectivity," 43.

53. Mott, *American Journalism*, 243.

54. Seitz, *The James Gordon Bennetts*, 73–101; Hudson, *Journalism in the United States*, 456–461; James Crouthamel, "The Newspaper Revolution in New York, 1830–1860," *New York History* 45 (April 1964): 91–113; James Crouthamel, "*The New York Herald* and the Development of Newspaper Sensationalism," *New York History* 54 (July 1973): 294–316.

55. *Trial: Commonwealth vs. J. T. Buckingham*, 43.

56. *Niles Weekly Register*, September 5, 1835, 1; cited in Richards, "*Gentlemen of Property and Standing*," 12–13.

57. David Demers, "The Origins of Crime News in American Newspapers" (unpublished paper, 1981), discusses attitudes toward publishing crime news.

58. *St. Louis Reveille*, May 14, 1844. The editor indicated what he viewed as appropriate newspaper content: "We shall take due cognizance of all political matters presenting interest to the general reader, but remain neutral . . . summing up the news of the day . . . noticing all local events, paying especial attention to all matters connected with the interests of St. Louis. . . . We hold variety to be the sauce of a newspaper. . . ."

59. *Trial: Commonwealth vs. J. T. Buckingham*, 53.

60. Finnegan, "Defamation, Politics, and the Social Process of Law," 231ff., has found that plaintiffs fared better than defendants in New York defamation suits in this era, which suggests that responsibility was defined in support of traditional values, particularly deference. The most interesting trials during the era were of suits brought by James Fennimore Cooper; see Ethel R. Outland, *The "Effingham" Libels on Cooper: A Documentary History of the Libel Suits of James Fennimore Cooper Centering Around the Three-Mile Point Controversy and the Novel Home as Found, 1837–1845* (Madison: University of Wisconsin, 1929).

61. E. L. Bulwer and Sergeant Talfourd, "Literary Remains of the Late William Hazlitt," *American Quarterly Review* 20 (December 1836): 265, 267.

62. "The Newspaper and Periodical Press," 5–6.

63. Ibid.

64. *New York Sun*, November 29, 1833; the editor of the *New York Evening Post*, November 25, 1850, also argued against appointments of editors.

65. *Chicago Tribune*, July 3, 1841.

66. *Hannibal* (Missouri) *Courier*, November 1, 1842.

67. Quoted in Brown, *Raymond of "The Times,"* 25.

68. Quoted in Stoddard, *Horace Greeley*, 65.

Chapter Five: Press Criticism to 1850

1. James A. Casada, "Editor's Introduction," in E. M. Palmegiano, *The British Empire in the Victorian Press, 1832–1867* (New York: Garland Publishing, 1987): xi.

2. Walter E. Houghton, "Periodical Literature and the Articulate Classes," in Joanne Shattock and Michael Wolff, eds., *The Victorian Periodical Press: Samplings and Soundings* (Leicester: Leicester University Press, 1982): 3–4.

3. "The Newspaper and Periodical Press," 41–42.

4. Houghton, "Periodical Literature," 3.

5. Americans interpreted the power of public opinion more broadly than as a restraint on government, although they emphasized that. They believed that public opinion would, and should, serve as a restraint on activities and institutions, including the press. The defendant journalist in a libel trial in Massachusetts in 1822 denied that there could be any difficulty in distinguishing between press liberty and licentiousness because "public opinion has already drawn the line . . . thus far shalt thou go and no farther." Public opinion protected the virtuous, he argued, and if any printer attempted "to drag the pure and the honest" down, he would be "instantly pursued, overtaken and punished by public indignation." *Trial: Commonwealth vs. J. T. Buckingham*, 22.

6. Bulwer and Talfourd, "Literary Remains," 266, 267.

7. James Savage, *An Account of the London Newspapers, and of the Manner in Which They Are Conducted* (London: N.p., 1811).

8. *Observations upon Sunday Newspapers: Tending to Shew the Impiety of Such a Violation of the Sabbath, the Religious and Political Evils Consequent upon the Practice, and the Necessity Which Exists for Its Suppression* (London: J. Hatchard and Son, 1820).

9. Several sources deal with transatlantic circulation of publications during the eighteenth century. See, for example, Norman S. Fiering, "The Transatlantic Republic of Letters: A Note on the Circulation of Learned Periodicals to Early Eighteenth-Century America," *William and Mary Quarterly*, 3rd ser., 33 (October 1976): 642–660; Bernard Bailyn, *Ideological Origins of the American Revolution* (Cambridge: Harvard University Press, Belknap Press, 1967); Bailyn, ed., *Pamphlets of the American Revolution, 1750–1776* (Cambridge: Harvard University Press, Belknap Press, 1965). Similar work about literary exchanges in the early nineteenth century was not found, but some publishing houses in America specialized in supplying the English periodicals.

10. See Levy, *Freedom of Speech and Press in Early American History*, 1–17; Finnegan, "Defamation, Politics, and the Social Process of Law," 11–15, 95ff. American journalism histories generally begin with the English roots and treat developments principally from a political viewpoint emphasizing the struggle for press freedom.

11. "The Newspaper Press and Periodical Press," 59.

12. Hillhouse, *The Grub-Street Journal*, 106–108.

13. Ibid., 114.

14. Bleyer, *Main Currents*, 38–42.

15. Hillhouse, *The Grub-Street Journal*, 109. Elements in these accounts resemble America's penny press journalism, especially that of James Gordon Bennett, suggesting that a kind of eighteenth-century sensationalism was a forerunner and pattern imitated in what has been called America's "first burst" of sensationalism a century later.

16. Ibid., 110.

17. Charles Holden, former editor of the Portland *Eastern Argus*, quoted Ames in an address to the first meeting of the Maine Press Association in Portland on August 11, 1864.

18. Holden, [Address to the Editors and Publishers Association], 21–22.

19. Ibid.

20. *Observations upon Sunday Newspapers*.

21. The congressional debate on renewal of the Alien and Sedition Acts in 1801 reveals the tensions between the two sets of values. Several newspapers reported these debates; see especially the Baltimore *American Daily Advertiser* in late 1800 and early 1801.

22. William G. McLoughlin, ed., *The American Evangelicals, 1800–1900* (New York: Harper Torchbooks, 1968): 1–27; Paul E. Johnson, *A Shopkeeper's Millennium: Society and Revivals in Rochester, New York, 1815–1837* (New York: Hill and Wang, 1978): 1–14; Charles A. Johnson, *The Frontier Camp Meeting: Religion's Harvest Time* (Dallas: Southern Methodist University Press, 1955); William Warren Sweet, *Revivalism in America: Its Origin, Growth, and Influence* (New York: Abingdon Press, 1944); Tyler, *Freedom's Ferment*, 23–45; Pessen, *Jacksonian America*, 75–84; Timothy L. Smith, *Revivalism and Social Reform: American Protestantism on the Eve of the Civil War* (New York: Abingdon Press, 1957); Whitney R. Cross, *The Burned-Over District: The Social and Intellectual History of Enthusiastic Religion in Western New York, 1800–1850* (Ithaca: Cornell University Press, 1950); Perry

Miller, *The Life of the Mind in America from the Revolution to the Civil War* (New York: Harcourt, Brace and World, 1965); see especially Book 1, "The Evangelical Basis."

23. William A. Hachten, "The Metropolitan Sunday Newspaper in the United States: A Study of Trends in Content and Practice" (Ph.D. diss., University of Minnesota, 1961): 14–25; Frank Luther Mott, "The First Sunday Paper: A Footnote to History," *Journalism Quarterly* 35 (Fall 1958): 443–446; Alfred McClung Lee, *The Daily Newspaper in America* (New York: Macmillan, 1937): 376–407; Hudson, *Journalism in the United States*, 337–341. Rosewater, *Cooperative Newsgathering*, 16, discusses the opposition to newsgathering on Sundays. Although there had been several previous attempts to establish Sunday newspapers, James Gordon Bennett's *New York Sunday Herald*, established in 1841, was the first regularly published Sunday paper that endured. Bennett first attempted it in 1835 but discontinued it because of opposition. Hachten finds that the greatest source of opposition to Sunday papers in America was the clergy and others who sought to protect the Sabbath for religious observance; the opposition reached a "religious craze" by 1830, and state laws were passed to prohibit Sunday sales.

24. Robert Donald, "Sunday Newspapers in the United States," *The Universal Review* 8 (September–December 1890): 78–89.

25. *Observations upon Sunday Newspapers*, 45–46.

26. Ibid., 46–47, 53.

27. Ibid., 53–54.

28. Ibid., 96–97, 47.

29. Ibid., 51–52, 57–60.

30. "Influence of the Newspapers," *Fraser's Magazine for Town and Country* 4 (September 1831): 127–130.

31. Ibid., 130–133.

32. Ibid., 130.

33. Ibid.

34. Ibid., 131.

35. Ibid., 131–132.

36. Ibid., 132.

37. Ibid., 131.

38. "The Influence of the Press," *Blackwood's Edinburgh Magazine* 36 (September 1834): 374.

39. Ibid., 373–374.

40. Ibid., 375–376.

41. Ibid., 374–375.

42. Ibid., 381–382.

43. "Influence of the Newspapers," 136, 139.

44. *Observations upon Sunday Newspapers*, 96–97.

45. "Influence of the Newspapers," 131.

46. Ibid., 130–131.

47. Ibid., 131.

48. Ibid., 139.

49. "The Influence of the Press," 373.
50. Ibid., 377, 383.
51. Ibid., 377–380.
52. Bulwer and Talfourd, "Literary Remains."
53. Ibid., 269.
54. "The Newspaper and Periodical Press," 10. Although not part of the body of critical literature, the Massachusetts libel trial in 1822—two years after publication of *Observations upon Sunday Newspapers*—presents a different view of crime news and the press's potential harm to youth. In the judge's opinion, "It can scarcely be said that an exposure of crime and vice . . . and influence, are not within the fair scope of the liberty of the press," especially in a country where "piety, virtue and morality lie at the foundation of society, and are declared by its constitution, to be its hope and cement"; *Trial: Commonwealth vs. J. T. Buckingham,* 53. British critics had warned of the press's dangers to youth by exposing them to "unseemly" content, but the plaintiff's argument sought rather to protect youth themselves from news reports about them, an idea related to what later became the concept of invasion of privacy; *Trial,* 43.
55. "The Newspaper Press," 8.
56. Rev. J. M. Peck, "The Power of the Press," *Christian Review* 9 (March 1844): 70–71.
57. "The Newspaper and Periodical Press," 5–6.
58. Ibid., 11, 8.
59. Ibid., 9–10.
60. Bulwer and Talfourd, "Literary Remains," 267.
61. "American and British Newspaper Press," 237–238.
62. "The Newspaper Press," 6, 15.
63. Ibid., 15–16.
64. Ibid., 16.
65. Ibid.
66. Ibid., 8–9.
67. "American and British Newspaper Press," 237.
68. *Southern Quarterly Review* (January 1842): 14.
69. Ibid., 12–15. The writer noted 38 newspapers published in London in 1795, 72 elsewhere in England, 13 in Scotland, and 35 in Ireland for a total of 138; in 1808, 63 were published in London, 93 elsewhere, 24 in Scotland, and 37 in Ireland for a total of 217. In 1837, 11 dailies and 27 weeklies were published in London; the aggregate circulation of the dailies was about 40,000, that of the weeklies 120,000—"making a total circulation, in round numbers," of 160,000 in London alone.
70. Ibid., 17.
71. Ibid., 25, 18.
72. "American and British Newspaper Press," 236–273. Among the "good" newspapers, British critics mentioned the *New York American,* the *New York Evening Post,* the *Boston Daily Advertiser,* and a few others. The worst were the *New York*

Herald and the *New York Courier and Inquirer*, called by the British critics "those Billingsgate prints."
73. "The Newspaper Press," 17, 24–25.
74. Ibid., 17–18.
75. Ibid., 7–8, 27.
76. Ibid., 26–28. The judge in the Massachusetts libel trial emphasized the differences between England and America regarding press freedom. In an extensive examination of whether truth could be permitted as a defense against a libel charge, since no precedent existed in Massachusetts, the judge concluded that although English common law "excludes the truth in these cases," the American Constitution did not; *Trial: Commonwealth vs. J. T. Buckingham*, 8–17.
77. Bulwer and Talfourd, "Literary Remains," 268–269.
78. Ibid., 268–269.
79. Ibid., 269.
80. Ibid., 270–271.
81. "American and British Newspaper Press," 237.
82. "The Newspaper and Periodical Press," 13.
83. "American and British Newspaper Press," 238.
84. "The Newspaper and Periodical Press," 20–24. In a single sentence extending over two pages, the author explained what this kind of history would be and seemed to name every trait (good and bad) of humankind.
85. Ibid., 25–26.
86. Ibid., 20.
87. Ibid., 21.
88. Ibid.
89. Ibid., 21–22.
90. *Trial: Commonwealth vs. J. T. Buckingham*, 8–17.
91. "American and British Newspaper Press," 238.
92. "The Newspaper and Periodical Press," 20, 13.
93. Bulwer and Talfourd, "Literary Remains," 270.
94. "The Newspaper Press," 22.

Chapter Six: Criticism, 1850–1889: Press Functions and General Problems

1. Sweet, *Revivalism in America*, 159; E. Douglas Branch, *The Sentimental Years, 1836–1860* (London and New York: D. Appleton-Century, 1934).
2. One of the first articles to try to detail how the press worked is W. F. G. Shanks, "How We Get Our News," *Harper's New Monthly Magazine* 34 (March 1867): 511–522. The intent at the outset, as noted in Chapter 4, was to treat journalists' criticism separately on the assumption that those who worked in the industry would have different insights about press conduct. Such separation proved impractical, however. It also became clear that, although the views differed in some respects—and although some divergence had appeared by the end of the 1880s —journalists emphasized the same themes as nonjournalists. Journalists' views are therefore interwoven in the analysis of criticism for the last half of the century.

3. Edwin Godkin, editor of *The Nation* until 1881 and of the *New York Evening Post* from 1883 until 1900 (he was associate editor, 1881–1883), has been called by the historian Morton Keller "the most distinguished journalist of his generation." Born in Ireland in 1831, the son of a Presbyterian minister, Godkin interrupted his law studies in 1853 to write a *History of Hungary*, which earned him a literary reputation and position as the London *Times* correspondent on the Crimean War from 1853 to 1855. Arriving in America in 1856, he apprenticed in David Dudley Field's New York City law office and joined the bar in 1858 but did not sustain interest in a legal career. Continuing as a correspondent, he became a consultant to the *New York Times*. Increasingly disaffected with the United States in later years, he moved to England in 1899 and died there in 1902.

Samuel Bowles III, the son of Samuel Bowles, Jr., who established the weekly *Springfield Republican* in 1824, was born in Springfield, Massachusetts, on February 9, 1826. He began to work with his father after leaving school at seventeen and soon became involved in editorial duties. He became editor of the *Republican* in 1851 and earned recognition as a leader of "independent" journalism. At his death on January 16, 1878, tributes hailed him as the "pioneer and leader of independent journalism in the United States" and the "*facile princeps* among his contemporaries" in all that constituted "taste in journalism,—good taste, condensation, dress, perspicuity, and elevation of tone." No other newspaper, one individual commented, had been "more diligently studied by editors than the Springfield *Republican*" during the previous two decades, for it represented all the best of journalism. See Morton Keller, ed., *Problems of Modern Democracy: Political and Economic Essays by Edwin Lawrence Godkin* (Cambridge: Harvard University Press, Belknap Press 1966): vi–xii; George S. Merriam, *The Life and Times of Samuel Bowles*, 2 vols. (New York: Century, 1885).

4. Thomas Connery, "Fusing Fictional Technique and Journalistic Fact: Literary Journalism in the 1890s Newspaper" (Ph.D. diss., Brown University, 1984): 10.

5. *Springfield Republican*, September 30, 1858.

6. Holden, [Address to the Editors and Publishers Association], 22–23.

7. James Parton, *Famous Americans of Recent Times* (Boston: Houghton, Osgood and Company, 1867; rpt. 1879): 264. The article "The New York Herald" was first published in the *North American Review* 102 (April 1866): 373–418.

8. White, "The Morals and Manners of Journalism," 840.

9. O. B. Frothingham, "Voices of Power," *Atlantic Monthly* 53 (February 1884): 176–182.

10. Dion Boucicault, "At the Goethe Society," *North American Review* 148 (March 1889): 336–337.

11. Lunt, *Three Eras of New England* (Boston: N.p., 1857), 66–68.

12. Parton, *Famous Americans*, 264.

13. *Springfield Republican*, January 4, 1851; quoted in Mott and Casey, eds. *Interpretations of Journalism*, 115–116.

14. *New York Herald*, September 5, 1858, p. 3.

15. Dion Boucicault, "The Decline and Fall of the Press," *North American Review* 145 (July 1887): 34.

16. George T. Rider, "The Pretensions of Journalism," *North American Review* 135 (November 1882): 471–474.

17. See Augustus A. Levey, "The Newspaper Habit and Its Effect," *North American Review* 143 (September 1886): 308–3102; Boucicault, "The Decline and Fall of the Press," 32–39. See also note 76 below.

18. Edwin L. Godkin, "The 'Judicious' in Journalism," *The Nation* 6 (February 6, 1868): 105–106. It is noteworthy that a short time later a writer in England, identifying himself only as "a cynic," asserted that Parliament had abandoned debate to newspapers, which he called "our supreme rulers." Newspapers, having "done away with" legislative debate, had "undertaken the management of . . . national affairs"; "Our Rulers—Public Opinion," *Cornhill Magazine* 21 (March 1870): 288–289. Although typical in aristocracies, Godkin wrote, legislating ahead of popular opinion was futile in a democracy, enumerating examples that no treaty since 1800 had succeeded without popular support and approval.

19. Edwin L. Godkin, "Opinion-Moulding," *The Nation* 9 (August 12, 1869): 126. The editorial, Godkin wrote, was prompted by a statement in the *New York Times* that the daily newspaper's purpose, to dispense the news that had "become of immense moral . . . social . . . commercial and political importance to the world," put more responsibility on editors than "any other class" was "called on to bear."

20. Dana, *The Art of Newspaper Making*, 20–21; quoted in Mott and Casey, eds., *Interpretations of Journalism*, 163.

21. *Springfield Republican*, December 23, 1851, quoted in Bleyer, *Main Currents*, 256.

22. *Springfield Republican*, February 3, 1855, quoted in Mott and Casey, eds., *Interpretations of Journalism*, 116.

23. Edwin L. Godkin, "Editorial Perspective," *The Nation* 10 (January 17, 1870): 54.

24. Levey, "The Newspaper Habit," 309–310.

25. Parton, *Famous Americans*, 263.

26. White, "The Morals and Manners of Journalism," 840–841, 846.

27. Richard Grant White, "The Pest of the Period: A Chapter in the Morals and Manners of Journalism," *The Galaxy* 9 (January 1870): 106–108.

28. Melville E. Stone, *Fifty Years a Journalist* (New York: Doubleday, Page, 1923): 53.

29. Frothingham, "Voices of Power," 176–182.

30. Boucicault, "The Decline and Fall of the Press," 34.

31. Dana, *The Art of Newspaper Making*, 12, 22–24; quoted in Mott and Casey, eds., *Interpretations of Journalism*, 159–164.

32. *Springfield Republican*, January 4, 1851, quoted in Mott and Casey, eds., *Interpretations of Journalism*, 115–116.

33. Lunt, *Three Eras of New England*: 66–67.

34. Two important themes, whether journalists should be required to use bylines and the press's usurpation of the role of the pulpit, are omitted from the analysis because of lack of space and to permit fuller treatment of what seemed more significant issues. The possible tension between the press and the pulpit re-

curs in criticism during the last half of the century, and a thorough analysis would fill at least a chapter. Discussions of the issue of bylines per se ended in America with the Civil War, but in later years a related issue emerged in criticisms of the editorial "we." Lunt, for example, did not agree that the press had more power than the pulpit, but the "finest and most cogent sermons" had little effect "till the press . . . sent them teeming through the world, blazing with light." He also condemned the editorial "We," which he said presupposed "editors and kings to represent the voice of the people, which is the voice of God," as empowering the "delusive oracles" to mislead and therefore make them ready to commit excesses. The most eloquent writing before the Civil War defended the right of journalists to withhold names (their own and their sources') from newspaper content. Although published in England in 1857, there is reason to believe that Americans at the time agreed with the author. See *The Press and the Public Service* (London and New York: G. Routledge, 1857).

35. Wilmer, *Our Press Gang*, 381. One chapter was devoted to two charges —that newspapers debased literature and retarded knowledge; all other charges occupied at least one chapter each.

36. Ibid., 18–49. One of his early editorial misadventures, for example, took place at the *Baltimore Saturday Visiter*, which he helped establish at the invitation of an editor who sought him as a partner. When expenses mounted, a third partner joined the firm. When still another individual volunteered to write editorials gratis, Wilmer, the principal editorial writer, was thrown overboard as his two partners seized the opportunity to cut expenses. Without consulting Wilmer, the partners announced the change in other papers and sought an injunction to prevent Wilmer's creating a disturbance over the matter—while retaining his name under the logo for several weeks. Wilmer continued, however, to submit articles without pay (and was told he would receive none), collecting past-due subscriptions to help pay his expenses. His former partners advertised that no one should give him money for the *Visiter*; Wilmer in turn advertised that no one should give *them* money for the paper. The partners then invited him to rejoin the firm. Wilmer insisted that they retract the charges they had published against him—such as that he had committed fraudulent acts. They refused and, rejecting their offer, Wilmer began a lawsuit to assert his partnership rights. While the case was pending the newspaper failed, and when the court finally decided in Wilmer's favor, there was nothing to collect—although, after suffering impoverishment for some time, he did receive a settlement of $500.

37. Ibid., 36; David K. Jackson, *Poe and the "Southern Literary Messenger"* (Richmond, Va.: Dietz Printing, 1934), xi, 1–4. While Wilmer was editor of the *Baltimore Saturday Visiter* the newspaper established literary contests, in one of which Poe was awarded a prize for his story "MS. Found in a Bottle." In late 1834 Poe, seeking to establish a new literary magazine, wrote to Wilmer, including a prospectus. Wilmer was penniless at the time, having been forced out of the *Visiter*, and could not join in the partnership. Poe's plan for a new literary magazine therefore failed; he became a contributor to the *Messenger* in 1835, and later that year assistant to the editor and founder, Thomas W. White. By December Poe was edi-

tor, remaining in that position until he resigned in January of 1837, after which he again became a contributor.

38. Richards, *"Gentlemen of Property and Standing,"* 7.

39. Wilmer, *Our Press Gang*, 51; Section 6, "Villainous Deceptions Practiced by the Newspapers," Section 7, "Villainous and Shameful Deceptions Practiced by Newspaper Editors," and Section 8, "Other Shameful and Wicked Deceptions Practiced by the Newspapers," 105–147.

40. Ibid., 53; Section 21, "Showing That the Newspaper Press Encourages and Justifies Mobbing, Treason and Rebellion," 353–373.

41. Ibid., 52–53; Section 17, "Editorial Duels," and Section 18, "Fights and Floggings of Editors," 294–326.

42. Ibid., 51; Section 4, "The Foreign and Anti-American Character of Our Newspaper Press," 73–89; the list of foreign newspapers appears on pages 85–87.

43. Ira M. Leonard and Robert D. Parmet, *American Nativism, 1830–1860* (New York: Van Nostrand Reinhold, 1971); Tyler, *Freedom's Ferment*, 363–395.

44. Wilmer, *Our Press Gang*, 51; Section 5, "The Treachery, 'Toryism,' and Anti-Republicanism of the American Press," 91–104; Section 9, "Showing That Imposters and Cheats of All Kinds Are Assisted by the Newspapers," 148–165.

45. Ibid., 53; Section 19, "American Intellect Disgraced by the Newspapers," 327–339.

46. Ibid., 53; Section 10, "The Demoralizing Influences of Journalism," 166–183.

47. Ibid., 51; Section 3, "Usurpation and Tyranny of the Newspaper Press," 60–72.

48. Ibid., 71.

49. Ibid., 52; Section 13, "Showing How the Newspaper Press Defeats the Purposes of Justice," and Section 14, "Horrid Effects of Editorial Interference with the Administration of Justice," 217–250.

50. Ibid., 52.

51. Ibid., Section 15, "A Vile Habit," and Section 16, "Motives, Modes, Examples and Effects of Newspaper Defamation," 251–293.

52. Ibid., 53; Section 20, "Showing That the Newspaper Press Is Leagued with Public Poisoners," 341–352.

53. Ibid., 71.

54. Ibid., 53; Section 11, "Political Villainies of the Newspaper Press," and Section 12, "Showing That Official Scoundrels Owe Their Power and Elevation to the Newspaper Press," 184–216.

55. Lunt, *Three Eras of New England*, 80, 103–105.

56. Holden, [Address to the Editors and Publishers Association], 20–21.

57. W. T. Harris, "Ought Young Girls to Read the Daily Newspapers?" *Addresses and Proceedings of the National Education Association* (1888): 86–89.

58. Holden, [Address to the Editors and Publishers Association], 20–22.

59. Levey, "The Newspaper Habit," 311–312.

60. Bleyer, *Main Currents*, 166, 173, gives examples of defenses.

61. Parton, *Famous Americans*, 293–294; Dana, *The Art of Newspaper Making*, 12.

62. Lunt, *Three Eras of New England*, 84–85.

63. Ibid., 78–79, 106–107.

64. Ibid., 79–80, 91.

65. Ibid., 68–69.

66. Levey, "The Newspaper Habit," 310. Levey (p. 312) noted that the newspaper-reading habit was least prevalent in two otherwise divergent classes: the working class, which found newspapers unsympathetic to its goals and which had learned to disregard them as subservient to capitalism, and the "highly cultivated and educated few," who blamed newspapers for all "modern superficial thought." Between these two extremes lay a "great mass of humanity" who, although they had been taught to read through popular education, had not learned judgment or discretion in choosing what they read.

67. Merriam, *The Life and Times of Samuel Bowles* 1: 193–194.

68. *Springfield Republican*, September 30, 1858. During the Civil War, Bowles believed that the newspaper's function should be to unite the public behind the cause. In an editorial published in 1864 he outlined a view of the press in this unifying role; the journalist's "power does not lie wholly or chiefly in the ability to convince or the gift to persuade," but he "has marvelous resource in the mere power of expression" and it "is his duty to give it voice." Merriam, *The Life and Times of Samuel Bowles* 2: 106, 348.

69. Godkin, "The Judicious in Journalism," 106.

70. Edwin L. Godkin, "The Adulteration of News," *The Nation* 31 (August 12, 1880): 107–108.

71. Ibid.

72. Payne, *History of Journalism*, 329.

73. Levey, "The Newspaper Habit," 309–310. Levey (p. 312) quoted an unnamed journalist, whom he called a "clear thinker" of the day, as saying that people no longer relied on newspapers for opinions, and that the age of newspapers was nearly over; pamphlets would supersede the newspaper because they had always been the medium for distributing information in "eras of transition and revolution" such as the nation was then entering.

74. Frothingham, "Voices of Power," 178–179.

75. Ibid. Frothingham said that partisan sympathies had grown annually "more generous" and political advocacy "more just and noble."

76. *Minnesota Newspaper Association Confidential Bulletin*, no. 20, May 17, 1988, 4–5 (cited with permission of the Minnesota Newspaper Association, Minneapolis).

77. Dana, *The Art of Newspaper Making*, 42.

78. White, "The Morals and Manners of Journalism," 845–846.

79. Rider, "The Pretensions of Journalism," 473.

80. Ibid., 473–474.

81. White, "The Morals and Manners of Journalism," 843, 846.

82. Godkin, "Opinion-Moulding," 126.

83. Dana, *The Art of Newspaper Making*, 20–21; quoted in Mott and Casey, eds., *Interpretations of Journalism*, 163.

84. Godkin, "Opinion-Moulding," 126.
85. Godkin, "Editorial Perspective," 54.
86. Warren Breed, "Social Control in the Newsroom," *Social Forces* 33 (May 1955): 326–335.
87. Godkin, "Editorial Perspective," 54.
88. Godkin, "The Adulteration of News," 107–108.

Chapter Seven: Criticism, 1850–1889:
Specific Journalistic Conduct, Remedies, and Standards

1. Emery and Emery, *The Press and America*, Chap. 10–13, provide insights about events and the press during the late nineteenth and early twentieth century and in a later chapter (pp. 577–582) note significant changes affecting press conduct.

2. Lunt, *Three Eras of New England*, 107, urged education for journalists and suggested training in ethics without suggesting an explicit code. Pray, *Memoirs of James Gordon Bennett*, 203, complained that, although lawyers and clergymen respected their offices and position, "There has yet been no recognition of a profession of journalism." He recommended a weekly meeting to allow a sharing of interests among journalists, "for [journalism's] code of courtesies can only be made in some such way."

3. Mott, *American Journalism*, 444–445, 547, describes personal journalism as the dominance of an editor's personality in newspaper content. Generally used to characterize the journalism of the era following and overlapping that of the penny press and lasting at least until the Civil War, the term seems to have originated with Samuel Bowles, who wrote in 1872 of the decline of personal journalism: "With the deaths of James Gordon Bennett and Horace Greeley, Personal Journalism also comes practically to an end. . . . Their personality was the necessity of their creative work, and it could not be suppressed by inks and types; but they have no successors, because there is no call for them . . . and henceforth, American Journalism, in its best illustrations, will exhibit its outgrowth both of Partyism and Personalism." See also Bleyer, *Main Currents*, 267–268.

4. Weisberger, *Reporters for the Union*, 42–43; Albert Smith, *"Press Orders": Being the Opinions of the Leading Journals on the Abolition of Newspaper Privileges* (London: W. Kent, 1853): 3–20.

5. Samuel D. Warren and Louis D. Brandeis, "The Right to Privacy," *Harvard Law Review* 4 (December 1890): 193–220. Morris L. Ernst and Alan U. Schwartz, *Privacy: The Right to Be Let Alone* (New York: Macmillan, 1962): 45, discuss the historical development of the concept of privacy and refer not only to press content before 1890 but also to Brandeis and Warren's having decided something should be done about it.

6. Emery and Emery, *The Press and America*, 226–243, refer to earlier sensationalism in discussing the yellow journalism of the late 1890s. See also *Special Issue on Sensationalism!! Journalism History* 12 (Autumn–Winter 1985).

7. Lunt, *Three Eras of New England*, 77, 80–81.

8. Godkin, "Opinion-Moulding," 127.
9. White, "The Morals and Manners of Journalism," 845–848.
10. Joseph B. Bishop, "Newspaper Espionage," *The Forum* 1 (August 1886): 535.
11. White, "The Morals and Manners of Journalism," 846–847.
12. Boucicault, "The Decline and Fall of the Press," 34–35.
13. Mott, *American Journalism*, 242–243.
14. *Springfield Republican*, September 30, 1858, p. 1.
15. Lunt, *Three Eras of New England*, 88–91.
16. Godkin, "Opinion-Moulding," 126.
17. White, "The Morals and Manners of Journalism," 106.
18. White, "The Pest of the Period," 844.
19. Rider, "The Pretensions of Journalism," 478.
20. Ibid., 479.
21. Lunt, *Three Eras of New England*, 92.
22. Godkin, "Editorial Perspective," 54–55.
23. Ibid., 55.
24. Rider, "The Pretensions of Journalism," 479, 474–475.
25. Ibid., 475.
26. William H. Bushnell, "Journalistic Barbarism," *The Inland Printer* 3 (January 1886): 201.
27. Ibid.
28. Ibid.
29. Bishop, "Newspaper Espionage," 529–530.
30. Ibid., 531–532.
31. Ibid., 532–533.
32. Ibid., 533.
33. Ibid., 533–534.
34. Lunt, *Three Eras of New England*, 97–102.
35. Ibid., 96–98.
36. Rider, "The Pretensions of Journalism," 475–476.
37. Boucicault, "At the Goethe Society," *North American Review* 148 (March 1889): 340–341.
38. James Parton, "Falsehoods in the Daily Press," *Harper's Magazine* 49 (July 1874): 271–272, 278.
39. Rider, "The Pretensions of Journalism," 472–473.
40. Godkin, "Opinion-Moulding," 126.
41. Quoted in Mott and Casey, eds., *Interpretations of Journalism*, 161–162.
42. Godkin, "Opinion-Moulding," 126.
43. Ibid.
44. Bishop, "Newspaper Espionage," 536.
45. White, "The Pest of the Period," 107.
46. Ibid., 102.
47. Ibid., 102–103. White (p. 111) wrote that American journalism, greatly elevated and developed by the experiences of the Civil War, showed vast improve-

ment in some areas over fifteen years earlier; for example, authors no longer dared to send "puffs" of their books to prestigious newspapers. But except for two or three newspapers, journalism had improved very little in other areas, especially in "personal abuse in revenge for personal wrongs," which was "one of the few things" that remained as before the Civil War.

48. Rider, "The Pretensions of Journalism," 479.

49. Bushnell, "Journalistic Barbarism," 201.

50. Levey, "The Newspaper Habit," 310–311.

51. See, for example, John Henderson Garnsey, "The Demand for Sensational Journals," *The Arena* 18 (November 1897): 681–686.

52. Godkin, "Opinion-Moulding," 126–127.

53. Rider, "The Pretensions of Journalism," 477–478.

54. Rider, "The Pretensions of Journalism," 476–477.

55. Levey, "The Newspaper Habit," 311.

56. Rider, "The Pretensions of Journalism," 479–480.

57. Bushnell, "Journalistic Barbarism," 202.

58. Bishop, "Newspaper Espionage," 534.

59. Rider, "The Pretensions of Journalism," 479.

60. Ibid., 475.

61. Roger Foster, "Trial by Newspaper," *North American Review* 144 (May 1887): 525–526.

62. Lunt, *Three Eras of New England*, 76–77; *Springfield Republican*, September 30, 1858; Holden, [Address to the Editors and Publishers Association], 24.

63. Stone, *Fifty Years a Journalist*, 57, 54.

64. White, "The Morals and Manners of Journalism," 843.

65. Ibid., 841.

66. William H. Sampson, "The Press, Its Relations to Its Patrons and the Public," *Proceedings of the Maine Editors and Publishers' Association for the Year 1876* (Portland, Maine: Brown Thurston, 1876): 15.

67. Frothingham, "Voices of Power," 177.

68. Dana, *The Art of Newspaper Making*, 11–12.

69. Quoted in Bleyer, *Main Currents*, 265.

70. Sampson, "The Press," 14–15.

71. Ibid., 15.

72. Frothingham, "Voices of Power," 177–178.

73. Stone, *Fifty Years a Journalist*, 54.

74. White, "The Pest of the Period," 112.

75. Bishop, "Newspaper Espionage," 535–537.

76. White, "The Morals and Manners of Journalism," 844.

77. Godkin, "Opinion-Moulding," 126.

78. Dana, *The Art of Newspaper Making*, 54.

79. Godkin, "Opinion-Moulding," 126.

80. White, "The Morals and Manners of Journalism," 843.

81. Stone, *Fifty Years a Journalist*, 52–53.

82. Godkin, "The Adulteration of News," 107–108.

83. Boucicault, "At the Goethe Society," 336.

84. White, "The Pest of the Period," 106, 109.

85. White, "The Morals and Manners of Journalism," 844.

86. Merriam, *The Life and Times of Samuel Bowles* 2: 370–371.

87. Godkin, "Editorial Perspective," 54.

88. Rider, "The Pretensions of Journalism," 476, 482–483.

89. Bushnell, "Journalistic Barbarism," 202.

90. Merriam, *The Life and Times of Samuel Bowles* 2: 99; Payne, *History of Journalism*, 329.

91. White, "The Pest of the Period," 111–112.

92. Bushnell, "Journalistic Barbarism," 201.

93. Foster, "Trial by Newspaper," 523–527.

94. Presbry, *History of Advertising*, 590–591.

95. White, "The Morals and Manners of Journalism," 846–847.

96. Sampson, "The Press," 15–19.

97. *Springfield Republican*, February 3, 1855; quoted in Mott and Casey, eds., *Interpretations of Journalism*, 116–117.

98. *Springfield Republican*, February 3, 1855; quoted in Mott and Casey, eds., *Interpretations of Journalism*, 117.

99. Quoted in Bleyer, *Main Currents*, 267–268.

100. Sampson, "The Press," 15–17.

101. Ibid., 17.

102. Lunt, *Three Eras of New England*, 107.

103. K. T. Wulfemeyer, "Butterflies or Gold Mines: The Development of Courses of Instruction for Journalism in American Colleges and Universities" (paper presented at a meeting of the Association for Education in Journalism, Boston, August 1980): 2–6. See also Mott, *American Journalism*, 406; Robert W. Jones, *Journalism in the United States* (New York: E. P. Dutton, 1947): 503–509; and Marshall W. Fishwick, *Lee: After the War* (New York: Dodd, Mead, 1963): 138.

104. Wulfemeyer, "Butterflies or Gold Mines," 4–5; Jones, *Journalism*, 505; see also Sidney Kobre, *Development of American Journalism* (Dubuque, Iowa: William C. Brown, 1969): 533.

105. E. J. Carpenter, "Journalism as a Profession," *Education* 7 (February 1887): 410–415.

106. Dana, *The Art of Newspaper Making*, 16–17. Dana maintained that a newspaper must have someone on the reporting staff who was scientific, who knew "electricity and chemistry" and could "really understand the inventions of Edison" and relate what was happening in the scientific world. Such a department, he said, was of "supreme consequence."

107. Stone, *Fifty Years a Journalist*, 54; quoted in Mott and Casey, eds., *Interpretations of Journalism*, 465–466.

108. Coblentz, ed., *Newsmen Speak*, 15–17; Seitz, *The James Gordon Bennetts*, 352–355. Hudson, *Journalism in the United States*, 478–479, lists the rules estab-

lished earlier by James Gordon Bennett, Sr., which are similar but much less detailed.

109. Dana, *The Art of Newspaper Making*, 18–20.

Chapter Eight: Implications of Historical Study of Journalistic Standards

1. Personals were not unusual in newspapers of the 1850s. See, for example, the *Boston Transcript*, February 12, 1858.

2. Lee Benson, "The Mistransference Fallacy in Explanations of Human Behavior," *Historical Methods* 17 (Summer 1984): 118–131.

Bibliography

Books

Ainsworth, Fred C., and Joseph W. Kirkley. *The War of the Rebellion: A Compilation of the Official Records of the Union and Confederate Armies.* Washington: Government Printing Office, 1902.

Allen, Robert P., ed. *The Eighteenth Century: A Current Bibliography.* New York: AMS Press, 1981.

Ambler, Charles H. *Thomas Ritchie: A Study in Virginia Politics.* Richmond, Va.: Bell Book and Stationery Company, 1913.

American Newspaper Annual. Philadelphia: N. W. Ayer and Son, 1880–1900.

American Newspaper Directory. New York: George P. Rowell, 1871–73, 1876, 1879.

Ames, William E. *A History of the "National Intelligencer."* Chapel Hill: University of North Carolina Press, 1972.

Andrews, J. Cutler. *The North Reports the Civil War.* Pittsburgh: University of Pittsburgh Press, 1955, 1985.

Andrews, J. Cutler. *The South Reports the Civil War.* Princeton: Princeton University Press, 1970; rpt. Pittsburgh: University of Pittsburgh Press, 1985.

Associated Ohio Dailies. *Proceedings* of the Eighth Annual Meeting. Springfield, Ohio: Hosterman, 1893.

Bailyn, Bernard. *The Ideological Origins of the American Revolution.* Cambridge: Harvard University Press, Belknap Press, 1967.

Bailyn, Bernard, ed. *Pamphlets of the American Revolution, 1750–1776.* Cambridge: Harvard University Press, Belknap Press, 1965.

Bailyn, Bernard, and John B. Hench, eds. *The Press and the American Revolution.* Boston: Northeastern University Press, 1981.

Baker, Russell, ed. *The Norton Book of Light Verse.* New York: W. W. Norton, 1986.

Bardeen, Charles W. *History of Educational Journalism in . . . New York.* Syracuse, N.Y.: C. W. Bardeen, 1893.

Baritz, Loren, ed. *Sources of the American Mind.* New York: John Wiley and Sons, 1966.

Barney, William L. *The Road to Secession: A New Perspective on the Old South.* New York: Praeger, 1972.

Barton, R. T., ed. *The Reports by Sir John Randolph and by Edward Barradall of the General Court of Virginia, 1728–1741.* Vol. 1 of *Virginia Colonial Decisions.* Boston: Boston Book Company, 1909.

Bartow, Edith M. *News and These United States.* New York: Funk and Wagnalls, 1952.

Bassett, John Spencer, ed. *Correspondence of Andrew Jackson.* 7 vols. Washington, D.C.: Carnegie Institution, 1929.

Belford, Barbara. *Brilliant Bylines.* New York: Columbia University Press, 1986.

Bennett, Charles O. *Facts Without Opinion.* Chicago: Audit Bureau of Circulations, 1965.

Bent, Silas. *Newspaper Crusaders: A Neglected Story.* New York: Whittlesey House, 1939.

Berkman, Ronald, and Laura W. Kitch. *Politics in the Media Age.* New York: McGraw-Hill, 1986.

Binkley, Wilfred E. *American Political Parties.* 3rd ed. New York: Alfred A. Knopf, 1958.

Black, Jeremy. *The English Press in the Eighteenth Century.* Philadelphia: University of Pennsylvania Press, 1987.

Bleyer, William G. *Main Currents in the History of American Journalism.* Boston: Houghton Mifflin, 1927.

Blythe, Samuel G. *Making of a Newspaper Man.* Philadelphia: Altemus, 1912.

Bok, Sissela. *Lying: Moral Choice in Public and Private Life.* New York: Vantage Books, 1979.

Bond, Donovan H., and W. Reynolds McLeod, eds. *Newsletters to Newspapers: Eighteenth-Century Journalism.* Morgantown: West Virginia University School of Journalism, 1977.

Boorstin, Daniel F. *The Americans: The National Experience.* New York: Vintage Books, 1965.

Borden, Morton. *Parties and Politics in the Early Republic, 1789–1815.* New York: Thomas Y. Crowell, 1967.

Bourne, Fox. *English Newspapers.* 2 vols. London: Chatto and Windus, 1887.

Branch, E. Douglas. *The Sentimental Years, 1836–1860.* London and New York: D. Appleton-Century, 1934.

Brigham, Clarence S. *History and Bibliography of American Newspapers, 1690–1820.* 2 vols. Worcester, Mass.: American Antiquarian Society, 1947.

Brigham, Clarence S. *Journals and Journeymen.* Philadelphia: University of Pennsylvania Press, 1950.

Brinton, Crane. *The Age of Reason Reader.* New York: Viking Press, 1956.

Brown, Charles R. *The Northern Confederacy: New England and the "Essex Junto," 1795–1814.* Princeton: Princeton University Press, 1915.

Brown, Francis. *Raymond of the "Times."* New York: W. W. Norton, 1951.

Brown, Stuart Gerry. *The First Republicans.* Syracuse: Syracuse University Press, 1954.

Buckingham, Joseph T. *Personal Memoirs and Recollections of Editorial Life.* 2 vols. Boston: Ticknor, Reed and Fields, 1852.

Buckingham, Joseph T. *Specimens of Newspaper Literature.* 2 vols. Boston: Redding, 1852.

Bullock, Penelope L. *The Afro-American Periodical Press, 1838–1909.* Baton Rouge: Louisiana State University Press, 1981.

Burlingame, Ward. *The Newspaper Press.* Topeka, Kans.: Commonwealth State Printing House, 1871.

Buttinger, Joseph. *Vietnam: The Unforgettable Tragedy.* New York: Horizon Press, 1977.

Carlyle, Thomas. *Heroes, Hero-Worship and the Heroic in History.* London: Chapman and Hall, 1840.

Catton, Bruce. *The Civil War.* New York: American Heritage Press, 1985.

Chamberlain, Joseph Edgar. *The Boston Transcript: A History of Its First Hundred Years.* Boston: Houghton Mifflin, 1930.

Chambers, William Nesbet. *Political Parties in a New Nation: The American Experience, 1776–1809.* New York: Oxford University Press, 1963.

Charles, Joseph. *The Origins of the American Party System.* Williamsburg, Va.: Institute of Early American History and Culture, 1956, rpt. New York: Harper & Row, 1961.

Christians, Clifford G., and Catherine L. Covert. *Teaching Ethics in Journalism Education.* Hastings-on-Hudson, N.Y.: Hastings Center, 1980.

Christians, Clifford G., and Gedmund Gzelsten. *Media Ethics and the Church.* Kristiansand, Norway: International Mass Media Institute, 1981.

Christians, Clifford G., Kim B. Rotzoll, and Mark Fackler. *Media Ethics: Cases and Moral Reasoning.* New York: Longman, 1983.

Clair, Colin. *A History of European Printing.* London and New York: Academic Press, 1976.

Clark, Allen Cullen. *William Duane.* Washington: Privately printed, 1905.

Clark, Mary Elizabeth. *Peter Porcupine in America: The Career of William Cobbett, 1792–1800.* Philadelphia: University of Pennsylvania Press, 1939.

Clive, John. *Scotch Reviewers: "The Edinburgh Review," 1802–1815.* Cambridge: Harvard University Press, 1957.

Coblentz, Edmond D., ed. *Newsmen Speak: Journalists on Their Craft.* Berkeley: University of California Press, 1954.

Cole, Donald B. *Martin Van Buren and the American Political System.* Princeton: Princeton University Press, 1984.

Commager, Henry Steele. *Era of Reform, 1830–1860.* New York: Van Nostrand Reinhold, 1960.

Congdon, Charles T. *Reminiscences of a Journalist.* Boston: James R. Osgood, 1880.

Congdon, Charles T., and Thomas Earle, eds. *Annals of the General Society of Mechanics and Tradesmen of the City of New York, from 1785 to 1880.* New York: Society of Mechanics and Tradesmen, 1882.

Congreve, Richard. *Essays, Political, Social, and Religious.* London: N.p., 1874.

Cross, Whitney R. *The Burned-Over District.* Ithaca: Cornell University Press, 1950.

Cunningham, Noble E., Jr. *The Jeffersonian Republicans.* Chapel Hill: University of North Carolina Press, 1957.

Curtis, William E. *The True Thomas Jefferson.* Philadelphia: N.p., 1901.

Czitrom, Daniel J. *Media and the American Mind: From Morse to McLuhan.* Chapel Hill: University of North Carolina Press, 1982.

Dana, Charles A. *The Art of Newspaper Making*. New York: D. Appleton, 1895.

Dann, Martin E. *The Black Press, 1827–1890*. New York: G. P. Putnam's Sons, 1971.

Davidson, Philip. *Propaganda and the American Revolution*. Chapel Hill: University of North Carolina Press, 1941.

Davis, Elmer. *History of the "New York Times," 1851–1921*. New York: New York Times Company, 1921.

Deitweiller, Frederick G. *The Negro Press in the United States*. Chicago: University of Chicago Press, 1922.

Dill, William A. *Growth of Newspapers in the United States*. Lawrence: University of Kansas Press, 1928.

Dill, William A. *The First Century of American Newspapers, 1690–1790*. Lawrence: University of Kansas, 1925.

Drechsel, Robert E. *News Making in the Trial Courts*. New York: Longman, 1983.

Eaton, Clement. *Freedom of Thought Struggle in the Old South*. Durham, N.C.: Duke University Press, 1940.

Eddy, Spencer L., Jr. *The Founding of the "Cornhill Magazine."* Muncie, Ind.: Ball State University, 1970.

Eisenstein, Elizabeth L. *The Printing Press as an Agent of Change*. New York: Cambridge University Press, 1979.

Elliott, Jonathan, ed. *The Debates in the Several State Conventions on the Adoption of the Federal Constitution*. 5 vols. Philadelphia: J. B. Lippincott, 1901.

Emery, Edwin. *History of the American Newspaper Publishers Association*. Minneapolis, University of Minnesota Press, 1950.

Emery, Michael, and Edwin Emery. *The Press and America: An Interpretive History of the Mass Media*. 6th ed. Englewood Cliffs, N.J.: Prentice-Hall, 1988.

Ernst, Morris L., and Alan U. Schwartz. *Privacy: The Right to Be Let Alone*. New York: Macmillan, 1962.

Facts and Figures About a Modern Newspaper. Chicago: Chicago Daily News, 1896.

Fader, Daniel, and George Bornstein. *British Periodicals of the 18th and 19th Centuries*. Ann Arbor, Mich.: University Microfilms, 1972.

Fassett, Frederick Gardiner, Jr. *A History of the Newspapers in the District of Maine, 1785–1820*. Orono: University of Maine Press, 1932.

Fenton, Alfred H. *Dana of "The Sun."* New York: Farrar and Rinehart, 1941.

Filler, Louis. *Crusaders for American Liberalism*. Yellow Springs, Ohio: Antioch Press, 1964.

Fine, Sidney. *Laissez-Faire and the General Welfare State: A Study of Conflict in American Thought, 1865–1901*. Ann Arbor: University of Michigan Press, 1956, 1964.

Fink, Conrad C. *Media Ethics: In the Newsroom and Beyond*. New York: McGraw-Hill, 1987.

Finkelman, Paul. *An Imperfect Union*. Chapel Hill: University of North Carolina Press, 1981.

Fishman, Mark. *Manufacturing the News*. Austin: University of Texas Press, 1980.

Flippen, C. C., ed. *Liberating the Media*. Washington, D.C.: Acropolis Books, 1974.

Foley, John P., ed. *The Jeffersonian Cyclopedia*. New York: Funk and Wagnalls 1900.

Foner, Philip S., and George E. Walker, eds. *Proceedings of the Black State Conventions, 1840–1865*. 2 vols. Philadelphia: Temple University Press, 1979.

Ford, Paul Leicester, ed. *The Writings of Thomas Jefferson*. 10 vols. New York: G. P. Putnam's Sons, 1898.

Ford, Worthington C., ed. *Thomas Jefferson and James Thomson Callender*. Brooklyn: Historical Printing Club, 1897.

Forsyth, David P. *The Business Press in America, 1750–1865*. Philadelphia: Chilton Books, 1964.

Fox, William Johnson. *The Morality of the Press*. London: N.p., 1835.

Frank, Joseph. *The Beginnings of the English Newspaper, 1620–1660*. Cambridge: Harvard University Press, 1961.

Franklin, John Hope. *Reconstruction After the Civil War*. Chicago: University of Chicago Press, 1961.

Freedom of the Press: What It Is, How It Was Obtained, How It Can Be Retained. New York: Newspaper-radio Committee, 1942.

Freneau, Philip. *Letters on Various Interesting and Important Subjects*. New York: Scholars' Facsimiles and Reprints, 1943.

Friedman, Jean E., and William G. Shade, eds. *Our American Sisters: Women in American Life and Thought*. 2nd ed. Boston: Allyn and Bacon, 1976.

Friendly, Alfred, and Ronald L. Goldfarb. *Crime and Publicity: The Impact of News on the Administration of Justice*. New York: Twentieth-Century Fund, 1967.

Gans, Herbert J. *Deciding What's News*. New York: Vintage Books, 1979.

Gilmore, William J. *Elementary Literacy on the Eve of the Industrial Revolution: Trends in Rural New England, 1760–1830*. Worcester, Mass.: American Antiquarian Society, 1982.

Goddard, D. A. *Newspapers and Newspaper Writers in New England, 1787–1815*. Boston: Williams, 1880.

Godwin, Eugene H. *Groping for Ethics in Journalism*. Ames: Iowa State University Press, 1983.

Godwin, Parke. *A Biography of William Cullen Bryant*. 2 vols. New York: D. Appleton, 1883.

Goodrich, Carter, ed. *The Government and the Economy*. Indianapolis: Bobbs-Merrill, 1967.

Griswold, W. M., ed. *Passages from the Correspondence of Rufus Griswold*. Cambridge, Mass.: W. M. Griswold, 1898.

Gurevitch, Michael, et al. *Culture, Society and the Media*. London and New York: Methuen, 1982.

Haig, Robert L. *The Gazetteer, 1735–1797: A Study in the Eighteenth-Century English Newspaper*. Carbondale: Southern Illinois University Press, 1960.

Hale, William Harlan. *Horace Greeley: Voice of the People*. New York: Harper and Brothers, 1950.

Hamilton, Frederick W. *A Brief History of Printing in America*. Chicago: United Typothetae of America, 1918.

Hamilton, John C., ed. *The Works of Alexander Hamilton*. 7 vols. New York: 1850–1851.

Hamilton, Milton W. *The Country Printer: New York State, 1785–1830*. New York: Columbia University Press, 1936.

Haney, Robert W. *Comstockery in America*. Boston: Beacon Press, 1960.

Hansen, J. L. *Wisconsin Newspapers, 1833–1850*. Madison: State Historical Society of Wisconsin, 1979.

Harper, Robert. *Lincoln and the Press*. New York: McGraw-Hill, 1952.

Harris, Joel Chandler, ed. *Life of Henry W. Grady, Including His Writings and Speeches*. New York: Cassill, 1890.

Hart, Jim Allee. *Views on the News: The Developing Editorial Syndrome*. Carbondale: Southern Illinois University Press, 1970.

Hawke, David. *The Colonial Experience*. Indianapolis: Bobbs-Merrill, 1966.

Herd, Harold. *The March of Journalism*. London: George Allen and Unwin, 1952.

Herford, C. H., Percy Simpson, and Evelyn Simpson, eds. *Ben Jonson*. Vol. 6. Oxford: Clarendon Press, 1938.

Herring, George C. *America's Longest War: The United States and Vietnam, 1950–1975*. New York: John Wiley and Sons, 1979.

Hillhouse, James T. *The Grub-Street Journal*. Durham, N.C.: Duke University Press, 1928; rpt. New York: Benjamin Blom, 1967.

Hofstadter, Richard. *The Age of Reform*. New York: Random House, 1955.

Hofstadter, Richard. *The Idea of a Party System: The Rise of Legitimate Opposition in the United States, 1780–1840*. Berkeley: University of California Press, 1970.

Hofstadter, Richard. *Social Darwinism in American Thought*. Rev. ed. Boston: Beacon Press, 1944.

Hooper, Osman Castle. *History of Ohio Journalism, 1793–1933*. Columbus, Ohio: Spahr and Glenn, 1933.

Horner, Harlan Hoyt. *Lincoln and Greeley*. Urbana: University of Illinois Press, 1953.

Hudson, Frederic. *Journalism in the United States from 1690 to 1872*. New York: Harper and Brothers, 1873.

Hugins, Walter. *Jacksonian Democracy and the Working Class: A Study of the New York Workingmen's Movement, 1829–1837*. Stanford: Stanford University Press, 1960.

Hulteng, John L. *Playing It Straight: A Practical Discussion of the Ethical Principles of ASNE*. Chester, Conn.: Globe Pequot Press, 1981.

Hunt, F. Knight. *The Fourth Estate*. 2 vols. London: D. Bogue, 1850.

Hunt, Gaillard, ed. *First Forty Years of Washington Society Portrayed by the Family Letters of Mrs. Samuel Harrison Smith*. New York: Charles Scribner's Sons, 1906.

Jackson, David K. *Poe and the "Southern Literary Messenger."* Richmond, Va.: Dietz Printing, 1934.

Jacobs, Robert D. *Poe: Journalist and Critic*. Baton Rouge: Louisiana State University Press, 1969.

Johannesen, Richard L. *Ethics in Human Communication.* 2nd ed. Prospect Heights, Ill.: Waveland Press, 1983.

Johnson, Charles A. *The Frontier Camp Meeting: Religion's Harvest Time.* Dallas: Southern Methodist University Press, 1955.

Johnson, Paul E. *A Shopkeeper's Millennium: Society and Revivals in Rochester, New York: 1815–1837.* New York: Hill and Wang, 1978.

Jones, Robert. *Journalism in the United States.* New York: E. P. Dutton, 1947.

Joyce, William L., et al. *Printing and Society in Early America.* Worcester, Mass.: American Antiquarian Society, 1983.

Keller, Morton. *Affairs of State: Public Life in Late Nineteenth Century America.* Cambridge: Harvard University Press, Belknap Press, 1977.

Keller, Morton. *In Defense of Yesterday: James M. Beck and the Politics of Conservatism, 1861–1936.* New York: Coward-McCann, 1958.

Keller, Morton, ed. *Problems of Modern Democracy: Political and Economic Essays by Edwin Lawrence Godkin.* Cambridge: Harvard University Press, Belknap Press, 1966.

Kerber, Linda K. *Federalists in Dissent: Imagery and Ideology in Jeffersonian America* Ithaca: Cornell University Press, 1970; rpt. 1980.

Kessler, Lauren. *The Dissident Press: Alternative Journalism in American History.* Beverly Hills: Sage, 1984.

Kirkland, Edward C. *Business in the Gilded Age.* Madison: University of Wisconsin Press, 1952.

Kirkland, Edward C. *Dream and Thought in the Business Community, 1860–1900.* Ithaca: Cornell University Press, 1956.

Kirkland, Edward C. *Industry Comes of Age: Business, Labor and Public Policy, 1860–1897.* New York: Holt, Rinehart and Winston, 1961.

Kobre, Sidney. *Development of American Journalism.* Dubuque, Iowa: William C. Brown, 1969.

Kobre, Sidney. *The Yellow Press and Gilded Age Journalism.* Tallahassee: Florida State University Press, 1964.

Labaree, Benjamin W. *America's Nation-Time, 1607–1789.* New York: W. W. Norton, 1972.

Lake, Anthony, ed. *The Vietnam Legacy: The War, American Society and the Future of American Foreign Policy.* New York: New York University Press, 1976.

Lambeth, Edmund B. *Committed Journalism: An Ethic for the Profession.* Bloomington: Indiana University Press, 1986.

Lee, Alfred McClung. *The Daily Newspaper in America: The Evolution of a Social Instrument.* New York: Macmillan, 1937.

Leonard, Ira M., and Robert D. Parmet. *American Nativism, 1830–1860.* New York: Van Nostrand Reinhold, 1971.

Levy, Leonard W. *Freedom of Speech and Press in Early American History: Legacy of Suppression.* New York: Harper and Row, 1963.

Levy, Leonard W., ed. *Freedom of the Press from Zenger to Jefferson.* Indianapolis: Bobbs-Merrill, 1966.

Linn, W. A. *Horace Greeley.* New York: D. Appleton, 1912.

Lipscomb, Andrew A., ed. *The Writings of Thomas Jefferson.* 20 vols. Washington, D.C.: Thomas Jefferson Memorial Association of the United States, 1904–1905.

Lockridge, Kenneth A. *Literacy in Colonial New England: An Inquiry into the Social Context of Literacy in the Early Modern West.* New York: W. W. Norton, 1974.

Luce, Robert. *Writing for the Press: A Manual.* Boston: Clipping Bureau Press, 1907.

Lunt, George. *Three Eras of New England.* Boston: N.p., 1857.

Luxon, Norval Neil. *"Niles' Weekly Register."* Baton Rouge: Louisiana State University Press, 1947.

Machlup, Fritz. *The Production and Distribution of Knowledge in the United States.* Princeton: Princeton University Press, 1962.

Mahin, Helen Ogden. *The Development and Significance of the Newspaper Headline.* Ann Arbor, Mich.: George Wahr, 1924.

Marcosson, Isaac F. *'Marse Henry': A Biography of Henry Watterson.* New York: Dodd, Mead, 1951.

Marvin, Frederic R. *Editors and Newspapers: A Sermon.* Portland, Oreg.: G. H. Himes, 1883.

Marzolf, Marion. *Up from the Footnote: A History of Women Journalists.* New York: Hastings House, 1977.

Maverick, Augustus. *Henry Raymond and the New York Press for Thirty Years.* Hartford, Conn.: A. S. Hale; Chicago: George W. Rogers, 1870.

Mayes, Martin. *An Historical-Sociological Inquiry into Certain Phases of the Development of the Press in the United States.* Richmond, Mo.: Rumford Press, 1937.

McCormick, Richard P. *The Second American Party System: Party Formation in the Jacksonian Era.* Chapel Hill: University of North Carolina Press, 1966.

McCulloch, Frank, ed. *Drawing the Line.* Washington, D.C.: American Society of Newspaper Editors, 1984.

McGiffert, Michael, and Robert Allen Skotheim, eds. *American Social Thought: Sources and Interpretations.* Vol. 1, *Colonial Beginnings to the Civil War.* Reading, Mass.: Addison-Wesley, 1972.

McJimsey, George T. *Genteel Partisan. Manton Marble, 1834–1917.* Ames: Iowa State University Press, 1971.

McLoughlin, William G., ed. *The American Evangelicals, 1800–1900.* New York: Harper Torchbooks, 1968.

McPhaul, John J. *Deadlines and Monkeyshines: The Fabled World of Chicago Journalism.* Westport, Conn.: Greenwood Press, 1962.

McQuail, Denis. *Analysis of Newspaper Content.* London: Her Majesty's Stationery Office, 1977.

McVicker, James Hubert. *The Press, the Pulpit and the Stage.* Chicago: Western News Company, 1883.

Media and the First Amendment in a Free Society. Reprinted from the *Georgetown Law Journal* for March 1972. Amherst: University of Massachusetts Press, 1973.

Merriam, George S. *The Life and Times of Samuel Bowles.* 2 vols. New York: Century, 1885.

Merrill, John C., and Jack S. Odell. *Philosophy and Journalism*. New York: Longman, 1983.

Meyer, Martin. *The Jacksonian Persuasion: Politics and Belief*. Stanford: Stanford University Press, 1957.

Meyer, Philip. *Editors, Publishers and Newspaper Ethics*. Washington, D.C.: American Society of Newspaper Editors, 1983.

Meyer, Philip. *Ethical Journalism*. New York: Longman, 1987.

Michener, James A. *Kent State: What Happened and Why*. New York: Random House, 1971.

Miller, Perry. *The Life of the Mind in America from the Revolution to the Civil War*. New York: Harcourt, Brace and World, 1965.

Mineka, Francis E. *The Dissidence of Dissent: The Monthly Repository, 1806–1838*. Chapel Hill: University of North Carolina Press, 1944.

Mitchell, Edward P. *Memoirs of an Editor*. New York: Charles Scribner's Sons, 1924.

Moore, John W. *Moore's Historical . . . Notes, Relative to Printers, Printing, Publishing and Editing*. Concord, N.H.: Republican Press Association, 1886.

Morgan, H. Wayne. *From Hayes to McKinley: National Party Politics, 1877–1896*. Syracuse, N.Y.: Syracuse University Press, 1969.

Morgan, H. Wayne. *Industrial America: The Environment and Social Problems, 1865–1920*. Chicago: Rand McNally, 1974.

Morgan, H. Wayne. *Unity and Culture: The United States, 1877–1900*. Baltimore: Penguin Books, 1971.

Morgan, H. Wayne, ed. *The Gilded Age*. Rev. ed. Syracuse, N.Y.: Syracuse University Press, 1970.

Moss, Sidney P. *Poe's Literary Battles: The Critic in the Context of His Literary Milieu*. Durham, N.C.: Duke University Press, 1963.

Mott, Frank Luther. *American Journalism: A History of Newspapers in the United States Through 160 Years: 1690 to 1950*. Rev. ed. New York: Macmillan, 1950.

Mott, Frank Luther. *The History of American Magazines, 1741–1850*. 5 vols. Cambridge: Harvard University Press, 1930.

Mott, Frank Luther. *Jefferson and the Press*. Baton Rouge: Louisiana State University Press, 1943.

Mott, Frank Luther. *The News in America*. Cambridge: Harvard University Press, 1952.

Mott, Frank Luther, and Ralph D. Casey, eds. *Interpretations of Journalism*. New York: F. S. Crofts, 1937.

Munson, A. J. *Making a Country Newspaper*. Chicago: Dominion, 1899.

Murray, Eustace Clare Grenville. *The Press and the Public Service*. London: N.p., 1857.

Myers, Joseph S. *The Genius of Horace Greeley*. Columbus: Ohio State University Press, 1929.

Nesbitt, George L. *Benthamite Reviewing: The First Twelve Years of the Westminster Review, 1824–1836*. New York: Columbia University Press, 1934.

Nevins, Allan. *The Emergence of Modern America, 1865–1878*. New York: Macmillan, 1927; rpt. Chicago: Quadrangle Books, 1971.

Nevins, Allan. *The Evening Post: A Century of Journalism*. New York: Boni and Liveright, 1922.

Nevins, Allan. *Ordeal of the Union*. 2 vols. New York and London: Charles Scribner's Sons, 1947.

North, S. N. D. *History and Present Condition of the Newspaper and Periodical Press of the United States*. Washington, D.C.: Government Printing Office, 1884.

Norton, Mary Beth, et al. *A People and a Nation: A History of the United States*. Boston: Houghton Mifflin, 1982.

Nye, Russel B. *Fettered Freedom*. East Lansing: Michigan State University Press, 1963.

Oates, Stephen B. *Our Fiery Trial: Abraham Lincoln, John Brown and the Civil War Era*. Amherst: University of Massachusetts Press, 1983.

O'Brien, Frank M. *The Story of "The Sun," New York: 1833–1928*. New York: D. Appleton, 1928.

Observations upon Sunday Newspapers. London: J. Hatchard and Son, 1820.

Ogden, Rollo, ed. *Life and Letters of Edwin L. Godkin*. 2 vols. New York: Macmillan, 1907.

Outland, Ethel R. *The "Effingham" Libels on Cooper: A Documentary History of the Libel Suits of James Fennimore Cooper Centering Around the Three-Mile Point Controversy and the Novel Home as Found, 1837–1845*. Madison: University of Wisconsin, 1929.

Palmegiano, E. M. *The British Empire in the Victorian Press, 1832–1867*. New York: Garland, 1987.

Parrington, Vernon L. *The Romantic Revolution in America (1800–1860)*. Vol. 2 of *Main Currents in American Thought*. New York: Harcourt, Brace, 1927.

Parton, James. *Famous Americans of Recent Times*. Boston: Houghton, Osgood, 1867; rpt. 1879.

Parton, James. *George W. Childs*. Philadelphia: Collins, 1870.

Parton, James. *The Life of Horace Greeley*. New York: Mason Brothers, 1855.

Parton, James. *The Life of Thomas Jefferson*. Boston, New York: Houghton Mifflin, 1874.

Payne, George Henry. *History of Journalism in the United States*. New York: D. Appleton, 1925.

Pessen, Edward. *Jacksonian America: Society, Personality, and Politics*. Homewood, Ill.: Dorsey Press, 1969.

Phelan, John M. *Disenchantment: Meaning and Morality in the Media*. New York: Hastings House, 1980.

Philips, Melville, ed. *Making of a Newspaper*. London and New York: G. P. Putnam's Sons, 1893.

Plomer, Henry R. *Short History of English Printing, 1476–1900*. New York: Empire State Book Company, 1900.

Pollard, James E. *The Presidents and the Press*. New York: Macmillan, 1947.

Poore, Ben P. *Reminiscences of Sixty Years in the National Metropolis.* 2 vols. Philadelphia: Hubbard Brothers, 1886.

Pray, Isaac C. *Memoirs of James Gordon Bennett and His Times.* New York: Stringer and Townsend, 1855; rpt. Arno Press and the New York Times Company, 1970.

Presbry, Frank. *History and Development of Advertising.* New York: Doubleday, Doran, 1929.

The Press and the Public Service. London: G. Routledge, 1857.

Reid, Whitelaw. *Some Newspaper Tendencies.* New York: Henry Holt, 1879.

Reynolds, Donald E. *Editors Make War: Southern Newspapers in the Secession Crisis.* Nashville, Tenn.: Vanderbilt University Press, 1970.

Richards, Leonard I. *"Gentlemen of Property and Standing": Anti-Abolition Mobs in Jacksonian America.* New York: Oxford University Press, 1970.

Rivers, William L., Theodore Peterson, and Jay W. Jensen. *The Mass Media and Modern Society.* 2nd ed. San Francisco: Rinehart Press, 1971.

Rivers, William L., Wilbur Schramm, and Clifford G. Christians. *Responsibility in Mass Communication.* New York: Harper and Row, 1980.

Roberts, Chalmers M. *"The Washington Post": The First 100 Years.* Boston: Houghton Mifflin, 1977.

Rosebault, Charles J. *When Dana Was the "Sun."* New York: Robert M. McBride, 1931.

Rosewater, Victor. *History of Cooperative News-Gathering in the United States.* New York: D. Appleton, 1930.

Roshco, Bernard. *Newsmaking.* Chicago: University of Chicago Press, 1975.

Ross, Charles G. *The Writing of News: A Handbook.* New York: Henry Holt, 1911.

Rowell, George P. *Forty Years an Advertising Agent, 1865–1905.* New York: Franklin, 1926.

Salisbury, William. *Career of a Journalist.* New York: Dodge, 1908.

Sandage, C. H., and Vernon Fryberger, eds. *The Role of Advertising.* Homewood, Ill.: Richard D. Irwin, 1960.

Savage, James. *An Account of the London Newspapers, and of the Manner in Which They Are Conducted.* London: N.p., 1811.

Schiller, Dan. *Objectivity and the News: The Public and the Rise of Commercial Journalism.* Philadelphia: University of Pennsylvania Press, 1981.

Schilpp, Madelon Golden, and Sharon M. Murphy. *Great Women of the Press.* Carbondale: Southern Illinois University Press, 1983.

Schlesinger, Arthur M., Jr. *The Age of Jackson.* Boston: Little, Brown, 1945.

Schlesinger, Arthur M. *Prelude to Independence: The Newspaper War on Britain, 1764–1776.* 1957; rpt. Westport, Conn.: Greenwood Press, 1979.

Schmuhl, Robert, ed. *The Responsibilities of Journalists.* Notre Dame, Ind.: University of Notre Dame Press, 1984.

Schudson, Michael. *Discovering the News: A Social History of American Newspapers.* New York: Basic Books, 1978.

Scott, James R. A. *The Influence of the Press.* London: N.p., 1893.

Seitz, Don C. *The James Gordon Bennetts: Father and Son, Proprietors of the "New York Herald."* Indianapolis: Bobbs-Merrill, 1928.

Seitz, Don C. *Joseph Pulitzer: His Life and Letters*. New York: Simon and Schuster, 1924.

Shattock, Joanne, and Michael Wolff, eds. *The Victorian Periodical Press: Samplings and Soundings*. Leicester: Leicester University Press, 1982.

Shaw, Archer H. *The Plain Dealer: One Hundred Years in Cleveland*. New York: Alfred A. Knopf, 1942.

Schuman, Edwin. *The Art and Practice of Journalism*. Chicago: Stevens and Handy, 1899.

Siebert, Fredrick S. *Freedom of the Press in England, 1476–1776: The Rise and Decline of Government Control*. Urbana: University of Illinois Press, 1952.

Siebert, Fredrick S., Theodore Peterson, and Wilbur Schramm. *Four Theories of the Press*. Urbana: University of Illinois Press, 1956.

Sinclair, Upton. *The Brass Check*. (Pasadena, Calif.: N.p., 1920; rpt. New York: Arno Press, 1970).

Smith, Albert Richard, ed. *Press Orders: Being the Opinions of the Leading Journals on the Abolition of Newspaper Privileges*. London: W. Kent, 1853.

Smith, Anthony. *The Politics of Information*. London: Macmillan, 1978.

Smith, Culver H. *The Press, Politics and Patronage*. Athens: University of Georgia Press, 1977.

Smith, Elbert B. *Francis Preston Blair*. New York: Free Press, 1980.

Smith, James Morton. *Freedom's Fetters: The Alien and Sedition Laws and American Civil Liberties*. Ithaca: Cornell University Press, 1956.

Smith, Timothy L. *Revivalism and Social Reform: American Protestantism on the Eve of the Civil War*. New York: Abingdon Press, 1957.

Smith, William Ernest. *The Francis Preston Blair Family in Politics*. 2 vols. New York: Macmillan, 1933.

Snyder, Louis L., and Richard B. Morris, eds. *A Treasury of Great Reporting*. 2nd ed. New York: Simon and Schuster, 1962.

Starr, Louis M. *Bohemian Brigade: Civil War Newsmen in Action*. New York: Alfred A. Knopf, 1954.

Stewart, Donald H. *The Opposition Press of the Federalist Period*. Albany: State University of New York Press, 1969.

Stickles, Arndt M. *The Critical Court Struggle in Kentucky, 1819–1829*. Bloomington: Indiana University Graduate Council, 1929.

Stoddard, Henry Luther. *Horace Greeley: Printer, Editor, Crusader*. New York: G. P. Putnam's Sons, 1946.

Stone, Candace. *Dana and the "Sun."* New York: Dodd, Mead, 1938.

Stone, I. F. *The Killings at Kent State: How Murder Went Unpunished*. New York: Vintage Books, 1970.

Stone, Melville E. *Fifty Years a Journalist*. New York: Doubleday, Page, 1923.

Strout, Alan Lang, *A Bibliography of Articles in "Blackwood's Magazine," 1817–1825*. Lubbock: Texas Tech Press, 1959.

Strout, Alan Lang, ed. *John Bull's Letter to Lord Byron*. Norman: University of Oklahoma Press, 1947.

Sutton, Albert A. *Education for Journalism in the United States from Its Beginning to 1940*. Evanston: Northwestern University Press, 1945.

Swados, Harvey, ed. *Years of Conscience*. Cleveland: Meridian Books, 1962.

Swanberg, W. A. *Citizen Hearst*. New York: Charles Scribner's Sons, 1961.

Swanberg, W. A. *Pulitzer*. New York: Charles Scribner's Sons, 1967.

Sweet, William Warren. *Revivalism in America: Its Origin, Growth and Influence*. New York: Charles Scribner's Sons, 1944.

Symonds, R. A. *The Rise of English Journalism*. Exeter: A. Wheaton, 1952.

Thayer, Lee, ed. *Ethics, Morality and the Media*. New York: Hastings House, 1980.

Thomas, Isaiah. *The History of Printing in America*. New York: Weathervane Books, 1970. Edited by M. McCorison from the second edition.

Thrall, Miriam M. H. *Rebellious "Fraser's": Nol Yorke's Magazine in the Days of Maginn, Thackeray, and Carlyle*. New York: Columbia University Press, 1934.

Tocqueville, Alexis de. *American Institutions and Their Influence*. New York: A. S. Barnes, 1851.

Trachtenberg, Alan, ed. *Democratic Vistas, 1860–1880*. New York: George Braziller, 1970.

Tredrey, F. D. *The House of Blackwood, 1804–1954*. Edinburgh and London: William Blackwood and Sons, 1954.

Trial: Commonwealth vs. J. T. Buckingham, on an Indictment for a Libel, from the Municipal Court of the City of Boston, December Term, 1822. Boston: 1822.

Tyler, Alice Felt. *Freedom's Ferment*. Minneapolis: University of Minnesota Press, 1944.

U.S. Bureau of Education. *Illiteracy in the United States in 1870 and 1880*. Compiled by Charles Warren. Washington, D.C.: Government Printing Office, 1884.

U.S. Bureau of the Census. First Census, 1790. *Return of the Whole Number of Persons Within the Several Districts of the United States*. Philadelphia: Childs and Swaine, 1791.

U.S. Bureau of the Census. Third Census, 1810. *A Statement of the Arts and Manufactures of the United States of America, for the Year 1810*. Philadelphia: A. Cornman, Jr., 1814.

U.S. Bureau of the Census. Fifth Census, 1830. *Abstract of the Returns of the Fifth Census*. Washington: Duff Green, 1832.

U.S. Bureau of the Census. Sixth Census, 1840. *Compendium of the Enumeration of the Inhabitants and Statistics of the United States*. Washington, D.C.: Thomas Allen, 1841.

U.S. Bureau of the Census. Seventh Census, 1850. *Statistical View of the United States*. Washington, D.C.: A.O.P. Nicholson, 1854.

U.S. Bureau of the Census. Seventh Census, 1850. *Report of the Superintendent of the Census for December 1, 1852: to Which Is Appended the Report for December 1, 1851*. Washington, D.C.: Robert Armstrong, 1853.

U.S. Bureau of the Census. Eighth Census, 1860. *Manufactures of the United States in 1860*. Washington, D.C.: Government Printing Office, 1865.

U.S. Bureau of the Census. Eighth Census, 1860. Joseph C. G. Kennedy, Superintendent. *Preliminary Report on the Eighth Census.* Washington, D.C.: Government Printing Office, 1862.

U.S. Bureau of the Census. Eighth Census, 1860. *Statistics of the United States.* Washington, D.C.: Government Printing Office, 1866.

U.S. Bureau of the Census. Ninth Census, 1870. *The Statistics of the Wealth and Industry of the United States.* Washington, D.C.: Government Printing Office, 1872.

U.S. Bureau of the Census. Tenth Census, 1880. S.N.D. North, comp. *The Newspaper and Periodical Press.* Ivan Petroff, comp. *Alaska: Its Population, Industries, and Resources.* Henry W. Elliott, comp. *The Seal Islands of Alaska.* Henry Hall, comp. *Ship-Building Industry in the United States.* Washington, D.C.: Government Printing Office, 1884.

U.S. Bureau of the Census. Twelfth Census, 1900. Census Reports, vol. VII. *Manufactures, Part I: United States by Industries.* Washington, D.C.: U.S. Census Office, 1902.

U.S. Bureau of the Census. Ben J. Wattenberg, comp. *The Statistical History of the United States from Colonial Times to the Present.* New York: Basic Books, 1976.

U.S. Department of Labor. E. Stewart, Comp. *Documentary History of the Early Organization of Printers.* Bulletin no. 61. Washington, D.C.: Government Printing Office, 1905.

U.S. Department of Labor. Bureau of Labor Statistics. *History of Wages in the United States from Colonial Times to 1928.* Bulletin no. 604. Washington, D.C.: Government Printing Office, 1929.

U.S. Department of Labor. Bureau of Labor Statistics. *Labor Through the Century, 1833–1933.* Bulletin no. 605. Washington, D.C.: Government Printing Office, 1934.

Vander Mirden, Anne, ed. *Ethics and Mass Communication.* Utrecht: State University of Utrecht, 1980.

Van Deusen, Glyndon. *The Jacksonian Era: 1828–1848.* New York: Harper and Brothers, 1959.

Virginia General Assembly. House of Delegates. *The Virginia Report of 1799–1800 Touching the Alien and Sedition Laws.* New York: De Capo Press, 1970.

Walker, Sydney F. *Anonymous Journalism.* London: N.p., 1894.

Ward, John William. *Andrew Jackson: Symbol for an Age.* New York: Oxford University Press, 1955.

Warner, C. D. *American Newspapers.* New York: Osgood, 1881.

Warren, Charles, ed. *Jacobin and Junto, or Early American Politics as Viewed in the Diary of Dr. Nathaniel Ames, 1758–1822.* Cambridge: Harvard University Press, 1931.

Weed, Harriet A. *The Life of Thurlow Weed.* 2 vols. Boston: Houghton Mifflin, 1883.

Weigle, Clifford F., and David G. Clark, eds. *The American Newspaper by Will Irwin.* Ames: Iowa State University Press, 1969.

Weisberger, Bernard. *Reporters for the Union.* Boston: Little, Brown, 1953.

Wertenbaker, Thomas J. *The Puritan Oligarchy: The Founding of American Civilization.* New York: Grosset and Dunlap, 1947.

Wharton, Francis. *State Trials of the United States During the Administrations of Washington and Adams.* Philadelphia: Carey and Hart, 1849.

Wheeler, Paul Mowbray. *America Through British Eyes: A Study of the Attitude of the "Edinburgh Review" Toward the United States of America From 1802 Until 1861.* Ann Arbor: Edwards Brothers, 1935.

Wiebe, Robert H. *The Search for Order, 1877–1920.* New York: Hill and Wang, 1967.

Wieder, Callie. *Daily Newspapers in the United States.* White Plains, N.Y.: H. W. Wilson, 1916.

Wilkie, Frank B. *Personal Reminiscences of Thirty-five Years of Journalism.* Chicago: F. J. Shulte, 1891.

Wilmer, Lambert A. *Our Press Gang.* Philadelphia: J. T. Lloyd, 1860.

Wingate, C. *Views and Interviews on Journalism.* New York: F. B. Patterson, 1875.

Winter, William. *The Press and the Stage: An Oration.* New York: Lockwood and Coombes, 1889.

Wolseley, Roland E. *The Black Press, U.S.A.* Ames: Iowa State University Press, 1971.

Articles

Adams, Edward F. "Newspaper Work: Limitations of Truth-Telling." *Arena* 20 (November–December 1898): 604–614.

"American and British Newspaper Press," *Southern Quarterly Review* 4 (July 1843): 235–238.

Ames, William E. "Samuel Harrison Smith Founds the *National Intelligencer.*" *Journalism Quarterly* 42 (Summer 1965): 389–396.

Ames, William E., and Dean Olson. "Washington's Political Press and the Election of 1824." *Journalism Quarterly* 40 (Summer 1963): 343–350.

Babcock, Havilah. "The Press and Civil War." *Journalism Quarterly* 6 (March 1928): 1–12.

Baldasty, Gerald J. "The Boston Press and Politics in Jacksonian America." *Journalism History* 7 (Autumn–Winter 1980): 104–108.

Baldasty, Gerald J. "The Charleston, South Carolina, Press and National News, 1808–1847." *Journalism Quarterly* 55 (Autumn 1978): 519–526.

Baldasty, Gerald J. "The Press and Politics in the Age of Jackson." *Journalism Monographs* 89 (August 1984).

Barrow, Lionel C., Jr. "'Our Own Cause': *Freedom's Journal* and the Beginnings of the Black Press." *Journalism History* 4 (Winter 1977–78): 118–122.

Beasley, Maurine. "The Curious Career of Anne Royall." *Journalism History* 3 (Winter 1976–77): 98–102, 136.

Benjamin, S. G. W. "Notable Editors Between 1776 and 1800." *Magazine of American History* 17 (February 1887): 97–127.

Benson, Lee. "The Mistransference Fallacy in Explanations of Human Behavior." *Historical Methods* 17 (Summer 1984): 118–131.

Berthoff, Rowland. "The American Social Order: A Conservative Hypothesis." *American Historical Review* 65 (April 1960): 495–514.

Betts, John Richards. "Sporting Journalism in Nineteenth-Century America." *American Quarterly* 5 (Spring 1953): 39–56.

Bishop, Joseph B. "Newspaper Espionage." *The Forum* 1 (August 1886): 259–537.

Blaikie, W. G. "Penny Newspapers and Their Power." *The Sunday Magazine* (1883): 179–181, 319–332.

Blanchard, Margaret A. "Press Criticism and National Reform Movements: The Progressive Era and the New Deal." *Journalism History* 5 (Summer 1978): 33–37, 54–55.

Bond, Donovan H. "How the *Wheeling Intelligencer* Became a Republican Organ (1856–1860)." *West Virginia History* 11 (April 1950): 160–184.

Bonney, C. C. "The Duties and Privileges of the Public Press." In *Echoes of the Sunset Club*, compiled by W. W. Catlin. Sunset Club, 1891. Pp. 12–17.

Botein, Stephen. "Printers and the American Revolution." In *The Press and the American Revolution*, edited by Bernard Bailyn and John B. Hench. Boston: Northeastern University Press, 1981. Pp. 11–57.

Boucicault, Dion. "At the Goethe Society." *North American Review* 148 (March 1889): 335–343.

Boucicault, Dion. "The Decline and Fall of the Press." *North American Review* 145 (July 1887): 32–39.

Bovee, Warren G. "Horace Greeley and Social Responsibility." *Journalism Quarterly* 63 (Summer 1986): 251–259.

Bradshaw, James Stanford. "George W. Wisner and the *New York Sun*." *Journalism History* 6 (Winter 1979–80): 112, 117–121.

Breed, Warren. "Social Control in the Newsroom." *Social Forces* 33 (May 1955): 326–335.

Bullen, Henry Lewis. "The Evolution of American Printing Presses from the Year of Independence, 1776, to the Present Year." *American Printer* 83 (July 1926): 70–71.

Bulwer, E. L., and Sergeant Talfourd. "Literary Remains of the Late William Hazlitt." *American Quarterly Review* 20 (December 1836): 265–291.

Bushey, Glenn-Leroy. "William Duane, Crusader for Judicial Reform." *Pennsylvania History* 5 (July 1938): 141–156.

Bushnell, William H. "The Antagonism of the Pulpit and the Press." *Inland Printer* 3 (June 1886): 528–530.

Bushnell, William H. "Journalistic Barbarism." *Inland Printer* 3 (January 1886): 201–202.

Calkin, Homer L. "Pamphlets and Public Opinion During the American Revolution." *Pennsylvania Magazine of History and Biography* 64 (January 1940): 22–42.

Cappeller, W. S. "The Nature and Limit of the Obligation of the Newspaper to Its Party." *Inland Printer* 7 (October 1889): 49.

Capper, Charles. "Margaret Fuller as Cultural Reformer: The Conversations in Boston." *American Quarterly* 39 (Winter 1987): 509–528.

Carey, James W. "Advertising: An Institutional Approach." In *The Role of Advertising*, edited by C. H. Sandage and Vernon Fryberger. Homewood, Ill.: Richard D. Irwin, 1960. Pp. 3–17.

Carlisle, Thomas. "Mud Moralists." *St. James's Magazine*, 3rd ser., 2 (February 1876): 493–497.

Carpenter, E. J. "Journalism as a Profession." *Education* 7 (February 1887): 410–415.

Carter, Edward L. "The Revolution in Journalism During the Civil War." *Lincoln Herald* 73 (Winter 1971): 229–241.

"The Casuistry of Journalism." *Cornhill Magazine* 28 (August 1873): 198–206.

Cater, Douglas. "The Survival of Human Values." *Journal of Communication* 31 (Winter 1981): 190–201.

Clement, E. H. "Nineteenth-Century Boston Journalism." *New England Magazine* 26 (November 1906–September 1907).

Crouthamel, James. "Did the Second Bank Bribe the Press?" *Journalism Quarterly* 36 (Winter 1959): 35–44.

Crouthamel, James. "James Gordon Bennett, the *New York Herald* and the Development of Newspaper Sensationalism." *New York History* 54 (July 1973): 294–316.

Crouthamel, James. "The Newspaper Revolution in New York, 1830–1860." *New York History* 45 (April 1964): 91–113.

Daniels, J. D. "Amos Kendall: Kentucky Journalist, 1815–1829." *The Filson Club History Quarterly* 52 (January 1978): 46–65.

Davidson, Cathy. "Towards a History of Books and Readers." *American Quarterly* 40 (March 1988): 7–17.

Davis, Elmer. "News and the Whole Truth." *Atlantic Monthly* 190 (August 1952): 32–38.

Davis, Horace G., Jr. "Pensacola Newspapers, 1821–1900." *Florida Historical Quarterly* 37 (January–April 1959): 419–445.

Dickerson, Donna. "William Cowper Brann: Nineteenth Century Press Critic." *Journalism History* 5 (Summer 1978): 42–45.

Donald, Robert. "Sunday Newspapers in the United States." *The Universal Review* 8 (September–December 1890): 78–89.

Dyer, Carolyn Stewart. "Census Manuscripts and Circulation Data for Mid-19th Century Newspapers." *Journalism History* 7 (Summer 1980): 47–48, 67.

Dyer, Carolyn Stewart. "Economic Dependence and Concentration of Ownership Among Antebellum Wisconsin Newspapers." *Journalism History* 7 (Summer 1980): 42–46.

Elliot, Chuck. "Conscience of England: The Unknown Side of William Cobbett." *Media History Digest* 2 (Summer 1982): 57–64.

Epstein, Edward Jay. "Journalism and Truth." *Commentary* 57 (April 1974): 36–40.

Eriksson, Erik McKinley. "President Jackson's Propaganda Agencies." *The Pacific Historical Review* 7 (January 1937): 47–57.

"An Evening with the Telegraph-Wires." *Atlantic Monthly* 2 (September 1858): 489–495.

Ewing, Gretchen. "Duff Green: Independent Editor of the Party Press." *Journalism Quarterly* 54 (Winter 1977): 733–739.

Fiering, Norman S. "The Transatlantic Republic of Letters: A Note on the Circulation of Learned Periodicals to Early Eighteenth-Century America." *William and Mary Quarterly*, 3rd ser., 33 (October 1976): 642–660.

Folkerts, Jean. "Functions of the Reform Press." *Journalism History* 12 (Spring 1985): 22–25.

Ford, Worthington C., ed. "Letters of William Duane." *Proceedings of the Massachusetts Historical Society*, 2nd ser., 20 (May 1906): 257–394.

Foster, Roger. "Trial by Newspaper." *North American Review* 144 (May 1887): 524–527.

Franke, Warren. "Sensationalism and the Development of 19th-Century Reporting: The Broom Sweeps Sensory Details." *Journalism History* 12 (Autumn–Winter 1985): 80–85.

Frothingham, O. B. "Voices of Power." *Atlantic Monthly* 53 (February 1884): 176–182.

Gage, Larry J. "The Texas Road to Succession and War: John Marshall and the *Texas State Gazette*, 1860–1861." *Southwestern Historical Quarterly* 62 (October 1958): 191–226.

Gardner, Dorsey. "Oratory and Journalism." *North American Review* 114 (January 1872): 39–87.

Garnsey, J. H. "The Demand for Sensational Journals." *The Arena* 18 (November 1897): 681–686.

Godkin, Edwin L. "The Adulteration of News." *The Nation* 31 (August 12, 1880): 107–108.

Godkin, Edwin L. "Diplomacy and the Newspaper." *North American Review* 160 (May 1895): 570–579.

Godkin, Edwin L. "Editorial Perspective." *The Nation* 10 (January 17, 1870): 54–55.

Godkin, Edwin L. "The 'Judicious' in Journalism." *The Nation* 6 (1868): 105–107.

Godkin, Edwin L. "Newspapers Here and Abroad." *North American Review* 150 (February 1890): 197–204.

Godkin, Edwin L. "Opinion-Moulding." *The Nation* 9 (August 12, 1869): 126–127.

Gorren, Aline. "The Ethics of Modern Journalism." *Scribner's Magazine* 19 (April 1896): 507–513.

Green, Fletcher M. "Duff Green: Industrial Promoter." *Journal of Southern History* 2 (February 1936): 29–42.

Green, Fletcher M. "Duff Green, Militant Journalist of the Old School." *American Historical Review* 52 (January 1947): 247–264.

Grotta, Gerald L. "Philip Freneau's Crusades for Open Sessions of the U.S. Senate." *Journalism Quarterly* 48 (Winter 1971): 667–671.

Harris, William T. "Ought Young Girls to Read the Daily Newspapers?" *Addresses and Proceedings of the National Education Association* (1888): 86–89.

Heinl, Frank J. "Newspapers and Periodicals in the Lincoln-Douglas County, 1831–1832." *Journal of the Illinois State Historical Society* 23 (October 1930): 371–438.

Hemanus, Pertti. "Objectivity in News Transmission." *Journal of Communication* 26 (August 1976): 102–107.

Holden, Charles. [Address to the Editors and Publishers' Association.] *Proceedings of the Maine Press Association for the Years 1867, 1865 and 1866.* Bar Harbor, Maine: Mount Desert Publishing, 1887. Pp. 12–25.

Howe, John R. "Republican Thought and the Political Violence of the 1790s." *American Quarterly* 19 (Summer 1967): 147–164.

Hudson, Robert V. "Will Irwin's Pioneering Criticism of the Press." *Journalism Quarterly* 47:2 (Summer 1970): 263–271.

Hunt, Gaillard, ed. "Office-Seeking During the Administration of John Adams." *American Historical Review* 2:2 (January 1897): 241–261.

"Influence of the Newspapers." *Fraser's Magazine* 4 (September–October 1831): 127–142; 310–321.

"The Influence of the Press." *Blackwood's Edinburgh Magazine* 36 (September 1834): 373–391.

"The Influence of the Press." *Westminster Review* 21 (October 1834): 498–505.

Irwin, Will. "The American Newspaper: A Study of Journalism in Its Relation to the Public; Part 1, The Power of the Press." *Collier's Magazine* 46 (January 21, 1911): 15–18.

Irwin, Will. "The American Newspaper: A Study of Journalism in Its Relation to the Public; Part 3, The Fourth Current." *Collier's Magazine* 46 (February 18, 1911): 14–17, 24, 27.

Irwin, Will. "The American Newspaper: A Study of Journalism in Its Relation to the Public, Part 5, What Is News?" *Collier's Magazine* 46 (March 18, 1911): 16–18.

Irwin, Will. "The American Newspaper: A Study of Journalism in Its Relation to the Public; Part 8, All the News That's Fit to Print." *Collier's Magazine* 47 (May 6, 1911): 17–19, 30.

"Journalists and Magazine-Writers." *Blackwood's Edinburgh Magazine* 125 (January 1879): 69–92.

Kaestle, Carl F. "The History of Literacy and the History of Readers." In *Review of Research in Education* 12 (1985): 11–53.

Kazin, Alfred. "Where Would Emerson Find His Scholar Now?" *American Heritage* (December 1987): 93–96.

Kielbowicz, Richard B. "Newsgathering by Printers' Exchanges Before the Telegraph." *Journalism History* 9 (Summer 1982): 42–48.

Kingsbury, Susan M., et al. "Measuring the Ethics of American Newspapers: A

Spectrum Analysis of Newspaper Sensationalism." *Journalism Quarterly* 10 (June 1933): 93–108.

Knights, Peter R. "'Competition' in the U.S. Daily Newspaper Industry, 1865–68." *Journalism Quarterly* 45 (Autumn 1968): 473–480.

LaCourse, Richard. "Native American Journalism: An Overview." *Journalism History* 6 (Summer 1979): 34–38.

Larson, Robin Fisher. "Cooper Union Speech: New York Media Launch a Candidate." *Media History Digest* 6 (Winter 1986): 2–7.

Leupp, Francis E. "The Waning Power of the Press." *The Atlantic Monthly* 105 (February 1910): 145–156.

Levermore, Charles H. "The Rise of Metropolitan Journalism, 1800–1840." *American Historical Review* 6 (April 1901): 446–465.

Levey, Augustus A. "The Newspaper Habit and Its Effects." *North American Review* 143 (September 1886): 308–312.

Levy, Leonard. "The Third President and the Press." *Media History Digest* 2 (Summer 1982): 18–26, 54.

Lilly, W. S. "The Ethics of Journalism." *The Forum* 7 (July 1889): 503–512.

List, Karen K. "Magazine Portrayals of Women's Role in the New Republic." *Journalism History* 13 (Summer 1986): 64–70.

Malone, Henry T. "The *Weekly Atlanta Intelligencer* as a Secessionist Journal (1860–1861)." *Georgia Historical Quarterly* 37 (December 1953): 278–286.

Malone, Kathryn R. "The Fate of Revolutionary Republicanism in Early National Virginia." *Journal of the Early Republic* 7 (Spring 1987): 27–51.

Marbut, F. B. "Decline of the Official Press in Washington." *Journalism Quarterly* 33 (Summer 1956): 335–341.

Marbut, F. B. "Early Washington Correspondents: Some Neglected Pioneers." *Journalism Quarterly* 25 (December 1948): 369–374.

Martin, L. John, and Harold L. Nelson. "The Historical Standard in Analyzing Press Performance." *Journalism Quarterly* 33 (Fall 1956): 456–466.

Masel-Walters, Lynn. "'Their Rights and Nothing More': A History of the *Revolution*, 1868–1870." *Journalism Quarterly* 53 (Summer 1976): 242–251.

Maurer, Oscar. "'Punch' on Slavery and Civil War in America." *Victorian Studies* 1 (September 1957–58): 5–28.

McCrorie, Ken. "Objectivity: Dead or Alive?" *Journalism Quarterly* 36 (Spring 1959): 145–150.

McFarland, C. K., and Robert L. Thistlethwaite. "Twenty Years of a Successful Labor Paper: *The Working Man's Advocate*, 1829–1849." *Journalism Quarterly* 60 (Spring 1983): 35–40.

McFaul, John. "Expediency vs. Morality: Jacksonian Politics and Slavery." *Journal of American History* 62 (June 1975): 24–39.

McKerns, Joseph P. "Media Ethics: A Bibliographical Essay." *Journalism History* 5 (Summer 1978): 50–53, 66–67.

McWilliams, Carey. "One Hundred Years of *The Nation*." *Journalism Quarterly* 42 (Spring 1965): 189–197.

Megargee, L. N. "Newspaper Sensation." *Lippincott's Magazine* 52 (December 1893): 719–736.

Miller, Aaron. "The Paradoxical Godkin, Founder of *The Nation*." *Journalism Quarterly* 42 (Spring 1965): 198–202.

Miller, Linda Patterson. "Poe on the Beat: 'Doings of Gotham' as Urban, Penny Press Journalism." *Journal of the Early Republic* 7 (Summer 1987): 147–165.

Monaghan, E. Jennifer. "Literacy Instruction and Gender in Colonial New England." *American Quarterly* 40 (March 1988): 18–41.

Moore, Jacob B. "History of Newspapers Published in New Hampshire, from 1756 to 1840." *American Quarterly Register* 13 (November 1840): 170–181.

Mott, Frank Luther. "The First Sunday Paper: A Footnote to History." *Journalism Quarterly* 35 (Fall 1958): 443–446.

Murphy, Paul V. "*Near* v. *Minnesota* in the Context of Historical Developments." *Minnesota Law Review* 66 (November 1981): 95–160.

"The *National Intelligencer* and Its Editors." *Atlantic Monthly* 6 (October 1860): 470–481.

"The Nature and Limit of the Obligation of the Newspaper to Its Party." *The Inland Printer* 7 (October 1889): 49.

Nelson, Harold L. "Seditious Libel in Colonial America." *American Journal of Legal History* 3 (April 1959): 160–172.

Nevins, Allan. "E. L. Godkin: Victorian Liberal." *The Nation* 171 (July 22, 1950): 76–79.

Newfield, Jack. "The 'Truth' About Objectivity and the New Journalism." In *Liberating the Media*, edited by C. C. Flippen. Washington, D.C.: Acropolis Books, 1974. Pp. 59–65.

"Newspaper Leaders." *St. James's Magazine*, new. ser., 4 (October 1869–April 1870): 425–430.

"The Newspaper and Periodical Press." *Southern Quarterly Review* 1 (1842): 5–66.

"Newspapers and the War." *Leisure Hour* 19 (December 1, 1870): 774–776.

"Newspapers, Magazines and Other Periodicals Published in the United States as of July 1, 1839." *American Almanac* (1840): 196.

Nilsson, Nils Gunnar. "The Origin of the Interview." *Journalism Quarterly* 48 (Winter 1971): 707–713.

Nord, David P. "The Evangelical Origins of Mass Media in America, 1815–1835." *Journalism Monographs* 88 (May 1984): 00–00.

Nord, David P. "A Republican Literature: A Study of Magazine Reading and Readers in Late Eighteenth-Century New York." *American Quarterly* 40 (March 1988): 42–64.

Nord, David P. "Tocqueville, Garrison and the Perfection of Journalism." *Journalism History* 13 (Summer 1986): 56–63.

Olasky, Marvin. "Late 19th-Century Texas Sensationalism: Hypocrisy or Biblical Morality?" *Journalism History* 12 (Autumn–Winter 1985): 96–100.

"Our Rulers—Public Opinion." *Cornhill Magazine* 21 (March 1870): 288–298.

Park, Robert E. "The Natural History of the Newspaper." *American Journal of Sociology* 29 (November 1923): 273–289.

Parton, James. "Falsehoods in the Daily Press." *Harper's Magazine* 49 (July 1874): 269–280.

Parton, James. "*The New York Herald.*" *North American Review* 102 (April 1866): 373–418.

Peck, J. M. "The Power of the Press." *Christian Review* 9 (March 1844): 70–92.

"Periodical Literature" and "The Periodical Press." *American Almanac* (1835): 97–106, 266–282.

Perry, Wilder W. "The Printed Page and Journalism—Its Growth and Influence." *Report of the Maine Press Association, for the Year 1878*. Portland, Maine: Brown Thurston, 1878. Pp. 9–16.

Pessen, Edward. "George Washington's Farewell Address, the Cold War, and the Timeless National Interest." *Journal of the Early Republic* 7 (Spring 1987): 1–25.

Pessen, Edward. "Society and Politics in the Jacksonian Era." *Kentucky Historical Society Register* 82 (Winter 1984): 1–27.

Phillips, E. Barbara. "Approaches to Objectivity: Journalistic and Social Science Perspectives." In *Strategies for Communication Research*, edited by Paul M. Hirsch et al. Beverly Hills: Sage, 1977. Pp. 63–77.

"The Political Press—French, British and German." *North British Review* 34 (February 1861): 184–209.

"Politics and the Press." *Fraser's Magazine*, new ser. 12 (July 1875): 41–50.

Pratt, Julius W. "John L. O'Sullivan and Manifest Destiny." *New York History* 14 (July 1933): 213–234.

Pratt, Julius W. "The Origin of 'Manifest Destiny.'" *American Historical Review* 32 (July 1927): 795–798.

"The Press and the Public Service." *Fraser's Magazine* 55 (June 1857): 649–662.

"The Press and the Tories." *Fraser's Magazine* 8 (September 1833): 330–338.

"The Press—Its Power and Mission." *Southern Literary Messenger* 19 (September 1853): 561–564.

Price, Warren C. "Reflections on the Trial of John Peter Zenger." *Journalism Quarterly* 32 (Spring 1955): 161–165.

Prince, Carl E. "The Federalist Party and Creation of a Court Press, 1789–1801." *Journalism Quarterly* 53 (Summer 1976): 238–241.

"Pulitzer and American Journalism." *Outlook* 99 (November 11, 1911): 608–609.

Pulitzer, Joseph. "College of Journalism." *North American Review* 178 (May 1904): 641–680.

Raymond, James H. "The Rights and Duties of the Newspaper Press." In *Echoes of the Sunset Club*, compiled by W. W. Catlin. Chicago: Sunset Club, 1891. Pp. 23–30.

Rider, George T. "The Pretensions of Journalism." *North American Review* 135 (November 1882): 471–483.

Riley, Sam G. "The Short Unhappy Life of the First American Indian Newspaper." *Journalism Quarterly* 53 (Winter 1976): 666–671.

Robinson, Elwyn B. "The *Public Ledger*: An Independent Newspaper." *Pennsylvania Magazine of History and Biography* 64 (January 1940): 43–55.

Sampson, William H. "The Press, Its Relations to Patrons and the Public." *Proceedings of the Maine Editors and Publishers' Association for the Year 1876*. Portland, Maine: Brown Thurston, 1876. Pp. 9–21.

Saxton, Alexander. "Problems of Class and Race in the Origins of the Mass Circulation Press." *American Quarterly* 36 (Summer 1984): 211–234.

Schwarzlose, Richard A. "Harbor News Association: Formal Origin of the AP." *Journalism Quarterly* 45 (Summer 1968): 253–260.

Scott, Frank W. "Newspapers, 1775–1860." In *Cambridge History of American Literature*, edited by William P. Trent et al. 3 vols. New York: Macmillan, 1933. Vol. 2: 176–195.

Shanks, W. F. G. "How We Get Our News." *Harper's New Monthly Magazine* 34 (March 1867): 511–522.

Shaw, Donald. "At the Crossroads: Change and Continuity in American Press News 1820–1860." *Journalism History* 8 (Summer 1981): 38–50.

Shaw, Donald. "News About Slavery from 1820 to 1860 in Newspapers of the South, North and West." *Journalism Quarterly* 61 (Autumn 1984): 483–492.

Shaw, Donald. "News Bias and the Telegraph: A Study of Historical Change." *Journalism Quarterly* 44 (Spring 1967): 3–12.

Shaw, Donald L., and John W. Slater. "In the Eye of the Beholder? Sensationalism in American Press News, 1830–1860." *Journalism History* 12 (Autumn–Winter 1985): 86–91.

Silver, Rollo G. "Apron Instead of Uniform: The Practice of Printing, 1776–1787." *Proceedings of the American Antiquarian Society* 87 (april 1977): 111–194.

Singletary, Michael W. "The New Editorial Voice for Andrew Jackson: Happenstance, or Plan?" *Journalism Quarterly* 53 (Winter 1976): 672–678.

Sloan, William David. "George W. Wisner: Michigan Editor and Politician." *Journalism History* 6 (Winter 1979–80): 113–116.

Smalley, G. W. "Chapters in Journalism." *Harper's Monthly* 89 (August 1894): 426–435.

Smalley, G. W. "Notes on Journalism." *Harper's Monthly* 97 (July 1898): 213–223.

Smith, Culver H. "Propaganda Technique in the Jackson Campaign of 1828." *East Tennessee Historical Society Publications* 6 (1934): 44–46.

Smith, Henry Ladd. "The Beauteous Jennie June: Pioneer Woman Journalist." *Journalism Quarterly* 40 (Spring 1963): 169–174.

Smith, William E. "Francis P. Blair, Pen-Executive of Andrew Jackson." In *Highlights in the History of the American Press*, edited by Edwin H. Ford and Edwin Emery. Minneapolis: University of Minnesota Press, 1954. Pp. 138–149.

Smythe, Ted Curtis. "The Reporter, 1880–1900: Working Conditions and Their Influence on the News." *Journalism History* 7 (Spring 1980): 1–10.

"Some Corruptions of the Press." *St. James's Magazine*, 3rd ser., 1 (April–September 1875): 249–254.

"South Carolina in the Presidential Election of 1800." *American Historical Review* 4 (October 1898): 111–129.

Stead, William Thomas. "Government by Journalism." *Contemporary Review* 49 (May 1886): 653–674.

Steen, Ralph W. "Texas Newspapers and Lincoln, 1860–1946." *Southwestern Historical Quarterly* 41 (January 1948): 199–212.

Steffens, Lincoln J. "The Business of a Newspaper." *Scribner's Magazine* 22 (October 1897): 447–467.

Stephens, Mitchell. "Sensationalism and Moralizing in 16th and 17th-Century Newsbooks and News Ballads." *Journalism History* 12 (Autumn–Winter 1985): 92–95.

Stevens, John D. "Sensationalism in Perspective." *Journalism History* 12 (Autumn–Winter 1985): 78–79.

Stewart, Donald H. "The Press and Political Corruption During the Federalist Administrations." *Political Science Quarterly* 47 (September 1952): 426–446.

Stone, Sue Lynn. "Blessed Are They That Mourn: Expressions of Grief in South Central Kentucky, 1870–1910." *Kentucky Historical Society Register* 85 (Summer 1987): 213–236.

Thompson, Slason. "Newspapers: Their Rights and Duties." In *Echoes of the Sunset Club*, compiled by W. W. Catlin. Chicago: Sunset Club, 1891. Pp. 18–22.

Thwaites, Reuben Gold. "The Ohio Valley Press Before the War of 1812–15." *Proceedings of the American Antiquarian Society* 19 (April 1909): 309–368.

Trendel, Robert. "The Expurgation of Antislavery Materials by American Presses." *Journal of Negro History* 58 (July 1973): 271–290.

Trumbull, M. M. "The Press as It Is." In *Echoes of the Sunset Club*, compiled by W. W. Catlin. Chicago: Sunset Club, 1891. Pp. 31–33.

Tuchman, Gaye. "Objectivity as Strategic Ritual: An Examination of Newsmen's Notions of Objectivity." *American Journal of Sociology* 77 (January 1972): 660–679.

Turnbull, George S. "Some Notes on the History of the Interview." *Journalism Quarterly* 13 (September 1936): 272–279.

Warren, Samuel D., and Louis D. Brandeis. "The Right to Privacy." *Harvard Law Review* 4 (December 1890): 196–220.

Welter, Barbara. "The Cult of True Womanhood, 1820–1860: Part 1." *American Quarterly* 18 (Summer 1966): 151–174.

White, David Manning. "The 'Gatekeeper': A Case Study in the Selection of News." *Journalism Quarterly* 27 (Fall 1950): 383–390.

White, Richard Grant. "The Morals and Manners of Journalism." *The Galaxy* 8 (December 1869): 840–847.

White, Richard Grant. "The Pest of the Period: A Chapter in the Morals and Manners of Journalism." *The Galaxy* 9 (January 1870): 102–112.

Wicek, William. "A Peculiar Conservatism and the Dorr Rebellion," *American Journal of Legal History* 22 (1978): 237–253.

Wilcox, D. F. "American Newspaper." *Annals of the American Academy* 16 (July 1900): 56–92.

Williams, Samuel Q. "The First Abolition Journals." *New England Magazine*, new ser., 10 (July 1894): 633–636.

Wilson, C. Edward. "Egregious Lies from Idle Brains: Critical Views of Early Journalism." *Journalism Quarterly* 59 (Summer 1982): 260–264.

Wilson, C. Edward. "The *First* Daily Newspaper in English." *Journalism Quarterly* 58 (Summer 1981): 286–288.

Wilson, C. Edward. "The Boston Inoculation Controversy: A Revisionist Interpretation." *Journalism History* 7 (Spring 1980): 16–19.

Wilson, Quintus. "The Confederate Press Association: A Pioneer News Agency." *Journalism Quarterly* 26 (June 1949): 160–166.

Winslow, H. M. "Some Newspaper Women." *The Arena* 17 (December 1896): 127–142.

Witten, Manley. "Hamilton, Andrew: Light on the Horizon." *Media History Digest* 2 (Summer 1982): 42–44.

Wood, Gordon S. "The Significance of the Early Republic." *Journal of the Early Republic* 8 (Spring 1988): 1–20.

Woodbury, Margaret. "Public Opinion in Philadelphia, 1789–1801." *Smith College Studies in History* 5 (October 1919–January 1920): 7–138.

Yodelis, Mary Ann. "Who Paid the Piper? Publishing Economics in Boston, 1763–1775." *Journalism Monographs* 38 (February 1975).

Zboray, Ronald J. "Antebellum Reading and the Ironies of Technological Innovation." *American Quarterly* 40 (March 1988): 65–82.

Theses and Dissertations

Abramoske, Donald J. "The *Chicago Daily News*: A Business History, 1875–1901." Ph.D. diss., University of Chicago, 1963.

Baldasty, Gerald J. "The Political Press in the Second American Party System." Ph.D. diss., University of Washington, 1978.

Berryman, Jack W. "John Stuart Skinner and Early American Sport Journalism, 1819–1835." Ph.D. diss., University of Maryland, 1976.

Butler, Randall R. "New England Journalism and the Questions of Slavery, the South, and Abolitionism: 1820–1861." Ph.D. diss., Brigham Young University, 1980.

Connery, Thomas B. "Fusing Fictional Technique and Journalistic Fact: Literary Journalism in the 1890s Newspaper." Ph.D. diss., Brown University, 1984.

Dooley, Patricia L. "Minnesota Journalists as Elected Officials, 1923–1938." M.A. thesis, University of Minnesota, 1985.

Finnegan, John, Jr. "Defamation, Politics, and the Social Process of Law in New York State, 1776–1860." Ph.D. diss., University of Minnesota, 1985.

Hachten, William A. "The Metropolitan Sunday Newspaper in the United States: A Study of Trends in Content and Practice." Ph.D. diss., University of Minnesota, 1961.

Harrison, James G. "American Newspaper Journalism as Described in American Novels of the Nineteenth Century." Ph.D. diss., University of North Carolina, 1945.

Holtzheuter, J. O. "The Wisconsin Editors' and Publishers' Association, 1853–1877." M.A. thesis, University of Wisconsin, 1965.

Melton, Baxter Ford, Jr. "Amos Kendall in Kentucky, 1814–1829: The Journal-

istic Beginnings of the 'Master Mind' of Andrew Jackson's 'Kitchen Cabinet.'"
Ph.D. diss., Southern Illinois University, 1978.

Middleton, Kent R. "Commercial Speech and the First Amendment." Ph.D. diss.,
University of Minnesota, 1977.

Mikkelson, Dwight L. *Kentucky Gazette*, 1787–1848: The Herald of a Noisy
World." Ph.D. diss., University of Kentucky, 1963.

Shilen, Ronald. "The Concept of Objectivity in Journalism in the United States."
Ph.D. diss., New York University, 1955.

Smith, Victoria. "Newspapers and Freedom of Expression: Minnesota Press Reaction to Suppression During the World War I Era, 1912–1918." M.A. thesis,
University of Minnesota, 1985.

Unpublished Papers

Bensen, Joe. "Visual Reporting of the Civil War." Lecture given at the University
of Minnesota, Minneapolis, November 1986.

Demers, David. "The Origins of Crime News in American Newspapers." Department of Journalism, Ohio State University, 1981. Photocopy.

Dooley, Patricia. "Newspaper Professionals and Political and Community Involvement: Ignorance Is Bliss." Department of Journalism, University of Minnesota,
1983. Photocopy.

Finnegan, John, Jr. "Effects of the Civil War on American Journalism." Lecture
given at the University of Minnesota, Minneapolis, November 1986.

Nowell, Bob. "Amos Kendall's Role in the Election of Andrew Jackson as President
of the United States, 1828." Paper presented at a meeting of the Association for
Education in Journalism, 1981.

Pearson, Kelly L. "The Sedition Law: A Silent Death?" School of Journalism and
Mass Communication, University of Minnesota, 1986. Photocopy.

Rutenbeck, Jeffrey B. "Partisan Press Coverage of Anti-Abolitionist Violence—A
Case Study of Status Quo Journalism." Paper presented at a meeting of the Asso-
ciation for Education in Journalism and Mass Communications, San Antonio,
Texas, August 1987.

Smith, Jeffrey A. "Impartiality and Revolutionary Ideology: Editorial Policies of
the *South Carolina Gazette*, 1732–1775." Paper presented at a meeting of the
Association for Education in Journalism, Athens, Ohio, August 1982.

Stensaas, Harlan S. "The Rise of Objectivity in U.S. Daily Newspapers, 1865–
1934." Paper presented at a meeting of the American Journalism Historians
Association, St. Louis, Missouri, 1986.

Wulfemeyer, K. T. "Butterflies or Gold Mines: The Development of Courses of
Instruction for Journalism in American Colleges and Universities." Paper pre-
sented at a meeting of the Association for Education in Journalism, Boston,
August, 1980.

Newspapers

Note: Asterisks indicate newspapers and years for which scattered issues were read in addition to those in the sample.

Baltimore *American and Daily Advertiser* (1801, 1809).
Baltimore Sun (1852, 1858).
Boston Transcript (1852, 1858).
Boston Gazette, Commercial and Political (1801).
Burlington (Iowa) *Free Press* (1851–1852).
*Burlington, Iowa, *Territorial Gazette and Burlington Advertiser* (1837–1840).
*Cape Girardeau, Mo., *Eagle* (1849–1851).
Cincinnati Post (1891).
Chicago Daily Journal (April–June 1849).
Chicago Tribune (1840–1841, 1849–1853).
Columbus (Ga.) *Enquirer* (1832).
*District of Columbia *United States Telegraph* (1826).
Dubuque (Iowa) *Visitor* (1836–1838).
Easton, Md., *Republican Star* (1809).
*Edenton, N.C., *Post-Angel or Universal Entertainment* (1800).
Elizabethtown *Maryland Herald* (1801, *1802, 1809).
Elizabethtown *New-Jersey Journal* (1801, 1809).
*Frankfort, Ky., *Argus of Western America* (1818–1837).
*Galena, Ill., *Galenian* (1834–1837).
*Galena, Ill., *Northwestern Gazette* (1834–1850).
*Hallowell, Maine, *Liberty Standard* (1841).
*Hannibal *Missouri Courier* (1842, 1849, 1850–1851).
Hartford, Conn., *American Mercury* (1801, 1809).
Middletown, Conn., *Middlesex Gazette* (1801, 1809).
*Montgomery, Ala., *Tri-Weekly Flag and Advertiser* (1847).
Newark, N.J., *Centinel of Freedom* (1801, 1809).
New York Commercial Advertiser (1833).
*New York *Courier and Enquirer* (1833, 1838).
New-York Evening Post (1830–1831, 1836, 1850).
New York Herald (*1835, *1837, 1852, 1858).
New York *Spectator* (1801, 1809).
New York Sun (*1833, *1834, 1891, 1899).
New York Times (1852).
New York Tribune (*1844, *1845, *1849, 1852, *1855, 1858).
Northampton, Mass., *Hampshire Gazette* (1801, 1809).
Philadelphia Evening Bulletin (1891, 1899).
Portland, Maine, *Gazette* (1806, 1809).
Portsmouth *New-Hampshire Gazette* (1801, 1809).
St. Louis Beacon (1829–1830).
*St. Louis *Missouri Argus* (1835–1839).

*St. Louis Reveille (1844, 1849–1850).
St. Paul, Minn., Daily Pioneer Press (1891).
Salem (Mass.) Gazette (1801, 1809).
Savannah, Ga., Columbian Museum (1806, 1809).
Springfield (Mass.) Republican (1852, 1858).
Trenton, N.J., True American (1801, 1809).
*Tuscaloosa Alabama State Intelligencer (1833).
Walpole, N.H., Farmer's Museum (1801, 1809).

Index

Abolition crisis: created new sensitivity to the role of the press, 51; journalists' efforts reflect value structure during, 98; the press blamed for violence during, 167

Abstract press criticism, 121; British examples of, 124–34; American examples of, 137–145, 166–182; intensifying themes of, 166; mentioned, 124, 186

Accessibility of newspapers: expansion of, 23; during mid-nineteenth century, 44–45, 263n52: James Gordon Bennett quoted on, 45; *Southern Quarterly Review* quoted on, 45–46; for blacks, women, 23, 263nn52,53

Accountability: regarding sources, 68

Accuracy: as a theme in early press criticism, 18; difficulty of determining from newspaper content, 68, 279n3; irrelevance to the party press role, 97, 233; as a news value, 113; critics argue that journalistic goals preclude, 199, 202; critics' views of, 210–212, 233; relationship to truth as a construct, 238, 239

Advertising: rates, 26, 39, 43; as support for early American newspapers, 39; circulation as medium for "buying," 58; post-Civil War growth of, 62, 215; in sample newspapers, 1800–1810, 72; 1850–1860, 83; in 1890s newspapers, 91; related to profit motives by critics, 123, 184, 188; critics' attempts to resolve issue of, 215, 216, 222

Alien and Sedition Acts: effect on freedom of the press, 34; as test of the First Amendment, 34; debate about in newspapers, 75–76; mentioned, 72, 102, 234, 279n9, 286n21

"Alternative" press: in early America, defined, 51; influences American journalism, 51

Ames, Fisher: criticizes the American press, 123–125

American Indian press: influences on American journalism, 51

American Newspaper Publishers Association: code of ethics, 240

American press: effect of value structure on, 22, 23, 36, 233–234; changing roles described, 30–40, 40–51, 51–62; English influences on, 32; factors shaping political role of, 32–40; controls on, during colonial period, 33; as part of political structure, 36–40; financial base of, in early America, 39–40; structure, 20, 26, 43, 60–62, 224; orientation to individual, 44–46; partisanism decried, 48; growth of, related to understanding of the press, 49–51; importance during the Civil War, 51–52; erosion of partisanism in, 52; concentration of ownership, 61; blamed for violence during abolition crisis, 167; in transition in mid-nineteenth century, 227. *See also* Newspapers; Press, the

American press criticism: before 1850, 136–148; contrasted with British criticism, 136–137, 148–149; examples of, 137–145; characterized, 154; after 1850, 155 *passim*

American Quarterly Review, 136

American Revolution: marks involvement of the press in political issues, 22, 23

Ames, William: on patronage income of the *National Intelligencer*, 40

Andrews, J. Cutler: on antebellum journalism, 54

Anti-federalists: values represented, 36, 73; criticisms of Federalists, 76–77; opposition to Alien and Sedition Acts, 76

Associated Ohio Dailies: eighth annual meeting statement on effects of business aspirations of the press, 9